One Hundred Years of Communist Experiments

ONE HUNDRED YEARS OF COMMUNIST EXPERIMENTS

Edited by Vladimir Tismaneanu and Jordan Luber

Central European University Press
Budapest–New York

Published in 2021 by

Central European University Press

Nádor utca 9, H-1051 Budapest, Hungary
Tel: +36-1-327-3138 or 327-3000
E-mail: ceupress@press.ceu.edu
Website: www.ceupress.com

ISBN 978-963-386-405-0 (hardback)
ISBN 978-963-386-406-7 (ebook)

Library of Congress Cataloging-in-Publication Data

Names: Tismaneanu, Vladimir, editor. | Luber, Jordan, editor.
Title: One hundred years of communist experiments / edited by Vladimir
Tismaneanu and Jordan Luber.
Other titles: 100 years of communist experiments
Description: Budapest ; New York : Central European University Press, 2021.
| Includes bibliographical references and index.
Identifiers: LCCN 2021009743 (print) | LCCN 2021009744 (ebook) | ISBN
9789633864050 (hardcover) | ISBN 9789633864067 (ebook)
Subjects: LCSH: Communism.
Classification: LCC HX21 .O53 2021 (print) | LCC HX21 (ebook) | DDC
335.4309—dc23
LC record available at https://lccn.loc.gov/2021009743
LC ebook record available at https://lccn.loc.gov/2021009744

CONTENTS

INTRODUCTION

Why a 20th Century Exercise in the 21st Century

Vladimir Tismaneanu and Jordan Luber

Making sense of communism remains a simultaneously incomplete and urgent task. We need to understand precisely why communism's humanist quest for freedom without exception results in a reign of terror and lies. Such an answer is even more necessary in dark times like today.[1] This volume brings together the discussions of the conference "100 Years of Communist Experiments," held at the University of Maryland, College Park on 15–17 November 2017. This was a gathering of top international experts on various aspects of communism to present and vigorously debate new theories on the first century of communist governments. Recent years have proven the ideology is not dead, and that in fact communism and fascism remain not only cynically viable for a power-seeking elite, but genuinely tempting for masses of people in a horrifyingly modern world. Indeed, our intent to look back on the past one hundred years coincided with a rising need to understand why the communist millenarian project is so compelling in theory and so terrifying in reality. Studying communism remains important at this milestone because we still have much to understand about the past, and if we are to avoid a similar future we must clarify exactly what is wrong with the Marxist dream.

Our conference, held exactly a century after Lenin's coup brought the first communist regime to power in St. Petersburg, Russia in November 1917, seemed like a good time to take stock. This is true despite the fact that all communist regimes rusted around five decades ago, and most finally died rapidly between 1989 and 1991. For a while, it seemed this collapse was decisive.

---

[1] "Nothing in our time is more dubious, it seems to me, than our attitude toward the world… the public realm has lost the power of illumination which was originally part of its very nature." Hannah Arendt, *Men in Dark Times* (San Diego: Harcourt Brace & Company, 1968), 4. We emphatically assert that these are "the new dark times." Kate C. Langdon and Vladimir Tismaneanu, *Putin's Totalitarian Democracy: Ideology, Myth, and Violence in the Twenty-First Century* (Cham, Switzerland: Palgrave MacMillan, 2020), 1–2, 225–244.

True, the Chinese Communist Party slaughtered thousands of students with tanks in June 1989, and is reinvigorating its fascist genocidal imperialist project, and Cuba continued to choose famine over freedom. And this is not to mention the utter nightmare of North Korea's frozen, morbidly bizarre society. Vietnam and Laos appeared to be little more than mafiosos posing in front of portraits of Marx. At first, it seemed any remaining communist regimes were holdovers, having lost all pretense of ideology and chance of success. Communism appeared to be no more than the attempt of old tyrants to continue their iron grip. Ideology seemed to be gone. That's what the consensus said.

No one thing definitively proved this widespread theory wrong, and there was no clear first warning or proof that suddenly revealed the truth. Rather throughout this new century, and exponentially over the past few years, we have seen that ideology is alive and well—real, popular, strong, and destructively active. There has been a refusal to realize that we again live in an era fraught with the tragedy of Marxism. Chávez promised "socialism of the 21st century," and he seemed much closer to Lenin than to Bernstein or even Marx. Putin went from nationalism to fascism, from dictatorship to totalitarianism. China went from crony capitalism to genocidal imperialism. Hungary became the European Union's first dictatorship, something Poland, Romania, Austria, and Italy variably strive to emulate.[2] Half of Americans went for the xenophobic strongman Trump, and after years of crime and ruin they adore him with even more loyalty. The Sandinistas took power again, carried out an auto-golpe to end democracy, and once again began to slaughter. Every continent is now alight with mass movements which promise to restore justice through intoxicating unity and purifying removal.[3] Not all of the new dictatorships are Marxist or communist. But some are. And the rest cannot be understood without comprehensively evaluating modern ideological authoritarianism. Communism is a core pillar of modern dictatorship, so these new regimes make an examination of communism a practical endeavor.

So, while one hundred years is naturally a good time to take stock—we have had almost three decades to consider communism ex post facto—it has suddenly become an urgent task. This volume does not seek to be an encyclopedia, nor a traditional history book. Instead, it is both a radiography

---

[2]　For example, at the time of us drafting this "Introduction," the Romanian government deployed black-clad and armored gendarmes to attack protests in the streets, sending over 400 to the hospital.

[3]　Populism, such redemptive movements are often called. See Jan-Werner Müller, *What is*

and a warning. We and our contributors combine scholarship with political judgment, and invite our readers to do the same. This collection combines individual case studies on communist experiments of the past and general theoretical treatments of communism. In attempting to demonstrate what exactly was the catalyst for the man-made apocalypse under communism, we ask how this better understanding of the past can be employed to better resist authoritarian and totalitarian projects in an increasingly atrocious future.

Our intention is not to produce a complete history of communism. How large would that book be and yet still eternally incomplete? The number of victims—the dead and the de-humanized—alone make an exhaustive story impossible to tell. Unfortunately, there have been many communist experiments over the last century. It is neither our goal to be thoroughly historical, even for the cases we have decided to include. This has all been done before. Rather, our goal is to highlight key themes of communism, to show its fundamental character. The framework we use is outlined by our sections: *Fantasies of Salvation, Economics, Politics,* and *Society and Culture*.[4] We have thinkers who come from a variety of fields and countries. This volume is of course incomplete, as any volume on communism will always be. We do not aim to be definitive, but rather comprehensive enough to be conclusive on some general findings on the nature of communism, and possibly on ideologically authoritarian movements broadly.

Our comparative method spans a variety of subjects and strategies of inquiry, rooted in a conclusion reached by all participants at our conference: communism was an mass, eschatological project that sought freedom through redemption, which by its own logic could only come into being by force

---

Populism (Philadelphia: University of Pennsylvania Press, 2016). But the critical elements of populism are nothing more than the foundations of totalitarian movements. If there is any distinction at all between these clowns now and the terrors of the last century, we believe it is merely that today's populists are yesterday's communists and fascists who have not yet achieved the inevitable conclusion of their intolerant and frantic worldview, which always leads to the industrial human rights abuse and atrocity.

[4] The first section takes its name from a book published by Vladimir Tismaneanu twenty years ago. The book argued that from the political, social, and moral ruin which Leninist society left behind, new neo-fascist, redemptive nationalist, and radical racist ideas would rise in post-communist countries—and not as fringe hooligans, but as movements with widespread elite and mass popularity. It took slightly longer than predicted but the forecast turned out to be right. This serves as the heading for our first section because communism, like these neo-fascist efforts, is nothing but a fantasy of salvation, the fanatic and frantic attempt to fix everything through overwhelming lies and fear. "The stronger the feelings of isolation, historical marginality, and social stress, the greater the temptation to scapegoat those who

through a massive restructuring of both human civilization and human nature itself. Every communist project shared this goal, while also at the same time adapted to the situation of the time of the country where it operated. Lenin's communism at first screamed anti-war propaganda (then became "war communism"), while East Germany fabricated a Spartan military state of propaganda and militarization against West Germany for its entire existence. The Maoist project notoriously exhausted (and ironically exterminated) the peasant.[5] Each communist experiment had tremendous variations, but also the same fundamental goals (among which are always mass murder and elite enrichment). This is evident in their results. Without fail, whether in Asia in the 60s, Africa in the 70s, or Latin America in the 80s and 2010s, communism pursued a course of totalitarianism. Communism has had a long life, across many different periods and regions, but certain principles were present in every manifestation.

Despite its long life span and inherent variation in a project that spanned seven decades and five continents, the reader can be sure that the communist millenarian promise was always constant. The ideology varied in its specifics, but its general lines of thinking were without fail the same: exterminate the enemies, purify those who remain, and then freedom will be forever. Who specifically the enemies were, and what specifically the chosen people had to learn differed, but what was constant was that the category of enemies was virtually limitless, and the intensity of this forced enlightenment unprecedented. Communism was never a basic dictatorship, where a cynical and selfish elite exploited a resentful population merely for their simple love of power and riches. Unfortunately communism, like fascism, was always an exhilarating mass action, where the majority of people embraced its idea of struggle. All the terror and propaganda was justified—and celebrated—in the fight against democratic forces, because according to the communist world-

---

are perceived as different, 'abnormal.'" This is the same on the right or the left. Vladimir Tismaneanu, *Fantasies of Salvation: Democracy, Nationalism, and Myth in Post-Communist Europe* (Princeton: Princeton University Press, 1998), 91.

5   See Yang Jisheng, *Tombstone: The Great Chinese Famine*, eds. Edward Friedman, Guo Jian, and Stacy Mosher, trans. Stacy Mosher and Guo Jian (New York: Farrar, Straus, and Giroux, 2008); and Frank Dikötter, *Mao's Great Famine: The History of China's Most Devastating Catastrophe, 1958–1962* (London: Bloomsbury, 2010). It has been shown that likely around 60 million, and at least 40–45 million, were killed in China's manufactured famine. We affirm also that the number of slaughtered is a human truth, a crime perpetrated by the regime and suffered by the people, and academic findings have no effect on what happened.

view, democracy is only capitalism, an capitalism is pure evil.

It was an alternative idea of morality.[6] The rights of individual citizens did not matter because, philosophically, communism saw value only in collectivism. Comfort, security, justice, and freedom could only come to the proletariat as a class. This meant that crime was impossible, because no individual had rights when the fate of humanity itself was on the line. Prominent aspects of communism—cults of personality, mass mobilization, concentration camps, censorship, imperialism, exploitation, indoctrination, etc.—were all part of this basic conception of collectivism. The enemies had to be exterminated so that the proletariat could be saved. This is why "mistakes" were never ruinous to the legitimacy of the Party and its regime. Frantic efforts for human salvation may have resulted in mass murder and large-scale corruption, but this was always acceptable because the goal was so worthy and the enemies so near. Equality was that goal, but the version implemented was a twisted one, where citizens and society had no rights.

Communism offered mental comfort for believers: a clear plan for how to address what were, and in truth are still even today, real injustices and inequalities in the liberal-democratic world. But beyond reform or progress, which all those who believe in freedom and rights should strive for, Leninism meant eternal self-confidence and a fatalist hubris. No longer would people be ashamed to be stuck in their low class, and no longer would people feel helpless at exploitation and oppression. Such was the strength of communist indoctrination and mobilization (the totalitarian extreme of authoritarian propaganda and terror), that though worker were never more exploited than under communism,[7] and citizens never more oppressed, people believed

---

6   Again, this lie presents an eerie similarity to Trump. For his administration the similarity lies in his straight-faced proposal of "alternative facts," which are literally impossible, unless truth and morality count for nothing.

7   Hungarian dissidents provide much on this topic: "Here I am, stuck in front of my machine, bound hand and foot by piece-rates. Workers on the conveyor belt and those who run the automatic machines are tied by the machine themselves, the rest by discipline." "Mutual rights and obligations" are "a collective agreement: almost everybody knows that, but nobody knows what is in it." Miklós Haraszti, *A Worker in a Worker's State*, trans. Michael Wright (New York: Universe Books, 1978), 147–148, 95.

"As a *dictatorship* over needs we consider it is a value degradation, a demolition of the potentially free individual who voluntary association would form an emancipated society, in the imagination of Marx and every socialist." "It actually realizes the total subjugation of the workforce to the commanding centres of industrial development." Ferenc Fehér, Ágnes Heller, and György Márkus, *Dictatorship Over Needs* (New York: St. Martin's Press, 1983), 221, 232.

under communism they were standing upright while every other system would have them bowed. That this was precisely the opposite of reality merely demonstrates the frightful truth of communism—it was not only among the greatest crimes in history, the sincerity of its perpetrators and victims was and is an absurdity.

The Old Regimes were not the only targets of communism. The Reign of Terror, first attempted by Robespierre and the jacobins in the 1790s (a strong inspiration for Lenin),[8] was implemented to target the enemies of their new society. All communist experiments have employed this strategy as well.[9] Meanwhile, the reign of lies was induced to straighten out those who remain. Even the worthy people who were admitted to this new utopia were suspect. Only total reeducation could ensure that the citizens who were not exterminated as enemies were then able to become the kind of New Man (communism is always sexist) that this New World required. Workers had to spend their precious free time not with their families and communities but in party "meetings," soldiers had to obey battlefield orders from political commissars rather than knowledgeable officers, writers and artists had to follow the lines of thinking of "dialectical experts," because nothing was permitted—even success—if it was not done in the correct way. Perhaps communism failed at everything it did, aside from violence, not merely because of the paradoxes of the command economy, but because no one was permitted to actually work. Everything was dictated by dialectics and the class struggle, leaving genuine talent and honest effort forbidden. So human beings were

---

[8]   There is a bizarre, and when put into context revolting, anecdote about Lenin while he lived in Paris. He spent six months in the City of Light, and never once visited the Louvre. Meanwhile, he visited the Museum about the Commune Insurrection dozens of times. This was during Lenin's exile, when he was sure he would never see the Revolution. That is, he did this not out of research or planning, but mere personal interest—violence was everything, and culture, the beautiful potential of the human mind and emotions, nothing. He would institute these values rigorously upon his population.

[9]   Notably, the *Wall Street Journal* has just recently classified Ortega's regime in Nicaragua this way. Whether Ortega is a neo-communist resurrection or a post-communist degeneration is debatable, but it is objective that his Sandinista Front was a communist movement and he continues to use this as his foundation of power as he shoots to death hundreds of workers, students, and mothers in the street. The Editorial Board, "Ortega's Reign of Terror," *Wall Street Journal*, July 20, 2018, online edition, https://www.wsj.com/articles/ortegas-reign-of-terror-1532127542. Two years after the crushed rebellion, Ortega's machine brutally enforces a violent silence across the land. Frances Robles, "Nicaragua Has a Simple Message for Protesters: Don't," *New York Times*, December 26, 2019, online edition, https://www.nytimes.com/2019/12/26/world/americas/nicaragua-ortega-protests.html.

ultimately superfluous.

Communism went through a complicated history, and it is not linear. There was the Bolshevik coup and the crumbling of the Russian Empire into civil war and its colonies' wars of independence. This was a heady time of optimism for Russian communists and exhilaration for intellectuals across the West.[10] During the 20s and 30s under Stalin, Soviet communism focused on "socialism in one country." Europe and America were locked into either fascism or ailing democracy, and the rest of the world was drowning in the West's imperialism. So, communism only had success in the Soviet Union, along with admiration from fellow-travelers throughout the West. After World War II, when Soviet communism's stock had risen exponentially during its titanic (but in many ways exaggerated) fight against fascism in the 30s and 40s (for example, more Ukrainians were killed fighting Hitler than Russians, and the Germans killed more Ukrainian civilians than Russian civilians), Stalinism again returned to its revolutionary imperialism in Eastern Europe. The Soviet Union's explosive introductory violence in its new Eastern European colonies was matched by a reignited popular and intellectual enthusiasm, both from Stalin's own new subjects and fellow-travelers elsewhere. A decade later, as Khrushchev struggled to maintain anti-Stalinist Leninism, communism found new life in Latin America and Asia. Much of Africa joined the class struggle in the 60s, 70s, and 80s because people there were desperate for inspiration during the horrors involved in liberating themselves from Western imperialism. Communism went through waves of triumph in Latin America and Asia during these decades as well. At the same time, communism in Europe became a joke. But communism's terror was so powerful that no one challenged it, and its indoctrination so clever that few wanted to. Brezhnev and Gorbachev may have been failures, but still much of the masses of the Soviet Empire believed that surely this was better than "capitalism." Meanwhile, terrorism and genocide rocked the developing world—China, Cambodia, Zimbabwe, Ethiopia, Cuba, Nicaragua, Argentina, Peru, and more

---

[10] The thoughtless cruelty and radical ideology of the Red Army at the time is hauntingly revealed in Isaac Babel's *Red Calvary*. Consider "the dead fighters of the First Calvary, that proud phalanx which pounds the anvil of future centuries with the hammer of history." Isaac Babel, *Red Calvary* (New York: W. W. Norton & Company, 2002), 126. Stephen Kotkin shows how Lenin and his Bolsheviks saw the Invasion of Poland as the first steppingstone to global communist victory. From Poland to Germany, Germany to France, Italy to Britain, Britain to America, and then automatically the colonized world, leaving nothing remaining but red. They were mad with delusions of imminent global, final, eschatological triumph. Stephen Kotkin, *Stalin—Volume I, Paradoxes of Power* (New York: Penguin Press, 2014), 352–379.

all got to momentarily experience ultimate happiness.

For so many reasons, the overarching one being communism's incompatibility with the free nature of human beings and the messy but righteous diversity of human society, communism eventually collapsed. A large part of this, at least in the Soviet Empire, was the long struggle of dissidents. After decades of public resistance,[11] the masses finally started to hear them when they said that communism, a system of deprivation, lies, humiliation, and murder, made no sense, and that democracy was not "capitalist exploitation" but simple human decency. When the people finally found the courage to walk onto the street and face the rifles and tanks pointing at them, the Soviets and their colonies carried out half-hearted massacres and then surrendered (barely having enough backbone to take the time to pack up their plunder to take it with them as they fled). In the developing world, the lack of material progress that communism had managed, in increasingly pathetic contrast to the rest of the "capitalist" world, along with the mounting toll of their mass murder and the growing intolerability of their lies, combined with the end of Soviet inspiration and assistance to mean communism had neither the means nor the motives to fight on. After seven decades, people (perhaps only momentarily) chose democracy and plurality over the totalitarian struggle for utopia. Of course, part of the ensuing problem which quickly erased such advances in global human dignity was the widespread drift from democracy back to capitalism as the political, social, and moral system.

This, broadly, is the history of communism. The local situation mattered immensely. Time and space determined so much about the movement. For any given communist experiment, the crucial question is what era or wave of communist euphoria was it taking place in, and what region? Then of course there are national and social individualities distinct even from its neighbors and peers. By deeply investigating some case studies, this volume seeks to draw out the main lessons of the world's experience of communism overall. For, while there have been countless communist experiments and they were all so diverse, the basic character and performance of all is eerily similar. There is a common thread of ideology in every communist experiment, and this shared foundation is always dominant.

---

[11] Havel relays how society, and the dissidents, themselves all thought "we are madmen who are beating our heads against a wall." For decades, they were, with no mass response. Elzbieta Matynia, ed. and trans., *An Uncanny Era: Conversations Between Vaclav Havel and Adam Michnik* (New Haven: Yale University Press, 2014), 51.

Remarkably few efforts at a grand examination of communism have taken place around this grim centennial. Most notably, *The New York Times* has intermittently published its "Red Century" series. There was very little attempt from the *Times* to highlight the important lessons of what it calls the "Red Century," a name which is perfectly appropriate, nor to extrapolate the lessons that the fanaticism of communism clearly offers in our current era. Most disturbing of all was the assertion that women had more orgasms under communism.[12] For women, communist ideology and reality were based in subjugation, sexual harassment, and rape.[13] Slavenka Drakulic, for instance, admonished American fellow-travelers for ignoring that, "women there [in Communism] don't have either napkins or Tampaxes."[14] The *Times* piece was followed by no refutation, but it is such an insane, untrue, and disrespectful claim to make that a leading publication in American and the world should never have given credence to it, even if had inclined to publish a response to it. An equivalent to this claim would be to say that we should admire the civic youth culture of Hitler's Germany, or to praise the sense of community solidarity allegedly produced by Saudi Arabia and Iran's piety.

It is this failure of understanding, the insistence that there is nothing necessarily wrong with communism, only in how it has (erroneously, its proponents assure) been attempted so far, that must be addressed, for the sake of the past and the future. This kind of thinking is an insult to communism's victims past and present, and an invitation for radical ideologies, communist and fascist, to return to ravage the people of the world not privileged enough to live in democratic countries where they can make intellectual calls for communism from the safety of their armchairs. Without a firm comprehension of the reality and morality of totalitarianism, we will prove unable to

---

12   Kristen Ghodsee, "Why Women Had Better Sex Under Socialism," *New York Times*, August 12, 2017, online edition, https://www.nytimes.com/2017/08/12/opinion/why-women-had-better-sex-under-socialism.html. One of our own contributors, Venelin Ganev, investigated her research and found her data to be completely false. See Venelin Ganev, "Orgasmic Communism??? Critical Reflections on Kristen R. Ghodsee's New York Times Op-Ed," *The New Contemporary: Notes from the Havighurst Center*, January 09, 2018, online edition, https://blogs.miamioh.edu/havighurst/2018/01/09/orgasmic-communism/.

13   See Maria Bucur hauntingly describe constant sexual assault in public, beginning at the age of 7. Maria Bucur, "Sex in the Time of Communism: the ripple effect of the #metoo campaign," *Public Seminar*, December 07, 2017, online, https://publicseminar.org/2017/12/sex-in-the-time-of-communism/.

14   Slavenka Drakulić, *How We Survived Communism and Even Laughed* (New York: Harper Perennial, 1991), 124, 123–132.

successfully confront the newest challenges to diversity and tolerance.

Beyond *The New York Times*, little other efforts have been made at all to commemorate the horror that was communism; to use this centenary of its birth to conveniently take stock of this block of history, and to draw lessons which are so needed at the moment. Our project asserts the necessity of re-membering the communist period, to investigate its main features, and to take these as lessons for dealing with neo-communism and neo-fascism in the present. This conference and volume were originally conceived as a timely study of the past, and by the time they came to fruition, they had become an urgently needed exercise for an increasingly troubled world. Even if our world was not so exponentially plagued by mass ideological hu-bris as is definitive, not in scope but in conclusions. No such retrospective of one hundred years of communism has been done. As communist power and memory has faded, so has interest and attention to its faults. There remains much to learn. This volume cannot be the end, but it does hope to be the first of an effort to finally say that we have understood communism, and that we condemn it.

Fresh evaluations are rife within this book, even if most people consider the study of communism long ago finished. What remains to be said about this volume is that the findings of each contribution are beyond the specific and extend to the general. The theme of this book is lessons, urgently needed. Besides the specific look at communisms past, and considerations of common communist characteristics and strategies, this book also provides something new—a look at modern communism. In chapters on Xi's China and Chávez and Maduro's Venezuela, this book explicitly asserts that we are seeing a new wave of communism. Sadly, current regimes, as successor states to communist societies, also form the concluding section of many of the chapters. The con-tributors to this volume agree that we are, as Arendt said, "between past and future." That we are seeing a new communist wave may seem surprising to some, but judging by the reality of these places, of the crimes committed there and the ideology of the perpetrators and the supporting masses behind them, we uphold this thesis. And no one should doubt that we are seeing a new fascist wave as well. We also believe that the two are related, in fact hardly distinct, and that the lessons of communism are applicable to fighting both communism and fascism today. Maduro may be a clown, Orbán may be rabidly anti-communist, Xi may be a capitalist oligarch, and Castro may be a decrepit relic, but the attempted totalitarianism of all of them and any others of their cohort can be understood, and therefore resisted, only by considering the themes and arc of the first one hundred years of communism. Themes of fascist experiments are equally required to fully understand these new dictators.

The key issue of each chapter is to understand how the reconstruction of human civilization and human nature was pursued in a given communist experiment. Every communist experiment is a genuinely mass ideological project.[15] Unfortunately, this volume is not as wide in scope as we would like. But that is only because there has been truly too many communist experiments to capture even a mere geographic sample in one book. However, we are confident that the case studies provided are various, and the strategies of the contributors intentioned enough, that this can be a representative sample and a good starting point for thinking about communism overall. In many communist experiments, Marxism played merely a supporting, even a fabricated, role to local history, issues, crises, ideologies, despots, and clowns. Either way, this volume presents incisive examinations of specific examples of Leninist politics.

The first part of this volume, "Fantasies of Salvation," makes clear the point of this project, and highlights the goal and thesis of all our contributors. Communism was an ideological ecstasy. Passion for justice led to hubris in oppression. We see this in the first chapter, Jeffrey Herf's look at German communism. First, German communism was about anti-fascism. Many Central European Jews were drawn to communism because they saw it as an attempt to destroy anti-Semitism, and to destroy the reactionary influence of religion, including Judaism. After the war and Stalinization, German communism then saw resisting Israel as the fight against global, now American-led, imperialism. East Germany supported Arab "anti-imperialism," sent massive amounts of heavy weaponry to the states fighting against Israel, and did not denounce Palestinian terrorism. In East Germany anti-fascism led to anti-Semitism; this clearly demonstrates our thesis that ideology not only clouded communists' worldview but led them to attempt to devastate the world itself. Similarly, Vladimir Tismaneanu looks at the arc of communist ideological conviction in Eastern Europe. For the first three decades of communism, Marxist-Leninist ideology was cherished by intellectuals. For two decades after Stalin's conquest, it was the exhilaration of the masses as well.

---

15   We agree with Eric Hoffer that these projects are the willful choice of the masses. See Eric Hoffer, *True Believer: Thoughts on the Nature of Mass Movements* (New York: Harper Perennial, 1989).

But eventually the truth became obvious. As a result, intellectuals shifted to Marxism (without Leninism) and eventually to post-Marxism and even liberalism. The masses fell into cynicism and submission. Meanwhile the Eastern European state bureaucracies succumbed to corruption, thuggery, and blind power. This breakdown in ideology led to a breakdown in communist society and power. That the end of ideology was the definitive cause of death of communism reveals how necessary a utopian faith is for totalitarianism to take place. Mykola Riabchuk looks at how Ukrainian communism enthusiastically got on, and then eventually got off, "the red tram of socialism," as Józef Piłsudski called it. Ukrainian communism started a debate in 1918 between those who wanted independence and those who decided that the humanist hopes of socialism could be pursued within the Soviet Union. It took decades of Soviet imperialism for the Ukrainian leftists to eventually recognize the reality that progress in Ukraine could never come while their country was occupied by Moscow. Russian Bolshevik chauvinism and racism made any alternative impossible. The Bolsheviks' similarities with the Tsarist and reactionary regimes they hated so much was unimportant if their actions were in pursuit of their worldview, in their eyes. Finally, Mark Kramer concludes Part One by exploring how the tyrannical nature of Bolshevik ideology lead to the mass crimes of the Soviet Union, as well as its downfall. Gorbachev's modest reforms terminally infected Soviet communism because the ideology was ruined if it was diluted, and without ideology the totalitarian system was feeble. After communism, the liberal thought that was present in Russia was so shallow and artificial that it could not succeed. Putin's authoritarianism returned, and in fact co-opted "democracy," disproving the providence of liberalism in the eyes of most Russians and therefore returning Russia to authoritarian rule. The four chapters of Part One show us how communism was more than anything an ideology, and precisely what it was and what this means is the most fundamental explanation of the history of all communist experiments.

Part Two looks at the economics of communist regimes. Paul Dragos Aligica and Vlad Tarko examine the widespread belief that many people are nostalgic for the communist era. The contributors use data on the material and social realities of countries during communist and post-communist regimes to examine if there is any truth to the cliché that economically, life was stable and bearable under late communism. By looking at many factors such as health, consumption, labor productivity, and general studies of happiness, they come to the conclusion that "the record of communism is mixed at best," but it is clear that "life seems significantly better during post-communism than it was during communism." Their detailed research leaves little room for doubt, they are able to say conclusively that any nostalgia for communism is irrational, any longing merely ideological, rather than material or economic. Next, Steven Rosefielde surveys the historical idea that communism was a push for a workers' paradise. Instead of freedom there was oppression, and instead of paradise there was exploitation and failure. "Twentieth century communism went wrong because the vanguard of the proletariat was ruthless," Rosefielde argues, and left no possibility for political freedom or economic liberation, as the "verdict of history" has shown. Central planning was a miserable failure, and there was no way it could not be. Any vision for a command economy remains doomed to fail. Next, Peter Rutland specifically looks at the fate of the Soviet economy. To a tyrannical elite, economic planning gave political benefits—industrialization, militarization, modernization. Economically, however, the system could not function. Furthermore, the highly structured system was so vertically-bound that it was not capable of reform. So the system would always fail. Countering some rival assertions in scholarship, Rutland shows that the Party stayed in control, and no technocracy could ever develop to ease the inefficiencies of such a system. Following this, Rutland argues that the myth of the plan cannot be replaced by the myth of the market. This urgent advice for the future demonstrates that any blind faith to an unyielding economic vision is bound to cause disaster. Building on the same theme, Michael Bernstam compares centrally planned economies to the market economies of the West and the developing economies of the non-communist world. Making use of extensive data, he shows that through coercion, communism did create economic modernization and performed better than the un-planned economies of the developing world. But compared to the incentive-based and open market economies of the West, communist economies could never overcome the limits and inefficiencies of the planned economy. Long-term economic growth was impossible from a planned system. Coercion proved inadequate in motivating production, consumption, and prosperity. Finally, Part Two concludes with Serguey Braguinsky tracing at the rise and fall of the planned economy and its impact on the post-communist transition. Braguinksy starts with the fact that the Soviet Union was a totalitarian dictatorship. As such, its goal was to preserve totalitarian control. So, all the "deadweight" of the planned economy was tolerated because it prevented the road from economic development to political reform that Europe had experienced in the nineteenth and twentieth centuries. Welfare of citizens was irrelevant. With the (self-imposed) goals and constraints of the communist system, the planned economy was their only option. Today, Putin's kleptocracy and dictatorship are the newest, and hopefully final, stages of the communist economy. The five chapters in Part Two serve to definitively evaluate communist economies. Furthermore, sticking to the goal of this volume, our contributors' demonstration of the irrational, unbending commitment of the communist states to such disastrous economic regimes further shows that this was an ideological project, in which ruin and collapse were acceptable collateral damage.

Part Three looks at the politics of communist regimes. First, Leon Aron compares the Bolsheviks in the time of Lenin to ISIS today. Both were millenarian projects. Rather than being redemptive, a more accurate description of each ideology is fatalistic—both saw the end of the world, through indulgent violence, which would then bring Heaven on Earth. Aron's comparison is particularly striking, juxtaposing Lenin's small group of a century ago with current fanatics, whose barbarism we are quite familiar with. This exterminatory violence among Bolsheviks and ISIS members comes from their dedication to introducing a radically new world. Next, Marius Stan looks at "Tito's Leninism." Essentially, this heretic from Stalinism remained a Leninist-Stalinist himself, the only disagreement being he did not want to be a colony of Moscow. Despite the split from Stalin, this did not mean Tito wanted to liberalize, and if anything, especially after Stalin's death, Yugoslavia remained more Stalinist than the Soviet Union. Stan concludes by looking at the dissident Djilas, giving us a ray of hope, something rare in the story of this volume. Turning back to the contemporary, Margaret Pearson looks at China today and of the future. Explaining China's "continued utilization of the Leninist party toolkit" and "the willingness to employ coercive tools to undermine" free thinking and any non-Party organization, Pearson asserts some conclusions which are shocking but absolutely true. Ideology is alive and well in China, the result being a dictatorship which is increasingly among the worst on earth at the moment. Propaganda and terror remain trusted arms of a truly Leninist regime. This trend is only continuing and escalating as China enters neo-Maoism under Xi Jinping. Pearson urges us to immediately recognize that Leninism is not a corrupted pillar of legitimacy, but a real source of motive in the rule of the Chinese Communist

Party and the continued subjugation of China's people. Meanwhile, Venelin Ganev asks a simple question: Jim Crow and Nazism receive no mainstream reconsideration today, so why does communism? Why does leftist extremism, which was just as totalitarian as the worst utopias of the far right, still inspire such "enduring ideological invincibility?" A large part of the reason is the systematic de-legitimatization of anti-communism, Ganev says, reducing any anti-communist thinking, even from the left, as being a cover for Ronald Reagan-like conservatism. "Anti-anti-communism" remains strong even after the Cold War, and the passage of time seems to be redeeming, rather than condemning, communism—ignoring the real practices of Marxist regimes toward their own subjects. To conclude Part Three, Jordan Luber considers Venezuela under Chavismo, looking first at how Chávez was elected: harping on about enemies, the beauty of the people, and the need to mobilize, unite, and struggle to achieve. Dictatorship followed. An impressive indoctrination state reached totalitarian levels of control with relatively little violence. Now under Maduro, the state's rhetoric is less compelling and the violence more expansive, but the Chavista masses remain fanatically faithful all the same. Luber ends comparing Maduro to Chávez, the difference being Maduro is a jacobin, something worse than the average communist. The five chapters of Part Three leave us with a haunting sense of exactly how fervent communists are, and how important manipulation and power are in achieving not only state control but also actual popular support.

Part Four looks at how communist experiments reshape society and culture. First, Noemi Marin considers communist rhetoric. While immensely diverse from one experiment to the next, communist discourse always shares fundamental similarities. The point is always to convince its population and the world of the state's legitimacy, and the general strategy is always the same. Marin categorizes communist rhetoric "within the epideictic frame-work of praise and blame, without any intervention from deliberative and/or argumentative discursive paradigms." Communist rhetoric, employed without restraint and never allowing of rival voices, often finds success. Since "history is appropriated correctly only by and within communist narratives of salvation," communist discourse presents itself as naturally infallible. Such public dis-courses also explain why nationalism is so mainstream in post-communist countries. Next, András Bozóki looks at the history of intellectuals and the state in post-totalitarian communist Hungary. The post-Revolution Kadar state tried to keep intellectuals from threatening the Party's hold on society without resorting to overwhelming and risky violence. Censorship could not prevent an underground, illegal culture developing in parallel to the official communist one. Years of manipulation, struggle, and control evolved into the age of dissidents, who eventually ignited the spark that toppled the regime. Despite what Hungary is experiencing now, Bozóki leaves us a slightly hopeful picture of how thought and truth can overcome ideology. Moving across the border to Romania, Mircea Mihaies then looks at one of the key ideological pillars of the bizarre Ceauşescu regime, "protochronism." Simply put, this was the insistence that the Romanian nation was the greatest one in history—responsible for modern technology, communist courage, and essentially every development and progress in human history. This was absurd, but employed so fervently by obedient court intellectuals that this was the dominant narrative in Romania's frozen society. "An archipelago of madness" and "the perversity of the system" is all that can be said of thought and speech in Ceauşescu's times. Today in Romania, nationalist discourse remains ubiquitous and successful. Turning to religion, Piotr H. Kosicki considers Catholic views on communism during the twentieth century. From the earlier era of Catholic resistance to modernity and the left, "we see… the origins of the hybrid grammar of Catholic socialism." Catholics were taking Marx seriously because, given the social reality, a reconsideration of class conflict made sense to their non-secular approach to the world. During Stalinism, Polish Catholic socialists insisted on working with Marxists, while later in Latin America this evolved into Catholicism itself openly embracing the class struggle. Eventually, after communism fell, Catholicism again turned its attention to anti-liberalism, demonstrating that above all it shared with communism anti-liberal and anti-modern sentiments. Finally, in the last chapter of Part Four and of the volume Marci Shore's re-examines one of the critical pillars of Marx's thought, alienation. Alienation is modern society's scourge. All philosophers have wrestled with it; Marx's response was to eliminate private property. The Bolsheviks thought this meant to wipe out all those who allegedly had any real or perceived attachments to the old system. But, Shore says, Marx was wrong because the problem of alienation is not about private property or even modernity at all, but that merely existing as a human being inherently comes with an unsettled subjectivity. Marx misunderstood human nature. Ending alienation can only be done by trying to overcome human nature itself—hence the communists' insatiable violence and lies.

We are proud of the contributions these authors have made to this book. We are pleased with the picture that has been constructed, and believe it puts forward a strong argument. The flow of this book will guide the reader through a dismal but critical period in human history, and hopefully will help prepare the reader for this new age of madness. The debates at the conference were exciting affairs, and we are happy to share these challenging and complex conversations with our reader now. Hannah Arendt, Milovan Djilas, María Elena Moyano, Wei Jingsheng and so many others—with whose words can we conclude? Somewhat arbitrarily from this expansive and stunning group, we chose Havel, the quote which was the original motto of our conference: "In spite of this, I think the world now faces a huge opportunity that is offered by this vacuum,"[16] the vacuum of dignity and humility offered by those who resist the comfort and anger of communism.

---

[16] Elzbieta Matynia, ed. and trans., *An Uncanny Era: Conversations Between Vaclav Havel and Adam Michnik* (New Haven: Yale University Press, 2014), 52.

PART ONE

Fantasies of Salvation

GERMAN COMMUNISM, THE JEWS, AND ISRAEL

From the Anti-fascism of World War II to the Undeclared Wars of the Cold War

Jeffrey Herf

The promise of communism in 1917 was a world without war, social classes and, to quote the other Lenin, John Lennon, "no religion too." Religion was as Marx put it, the opiate of the people, while Judaism the essence of a despised capitalism. Part of communism's fantasy of salvation was to end the false consciousness of religious faith by ending the class oppression from which it supposedly sprang. Yet communism in Russia also emerged in opposition to Tsarism and to the antisemitic policies it implemented. In Central and Eastern Europe, communism was attractive to some Jews because they associated it with the fight against antisemitism. Or, as in the case of the Hungarian theorist Georg Lukacs, they were drawn to the Communist Party in hopes of replacing what he called a reified world of alienation with a classless society and human community that would finally smash the false consciousness that religion had nourished for centuries. These two impulses, fighting against antisemitism yet also smashing the myths of religion, including those of Judaism, both contributed to the communist project. Though as we will see, the latter was from beginning to end the norm and orthodox core of Marxism-Leninism. The former, the attack on antisemitism, became dominant only in two exceptional periods of the history of European communism.

In 1935, when the comintern abruptly ended the "class against class" attack on "social fascism" and began the popular front of anti-fascism in 1935, the appeal of communism for secular Jews deepened as the Soviet Union called for collective security against Hitler, while France and Britain adopted a policy of appeasement. As Francois Furet reminded us in *The Passing of an Illusion*, anti-fascism was central to the appeal of communism in Europe before and during World War II. Yet anti-fascism was also a chapter in what the German historian Karl Bracher called the history of the underestimation of Hitler's ideology. For communists, Nazism was first of all a product of capitalism and its primary targets were first the radical left in Germany and then the Soviet Union, not the Jews of Europe. Rather than see antisemitism for what it was, the ideological core of Nazism and the key to its policies, the dominant view in the Comintern was that Jew-hatred was a cynical tool of the German ruling classes whose purpose was to mystify the working classes. Yet Hitler and Goebbels' denunciation of "Jewish Bolshevism" had the result of fostering a solidarity of sorts among those who were the Nazis intended victims, communists and Jews.

For millions who had been drawn into the orbit of the Popular Front, Stalin's non-aggression pact with Hitler in August 1939 came as a shattering blow to the communist-Jewish solidarity of the previous four years. The pact made it possible for Hitler to begin World War II, one indispensable precondition for the Holocaust to come. It was Hitler, not Stalin who reignited the communist rapprochement with the Jews. He did so by launching the war of extermination on the Eastern Front in June 1941 and implementing the Holocaust until the end of the war in spring 1945. The two years of Soviet alliance with the Nazis was forgotten as the Red Army and Red Air Force decimated the Wehrmacht and Luftwaffe at the enormous cost of eight million military deaths and sixteen million civilian deaths. The Nazis waged war on "Jewish Bolshevism" yet it was the Soviet Union and its armed forces that played a major role in the defeat of Nazi Germany and the liberation of Eastern Europe from Nazi occupation and mass murder.

World War II was a return to the popular front anti-fascism of 1935–1939. Furet pointed out that the wartime alliance with Britain and the United States seemed, for some, to associate the Soviet dictatorship with democracy and the common fight against the Nazis. The anti-Hitler coalition also raised hopes among a minority of communists that Marxism-Leninism might find room for the particularity of Judaism and the Jews and the specificities of antisemitism. After all, the war was one waged against a racist and antisemitic regime so was not its logical implication support for Zionism and a state of the Jews? These were conclusions reached by Paul Merker, a member of the Politburo of the German Communist Party who found refuge in Mexico City. In his essays in Mexican emigration, Merker drew attention to Jew-hatred as the ideological core of the Nazi regime using reports of the mass murder of the Jews, and argued for financial restitution to Jewish survivors and support for Zionist plans for a Jewish state in Palestine.[1]

This minority tradition in European communism that focused on Jewish questions was evident as well in the journalism of the Soviet war correspondent, Vasily Grossmann, as well as in his novel *Life and Fate*. Grossmann and Merker stood in sharp contrast to the generalizing abstractions of wartime anti-fascism, which often marginalized the Jewish catastrophe or subsumed it as one among many of Nazism's crimes. Orthodox Marxist-Leninists found Jewish questions to be uncomfortable at best and at worst an ideological deviation that undermined the class struggle, diverted attention from Nazism's many other victims, and was an irritating barrier to their vision of a world without religion. In Los Angeles in 1944, Max Horkheimer and Theodor Adorno described fascism as the product of a dialectic of enlightenment, a philosophy which prizes tolerance and complexity. Yet a rage against otherness and irritation with the persistence of the Jewish question interfering with the simplistic narrative of the class struggle was also, perhaps even more so, a component of communist rationalism.

After the war, the deviations from the party line advocated for by Merker and Grossmann reached high into the Soviet regime to the office of Andrew Gromyko, its long serving Foreign Minister. In 1947 at the United Nations in New York, he famously supported the UN Partition Plan for a Jewish and an Arab state in Palestine, the original "two-state solution," accepted by the Jews but rejected then by the Arab states and the Palestinian Arabs. Gromyko blamed the "bourgeois powers" for their failure to save Europe's Jews, thereby repressing discussion of what the Soviet Union, with its vast armed forces and their physical proximity to the death camps and killing fields, could have done to stop the Final Solution. Yet the key point was that for Gromyko and many other communists, and certainly most leftists such as Jean Paul Sartre or the editors of the *Manchester Guardian* in Britain and *The Nation*

---

[1] Faced with the horrendous loss of life by the armies and peoples of the Soviet Union and the horror of Nazism's rule in Europe, few were eager to ask why the Soviet Union's vast land army and huge air force did not intervene to stop the mass murder of Europe's Jews, especially after the Battle of Stalingrad in early 1943 as the front moved West and the death camps in Poland came within range of Soviet planes. In 2003, in the journal *Kritika* I published an essay on this topic. As far as I know, neither scholars of the Soviet Union or those who ask what the United States and Britain could have done have pursued the issue. Yet it was the Soviet army and air force, not those of the Western allies that was within range and by 1943 had command of the air over the Eastern Front. Stopping the Holocaust, the details of which must certainly have been known to the Soviet regime, was simply not a priority. Jeffrey Herf, "The Nazi Extermination Camps and the Ally to the East: Could the Soviet Armed Forces Have Stopped or Slowed the Final Solution?" *Kritika: Explorations in Russian and Eurasian History* 4, no. 4 (2003): 913–30.

in this country, support for establishment of a Jewish state in Palestine was the seemingly obvious moral consequence of the Holocaust. The Israeli delegation at the United Nation used the term "Soviet Zionism" to describe the link between wartime anti-fascism and postwar communist support for the Zionist project.

For the Czech communists, support extended beyond voting for a UN resolution. It encompassed delivery of weapons to the Yishuv, the pre-state Jewish organizations in Mandate Palestine in 1947 and 1948, deliveries that were indispensable for the survival and then victory in the war of 1948. The Czech communists, like Merker and Gromyko, saw support for Zionism and Jewish national self-determination as a continuation of wartime anti-fascism. While there were Arabs who fought with the British, memories were still vivid of the Haj Amin al-Husseini's radio addresses for the Nazi regime and fears in 1942 that defeat at the Battle of Al Alamein might lead to Arab collaboration with the Nazis. For leftist and liberal sentiment in Europe in the immediate postwar years, the Arab regimes appeared to be bastions of political reaction, authoritarianism and, yet again, hatred of the Jews.

Communism's sympathy for Zionism and Israel did not last long. The orthodoxy of Marxism-Leninism returned with a vengeance against the Jews, first in the Doctor's Plot in Moscow in 1949 and then in the "anti-cosmopolitan" purges that spread throughout the Soviet bloc from 1949 to 1953. The trials recycled conspiracy theories about powerful Jews linked to capitalism that had been standard fare for fascist and Nazi conspiracy theories, now presented in the language of Leninist anti-imperialism. In 1952, the Czech communists paid the bill for decisions in 1947 and 1948 to send military assistance to the Jews in Palestine, which in retrospect seemed inexplicable. In November of that year, in a farce of a trial in Prague that featured confessions produced by torture, Rudolf Slánský, the General Secretary of the Czech Communist Party, and thirteen other defendants, eleven of whom were Jews, were found guilty of being agents of American imperialism and Zionism. By then, within the communist world, "Zionism" had become a term of abuse. On November 30, 1952, Slánský and ten others were executed by hanging. They paid with their lives for their contribution to the era of Soviet Zionism. The organizers of the purges redefined the anti-fascism and subsequent pro-Zionism of 1947–1948 as an embarrassing and regrettable deviation from the global struggle against American imperialism, global capitalism and its alleged Zionist "spearhead." The Slánský trial brought the era of Soviet Zionism to a violent ending.

On December 3, 1952, Stasi agents arrested Paul Merker in East Germany. On December 20, 1952 the Central Committee of the Socialist Unity Party, that is, the East German communist Party, published "Lessons of the Trial against the Slansky Conspiracy Center." It author, Central Committee member Herman Matern, denounced "the criminal activity of Zionist organizations" who were supposedly in league with "American agents" in an effort to destroy the "people's democracies" of Eastern Europe.[2] As was the case in Prague, the East German communists, in willing cooperation with directions from Moscow, reinterpreted Merker's empathy for the Jews and support for Zionism. Rather than view support for Zionism during the war as what it was, namely an expression of Communist wartime anti-fascism, Matern wrote that "the Zionist movement has nothing to do with the goals of humanity. It is dominated, directed and organized by US imperialism [and] exclusively serves its interests and the interests of Jewish capitalists."[3] So, overnight, the implementers of the purge turned the veteran communist Merker into an agent of American imperialism, one whose guilt was surely proven by the fact that he advocated support for Zionism even though he was not Jewish. As Marxist-Leninist ideology precluded such a stance, Merker's prosecutors concluded that he must have done so due to financial corruption in league with wealthy American Jews.

Attributions of great power, associations with a despised capitalism, and allegations of conspiratorial activity were all indictments of the anti-cosmopolitan purges. Indeed the name of the purges themselves echoed themes that had become familiar in the catalogue of European antisemitism, as did the assertion the Zionism had "nothing to do with the goals of humanity." The antisemitic essence of the anti-cosmopolitan purges was obvious then and has become more so with historical reconstruction of both public and previously secret documents of the time. One point I want to stress is that this revival of antisemitic discourse in the Soviet bloc in the first years of the Cold War was also a return to ideological normalcy in the history of communism and its guiding ideology, Marxism-Leninism. Empathy for the Jews and support for Zionism was due to the exceptional circumstances created by the coincidence of Nazi Germany's simultaneous

---

[2] On Merker's arrest and the indictment see Jeffrey Herf, *Divided Memory: The Nazi Past in the Two Germanys* (Cambridge, MA: Harvard University Press, 1997), 125–129.

[3] Herman Matern, "Lehren aus dem Prozeβ gegen das Verschwörerzentrum Slansky," *Dokumente der Sozialistische Einheitspartei, Band 4* ([East] Berlin: Dietz Verlag, 1954), 199–219; cited in Herf, *Divided Memory*, 125–126.

attack on communists, the Soviet Union and European Jewry. The far deeper structures of communist belief lay in hatred of capitalism, the belief that it required economic imperialism for its emergence and success, and the hopes ignited in October 1917 that world revolution would take place on the peripheries before conquering the metropoles.

The turn away from Zionism in the era of the purges also brought with it a change in the Soviet leadership's view of Arabs. Moscow was now placing its bets on the "anti-imperialism" of the Arab states and the Palestinians. The memories of Haj Amin al-Husseini's pro-Nazi, antisemitic and anticommunist radio diatribes during the war became an embarrassing memory as anti-imperialism came to replace and then redefine the meaning of anti-fascism. The communists transformed regimes they described as feudal, reactionary and Axis leaning during World War II into virtuous victims of Western and Zionist imperialism. For emotional and rhetorical reasons, the language of anti-fascism persisted in the communist movement, but it ceased to have any connection to empathy for the Jews. In the one hundred years of communism, the periods of the Popular Front from 1935–1939, and World War II and the immediate postwar years from 1941–1947, were exceptions to the norm of communist distrust and suspicion toward Jews and Judaism. The anti-Zionism from 1949 to 1989 was a return to ideological normalcy in the Marxist-Leninist interpretation of history and politics. One that moved away from at least some of the communist mentalities of World War II.

The postwar purges inaugurated four decades of increasing Soviet bloc antagonism to the state of Israel. Antagonism included hostile propaganda, and political warfare at the United Nations. From the 1960s to the collapse in 1989 it escalated to open and covert military support for both the Arab states and then the Palestinian terrorist organizations at war with Israel. As Isabella Ginor and Gideon Remez have recently documented, between the Six Day War of 1967 and the Yom Kippur War of 1973, about 50,000 members of the armed forces of the Soviet Union engaged in a shooting war with the Israelis along the Suez Canal.[4] For a historian of Germany the most astonishing chapter of communist antagonism to Israel was that written by the leaders of the German Democratic Republic or East Germany, a chapter I have examined in *Undeclared Wars with Israel: East Germany and*

---

[4] Isabella Ginor and Gideon Remez, *The Soviet-Israeli War, 1967–1973: The USSR's Military Intervention in the Egyptian-Israeli Conflict* (New York: Oxford University Press, 2017).

the West German Far Left, 1967–1989.[5] It was astonishing and disturbing that a German government after the Holocaust which defined itself as an anti-fascist regime never recognized the state of Israel nor had diplomatic relations with it and used its hostility—indeed hatred is not too strong a word—for Israel and Zionism as a playing card to gain friends in the Arab world. East Germany shattered what for the West German government became an unspoken eleventh commandment of German history after the Holocaust, namely to bring no more harm to the Jews or to the Jewish state. It brought plenty of harm to Israel.

During the Six Day War of 1967, the East German leader Walter Ulbricht, following the footsteps of Yakov Malik, the Soviet Ambassador to the United Nations, not only blamed Israel for the war and ignored the threats it faced from Arab states he also compared its policies to the occupation and expansionist policies of the Nazi regime. As my work in the archives of the East German Ministry of Defense, Council of Ministers and Ministry for State Security (the Stasi) revealed, that government sent tens of thousands of Kalashnikov assault rifles, rocket propelled grenade launchers, millions of bullets and hundreds of tanks and jet planes to Egypt, Iraq, and Syria when they were at war with Israel. In 1973 it became the first communist state in Europe to open an office of the Palestine Liberation Organization in its capital city of East Berlin at a time when the PLO was openly at war with Israel. From then until 1989 it supplied weapons and offered military training to the PLO as well as members of its Executive Committee including the Popular Front for the Liberation of Palestine (PFLP) when these organizations were engaged in horrific terrorist attacks on Israeli civilians in the 1970s and 1980s.

East German officials never denounced PLO terrorism directed at Israeli civilians. Indeed they reacted with indignation at the mere suggestion that a German government supplying weapons to states and terrorist organizations at war with the Jewish state could have anything at all to do with centuries-long traditions of antisemitism in European and German culture. Further, as Peter Florin, then East Germany's Ambassador to the United Nations, said, to call the PLO a terrorist organization was a "defamation" of a legitimate national liberation struggle. One will look in vain through the pages of the official government paper, *Neues Deutschland* for any empathy for the Israeli

---

[5] Jeffrey Herf, *Undeclared Wars with Israel: East Germany and the West German Far Left, 1967–1989* (New York: Cambridge University Press, 2016).

victims of Arab aggression or Palestinian terror or for factual accounts of the attacks on Israel in the 1970s and 1980s. One will come across many denunciations of apparently unprovoked "Israeli aggression." In the frank privacy of conversations between leaders of the PLO and the East German Ministry of State Security we read of the East German support for Palestinian terrorism against Israel so long as it did not extend to terrorist attacks in Western Europe that could be traced back to East Berlin—and thus undermine Détente with West Germany and Western Europe. The files reveal what I called East Germany's Eurocentric definition of counter-terrorism: support for Arab and Palestinian terrorism aimed at Israel but opposition to terrorism in Europe that would damage East Germany's claims that it was not a state sponsor of terror.

The return to Marxist-Leninist orthodoxy in the purges of 1949–1953 and the forgetting of the embarrassing alliance with Britain and the United States entailed a redefinition of the meaning of anti-fascism. It was shorn of any connection to opposition against antisemitism, defined as antagonism to Jews or Judaism. The Soviet Union and its East European satellites went a step further, a step that Robert Wistrich called "Holocaust inversion." They did not deny the existence of the Holocaust. Rather they inverted the meaning of fascism and Nazism by associating its past German associations with the state of Israel. In the communist lexicon, anti-fascism from the 1960s to the 1980s described the fight against Israel. The Israeli as Nazi entered into communist propaganda.

A photo captures the inversion. In 1978, during one of his many trips to East Berlin, Yasser Arafat visited the memorial in East Berlin to the victims of fascism. The photo of the event shows him solemnly paying respects accompanied by East German military and political leaders. The photo captures the transformation of the meaning of anti-fascism that I have been discussing. Arafat, then at war with Israel, appears as the inheritor of the legacy of anti-fascism established by the armed forces of the Soviet Union in war against Nazi Germany. Just as the Soviets fought the Nazis, now he inherited the mantle of anti-fascism in his armed struggle against Israel. The Israeli or Zionist as Nazi, imperialist, colonist, and racist remained a constant theme of Soviet bloc propaganda and policy. (The habit of calling people who are not Nazis, "Nazis" is one that survived the Soviet Union's collapse and is evident in Russia's attacks on Ukraine.) Had the Soviet policy that East Germany eagerly supported been successful, had the United States and the Western

Alliance lost the Cold War in the Middle East, it is likely that the state of Israel would have been destroyed by force of arms. The Western victory in the Cold War and the collapse of communism in 1989 was a disaster for the Arab governments and organizations seeking to destroy Israel. 1989 meant the loss of their major supplier of weapons and of diplomatic support for a radical attack on Israel. These are consequences that are rarely noted in the vast commentary on the revolutions and implosions of 1989.

The German term *Binsenwahrheit* refers to a truism. One of the most common is that not all criticism of Israel and Zionism is due to antisemitism. Yes, but some of it was and is and much of the communist assault on Zionism drew on vicious clichés and stereotypes of Jews with deep cultural roots in European history. Thus I want to conclude with a comment on the weight of the past and do so by calling on the authority and stylistic brilliance of an author who has some connection to the themes of this conference. As you may recall, in the *Eighteenth Brumaire of Louis Napoleon*, Karl Marx wrote "Men make their own history, but they do not make it as they please; they do not make it under self-selected circumstances, but under circumstances existing already, given and transmitted from the past." Yet the following two sentences, cited a bit less often, are more pertinent to the subject at hand. He continued: "The tradition of all dead generations weighs like a nightmare on the brains of the living. And just as they seem to be occupied with revolutionizing themselves and things, creating something that did not exist before, precisely in such epochs of revolutionary crisis they anxiously conjure up the spirits of the past to their service, borrowing from them names, battle slogans, and costumes in order to present this new scene in world history in time-honored disguise and borrowed language."

When one reads Marx's hackneyed and embarrassingly ignorant comments about Judaism in his famous essay on the Jewish question, the above quote sounds like unconscious self-reflection on the antisemitic "traditions of dead generations" that weighed like a nightmare in his own brain in 1843. From 1949 to 1989, as the communist leaders of the Soviet Union and world communism compared the Israelis to Nazis and praised those who were at war with them, they too offered evidence of the traditions of dead generations which Marx and Lenin thought they had consigned to the trash bin of history were, in fact, persisting in the language of anti-fascism and the policy of the undeclared war on Zionism and the state of Israel.

EUPHORIA TO DECAY

Post-Marxist Revision's Mortal Threat to Communism

Vladimir Tismaneanu

> *"I don't agree...with the complacency of most Western observers,*
> *especially now with the advent of Gorbachev, who would confine us within*
> *the limits of a mildly reformed communist system where power still lies*
> *with the Party, but where some other people can also shout a bit. If people*
> *don't have to suffer for their views but nevertheless have no real influence*
> *over what happens, the longer such a situation continues and the greater*
> *the difference develops between words and deeds. We cannot develop*
> *a normal life for the future on such a basis."*[1]

The Hungarian dissident philosopher G. M. Tamás expressed a widespread feeling among East European independents when he refused, unlike the majority of Western observers then and now, to consider Gorbachevism as God-sent. His stance here also reveals the crux of communism—it is the story of ideology. The communists had a collectivist view of a utopian society, in contrast to a belief in human thought and civic activity. At their core these are two fundamentally incompatible visions of the destiny of human civilization. Soviet communism was popularly and intellectually endorsed first by enthusiastic fantasies, followed by naïve pleading for reform, then cynical surrender and despair, and finally a moral stance on the necessity of a civic revolution—knowingly and explicitly at the cost of the final death of the "classless society." Examining the twin arcs of who were the true believers, from interwar intellectuals to Brezhnev-era bureaucrats, and who were the humanist activists, from Stalinist intellectuals to liberal (sometimes post- Marxist) dissidents, reveals the battle of communism across the twentieth century. Tracing communism's ideological decay reveals both why the millenarian project failed, and even why our own century continues to witness Leninist terror, and, increasingly, Leninist fantasies.

---

[1] "Human Rights Is Not Enough: An Interview with G.M. Támás," *Uncaptive Minds* 1, no. 1 (April–May 1988): 12.

Communist regimes were partocratic ideocracies (as discussed by authors such as Leonard Schapiro, Alain Besançon, A. Avtorkhanov, and Martin Malia). Their claim to legitimacy was purely ideological. It relied upon a belief-system shared by the elites and inculcated into the masses centered upon the Party's claim to incarnate historical truth. If this interpretation is correct, then de-radicalization (Robert C. Tucker), primarily in the field of ideological monopoly, explains the increased vulnerability of these regimes after the XXth Congress. The demise of the Supreme Leader ushered in ideological anarchy and a loss of self-confidence among the rulers. Attempts to restore the "betrayed values" of the original project (Khrushchev, Gorbachev) resulted in disarray, change of mind among former supporters, desertion of critical intellectuals from the "fortress," criticism of the old dogmas, awakening, breaks with the past, and eventually, as in the case of Kołakowski or the Budapest School, apostasy. The following essay draws upon and develops my theses, formulated in the 1980s and early 1990s, about the role of ideological disillusionment in the ultimate decline (de-radicalization) of Leninist regimes.[2]

Communist ideology substituted religious symbols and values. Raymond Aron was right when he described communism as *religions séculières* or even as a "Christian heresy." According to Emilio Gentile, a political religion is

> a form of the sacralisation of politics of an exclusive and integralist character. It rejects coexistence with other political ideologies and movements, denies the autonomy of the individual with respect to the collective, prescribes the obligatory observance of its commandments and participation in its political cult, and sanctifies violence as a legitimate arm of the struggle against enemies, and as an instrument of regeneration.[3]

---

[2]   See Vladimir Tismaneanu, "Critical Marxism and Eastern Europe," *Praxis International* 3, no. 3 (October 1983), 235–247; Vladimir Tismaneanu, *The Crisis of Marxist Ideology in Eastern Europe: The Poverty of Utopia* (London, New York: Routledge, 1988); Vladimir Tismaneanu, "The Neo-Leninist Temptation: Gorbachevism and the Party Intelligentsia," in eds. Alfred J. Rieber and Alvin Z. Rubinstein, *Perestroika at the Crossroads* (New York: Routledge, 1991), 31–51; Vladimir Tismaneanu, "From Arrogance to Irrelevance: Avatars of Marxism in Romania," in Raymond Taras, *The Road to Disillusion: From Critical Marxism to Postcommunism in Eastern Europe* (Armonk, N.Y.: M.E. Sharpe, 1992), 135–50; Vladimir Tismaneanu, *Reinventing Politics: Eastern Europe from Stalin to Havel* (New York: The Free Press, 1992).

[3]   Emilio Gentile, "Political Religion: A Concept and its Critics—A Critical Survey," *Totalitarian Movements and Political Religions* 6, no. 1, (June 2005): 30. See also Emilio Gentile, "Fascism as Political Religion," *Journal of Contemporary History* 25, no. 2/3 (May–Jun. 1990): 229–51; Emilio Gentile, *The Sacralization of Politics in Fascist Italy* (Cambridge, MA: Harvard University Press, 1996).

Dialectical and historical materialism were indeed the official outlook, the main political, philosophical, ethical, aesthetic corpus of hypotheses, theses, values, norms, and opinions which guided, inspired, and motivated the political-intellectual development of East European societies. In communist regimes, Marxism, i.e. its Leninist avatar, was imposed as the philosophy *par excellence*, the unique scientific world view, the spiritual complement of the technological-industrial evolution of the society. Moreover, under the specific circumstances of the Stalinist period, Marxism converted into *Diamat*, a *simulacrum* of dialectics combined with a pseudo-scientific vocabulary. The latter was gradually instituted as a monopolistic orthodoxy imagined according to the requirements of self-sufficient, non-contradictory, and *a priori* infallible religious dogmas. Conceived as such, it brought about a continual stiffening of intellectual life in those countries.

The Stalinist functionalist-pragmatic *Weltanschauung* succeeded in emphasizing as altogether certain and genuinely axiomatic a number of theses from *The German Ideology* (e.g., economic determinism, the assumption that the dominant ideas within a social organization are the ideas of the hegemonic group, etc.) as well as several naïve materialist positions defended and promoted by Lenin in *Materialism and Empiriocriticism*: above all Lenin's vulgar representation of the philosophical parties. Under Stalin, dialectics suffered a strange metamorphosis, a process of *refunctionalization*, the result of which was the transformation into a purely ideological weapon, a mythological instrument supporting each political step of the regime, each tactical turning. According to Klaus Riegel, the structural challenges of utopia in power (take-over, fulfillment of ideals, and adaptation to the world) brought about, under Stalin, the "hierocratic domination of the church-dispensed grace." In the physical absence of the numinous leader incarnating the absolute power of the party, Lenin, "the imagined community of Leninist disciples"[4] had to re-invent itself by means of basing its charisma on the scriptures and delusions of its founding fathers.

Within this construct, morality was defined in terms of loyalty to a sense of ultimate historical transcendence. First Leninism, then Stalinism, codified the total commitment to an apocalyptic scenario dedicated to bringing about not only a new type of society but also a new type of person. With its ambition

---

[4]   Riegel Klaus-Goerg, "Rituals of Confession within Communities of *virtuosi*: An Interpretation of the Stalinist Criticism and Self-Criticism in the Perspective of Max Weber's Sociology of Religion," *Totalitarian Movements and Political Religions* 1, no. 3 (Winter 2000): 16–42.

to initiate an anthropological revolution, Marxism was a form of utopian commitment. Moreover, in its Bolshevik application, this radicalism turned into "a set of values and beliefs, a culture, a language, new forms of speech, more modern customs and new ways of behaving in public and in private." And the name under which all this came together was Stalinism—a civilization self-identified as separate and superior.[5] Marxism-Leninism as mythology therefore relied on two mutually conditioning myths: a sustaining one and an eschatological one.[6] This triumphant tale of humanity's renewal was provisioned only by the surrender and self-sacrifice to the will of the leader (unqualified yet).[7] It was the "scientific" answer to the paradox of *theodicy* intrinsic to Marxism: the eschatological subject was identified, but its coming of age needed leadership: the Kautskian intervention from without, Lenin's party of a new type, and, why not, ultimately Stalin's revolution from above. Marxism-Leninism was the formula used to reconcile the ever-expanding rational mastery of the world with the aspiration for individual liberation.

The climax of this degeneration was the "dialectical confessions" during the Stalinist show-trials, abject self-flagellations meant to give totalitarianism a moral legitimacy: if all the opponents (real or invented) were nothing but scoundrels, loathsome agents of the West, despicable traitors, and infamous saboteurs, then the Stalinist leadership, benefiting from a perfect political purity, was entitled to invoke the alibi of an "objective" historical rationality. These "poetics of purge" regulated ideological space within the body social and politics of the Soviet-type polity, re-defining the "elect" within the community and re-emphasizing their messianic role. The Purged communists stayed loyal to Stalin because they knew it was history asking them to pretend to be guilty, so that it can be easier to catch the bourgeois enemies. They were duty-bound to do this. The Party was never wrong, any Terror and lies were dialectical privileges.

---

[5]   Astrid Hadin, "Stalinism as a Civilization: New Perspectives on Communist Regimes," *Political Studies Review* 2, no. 2 (Feb. 2004): 177.

[6]   For a discussion of myth vs. ideology in relation to Marxism-Leninism see Carol Barner-Barry and Cynthia Hody, "Soviet Marxism-Leninism as Mythology," *Political Psychology* 15, no. 4 (Dec. 1994): 609–630.

[7]   Peter Ehlen, "Communist Faith and World-Explanatory Doctrine: A Philosophical Analysis," in eds. Hans Maier and Michael Schäfer, *Totalitarianism and Political Religions, Volume II: Concepts for the Comparison of Dictatorships* (New York: Routledge, 2007), 124–137.

The Stalinist epoch of Marxism can be therefore branded as the age of *sacrificial dialectics*. The obsessions with the *interior enemy* and the *potential traitor* seemed to occult, and eventually to annul, any moral considerations. Force lay at the center of utopia and became the main realization of ideological power. The fact that such distinguished Western intellectuals as Maurice Merleau-Ponty or Jean-Paul Sartre did not hesitate to share many of the delusive communist arguments, that they trusted the statements of the Stalinist *haut-parleurs* and rejected the anti-totalitarian demonstrations as hysterical anticommunism, was all the more revealing.

Undoubtedly, Stalinism knew how to speculate on the ethical capital of the intelligentsia, the fervor of the heroic rebellion, the glory of the radical challenge to the abhorred existing order. As Arthur Koestler put it, "the sacrifice to the sheer utopia and the revolt against a corrupted society are then the two poles which provide the tension of all the militant faiths."[8] Leninism's push for a regeneration of politics and society, its function as a "palingenetic myth" (Roger Griffin),[9] thickened the veil of ignorance on the part of the "progressive" European intelligentsia. Furthermore, the anti-Fascist campaigns actually furnished the necessary moral incentives to strengthen the Stalinist passion of many outstanding Western intellectuals and covered their political and axiological capitulation with the magic veil of the Resistance.[10]

Conceived by its founding fathers as an anti-statist philosophy, Marxism culminated in the Soviet apotheosis of the party and state machine. Under Lenin and Stalin, ideology represented a major source of power for communist elites. The legitimacy of the Bolshevik elite derived primarily from its relationship to the Marxist doctrine. Arcane as they sounded to external observers, the squabbles of the 1920s touched on the most sensitive points of what Czesław Miłosz has called the New Faith, an ideology "based on the principle that good and evil are definable solely in terms of service or harm to

---

[8] Arthur Koestler, Raymond Aron, Richard Howard, Stafford Crossman, et al., *Le dieu des ténèbres: (The God that Failed)* ([Paris: Calmann-Lévy, 1950] New York: Columbia University Press, 2001), 22; Richard Pipes, *Communism: A History* (New York: Modern Library, 2001); Eric Hoffer, *The True Believer: Thoughts on the Nature of Mass Movements* (New York: Harper Perennial, 1966).

[9] Roger Griffin, "Cloister or Cluster? The Implications of Emilio Gentile's Ecumenical Theory of Political Religion for the Study of Extremism," *Totalitarian Movements and Political Religions* 6, no. 1 (June 2005): 37–46. See also Roger Griffin, *The Nature of Fascism* (London: Pinter, 1991).

[10] Herbert R. Lottman, *La Rive gauche: Du Front Populaire à la guerre froide* (The Left Bank) (Paris: Seuil, 1981); François Furet, *Le passe d'une illusion: Essai sur l'idee communiste au XXe siecle* (Paris: Robert Laffont & Calmann-Levy, 1995).

the interests of the Revolution."[11] The Revolution was idealized as a cathartic event, the advent of a new age of social justice. In an age of extremes, intellectuals became blinded by a love of determinism.

At least throughout the first decade of the new revolutionary regime people were enthusiastically ready to espouse Leninist dogma. The social promises and revivalist spirit of Bolshevism were invoked as arguments against those who deplored the violence by dictatorial power. Many intellectuals, including some famous names like Maxim Gorky, André Gide, Arthur Koestler, Manès Sperber, Romain Rolland, André Malraux and Ignazio Silone, were fascinated by what seemed to be a heroic historical adventure. Some of them grew disappointed with the cynicism of the communist commissars and left the Leninist chapels; others, like Pablo Neruda and Louis Aragon, refused to abjure their faith and remained attached to hackneyed communist tenets. Two decades later, upon the Sovietization of Eastern Europe, Leninism became an *alternative* for national rebirth. Even under Stalin, the conviction that the unprecedented state of terror of propaganda remained strong because of the redemptive mission of defying democracy's alleged civilizational failure.

The Short Course of History of the CPSU, published in 1938, represented the paradigm of the Bolshevik intellectual debasement. Turned into a gospel for the international communist movement, this parody of Marxism was extolled as the pinnacle of human wisdom. It was the literary reflection of the "monopoly of the legitimate use of hierocratic coercion" (M. Weber) exercised by Stalin in the show-trials. To paraphrase Souvarine, the *Short Course* paradigm[12] officially transformed Leninism into a *religion d'état*. The human being that Stalinism wanted to build up was supposed to repudiate the classical distinctions between *good* and *evil*, scornfully discredited as obsolete through the exposure to another moral code, in many points suggestive of the Nazi Übermensch. His ideology should have been rooted in hatred and resentment, a cynical logic of *manipulation*, *domination*, and *survival*. Continuous brain-washing, a progressive conditioning of the intellect and the destruction of the autonomous will were the *sine qua non* for the fulfillment of this project. All the state-ideological apparatuses, to use Althusser's term,

---

[11]   See Czesław Miłosz, *The Captive Mind* (New York: Vintage Books, 1981), 75.

[12]   On the features of the historical-ideological profile of the *Short Course* and the revision of its main tenets within the Soviet historical field in the 1960s and 1970s see Roger D. Markwick, *Rewriting History in Soviet Russia: The Politics of Revisionist Historiography, 1954–1974* (New York: Palgrave MacMillan, 2001).

were mobilized and subordinated to this prevailing task. The goal of the propaganda was to purify the minds; it was like an exorcising ritual through which the régime attempted to eliminate all the vestiges of Western culture and to create the human instrument of perfect social reproduction. Its content consisted in a few mechanically reiterated themes; its method was symbolic aggression, ideological violence. Earlier, in 1929, Stalin proclaimed the "year of the great break" (*god velikogo pereloma*) that, according to Bernice Glatzer Rosenthal connoted "the Marxist leap from 'necessity' to 'freedom' (…) a complete rupture with the accursed old world (…) Under Stalin's leadership, the masses were building an earthly paradise."[13] What was really happening at the time was an annihilation of the free-will, the total intoxication, moral dereliction, and, thereby, absolute identification with the system. It was the Soviet version of an individual *Gleichschaltung*.

After the occupation of East-Central Europe by the USSR, the same form of primitive Leninism—they never dared to call it Stalinism—was decreed the unique interpretation of Marxism. The East European countries, dominated by Stalinist parties, were compelled to embark on the same political and economic platform as the Soviet Union and submitted to all the practices involved in the Stalinist socio-political paradigm: an aberrant industrialization, forced collectivization, rabid cultural revolution, i.e., the violation of all the spiritual heritage of those peoples in behalf of the rough materialism encouraged and generated by the system. From Rákosi to Gheorghiu-Dej, from Bierut to Gottwald, all those Stalins in miniature competed for implementing the Soviet institutions in their own countries. The *ersatz* Marxism of the epoch was subsequently the ideological framework created by Stalin and by his followers and was, in fact, a compendium of trivial metaphysical ideas interwoven with pragmatic rules and mythological fixations. In the communist countries, the mind agonized in the captivity of the thought police.

Stalin's death and the promises of the thaw caused certain semantic modifications within the rigid structure of the dogmas, especially in the context of Nikita Khrushchev's fulminating attack on Stalinism at the 20th Congress of the CPSU in February 1956. The totalitarian imagery functioning on a mechanism of "*tremendum et fascinosum* (the alternation of fear and hope, terror and salvation)"[14] found its spell radically dimmed. It permitted a slight

---

[13]   Bernice Glatzer Rosenthal, *New Myth, New World: From Nietzsche to Stalinism* (University Park: Pennsylvania State University Press, 2002), 238.

[14]   Hans Maier, "Political Religions and Their Images: Soviet Communism, Italian Fascism and

move away from the petrified doctrine corpus toward the origins of Marxism as philosophy, toward the so-called "young Marx" as an archetype of a pure, unadulterated socialist impetus. "Revisionism," a term coined by neo-Stalinist orthodoxies to stigmatize critical currents of thought and the main adversary encountered by ruling bureaucrats since the factional struggles of the mid and late 1920s, became the main foe of the neo-Stalinist ideological construct.[15] The political radicalization of the East European intellectuals coincided with—and was catalyzed by—the wave of liberalization touched off by Khrushchev's historical revelations.[16] All the Stalinist theoretical and political constructions had been denounced as a horrible hoax: the illusions could no longer cover the squalid reality. The dogmas had proved their total inanity. The yearning for a moral reform of communism was the basic motivation for the neo-Marxist revival in Eastern Europe. State Marxism was correctly identified as an "instrument of apology" (Kołakowski) for those in power. The intellectuals' rebellion against totalitarian controls was one of the major threats experienced by Soviet-type regimes. The dubious legitimacy of these governments was questioned by critics who could not be accused of belonging to the defeated social classes. With their outspoken advocacy of humanism and democracy, they contributed to the erosion of the apparent monolithic consensus.

The most active in the struggle against Stalinist obscurantism were Hungarian and Polish intellectuals, the exponents of a radical political outlook which was able to inflame the masses throughout the hectic months after the 20th Congress of the Communist Party of the Soviet Union. This fact has to be related to the traditions of the Left in those countries, but also to the existence of a specific confusion within the communist *nomenklatura* heightened by the growing anti-bureaucratic radicalism of the working-class. We have to take into consideration, in this respect, the evolution of the class-consciousness

German National Socialism," *Totalitarian Movements and Political Religions* 7, no. 3 (September 2006): 267–281.

[15]   Leszek Kolakowski, *Main Currents of Marxism: The Founders, the Golden Age, the Breakdown*, trans. P.S. Falla (New York: Norton, 2005); Andrzej Walicki, *Marxism and the Leap to the Kingdom of Freedom: The Rise and Fall of the Communist Utopia* (Stanford: Stanford University Press, 2005). Two classics on the topic of Marxist revisionism in Eastern Europe are: Leopold Labedz, ed., *Revisionism: Essays on the History of Marxist Ideas* (New York: Praeger 1962), online edition, https://www.jstor.org/stable/1904552?seq=1 and Wolfgang Leonhard, *Three Faces of Marxism: the Political Concepts of Soviet Ideology, Maoism, and Humanist Marxism* (New York: Paragon books, 1979).

[16]   William Taubman, *Khrushchev: The Man and His Era* (New York: W.W. Norton, 2002).

of both the working-class and the intellectuals and the existence of a certain
psycho-emotional communication, and even osmosis, between these two
social groups. I stress all these facts in order to also suggest an explanation -
beyond the sheer force of the political police—for the relative political passivity
of the working-class in other communist countries (Romania, Bulgaria) and
for the astonishing neutrality of the Czech and Slovak intellectuals during the
Hungarian and Polish revolt movements in the 1956.

More than a decade after Stalin's death, the East European intelligentsia
was experiencing a period of ethical reconstruction, an invitation to the
rehabilitation of the whole historical evolution of Western Marxism and to
the critical approach to "institutional dialectics." Leszek Kołakowski, in his
1957 manifesto "Permanent vs. Transitory Aspects of Marxism," made the distinction between "institutional Marxism" and "intellectual Marxism." While
the first was mere religious dogma instrumentalized by those in power, the
second was characterized by "radical rationalism in thinking; steadfast resistance to any invasion of myth in science; an entirely secular view of the
world; criticism pushed to its ultimate limits; distrust of all closed doctrines
and systems ... a readiness to revise accepted theses, theories and methods."[17]
Freedom had become again the highest good for man independent of the
detour imposed through party mediated self-determination.

The favorite theme in the discourses of East European philosophers was
the return to Marx: the attempt to detect those elements in Marx's original
design which could justify the claims for the political changes within the system. Moreover, that endeavor was conceived as a *re-discovery* and *re-inter-
pretation* of Marx's early works, of the whole philosophical Marxian legacy
detested by the Stalinist ideologues. The concept of *alienation* became the
basis of the most impassioned philosophical controversies, fostered the case
for liberalization, and provided the theoretical basis for political criticism.
In fact, the "dictatorship of the proletariat" was felt as exactly the opposite of
the "bright future" promised by the founders of Marxism. It was viewed as a
caricature of the project of emancipation which had been announced by the
Communist Manifesto.

The immediate effect of the general intellectual unrest was the revival
of the class-consciousness of the working-class. One of the most interesting
manifestations of this phenomenon was the 1964 *Open Letter of the Basic*

---

[17] Kołakowski quoted in Stanley Pierson, *Leaving Marxism: Studies in the Dissolution of an
Ideology* (Stanford: Stanford University Press, 2001), 134–135.

Party Organization of PZPR and to Member of the University Cell of the Union of Socialist Youth at Warsaw University. The document, an excellent example of critique of the party from the left, claimed to uphold the true principles of Marxism-Leninism as against the practically fictitious party democracy, to defend the workers' rights against top-down decision-making.[18] The same year, Zdeněk Mlynář drafted his *The State and the Individual* (an anticipation of his 1968 "Towards a Democratic Political Organization of Society"), in which he tried to reconcile democracy and socialism. Moreover, the leading role of the party could be maintained, according to Mlynář only if, first, it was made up of a truly "conscious vanguard" in service to the "overall interests and socialist goals of the entire society"; and second, only if it didn't take for granted its leadership and it led by means of "tireless persuasion."[19]

It was an exhilarating search for the "realm of freedom" prophesized by Marx, an explosion of the *unglückliche Bewusstsein* (unhappy consciousness), the revolt of the libertarian undercurrents that succeeded in surviving the mortifying experience of Stalinism. The crushing of the Hungarian Revolution, the attempt to tame the Polish intelligentsia, the hardening of the political line in all East European countries between 1957–1961 (and the two and a half decades of bureaucratic stagnation after), and the harsh anti-revisionist campaign after the publication of the Program adopted by the Communist League of Yugoslavia could not obstruct the creative philosophical openings nor hinder the anti-dogmatic impetus which has resulted in the *humanist-ethical outlook* execrated by the impenitent Stalinists and neo-dogmatics.

Revisionism was nearly suppressed because of its own commitment to values fatally perverted through official manipulation. It was a fallacious strategy based on wishful thinking and impossible desiderata of moral regeneration of the ruling elite. It foolishly yearned for dialogue with those who valued only brutal force. Adam Michnik aptly describes the inescapable dilemma of neo-Marxist revisionism in East-Central Europe:

> The revisionist concept was based on a specific intraparty perspective. It was never formulated into a political program. It assumed that the system of power could be humanized and democratized and that the official Marxist

---

[18] Jacek Kuron and Karol Modzelewski were arrested for their involvement in the distribution of this document. See *The Dilemmas of Dissidence in East-Central Europe: Citizen Intellectuals and Philosopher Kings* (Budapest: Central European University Press, 2003), 17.

[19] Mikhail Gorbachev and Zdenek Mlynar, *Conversations with Gorbachev: On Perestroika, the Prague Spring,* trans. George Shriver (New York: Columbia University Press, 2002), 56–58.

doctrine was capable of assimilating contemporary arts and social sciences. The revisionists wanted to act within the framework of the Communist Party and Marxist doctrine. They wanted to transform "from within" the doctrine and the party in the direction of democratic reform and common sense.[20]

The ideological apparatuses of the East European communist parties (to use Althusser's concept) became rapidly aware of the subversive implications of the Marxist "return to the source." "Revisionism" became the obsessional projection of the Stalinist ideologues, the embodiment of their secret anguishes. Against the attempt to mediate on the negative potential offered by dialectics as a method opposed to any positivistic-functionalist perspective, the apparatchiks, mobilized all the possibilities available within a totalitarian régime: the "revisionist" temptation was anathemized and its exponents were stigmatized as "nihilist-destructive" elements. It was only the outburst of the Sino-Soviet conflict, as well as the necessity to rebuke the Chinese and Albanian "dogmatic" positions, which compelled Khrushchev and other leaders of the Soviet bloc to take into account the possible advantages of an *ideological de-Stalinization*, a process which permitted such essential steps as the publication of Solzhenitsyn's "Ivan Denisovitch" in the Soviet Union and in other communist countries as well as the beginning of a new cultural liberalization (e.g., the "reconsideration" of Kafka's works in Czechoslovakia, despite the official opposition of the dogmatic *chiens de garde*, an event with many spiritual and political repercussions). Nevertheless, the "antagonistic Marxism" promoted by the partisans of the liberalization became the main target of the dogmatic attacks: the "jester" could not avoid the confrontation with the intolerant reaction of the wrathful "priests," he had to radicalize his "attitude of negative vigilance in the face of any absolute."[21]

I believe it would be inaccurate to consider, like Kołakowski, that the traditional exclusive-dogmatic mentality has been almost completely substituted by a cynical, strictly pragmatic approach, specific for the new type of communist bureaucrat. Certainly, the most intolerant generation of ideological clerks vanished after 1960, but one should not suspect the subsequent cohorts of apparatchiks of any liberal or humanistic leanings. Morally and

---

[20] See Adam Michnik, *Letters from Prison and Other Essays* (Berkeley: University of California Press, 1985), 135.

[21] Leszek Kołakowski's famous dichotomy quoted in *The Modern Polish Mind: An Anthology*, ed. Maria Kuncewiczowa (London: Secker and Warburg, 1963), 326.

psychologically, they belonged to another generation than the "priests" once evoked by Kołakowski. They were not personally involved in the Stalinist crimes, they have no reason to look for all kinds of historical rationalizations, but politically they must share the same values as their forerunners. They were "objectively" the prisoners of the same fallacious logic.[22] The indifferent, amoebic ideological apparatchik, with his or her simulated axiological aloofness, was actually an efficient element of the well-functioning authoritarian-bureaucratic superstructure: he or she had nothing in common with Marxist philosophy or with Socialist ethics; he/she superbly ignored the embarrassing problems of historical responsibility. To paraphrase Engels, their main task was to correct the logic of conflicting facts, to fashion and expound history, against all hope, as immutably marching towards communism. They had only one faith, one absolute *credo*; they paid tribute only to one God; they honored but one political value: their own bureaucratic survival, their right to dominate, to dictate, and to terrorize, their enduring access to power. They gave up on the pretense of credible, trustworthy communication of faith, therefore provoking the caving in of the sustaining and eschatological myths of Marxism-Leninism.

In this respect, the late Soviet dissident and philosopher Alexander Zinoviev was right to decipher a perfect continuity from the first Stalinist generation – those people who perpetrated the crimes and/or supported the whole terrorist system – to the contemporary distant, cold, pseudo-sophisticated cultural (ideological) clerk making use of Marxist rhetoric in order to cover his moral and intellectual vacuum. In line with these murderous technocrats stood the Soviet and East European intellectuals, who contained a general metaphysical malaise, expressed in their dissatisfaction with the "democratic illusions" and Socialist strategies promoted by the "radical humanist opposition" in the advanced industrial societies. Yet still, for many intellectuals, there was an absolute divorce between this alternative outlook and the bureaucratic-institutional orthodoxy. Anti-totalitarian Marxist arguments were compelling and pervasive among a wide swath of intellectuals. The necessary criticism of neo-Stalinist régimes and attempts to do away with a whole tradition of utopian-emancipatory thought cannot be discounted in a broad attack on "Stalinist-Marxism."

---

[22] Leszek Kołakowski, *Main Currents of Marxism, Vol. III: The Breakdown* (Oxford: Oxford University Press, 1978).

The publication of Marx's young philosophical contributions had a tremendous impact in all East European societies, because they were perceived as a true manifesto for the freedom of subjectivity, for the emancipation of revolutionary praxis, for an unbound approach to the social, economic, political, and cultural problems of the Soviet-type regimes. Beyond the present skepticism of certain disaffected intellectuals, one has to recognize the fact that the young Marx, at the time, was a precious ally of the liberal forces against the political conservatism of the dominant bureaucracies of Eastern Europe; he furnished, through a sensitive reading, a number of irrefutable arguments against the oppressive prevailing order. To use Dick Howard coinage, "Marx did announce that the specter of democracy is haunting Europe." In rediscovering Marx, the Eastern European revisionists discovered the democratic implications of his theory.[23]

The entire heterodox Marxist tradition was eventually summoned to participate in the struggle against the sclerotic social and economic structures: from Rosa Luxemburg to Trotsky, from the young Lukács and Karl Korsch to Wilhelm Reich and Erich Fromm, from Gramsci to Sartre to the Frankfurt School, a whole intellectual thesaurus was invoked and developed due to this offensive against the authoritarian bureaucracies. It was like an unexpected revival of a forgotten tradition, an evanescent osmosis with the *impossible utopia*, a tragic endeavor to recreate a spirit and a mentality altogether opposed to the self-satisfactory, philistine logic of the monopolistic communist elite. It was, therefore, logical that the counter reaction of the ideological apparatus consisted of supporting regimented philosophical and sociological investigations, those research-areas which avoided the collision with the power-monopoly of the Communist Party. It is already well known, above all the Czecho-Slovak experience with the liberalization process, as well as from the repeated Polish crises after 1956, that the advocates of critical Marxism were among the most aggressive representatives of the anti-bureaucratic wave in Eastern Europe, and their theses functioned as a catalyst for the liberalization and "democratization" movement.[24] Konrád and

---

[23] Dick Howard, *The Specter of Democracy* (New York: Columbia University Press, 2002), vii–xvii.

[24] Pavel Tigrid, *Le Printemps de Prague* (Paris: Seuil, 1968). For the history of the intellectual commitment to the Hungarian anti-Stalinist insurrection in 1956 see: Imre Nagy, *On Communism: In Defense of the New Course* (New York: Praeger, 1957); Tibor Meray, *Ce jour-là: Budapest (23 Octobre 1956)*, (Paris, 1966), including Albert Camus' impressive anti-totalitarian discourse (*The Truth about the Nagy Affair*, preface by Albert Camus, London: Secker & Warburg, 1959, vii-ix), *Kadar a eu son jour de peur*. For the history of socio-political dissent in Eastern

Szelényi observed that "the ruling Communist Parties have a dual class base. They are at the same time mass parties of the intellectual class and cadre parties of the working class."[25] There was, though, a *silent intellectual majority* whose exponents succeeded from time in expressing different and even subversive opinions, who refused the mental captivity imposed by the régime and dared to defy its faked infallibility. This stratum promoted a radical criticism of the bureaucracy and was the most interested in the symptoms of the growing social crisis, subsequently giving birth to a challenging sub-group of dissidents.

Providing a different matrix than its counterpart in the Western world, the critical Marxist paradigm developed by East European radical thinkers offered the main epistemological and historical-political categories and concepts necessary for a thorough comprehensive criticism of the authoritarian-bureaucratic institutions and methods and provided as well as the prerequisites for a project of essential change. The Party ideological watchdogs realized immediately the danger, and their violent, intolerant, and repressive reaction aimed at neutralizing, at all costs, this threatening tendency. That was the reason for the angry attack against Rudolf Bahro in the GDR, for the unexpectedly enraged attitude of the alleged "liberal" Kádár régime toward the theoretical conclusions of Konrád and Szelényi, and the "moderate" persecution of the Budapest school. There was no greater fear of the State-ideological apparatuses in the Soviet-type régimes than the crystallization of the interior resistance, the structuring of a critical social consciousness, the radicalization of the intelligentsia. The latter was perceived as the most perilous evolution, a menace to the stability of the dominant institutions and values. Henceforth, the régimes in Eastern Europe did not hesitate to exploit any possible political-manipulative device in order to avoid the ascent of an *oppositional coalition* between the *seditious intelligentsia* and the *dissatisfied working-class*.[26] The classical situation, from this point of view, was that of Czechoslovakia during the last years of the Novotny's régime when the Communist Party could not spare any effort in slandering and discrediting

---

Europe see J. Kurón and K. Modzelewski, *An Open Letter to the Party* ("A Revolutionary Socialist Manifesto Written in a Polish Prison") (London, 1969); Jiri Pelikán, ed., *The Czechoslovak Political Trials,1950–1954* (Stanford: Stanford University Press, 1971).

[25] György Konrád and Iván Szelényi, *The Intellectuals on the Road to Class Power* (Brighton: Harvester Press, 1979), 179.

[26] Walter D. Connor, "Dissent in Eastern Europe: A New Coalition?" *Problems of Communism* 29, no. 1 (Jan.–Feb. 1980).

the critical intellectuals, in compromising their attempt to set up an alliance with the radicalized elements of the working-class. Just a few examples: the exasperation and the furious reaction of the Party apparatchik Jiři Hendrich during the Congress of the Writers' Union in 1967; the perfidious attacks against such prominent Czech and Slovak liberal intellectuals as Ludvik Vačulik, Ladislav Mnačko, Antonin Liehm, Ivan Svitak, Pavel Kohout, and Eduard Goldstücker; and the vindictive persecutions organized after the Soviet invasion in August, 1968.

On the other hand, we should mention the contradictory relation between certain East European critical Marxists and the Western New Left, suspected of despotic temptations for terrorism and accusations, more than once, of messianic sectarianism. The merciless criticism of any utopian millenarianism offered by Kołakowski in his *Main Currents of Marxism*, expressed more than a dissatisfaction with the desperate powerlessness of negative dialectics: it was an invitation of sorts for critical Marxists to go beyond their ideological and emotional attachments, to assume the basic ambivalence of their doctrine, to accept the honest examination of the Marxist false consciousness, to transcend the metaphysical paradigm of Hegelian-Marxist radicalism. The only possible conclusions form this kind of logic were obvious.

East European critical Marxism attempted to counter-balance the inept official "dialectical triumphalism," the conservative-dogmatic functionalism assumed and promoted by the ruling communist parties. Its project was to offer the spiritual arms for the criticism of the system in order to engender a more humane, less asphyxiating, eventually democratic socio-political order. Unfortunately, it had to compete with a perverse adversary, an enemy ready to make use of whatever weapon to keep unaffected its privileges. Against the Machiavellian bureaucrats, viscerally attached to their dull prejudices and obtuse dogmas, the critical Marxists were left in purgatory: either to go toward an all-embracing, general criticism of Soviet-type despotic societies, a position resulting in the radical rejection of their alleged "socialist" and "democratic" potentialities, or to persevere in their generously humanist discourse, being eventually integrated into the manipulative technology of the system.[27] Ultimately, critical Marxists did manage, as correctly shown by

---

[27] For a general theoretical framework of this study, I would like to indicate several illuminating sources: Theodor W. Adorno, *Dialectique négative* (Paris: Éditions Payot, 1978); Max Horkheimer and Theodor W. Adorno, *La Dialectique de la Raison. Fragments philosophique* (Paris: Gallimard, 1974); Herbert Marcuse, *Le Marxisme soviétique. Essai d'analyse critique* (Paris: Gallimard, 1963);

Ferenc Fehér, to transform "the semantic potentialities of their vocabulary into the language of an actual politics of dissent."[28] They escaped the trap of a fanciful pluralism in Marxism and succeeded in creating and alternative discursive space outside the logocracy of the Party.

As the erosion of the Leninist Totalitarian monolith came to a head with Gorbachev's successful, albeit unintentional, dismantling of the Party's terrorist and propagandistic state, intellectuals and even the masses across the Soviet lands arrived at their final destination of the twentieth century, a realization of the inviolable political value of human rights and the necessity of respecting civil society. Despite the new euphoria that marked the downfall of communism and the unbridled confidence that civil society and tolerance had become a universal value, the Leninist debris remained stronger than all but a few had dared to imagine. Cynicism, dogma, xenophobia, nationalism, imperialism, and the search for unity and purpose continued to underlie the post-communist societies, even in the happiest of times, under the reign of the former dissidents in the early 1990s. As Eastern Europe's struggles with collectivist authoritarianisms intensify today, as nationalism and even a form of proto-Leninist redemptionism seem to hold the majority, a few major accomplishments of the civil school of intellectuals cannot be denied: they

---

Lucien Goldmann, *Marxisme et sciences humaines* (Paris: Gallimard, 1970); Hannah Arendt, *The Origins of Totalitarianism* (London: Allen &Unwin, 1967); Iring Fetscher, *Karl Marx und der Marxismus. Von der Philosophie des Proletariats zur Proletarischen Weltanschauung* (München: Piper, 1967); Jürgen Habermas, *Theorie und Praxis: Sozialphilosophische Studien* (Neuwied and Berlin: Luchterhand, 1963), Jürgen Habermas, *La technique et la science comme "idéologie"* (Paris: Gallimard, 1973), Jürgen Habermas, *Communication and the Evolution of Society* (Boston: Beacon Press, 1979); Alvin W. Gouldner, *The Dialectics of Ideology and Technology: The Origins, Grammar and Future of Ideology* (New York: Seabury Press, 1976). Last, but not least, I would like to evoke the unforgettable dialogues I had the chance to share with the brilliant, irresistible Romanian *home de letters* and philosopher, himself a solitary critical Marxist, Alexandru Ivasiuc, absurdly killed during the earthquake in Bucharest in March 1977. During our conversations, Ivasiuc mentioned many hypotheses which could have become the substance of his future philosophical works. His "humanist-democratic" Marxist ideas deserve a special analysis, all the more so as he was one of the most influential and active intellectuals during the short Romanian "liberalization" (1967–71) and an extremely gifted essayist and novelist, fascinated by the dialectics of reality and possibility, by the tragic tension between *utopia* and *lucidity*. In a certain way, Ivasiuc's destiny is emblematic for the illusions of the Romanian intelligentsia, cynically speculated by the hegemonic bureaucracy: his last novel, *The Lobster*, speaks about power, revolution and dictatorship, about the intellectual dilemmas and anxieties in an age of violence and terror.

28 Ferenc Fehér, "The Language of Resistance: 'Critical Marxism' versus 'Marxism-Leninism' in Hungary," in Raymond Taras, *The Road to Disillusion: From Critical Marxism to Poscommunism in Eastern Europe* (Armonk, New York: M. E. Sharpe, 1992), 48.

brought down communism, they have permanently discredited Marxism-Stalinism, and no matter how dark the times they have ensured that a stubborn minority refuse to embrace anything but full tolerance and decency. Even as Europe struggles now, in large part due to its communist inheritance, we remain in a better situation than a century ago, because of the agonizing process of progress made from the celebration of torture and show trials to resistance and revolution in 1989.

GETTING OFF THE RED TRAM OF SOCIALISM

Mykola Riabchuk

Back in 1918, Józef Piłsudski, the founding father of the Second Polish Republic and undisputable national leader, allegedly made his most famous and frequently quoted dictum when talking to his former colleagues from the Polish Socialist Party (PPS): "Comrades, I took the red tram of socialism to the stop called Independence, and that's where I got off."

At that time, however, Piłsudski's defection was not a widespread phenomenon. The mass exodus from the "red tram of socialism at the stop called independence" did not start until seventy-plus years later, though the stream of defectors never went totally dry, especially after the Prague Spring was crushed in 1968 and the last hopes for a better kind of socialism vanished.

In 1918, "the red tram of socialism" actually acquired a new energy, vigor, and viability. Drawing on the revolutionary upsurge, the Bolsheviks had quickly become a heavily armored train, ready to liberate the global proletariat from their capitalist oppression. As the Russian empire collapsed, many socialists of non-Russian ethnicity faced the "Piłsudski dilemma". Some, like Piłsudski, got off the red tram, but most stayed on board, either by choice or by default—as the choices were increasingly limited.

The Ukrainian socialists split dramatically on the issue of the red tram. Aligning with the Bolsheviks or continuing down the path of socialism meant the same thing. "Aligning with the Bolsheviks" meant (officially) "continuing down the path of socialism". The real choice was between socialism (promoted by Bolsheviks) and the national cause. Pilsudski reneged on socialism and opted for nationalism—Polish independence. Some of Ukrainian socialists followed Piłsudski's suit and clearly opted for Ukrainian independence (Petliura et al.) but some tried to promote the national cause within the communist party and ideology. They are objects of this study. Some of those who got off the tram, like Symon Petliura, clearly opted for independence and took to arms to defend it. Some, like Volodymyr Vynnychenko, became completely bewildered and opted for emigration. But the majority tried to find some resolution with the dominating Bolsheviks, who effectively hijacked the "red train" and made their leftist allies mere hostages in their neo-imperial policy.[1]

Ukrainian "national communism" of the 1920s represented an interesting and largely underestimated phenomenon that preceded all other versions of "national communism" worldwide, including in Yugoslavia (still considered by many to be the first and most paradigmatic example). As Stephen Velychenko, one of the most diligent students of the Ukrainian "national communism" aptly remarked, "it was they [the Ukrainian Marxists], not the Yugoslavs, who created the world's second "national communist" movement after the Russians. They also initiated the world's first intra-communist war when they took up arms against the RCP in March 1919—fifty years to the month before the Chinese did so... Ukrainian Marxist writings on capitalism, national oppression, Russian colonialism, and imperialism, accordingly, should be included within the corpus of "anti-colonialist Marxism."[2]

Indeed, Ukrainian Marxists' encounter with Bolshevism revealed clearly the neo-imperial essence of the Soviet system, its hypocrisy in regard to its proclaimed attitude toward nationality politics, and its fundamental incompatibility with cultural-cum-political aspirations of non-Russian nationalities. Regretfully, the lesson of Ukrainian "national communism" remained largely unnoticed and largely unlearned. Even though, if properly taken, it may have prevented many wrong choices and false illusions. It may also have contributed to the proper (anti-colonial) understanding of the Soviet empire, and eventually made its collapse not so unexpected and confusing.

---

[1]   For a good introduction to the revolutionary developments in Ukraine see John Reshetar, *The Ukrainian Revolution, 1917–1920: A Study in Nationalism* (Princeton: Princeton University Press, 1952). The aftermath is covered comprehensively in Serhii Plokhy's *The Gates of Europe: A History of Ukraine* (New York: Basic Books, 2015), specifically in chapter 20, "Communism and Nationalism." Olena Palko, in a short but informative article on Ukrainian National Communism, focuses mostly on the period of 1917–1925, when Bolsheviks tolerated a relative political pluralism, so that various left-wing parties and groups could exist legally in Ukraine. She considers Ukrainian national communism as "an original quest for an appropriate local model for implementing Marxism," but stops short of examining the phenomenon in anticolonial terms—as a local attempt to complete the suppressed processes of national liberation and decolonization. Olena Palko, "Ukrainian National Communism in International Context," in *Disappearing Realities: On the Cultural Consequences of Social Change*, eds. Anna Dwyer and Maria Bucholc (Vienna: IWM Junior Visiting Fellows' Conferences, 2011), http://www.iwm.at/publications/5-junior-visiting-fellows-conferences/vol-xxx/olena-palko-ukrainian-national-communism-in-international-context/.

[2]   Stephen Velychenko, "Ukrainian Anticolonialist Thought in Comparative Perspective: A Preliminary Overview," *Ab Imperio* 4 (2012): 25.

Ukrainian Marxists never attained power and therefore never had the privilege of writing their own history as victors do. They neither wrote nor were translated into major world languages, so this inevitably limited access to their work. But the main reason for their relative obscurity stems, most likely, from the double bias against them on behalf of both the international Left and the international academic community. In one case, the bias is grounded in deep and blind Russophilic, Moscow-centric feelings, projected today even upon the essentially far right, hyper-nationalistic regime in Kremlin. In the second case, the bias results from the long-time perception of Russia (and the Soviet Union) as a multinational state, rather than an empire with exploited and developmentally stunted colonies. Both biases often are intertwined and interdependent in so much as they share the Enlightenment paradigm that equates progress with economic development and sets an alleged universalism of "historical" nations and their cultures against any national particularism, deemed a retrograde, anti-modernizing phenomenon.

Back in 1993, the renowned Canadian-Ukrainian historian Orest Subtelny complained of a "considerable skepticism" that specialists in Ukrainian history encountered among their colleagues in Russian and Soviet studies throughout much of the postwar period:

> Most American historians who were trained in the 1950s and 1960s by the influential Russian emigre historians (…) shared their teachers' 'one and indivisible' view of East Slavic history. Meanwhile the left-leaning revisionists who appeared in the 1970s were also ideologically predisposed to downplay the history of the non-Russian nationalities. More often than not, both camps assumed that a historian of Ukraine was, almost by definition, a Ukrainian nationalist. Thus, well into the 1980s, Ukrainian history was considered not only a peripheral but even intellectually suspect area of specialization.[3]

This might be the reason why James Mace's 1983 book on Ukrainian national communism published by the Harvard Ukrainian Institute did not get the attention it deserved. The author's unequivocal view of Ukraine as a colony of czarist Russia and, eventually, Soviet Union left him little chance to be heard and appreciated.[4] And his brief but substantial coverage of the Stalin's

---

[3] Orest Subtelny, "The Current State of Ukrainian Historiography," *Journal of Ukrainian Studies* 18, nos. 1–2 (1993): 37. For a broader discussion of the problem see Mark von Hagen, "Does Ukraine Have a History?" *Slavic Review* 54, no. 3 (1995): 658–73.

[4] As George Grabowicz, a long-time director of the Ukrainian Research Institute in Harvard, argued: "Until recently leading scholars in the West considered references to the Soviet Union

genocidal famine in Ukraine (that effectively sealed the story of Ukrainian national communism in 1933)—made the book even more unpalatable for most Sovietologists of the time. Even his reference to the "Ukrainian connection" in Yugoslavian national communism, featured strategically at the very beginning of the book, proved to be of no avail.[5]

Today, with the formidable communist system gone and communist ideology to a large degree antiquated, it appears ironically that the only kind of communism that has retained some attractiveness and relevance, at least theoretically, is the "national" kind—despite, or perhaps because of, the fact that it had been condemned and disgraced long ago by true believers. It is not so much the class struggle that invigorates the creed nowadays but, rather, the daunting (neo)colonial problems of economic extortion, political dominance, and cultural supremacism that confer some relevance on national forms of communism with a strong anti-hegemonic, national-liberation agenda.

The following essay discusses two aspects of Ukrainian national communism that still seem to be topical. One of them relates to Ukrainian Marxists' encounter with strong imperialist-cum-chauvinist presuppositions in Russian Bolshevism, and attempts to resist or to accommodate the victors. The second touches upon the highly ambiguous policy of "Ukrainization," in which Ukrainian national communists played a major role and, though ultimately extinguished, left an important institutional spin-off that later facilitated Ukraine's independence in 1991.

---

as a malevolent genocidal experiment to be unscholarly, indeed a form of anti-scholarship. Up to the end of the 1980s the very term 'Soviet empire' was seen as an obvious sign that the text in which it was used was not very serious—the author being either 'right wing' or not all there. One can check this in the bibliographic sources: up to 1989 studies or overviews that use this term can be counted on the fingers of both hands (with a number of them appearing in the Congressional Record); after 1989 they number in the hundreds." Hryhory Hrabovych, "Ukraina: pidsumky stolittia," *Krytyka* 11 (1999): 6.

5   Mace points out that Milovan Djilas' seminal article "Lenin on the Relations Between Socialist States" was designed to justify Broz Tito's break with the Soviet Union and "consisted largely of Lenin's assurances to the Ukrainians that their rights and aspirations would be respected." In Mace's view, "it was quite appropriate that the Yugoslavs turned to Ukraine for a precedent, for it was the Ukrainians who first attempted to find their own national road to socialism." See James E. Mace, *Communism and the Dilemmas of National Liberation: National Communism in Soviet Ukraine, 1918–1933* (Cambridge, MA: Harvard University Press, 1983), 1.

Encounter with a 'red imperialism'

Perhaps the most remarkable and long-lasting legacy of Ukrainian Marxism was its unrelenting exposure and deconstruction of Russian Bolshevism as an imperialism "painted red" and disguised under quasi-proletarian, "internationalist" rhetoric. This deconstruction was based on three major premises, each uncontestably Marxist in its core. First, the Marxist concept of basis and superstructure was employed to argue that all the Moscow concessions regarding language and culture were worth little without a full-fledged national economy, real ownership and management of national resources, and a large-scale and thorough institutional devolution.

Second, fully in line with Marxist social historicism, Ukrainian national communists contended that proletariat is not an abstract category but a product of the concrete social-historical circumstances and specific national cultures. Hence, there was no reason to believe that the class consciousness would inevitably supersede national consciousness, and even less reason to expect that the national consciousness, with all its cultural codes and ethnic stereotypes, would have no significant impact on class consciousness.

Third, Ukrainian Marxists claimed, with facts and figures, that the so-called "Communist Party of Ukraine" did not represent the interests of the Ukrainian nation because its ethnic composition, its language and cultural background, and its explicit policies in Ukraine made it a party of settler-colonists, with a rather typical contempt for the autochthons of Ukraine and a deeply engrained "banal" (to paraphrase Michael Bilig's insightful term) great power chauvinism in their mentality. Moreover, even by its social composition, the CPU was not a proletarian party but, primarily, the party of petite-bourgeois functionaries and déclassé intellectuals preoccupied with their hegemonic position and career opportunities in Ukraine. (The claim seems to foreshadow the eventual discovery of the "new class" by Milovan Djilas).

Ukrainian "national communism" as a discernable intellectual and ideo-logical trend can be traced from 1917 to 1933, with a minor rebirth in the 1960s and some marginal appearances among Ukrainian emigres writing in Europe and North America. In a politically institutionalized form, it was primarily evident in the short-lived Ukrainian Communist Party (UCP, 1920–1925) and in the activity of some Ukrainian intellectuals, including the CPU members, engaged in the Soviet policy of "indigenization." The UCP was created in January 1920 by former members of the Ukrainian Social Democratic Labor Party (Sovereigntists) as a national alternative to the Communist Party of Ukraine (Bolsheviks)—a regional sub-branch of the Russian Communist Party rebranded in 1918. From its very inception, the UCP considered the CPU non-Ukrainian in both its ethnic composition and for its arguably pro-Russian, neocolonial policies. The UCP absorbed some pro-Ukrainian members of CPU(b)—the so called "federalists," as well as the partly left-wing Ukrainian socialist-revolutionaries (Borotbists), dissolved in 1920.

The UCP membership never exceeded 3,000 persons, but they drew on a number of prominent Ukrainian intellectuals and had their own newspaper "Chervony prapor" (The Red Flag). There and elsewhere, they waged systemic and well-grounded criticism of the CPU(b), deeming it a mere arm of the Russian imperial rule in Ukraine, and developed (actually pioneered) what can be considered today a rather coherent anti-colonialist Marxist critique of Russian imperial dominance. Unlike all their predecessors and many followers, they did consider Ukraine a "colony" and used that term explicitly. The strongest exponents of this critique were Ukrainian communists Vasyl Shakhrai and Serhiy Mazlakh who as early as 1919 published a pamphlet "Do Khvyli. Shcho diyetsia na Ukraini i z Ukrainoyu" ("On the Current Situation in Ukraine").[6]

There, they analyzed the Bolshevik policy in Ukraine and asserted: "The Russian proletariat made a social revolution and praise and respect is therefore due it. But this does not mean that it did not inherit from tsarist Russia a bit of imperialism or [so-called] historical and ethnographic rights." Because the overwhelming majority of Bolsheviks in Ukraine were Russian or Russified, their party logically could not represent an "oppressed nation" and obviously avoided the issue of national liberation.[7]

A year later, in the Memorandum to the Second Congress of the III Communist International (July–August 1920) the UCP explicitly referred to Bolshevik rule in Ukraine as "Russian occupation" because it arguably ignored national issues and imagined that these could be placated by simple

---

[6]   Serhii Mazlakh and Vasyl' Shakhrai, "Do khvyli: Shcho diyetsia v Ukraini i z Ukrainoyu?" (Saratov, 1919), http://chtyvo.org.ua/authors/Mazlakh_Serhii/Do_khvyli_Scho_diietsia_na_Vkraini_i_z_Ukrainoiu7/.

[7]   Serhii Mazlakh and Vasyl' Shakhrai, *On the Current Situation in Ukraine* (Ann Arbor: University of Michigan Press, 1970). Quoted in Velychenko, "Ukrainian Anticolonialist Thought," 19.

"bourgeois cultural-national autonomy." It described the CPU as totally dependent on the RCP but explicitly accused only the former of being unable to overcome "the imperialist legacy of old Russia."[8]

The Bolshevik reaction to all the "nationalistic deviations" had been rather predictable, though not always unanimous and uniform. It reflected, on one hand, the lack of unity in the Bolshevik ranks on nationality issues and on the Ukrainian problem in particular.[9] On the other hand (and on a deeper theoretical level), it reflected the absence of a coherent approach to the nationalities problems in the writings of Marx and Engels. They failed, in Roman Szporluk's words, "to speak clearly and comprehensively" on the complex issue.[10] Lenin followed suit, picking up different arguments from his mentors ad hoc and adjusting them "dialectically" to the specific needs of a current moment. In sum, one may distinguish three major factors that determined the Bolshevik policy toward Ukraine: "strategic-political considerations, Marxist principles, and Russian imperialist preconceptions."[11]

However flexible and politically expedient were the Bolsheviks in their nationality policies, they claimed strong commitment to the Marxist principle of "proletarian internationalism" that stipulated supremacy of class consciousness (and identity) over all other forms of self-identification, including the national. As revolutionaries, committed to the Enlightenment notion of progress based on rational knowledge and universal laws, they professed equality of the people and supported the liberation of all oppressed groups, including subjugated nations. At the same time, they could not but feel that national feelings pave a way to national solidarity, which, in turn, blurs the dividing class lines and undermines international solidarity of proletarians, indispensable for the world revolution.[12] They condemned therefore nationalism

---

8   Mazlakh and Shakhrai, *On the Current Situation in Ukraine.*

9   "The Bolsheviks reached no consensus on nationality policy, and the conflict between those who, like Lenin, considered the national agenda of non-Russians and those who, like Stalin, subordinated the national to the 'proletarian' continued until the former's death and the latter's consolidation of power within the party." Ronald Grigor Suny, "Nationalism and the Russian Revolution: From Anti-Imperialism to a Soviet Empire," *H-Nationalism*, December 20, 2017, https://networks.h-net.org/node/3911/discussions/1118710/left-and-nationalism-monthly-series-%E2%80%9Cnationalism-and-russian.

10 Roman Szporluk, *Communism and Nationalism: Karl Marx versus Friedrich List* (New York and Oxford: Oxford University Press, 1985), 1.

11 Stephen Velychenko, *Painting Imperialism and Nationalism Red: The Ukrainian Marxist Critique of Russian Communist Rule in Ukraine, 1918–1925* (Toronto University Press, 2015), 7.

12 "As a rival of socialism, [nationalism] promoted the formation of distinct national communities with their own economic and political interests—communities that emphatically included the

as a sort of "bourgeois false consciousness serving to divide the workers along national lines, to divert attention from their class enemies, and thereby to inhibit the struggle for socialism."[13] And they applied a precarious dialectic to sort out their own ambivalent stances to various issues of national liberation and to develop ambiguous, highly opportunistic policies in the field. On one hand, they recognized, in principle, the right of all nations for self-determination. On the other hand, they made this "right" conditional on so many caveats, that its implementation became a matter of sheer arbitrariness. The Bolsheviks reserved for themselves the right to endow or revoke that entitlement any time at their convenience.[14]

The Marxist utopia envisioned communism as a global system that should be not only classless but also nationless. The Bolsheviks interpreted it literally, as a fusion of all "proletarian nations" into a single community that, in practical terms, meant the dissolution of all nationalities into the most advanced, the most "revolutionary," and "progressive" Russian nation. From this point of view, political independence of non-Russian nationalities made little sense in a long run since they sooner or later should be reunified again. But in the short term, some of them could be allowed to exercise their "right for a self-determination"—either to speed up the decline of the old European empires (as in the case of the national liberation movements in Asia or Africa), or to create buffer states at the vulnerable Russian borders (as in the case of Tuva or Mongolia), or to prove, usually by default, the much-touted Bolsheviks' commitment to the principle of self-determination (the ultimate goal of which was to persuade international revolutionaries to join a global communist confederation presided by the emphatically non-imperial Russia).[15]

Whatever Bolsheviks said and did, they shared in their hearts "the younger Marx's dismissive views on nationality—his notion that large, centralized economies were progressive, that nationalism was not progressive, and that

---

workers. By doing so, it ran counter to the attempts of the socialists to build a solidarity of workers along supranational lines." Szporluk, *Communism and Nationalism*, 15.

[13] Mace, *Communism and the Dilemmas of National Liberation*, 9.

[14] "On the ground, Communists themselves decided who was the carrier of the nation's will (...) A national liberation movement in one country might have to be opposed if it proved to be 'merely an instrument of the clerical or financial-monarchist intrigues of other countries.' The flexibility that [Lenin] proposed in 1916 would two years later... have enormous consequences for non-Russian nationalities." Suny, "Nationalism and the Russian Revolution."

[15] "The language of national liberation and anti-imperialism remained a potent discursive cloak under which an empire of subordinated nations was gradually built." Suny, "Nationalism and the Russian Revolution."

small national states were archaic. These elements of revolutionary messianism coincided with the educated opinion of the time that viewed minority nationalisms of small 'doomed' peoples as anomalies."[16] The traditional Russian messianism was not only wrapped in a Marxist "revolutionary" phraseology it was also crossbred with programmatic immoralism, based on a firm belief that the sacred goal—liberation of humankind—justified any means.

The main rift between Russian and Ukrainian communists ran along their fundamentally different views on what Ukraine was, is, and should be. As first of Russians, sharing all the imperial biases and phobias of the Russian population in general, Bolsheviks shared all the imperial stereotypes and biases against non-Russians. Even those who were ready to accept Ukrainians as a separate nationality, considered them through the prism of the primordialist myth of the so-called Russian-Ukrainian 'brotherhood' and tripartite East Slavonic unity. Even those who agreed that Russia was an empire, disagreed that its policies in Ukraine were colonial.

"Most Bolsheviks," Stephen Velychenko writes in a recently published book, "belonged to the ruling Russian nationality or identified with it by choice. They had been educated in Russian, they read Russocentric tsarist histories of the empire, and they lived in urban centres with Russian media... In keeping with the Hegelian Enlightenment zeitgeist of the time that led the educated in ruling imperial nations to equate progress and modernity with their respective cultures and languages and large states, learned imperialist ideas formed Bolshevik attitudes towards non-Russians.... Socialism, in their view, was incompatible with nationalism, and national identity was an invention of nationalists."[17]

Any concessions to the Soviet non-Russians like a limited use of local languages in education, publishing, and administration were considered just tactical and temporary—to pacify "leftover nationalist feelings among the working masses of oppressed or underprivileged nations." The same was their approach to Soviet federalism: most Bolsheviks saw it as just another concession to the politically immature natives—a means to satisfy their "nationalistic delusions" (in Georgiy Piatakov's words) in a way the remaining churches were to satisfy the religious superstitions of a backward folk.[18]

---

[16] Velychenko, *Painting Imperialism Red*, 86.
[17] Velychenko, *Painting Imperialism Red*, 91–92.
[18] Velychenko, *Painting Imperialism Red*, 68, 72.

Ukrainian communists felt increasingly exasperating tension between their being both communists and Ukrainians at the same time—something that Russian communists had never felt, because being a communist and a Russian was largely congruent and coterminous. Perhaps this is what Yuri Slezkine meant when remarked that "Russian Bolsheviks could never be more Russian than Bolshevik." "Not only was the Russian language the medium that cemented both the Soviet party/state and the Soviet imagined community," he wrote, "but the Russian cultural canon was eagerly maintained and promoted by state officials long before it was formally incorporated into official statements."[19]

Ukrainian communists, on the contrary, could be more Ukrainian than communist, but this was increasingly dangerous and punishable—so dangerous that by 1930s most of them tried to be as little Ukrainian as possible. This did not guarantee their survival but somewhat increased the chances. Ukrainian nationality at the time was the second most dangerous for its holders after the Polish.

In 1920s, however, quite a few Ukrainian communists were tempted, or even provoked to be more Ukrainian than communist—inasmuch as they tried to rescue the lost cause of national liberation, to fix the perceived (neo) colonial injustice, and to defend their national dignity and personal integrity against the institutionalized "red imperialism" that emanated from Moscow and the vernacular "plebeian imperialism" exposed extensively by local Russian and Russified urbanites.

In his well-researched, rich of primary sources book, Stephen Velychenko depicts a stifling atmosphere of the time as it was felt by his heroes in daily encounters with "banal" imperialism often expressed explicitly via Ukrainophobic statements like "Ukrainian is only a language for songs"; "[the language] is vulgar and unsuited for a subject like physics ... Ukraine now is nothing but a part of Russia"; "I won't Ukrainianize—the Revolution was in Russian"; "Ukrainian is a dog's language, I won't study it." Heorhy Lapchynsky, a leader of the "federalist" faction in the CPU, described the citizens of Kharkiv (the capital of Soviet Ukraine at the time) as "totally Russified and zoologically hostile to everything Ukrainian." Another Ukrainian communist depicted Odessa with a similar angst: "the Ukrainian population is small and totally terrorized... The fear is so great that they are afraid to speak Ukrainian and ask about what is happening in Ukraine in corners," i.e. they don't dare to speak

---

[19] Yuri Slezkine, "Commentary: Imperialism as the Highest Stage of Socialism," *Russian Review* 59, no. 2 (2000): 231.

Ukrainian in public and do it only in private, secretly, confidentially, only in a whisper. Speaking Ukrainian required much courage, "because everything Ukrainian is slandered as Petliurism" [i.e., named after the leader of the allegedly "bourgeois" and "counterrevolutionary" Ukrainian National Republic]. In 1922, the Kyiv Bolshevik newspaper "Komunist" had even to feature the article titled "The Ukrainian Language Is Not the Language of Petliura"—in an apparent attempt to soften the popular tendency of denigration of all things Ukrainian with a slanderous, ideologically charged label.[20]

Lenin himself was aware of ethnic presuppositions among many Russians and castigated occasionally some of his close associates for "great power chauvinism" and a "lack of national sensitivity." In March 1919, he famously quipped "Scratch some communists and you will find Great Russia Chauvinists."[21] The persistence of "plebeian imperialism," especially among Russian colonial settlers in ethnically non-Russian borderlands, increasingly worried Lenin and other Bolshevik leaders as it threatened their "indigenization" project, however limited and superficial it had to be. In a classified report, the CPU recognized that "the city" contemptuously regarded Ukrainian as coterminous with backwardness and peasantry. By 1918, they wrote, "we had full-blown hate in towns towards everything Ukrainian." Capitalism threw together into the city both Ukrainian peasants and Russian workers from Russia. As a result, the Ukrainian proletariat "acquired Russian culture, began to internalize Russian, including its attitude to everything Ukrainian as peasant and backward."[22]

In fact, Bolsheviks themselves contributed to the widespread association of Ukrainian language with the language of enemies, and the Ukrainian movement with a counterrevolution. This followed logically from their glorification of Russian as the "language of revolution" and their programmatic view of proletariat as a "progressive" class superior to the "conservative," or even "reactionary," peasantry.[23] In a predominantly peasant Ukraine it was

---

[20] Velychenko, *Painting Imperialism Red*, 22, 35, 93, 104.

[21] Lenin, *Polnoe sobranie sochineniy*, vol. 38 (Moscow: Izdatelstvo politicheskoy literatury, 1969), 183. The quip is a paraphrase of the popular saying attributed to Joseph de Maistre: "Scratch a Russian and you will find a Tatar."

[22] Quoted in Velychenko, *Painting Imperialism Red*, 93.

[23] Bolsheviks were not the first who employed this kind of argumentation. In 1794, the French revolutionaries averred that French was the "language of liberty" and that those other tongues spoken in France were means to perpetuate "the reign of fanaticism and superstition… the domination of priests and aristocrats." Cited in Szporluk, *Communism and Nationalism*, 80–81.

tantamount to the assertion of ethnic and cultural superiority of Russian/ Russified cities over Ukrainian/Ukrainophone province and of the Russian nationality over the Ukrainian. Russian supremacy was solidified additionally by the crude biological metaphor of the "brotherly nations" that assigned the role of the "older" and "wiser" (i.e., "politically mature," in the Bolshevik parlance) brother to Russians. "Brotherly" guardianship of one nation over the others went hand-in-hand with a similarly supremacist "class" guardianship of the "advanced" proletarians over the "retarded" peasantry.

As long as Russian and Russified population made up the absolute majority in Ukrainian cities, Bolsheviks could fully rely on them as their social base, especially due to the fact that most anti-Bolshevik urbanites retreated en mass with the White Guard. The firm control of the Ukrainian cities provided them with a huge strategic advantage, but the problem was that almost 90 per cent of the population at the time lived in small towns and villages. Ukrainians, however "backward" and "reactionary" they may have been, had to be catered to in so much as the Bolsheviks needed them to expand their social base into Ukraine and complete their ambitious program of modernization.[24] This might have been the primary reason for the Bolshevik "Ukrainization" campaign launched officially in 1923 (after the 12th Party congress) within the broader "indigenization" policy throughout the whole newly established Soviet Union. "The essentially imperialist undertaking of keeping the nations of the Russian Empire in the new state resulted in a program of nativization, endowing the toilers of various nationalities with presumably equal and full-fledged national institutions."[25]

It is very unlikely that sheer doctrinal purity determined that shift in communist policy. Bolsheviks, as we know from a great many cases, were quite flexible on nationality issues and conveniently solved any doctrinal problems and contradictions by means of whimsical Marxist-Leninist "dialectics." Ideological principles may have played some role in their policies, combined with the propagandistic need to enhance the attractiveness of the Soviet Union in the eyes of the international proletariat bound for the

---

[24] "Bolsheviks were a minority party representing a social class that had nearly disappeared in the civil war. With no political or cultural hegemony over the vast peasant masses and with exceptional vulnerability in the non-Russian regions, the communist parties moderated their own leap into socialism." Suny, "Nationalism and the Russian Revolution."

[25] Serhy Yekelchyk, *Stalin's Empire of Memory: Russian-Ukrainian Relations in the Soviet Historical Imagination* (Toronto: University of Toronto Press, 2004), 3.

world revolution. But the modernization argument seems the most feasible. As an American author aptly remarks, "other states may have other claims to legitimacy; the USSR had nothing but progress and modernity. What else, besides victory over backwardness, could the Soviet state claim as its raison d'etre as well as its crowning achievement?"[26] To modernize a largely illiterate village, Bolsheviks needed not just a support but commitment of local intelligentsia. During the civil war, they cooperated opportunistically with Ukrainian leftists in so much as the latter considered Bolsheviks a lesser evil than the staunchly anti-Ukrainian Denikin's White Guard. Now, as the White-imperial threat had presumably vanished, Bolsheviks had to offer Ukrainians something positive to keep them as allies.

Speaking Ukrainian and Bolshevik at the same time

Since the Bolsheviks programmatically considered nations and national independence to be temporary phenomena, they could not but treat the indigenization campaign as a mere tactical move and not a long-term viable strategy. However impressive the campaign may have looked on the surface, it did not affect the fundamentals of the heavily centralized totalitarian state— particularly the hierarchical, tightly controlled, and disciplined dictatorial party and omnipotent security apparatus. None of these *real* institutions of power had ever been "federalized" or "Ukrainized." (One may add to this list heavy industry, international trade, finances, military, and a crucial for the communist states centralized economic planning).

For the Bolsheviks the campaign was indeed a win-win game. On the one hand, it allowed them to attract and coopt quite a few left-oriented Ukrainians, and thereby revamp the CPU as a Ukrainian party and legitimize, to a degree, its grip over Ukraine. On the other hand, it helped to delegitimize the rival Ukrainian groups, primarily the UCP (dissolved in 1925 after two unsuccessful applications to Komintern), and to silence, repress, and marginalize those Ukrainians who did not buy into the Party-led "Ukrainization."

The two-tier design of the Soviet institutions largely disguised the superficial and very limited and constrained character of the process. "Ukrainization" indeed affected the Soviet system superficially to a degree, administration, culture, and education (i.e. the external parts of the Soviet

---

[26] Slezkine, "Commentary," 228.

system) but never reached its deep structures, like the party and security bodies. The dismissive, essentially colonial attitude of these *real* authorities to the natives is expressed most explicitly in internal classified documents of the so-called "Ukrainian" GPU (State Political Directorate, the successor of VChK and predecessor of KGB). It is not only the language, unwaveringly Russian, spared from any hypocritical "indigenization," but also the discourse and *Weltanschauung* behind it, that reveal a profound disdain of occupation authorities for locals—treated as suspects at best and enemies at worst.

Mykhaylo Hrushevsky's files provide plenty of examples (the prominent historian had many because he was under tight GPU surveillance after his return to Ukraine in 1924). Pick up any random document and one can see GPU officers describe "Ukrainians" as an alien, highly suspicious group, an ethnic and ideological "Other" with whom they have nothing in common: "As we are informed, the Ukrainian activists intend to transform the Hryshevsky's jubilee into a national political celebration... The Ukrainian circles close to Hrushevsky have already informed the Ukrainian activists in the periphery about the [forthcoming] jubilee... Now, we are sending a [forged] letter to Kiev to disseminate it in Ukrainian circles in order to discredit Hrushevsky. (...) We should use the emerging disagreements among Ukrainians to deepen them...."[27]

This language says much more about the essence of the Soviet regime in Ukraine than the touted but shallow and superficial "indigenization." It seems, however, that Bolsheviks underestimated the "subversive" power of institutions—however dummy, feckless and subservient they might have been in the tightly controlled and supervised "national" republics.[28] It was in particular manifest in Ukraine where the process of indigenization, as James Mace aptly remarked, went further than anywhere else and "enabled the Soviet Ukrainian government to seek and receive the support of a substantial part of the formerly hostile national intelligentsia. Ukrainization succeeded in giving Soviet Ukraine a measure of national legitimacy, but this success was achieved only at the cost of legitimizing Ukrainian national aspiration within the Party itself. Communists began to raise questions that Moscow found exceedingly awkward."[29]

---

[27] Yuri Shapoval and Volodymyr Prystayko, eds., *Mykhaylo Hrushevsky i GPU-NKVD. Trahichne desiatylittia: 1924–1934* (Kyiv: Ukraine, 1996).

[28] Valerie Bunce, *Subversive Institutions: The Design and the Destruction of Socialism and the State* (Cambridge: Cambridge University Press, 1999).

[29] Mace, *Communism and the Dilemmas of National Liberation*, 3.

Stalin had apparently a good reason to oppose Lenin's idea of federali-
zation since he noticed undesirable side-effects of the process as early as
1922. Broad autonomy, he complained, had created, "despite our intentions,"
people who "demanded real independence in all aspects." Young communists
"in the borderlands refuse to accept the independence game as a game." [30]
His associate Feliks Dzerzhinsky, the head of the notorious VChK, supported
the view arguing that the "borderland" governments unfortunately took
themselves too seriously "as if they could be independent governments."[31]

Whether Bolsheviks had any viable alternative to Lenin's plan in the early
1920s is another matter. The fact is, however, that even a partial weakening of
the imperial grip over Ukraine, at least in the sphere of culture and education,
allowed Ukrainians to quickly complete the Hrochian phase B of the nation-
building (arrested under the tsars) and predictably reach the phase C, i.e., the
phase of mass political mobilization.[32] The respective demands were carefully
but insistently worded by the 'national communists' as they remained, for
nearly a decade, the only political force able to articulate Ukrainian national
aspirations more or less openly.

Indeed, the process of indigenization, unleashed opportunistically by
Bolsheviks as a sheer tactical move, was taken seriously by their indigenous
partners as a long-term strategy. To much of Kremlin's chagrin, they pushed
"the Ukrainization policy too assiduously"—so that, in Mace's words,
"Ukrainians were quickly becoming a sociologically complete nation: Ukrainians became a majority in the Party, the industrial proletariat, and were
rapidly penetrating the elites of the society in which they had hitherto been
confined to the bottom level of the social hierarchy."[33]

---

[30] Joseph Stalin, "Iz istorii obrazovaniia SSSR," in *Works*, vol. IV, 371, quoted in Velychenko,
      Painting Imperialism Red, 52.
[31] Stalin, "Iz istorii obrazovaniia SSSR."
[32] Miroslav Hroch conceptualized the 19th-century development of "small," stateless nations in
      Europe in three-stages. First, at the phase A (of cultural interest) a tiny group of intellectuals
      "discover" the richness of local cultural heritage. Then, in phase B (of nationalistic agitation)
      they try to inculcate masses with the newly discovered, culture-based identity. And finally,
      at the phase C (of mass national mobilization) they raise the political demands supported
      by popular movement. Miroslav Hroch, *Social Preconditions of National Revival in Europe: A
      Comparative Analysis of the Social Composition of Patriotic Groups among the Smaller European
      Nations* (Cambridge UK: Cambridge University Press, 1985). See also a comprehensive debate
      on the issue in Alexander Maxwell, "Typologies and Phases in Nationalism Studies: Hroch's
      A-B-C Schema as a Basis for Comparative Terminology," *Nationalities Papers* 38, no. 6 (2010):
      865–880.
[33] Mace, *Communism and the Dilemmas of National Liberation*, 305.

The appearance of a full-fledged nation-building was really strong on the surface, to the extent that even today many scholars tend to accept it at face value. In his otherwise brilliant book, Terry Martin argues, for instance, that the Soviet state "literally seized leadership over all the three [Hrochian] phases: the articulation of national culture, the formation of national elites, and the propagation of the national mass consciousness. It still went further and initiated even 'phase D' measures typical of newly formed nation-states, establishing a new language of state and a new governing elite. To use more familiar Bolshevik terminology, the party became the vanguard of non-Russian nationalism."[34]

This is, alas, an overstatement. In actuality, the Soviets never permitted any phase C in their fiefdom, and there is definitely no reason to supplement Miroslav Hroch's model with any idiosyncratic phase D—the idea rejected, inter alia, by Hroch himself. The discussion was instigated several years ago by a Belarusian scholar Nelly Bekus who uncritically accepted Martin's assertion that "the initial process of national awakening typical for small nations in eastern and central Europe in the late nineteenth and early twentieth century… continued under Soviet rule after the Bolshevik revolution. Changes which were brought to Belarusian society together with socialist modernization in the Soviet state constituted 'Phase D' in Belarusian nation-building."[35]

Hroch responded that his Belarusian colleague had most likely misperceived "a significant peak in Phase B—a declaration of independence from enthusiastic activists [in 1918]—for the beginning of Phase C." In actuality, Hroch maintained, "if Bekus were right, then the identity issues in Belarus, and the development of this new independent nation state after the collapse of the Soviet Union, would be totally different. After having achieved Phase C, the nation forming process becomes irreversible and can no longer be stopped: consider the example of Baltic national movements under Soviet occupation. The sad story of Belarus is that the successes achieved during Phase B of their national movement were interrupted by Stalin's brutal Russification. The Belarusian movement started again after 1990, but remains an open-ended story. To call this repeated performance "Phase D" is only a matter of individual attempts to find a new description for a well-known situation."[36]

---

[34] Terry Martin, *The Affirmative Action Empire: Nations and Nationalism in the Soviet Union, 1923-1939* (Ithaca and London: Cornell University Press, 2001), 15.

[35] Nelly Bekus, "Nationalism and Socialism: 'Phase D' in the Belarusian Nation-Building," *Nationalities Papers* 38, no. 6 (2010): 829.

[36] Miroslav Hroch, "Comments," *Nationalities Papers* 38, no. 6 (2010): 888.

In other words, Bolshevik modernization had only briefly coincided in the 1920s with the nation-building efforts of Belarusian ethno-nationalists. Even then, however, the Bolsheviks aimed strategically at creating not so much a Belarusian nation as a Soviet multi-ethnic nation around the Russian ethno-cultural core. Throughout all the subsequent decades, there was transformation of "local" peasants not so much into Belarusians but first and foremost into a Belarusian ("local") kind of homo sovieticus. This pertains also to Ukrainians, even though they appeared to be a bit more advanced in terms of a nation-building than Belarusians.

It was probably the successful completion of phase B in Ukraine (and some other republics) and the looming specter of phase C that made Moscow thwart and rollback the phase B, supported initially at least in specific forms and to a certain degree. The Soviets actually never conceded any real power (like army, security service, or party apparatus) to the native elites, and never gave up close surveillance over the content of cultural and educational activity in ethnic peripheries. It could be "national in form," according to the Soviet dogma, but its "content" should have been definitely "socialist." And it was Moscow, of course, who decided the right proportion of "national"/"socialist" ingredients. For some time, this peculiar dialectic kept a room for embellishment of the "form" at the cost of the "content," and to smuggle some controversial "content" disguised in peculiar "form." By the 1930s, however, the space in that room shrank dramatically as a witch-hunt for ethnic "nationalists" went full stream, whereas the Russian nationalism became de facto the official ideology of the Soviet state.

The Bolsheviks might have been paranoid about Ukrainians' alleged conspiracy with the Poles and about many other things, but they were quite clear-minded about the strength and scale of the Ukrainian "national revival" unleashed by the revolution and catalyzed by the ambiguous policy of "Ukrainization." It was a real threat to the very existence of the empire, and the Bolshevik response to it was cruel, merciless but, in a way, adequate. First, they dealt with the old non-partisan intelligentsia and the national church, then with peasants, and finally with the national communists. The 1933 suicide of Mykola Khvyliovy and Mykola Skrypnyk, the cultural and political leaders of that movement, put both actual and symbolical end on Ukrainian communism as a genuine, intellectually and politically viable and vibrant phenomenon.

Conclusion

Ukrainian national communism emerged as a political and ideological movement that drew on the genuine need of Ukrainian society for both social and
national liberation. It reflected both the popularity of socialist ideas at the time
and the pragmatic need to cooperate with the victorious Bolsheviks, especially after all the hopes for Ukraine's independent development vanished.
The Ukrainian communists tried to pursue their own agenda but under
the tight Party control and GPU surveillance it was increasingly difficult.
Bolsheviks tolerated national communists in so much as they needed to broaden
their social base in non-Russian lands and pursue ambitious modernization
program. They launched an impressive indigenization campaign that did
not concede much power to national communists, but placated them with
substantial concession in the realms of culture and education, also, to a
degree, in administration and cadre policy. It appeared, however, that even
these limited and tightly controlled concessions produced a discernible
"nationalizing" effect, both in the society at large and in the CPU. The
tendency threatened the monolithic unity of the union Party and integrity
of the heavily centralized State. Within a few years, from 1929 to 1933, the
Ukrainian movement was totally and systemically crushed—in both its
intellectual, mostly communist leadership and its popular, mostly peasant
social base.

Ironically, the Soviet "national" institutions survived, however empty and
mostly decorative, and eventually played a role in all attempts at a "national
revival." In the late perestroika phase, this role became crucial, as not only the
Writers Union, the last refuge of "Ukrainianness" in the urban environment,
but also the bogus parliament and some city councils became champions
of the national cause. And, to add insult to injury, the communist party of
Ukraine that could hardly be called "national" in any meaningful sense, did
what the "national communists" of the 1920s would be happy to do if they
could—supported national independence. The ruling elite—predominantly
Ukrainian in ethnic terms but overwhelmingly Russian in terms of language
and culture—made a pact of convenience with indigenous anti-communists,
and conceived a hybrid "creole-cum-aboriginal" state based on institutional
continuity rather than ethnic or cultural unity and homogeneity.

A few years ago, the heirs of this elite who still run the country (even
though are dispersed today in various, mostly oligarchic factions), passed

the law under a long and whimsical title commonly known as the Law on Decommunization.[37] In fact, the law is much more about decolonization, since all the symbols, ideas and institutions condemned in this law are perceived today not so much as communist (nobody actually cares about communism any more) but first and foremost as Russian imperial. Ukrainian national communists of the 1920s were among the first who encountered this weird symbiosis of the communist and imperialist ideology in Russian Bolshevism, and denounced neo-imperial, hegemonic character of their political practices. As of today, this seems to be the most valuable and enduring legacy of Ukrainian "national communism." Regarding its other aspects, we would rather follow Piłsudski's advice. His next sentence after the often-quoted dictum about the "red tram," was: "You may continue your trip to the last stop, if you manage to, but in the meantime please let's address each other not as "Comrades" but "Sir" and "Mister.""

[37] "On the condemnation of the communist and national socialist (Nazi) regimes, and prohibition of propaganda of their symbols," Ukrainsky Instytut Natsionoi Pamiati [Ukrainian Institute of National Memory, official website], April 9, 2015, http://www.memory.gov.ua/laws/law-ukraine-condemnation-communist-and-national-socialist-nazi-regimes-and-prohibition-propagan.

THE RISE, DEMISE, AND PERNICIOUS LONG-TERM IMPACT OF SOVIET COMMUNIST IDEOLOGY IN RUSSIA

Mark Kramer

This essay discusses the origins, nature, and dissolution of Soviet Marxist-Leninist ideology, showing how the autocratic nature of the ideology blocked the development of deep-rooted democratic thought in the USSR and post-Soviet Russia. Soviet ideology was the best known of several millenarian versions of communist thought—versions that had their roots in the works of Karl Marx and Friedrich Engels and were later reshaped by Vladimir Lenin, Joseph Stalin, Mao Zedong, and other figures. The millenarian nature of the ideology is what links Soviet communism with extremist ideologies nowadays, notably radical Islam. In both cases, the millenarian quest to achieve a perfect human society (defined by class, religion, or some other criterion) becomes a grand rationalizer of tyranny, hatred, atrocities, and mass murder targeted against all those who are seen as standing in the way of the utopian end-goal.

By the term "ideology," I am referring to a set of doctrinal precepts that cumulatively determine how an individual views and understands the world. Widely shared precepts form the core of a state ideology, which serves as a broad guide to state actions. A state ideology is fostered via the state's political lexicon, rituals, ceremonies, and political and economic institutions.[1] The ideology helps shape the beliefs, perceptions, and actions of policymakers, political activists, and the wider public.

The modern notion of ideology as the basis for a mass political movement arose in the late eighteenth century with the French Revolution, which emphasized the use of ideas for political ends and mass mobilization. The leftwing *idéologues* who wrote political tracts in favor of the revolution (which they saw as a vehicle for utopian social-engineering) spurred a reaction from foreign observers (e.g., Edmund Burke) who had grave doubts about the

---

[1] Andrew Heywood, *Political Ideologies: An Introduction*, 5th ed. (London: Macmillan, 2012).

revolution. But one point on which all the commentators agreed was that the ideology of the event would serve basic sociopolitical goals.

The *idéologues* were uprooted by Napoleon, whose effort to eradicate revolutionary influences put a damper on leftwing ideological development for the next several decades. However, the rise of the German idealist school with Fichte and Hegel, and the inclusion of a materialist dimension by Feuerbach, provided all the elements necessary for the rise of Marxist ideology.[2] With Marx, the concept of ideology gained a champion whose influence came to affect large swaths of the world. Marx used "ideology" not in the sense of a worldview but to refer to "false consciousness" (i.e., the intellectual substructure encrusted on capitalism that kept workers from understanding the depth of the injustices they faced amid the existing system of ownership of the means of production). Only with Lenin did "ideology" come to mean either "capitalist ideology" or "socialist ideology," a distinction he first made in 1902.[3] In Lenin's view, capitalist ideology was equivalent to "false consciousness," whereas socialist ideology was the absence of false consciousness. Within Marxism, Antonio Gramsci completed the shift to current-day notions of ideology, with his concept of ideological hegemony.[4]

Soviet Marxist ideology had a much wider and deeper appeal than most observers nowadays would like to think, particularly during the years of Lenin and Stalin but also afterward. It provided a means for those who were dissatisfied with the existing order to think about how they could move to something better, and it cemented their conviction that they had come across the only true perspective for understanding and permanently changing the world. The intoxicating feeling of having found the "one true faith" caused many people to set aside their critical judgments about the direction the ideology was leading after the Bolsheviks seized power in Petrograd in November 1917.

---

[2]   Leszek Kołakowski, *Main Currents of Marxism*, vol. 1., trans. P. S. Falla (New York: Oxford University Press, 1978); George Lichtheim, "The Origins of Marxism," *Journal of the History of Philosophy* 3, no. 1 (April 1965), 96–105; and David McLellan, *The Young Hegelians and Karl Marx* (London: Macmillan, 1969).

[3]   Neil Harding, *Leninism* (Durham, NC: Duke University Press, 1996), 42–44; and Alfred G. Meyer, *Leninsim* (Cambridge, MA: Harvard University Press, 1957), 37–38. See Lenin's "What Is to Be Done?" (Chto delat?) pamphlet for the distinction.

[4]   On Soviet ideology as a hegemonic discourse, see Tom Casier, "The Shattered Horizon: How Ideology Mattered to Soviet Politics," *Studies in East European Thought* 51, no. 1 (March 1999), 35–59.

The founding of the Bolshevik regime, which converted Marxist-Leninist ideology into a guide and instrument of the Soviet state as well as a means of mass mobilization and social control, almost immediately gave rise to the Gulag and an oppressive state security apparatus. Bolshevik ideology itself, predicated on a millenarian conception of social and political organization, bred a murderous intolerance and antipathy toward those who were deemed to be obstacles to the millenarian vision. Lenin may not have been as wantonly cruel and sadistic as Stalin, but a great deal of research over the past 25 years has undermined the notion that Lenin's program was "betrayed" by Stalin.[5] Lenin repeatedly evinced his willingness to rely on brutal violence, and the same was true of all the potential successors to Lenin, including those who were somewhat less committed than Stalin to the use of systematic coercion and murder. Nikolai Bukharin, for example, mercilessly crushed the workers' revolt at Kronstadt in 1921 and accepted other measures to impose draconian controls on Soviet society both during and after the Russian Civil War. The Bolshevik regime, by its very nature, was a progenitor of mass repression— precisely the sort of regime that was bound to give a decisive advantage to figures like Stalin who were always willing to use harsh violence to eliminate their rivals and attain their goals. The ideology provided both a rationalization and an obligation to be ruthless.

The great writer Aleksandr Solzhenitsyn highlighted this point in a striking passage from the first volume of *Gulag Archipelago*:

> To do evil a human being must first of all believe that what he is doing is good, or else that it is a well-considered act in conformity with natural law. Fortunately, it is in the nature of the human being to seek justification for his actions.
>
> Macbeth's self-justifications were feeble—and his conscience devoured him. Yes, even Iago was a meek lamb, too. The imagination and the spiritual strength of Shakespeare's evildoers stopped short at a dozen corpses. Because they had no ideology.
>
> Ideology—that is what gives evildoing its long-sought justification and gives the evildoer the necessary steadfastness and determination. Ideology is the social theory that helps to make his acts seem good instead of bad in his own and other's eyes, so that he will not hear reproaches and curses but

---

[5] See, for example, Stephen Kotkin, *Stalin: Paradoxes of Power, 1878–1928*, vol. 1 (New York: Penguin Press, 2014), with its convincing refutation of such notions.

will receive praise and honors. That was how the agents of the Inquisition fortified their wills: by invoking Christianity; the conquerors of foreign lands, by extolling the grandeur of their Motherland; the colonizers, by civilization; the Nazis by race; and the Jacobins (early and late), by equality, brotherhood, and the happiness of future generations.

Thanks to ideology, the twentieth century was fated to experience evildoing on a scale calculated in the millions. This cannot be denied or passed over or suppressed. How, then, do we dare insist that evildoers do not exist? And who was it that destroyed these millions? Without evildoers there would have been no Archipelago.[6]

Although one would certainly need to define ideology more broadly than Solzhenitsyn does (to cover all millenarian religious, for example), it is certainly true that the most conspicuous feature of Stalinism in the Soviet Union—and of other communist polities that used ideology to rationalize mass slaughter and atrocities, such as China under Mao and Cambodia under the Khmer Rouge—was the use of violent mass repression to transform society. Stalin's lengthy tenure as the dominant leader in the USSR, from the mid-1920s until his death in March 1953, was geared toward rapid modernization, industrialization, and collectivization of agriculture. In pursuing these goals Stalin relied heavily on ruthless violence. He could have chosen other ways of fostering modernization and rapid industrialization— ways that are vastly less coercive and cruel than the approach he adopted— but he repeatedly chose to use the most extreme forms of coercion to achieve his objectives, never showing any qualms about it. Thanks in large part to ideology, his regime was imbued with an ethos of violence.

Post-Stalin developments

After Stalin died, Soviet ideology moderated, and the violent terror associated with his reign came to an end. What remained, however, was a repugnant dictatorship that continued to justify its hold on power by invoking ideology. Soviet elites from all over the USSR had been steeped in Marxism-Leninism and had been conditioned to believe that the Soviet system was legitimate. Until 1989, even those who were relatively cynical about communist ideology

---

[6]   Aleksandr Solzhenitsyn, *Arkhipleag GULAG, 1918–1956: Opyt khudozhestvennogo issledo-vaniya*, vol. 1 (Paris: YMCA Press, 1973), 111.

were intent merely on reforming it rather than jettisoning it altogether. As Peter Kenez has pointed out, ideological strictures in the Soviet Union exerted a stronger hold on the *nomenklatura* (privileged elite) than is often realized:

> Many of [the Soviet *nomenklatura*] were careerists, and some of them were corrupt, but it would be an error to blame most of these people for cynicism. The majority of them remained believers; they had a vested interest in believing, because their livelihood depended on it. Genuine hypocrisy is difficult, and few people are capable of it. It is better and easier to convince ourselves that what we say is true. There was a group of people who had become Communists long ago and had spent their lives remaining faithful to their original commitments.[7]

Mikhail Gorbachev was among the genuine believers. One of his main objectives from the time he came to office in 1985 was to "renew" Soviet ideology and adapt it to the challenges of the modern era.[8] By 1989 he had revised or even discarded some long-standing principles of Marxism-Leninism (e.g., with his suggestion that proletarian internationalism should be subordinated to "all-human values"), but he did so in the conviction that these adjustments would strengthen, not weaken, the "underlying virtues of socialism."[9] The Communist Party of the Soviet Union (CPSU) was still the only legal political party in the country, and its claim to power still rested on Marxist-Leninist ideology. Far from disavowing communism, Gorbachev repeatedly averred that he remained faithful to Lenin's teachings and was seeking only to improve the communist system. His decision to push for far-reaching change in Eastern Europe was based on the expectation that reform-minded communist leaders would emerge who would join him in pursuit of "socialism with a human face," the phrase used during the wide-ranging liberalization in Czechoslovakia in 1968 that was crushed by a Soviet-

---

[7] Kenez notes that in the Soviet Union "the people who consciously and completely repudiated the lies that are at the foundation of every repressive society were in a tiny minority.... People who were dedicated communists now think back and think of their beliefs as if they had always been Social Democrats. The past is malleable, and we recall what we want to recall." Peter Kenez, "Dealing with Discredited Beliefs," *Kritika: Explorations in Russian and Eurasian History* 4, no. 2 (Spring 2003): 374, 376, 377.

[8] M. S. Gorbachev, *Perestroika i novoe myshlenie dlya nashei strany i vsego mira* (Moscow: Politizdat, 1987), 3–7, 21–41, 68–79.

[9] "Na perelomnom etape perestroiki: Vystuplenie M. S. Gorbacheva na vstreche v TsK KPSS s rukovoditelyami sredstv massovoi informatsii," *Pravda* (Moscow), 30 March 1989, 1.

led invasion. That scenario, if realized, would have preserved—and even bolstered—key features of the Marxist-Leninist ideology that underpinned and legitimized communist rule in both the Soviet Union and Eastern Europe.

The downfall of Marxism-Leninism

The collapse of East European communism in 1989 undercut the ideological raison dêtre of the Soviet regime. For four decades, Soviet leaders had pointed to the "socialist commonwealth" in Eastern Europe as evidence that Marxism-Leninism was superior to Western democratic capitalist ideology. The massive protests against the East European regimes in 1989, resulting in the abrupt demise of the Soviet bloc, laid bare the fundamental illegitimacy of the communist systems that had been in place since the late 1940s. The inherent fragility of communist rule in Eastern Europe had been evident long before 1989—most notably during the crises in Czechoslovakia and East Germany in 1953, in Poland and Hungary in 1956, in Poland and Czechoslovakia in 1968, and in Poland in 1970, 1976, and 1980–1981—but the unrest in these cases was quelled either by the local communist authorities or by the Soviet Army. In the 1970s and 1980s some Western observers argued that the East European regimes had developed enough support and popular legitimacy to sustain themselves in power without Soviet military backing. The events of 1989 thoroughly discredited this argument and exposed the bankruptcy of the autocratic Marxist-Leninist ideology that underlay the Soviet bloc. In the wake of those upheavals, even some of the staunchest East European communists like Todor Zhivkov, who presided for thirty-five years over an orthodox Marxist-Leninist regime in Bulgaria, acknowledged that the ideological principles they had long espoused had turned out to be "utter nonsense." In a telling, if disingenuous, interview a year after being forced from office, Zhivkov claimed:

> If I had to do it over again, I would not even be a Communist, and if Lenin were alive today he would say the same thing.... I must now admit that we started from the wrong basis, from the wrong premise. The foundation of socialism was wrong. I believe that at its very conception the idea of socialism was stillborn.[10]

---

[10] Cited in Chuck Sudetic, "Bulgarian Communist Stalwart Says He'd Do It All Differently," *New York Times*, 28 November 1990.

When events in Eastern Europe moved much further and much more rapidly than Gorbachev had anticipated, one of the consequences was that orthodox Marxism-Leninism was fatally weakened through its link with the regimes, ideologies, and institutions that had collapsed. Even the more liberal ideological vision promoted by Gorbachev was thrown into disarray by the events of 1989.

A memorandum adopted by the CPSU Politburo in early April 1990 acknowledged that recent events in Eastern Europe had sparked a "profound ideological crisis" and had pushed the CPSU to a "critical threshold." The crisis facing the Soviet party, according to the document, was "intimately connected with, but deeper than, the demise of the command-administrative model of socialism."[11] This same point had been raised the previous day in the Soviet newspaper *Izvestiya* by two well-known political commentators, who wrote:

> Not only has the model of command-bureaucratic socialism in the East European region been rendered completely bankrupt, but also—and this is far more significant in terms of its long-run consequences—socialist values and the socialist idea as such have been seriously devalued. The very word "socialism" now evokes in people an allergic reaction and a sense of repugnance.[12]

In a similar vein, the Politburo memorandum concluded that "the changes in Eastern Europe and their influence on the rest of the world" would greatly alter "the contemporary understanding of socialism," not least in the Soviet Union:

> The authority of the Communist parties in [the East European] countries has been undermined among the masses, who now believe more than ever that socialism is incapable of fulfilling their basic needs. The Communists are dispirited, having lost confidence in the validity of the ideas for which they once struggled and made great sacrifices. . . . Public life in the countries of Eastern Europe is now dominated entirely by centrist and rightist parties that have set themselves against the Communist parties and have decisively rejected everything that was done during the [Communist] period. Even the

---

[11] "Vypiska iz protokola No. 184 zasedaniya Politbyuro TsK KPSS ot 5 aprelya 1990 goda: O linii KPSS i merakh v podderzhku kommunisticheskikh i rabochikh partii v vostochnoevropeiskikh stranakh," No. P184/38 (Top Secret), 5 April 1990, in Rossiiskii Gosudarstvennyi Arkhiv Noveishei Istorii (RGANI), Fond (F.) 89, Opis' (Op.) 9, Delo (D.) 103, Listy (Ll.) 1–9.

[12] Marina Pavlova-Silvanskaya and Sergei Yastrzhembskii, "Vostochnaya Evropa: Probil chas sotsial-demokratii?" *Izvestiya* (Moscow), 4 April 1990.

purely cosmetic attributes of socialism are being rapidly eliminated. Methodical efforts are under way to discredit the entire basis of the socialist idea itself.[13]

Although Gorbachev subsequently assured the CPSU that "socialist values and the socialist idea have retained their unique importance," his assurances seemed rather hollow after the upheavals of 1989. It is not surprising that many Soviet officials and intellectuals began to question and lose faith in the principles they had long held dear but were not yet able to embrace liberal democratic thought in a genuine way.

Soviet elites who only recently had been firm believers in Marxism-Leninism found it difficult to cope with their growing doubts. General Dmitrii Volkogonov, a high-ranking Soviet military officer who became disaffected with communist ideology at the end of the 1980s, later wrote that it was "agonizing" *(muchitel'no)* for him to "shed [his] illusions."[14] Volkogonov's anguish was typical of the confusion and self-doubt that a large number of Soviet elites were experiencing. Some had become skeptical about certain aspects of Marxism-Leninism well before 1989 (as far back as the 1960s and 1970s), but the scope and intensity of the ideological disillusionment increased drastically as a result of the events in Eastern Europe. The wholesale collapse of the East European regimes illustrated, as vividly as possible, the disjuncture between Marxist-Leninist rhetoric and the realities of life under communist rule. As General Volkogonov later recalled:

> When I was responsible for ideological training and propaganda in the armed forces, my belief in the official ideology did not waver. I was a loyal, convinced Communist. The discussions that followed the introduction of glasnost and the documents I saw when working on my biography of Stalin [after being appointed director of the Institute of Military History] created some uncertainty, but even then I retained many of my convictions. But when I saw what happened in Eastern Europe in 1989, how could I not realize that so much of what we had been told, so much of what we had believed in, was just a lie? My work on the Stalin biography [published in 1989] moved me away from orthodoxy, but the fundamental changes in Eastern Europe made me rethink everything. I had no choice.[15]

---

[13] "Vypiska iz protokola No. 184 zasedaniya Politbyuro TsK KPSS ot 5 aprelya 1990 goda," Ll. 3–4.

[14] Dmitrii Volkogonov, *Lenin: Politicheskii portret*, vol. 1 (Moscow: Novosti, 1994), 11.

[15] Interview with Dmitrii Volkogonov, by the author, in Moscow, 11 August 1995.

Numerous other high-ranking military officers went through an equally "agonizing" reassessment of long-held beliefs. Marshal Sergei Akhromeev, the former head of the Soviet General Staff who became the chief military adviser to Gorbachev, confided to US National Security Adviser Brent Scowcroft in the summer of 1990 that he was filled with misgivings about everything he had long taken for granted. Having been "a soldier . . . who dedicated his life to the Soviet Union and the principles he had been taught it represented," Akhromeev said that the profound changes sweeping through Eastern Europe and the USSR had left him "deeply confused."[16] In earlier years, he had never doubted the superiority of the communist system, but he now felt an increasing sense of bewilderment:

> Suddenly he was being told that everything for which he had stood and fought was wrong. The Soviet Union, its leaders, its actions, and motivation—had all been a lie. His world had been uprooted, his moral and national moorings destroyed. He no longer knew what to believe, what to defend. His children despised him and the system he had represented.[17]

A year later, in the wake of the failed coup d'état in Moscow (which Akhromeev supported), the Soviet marshal committed suicide.

The growing public ferment in the USSR and the collapse of East European communism shook the ideological convictions not only of Soviet military officers but also of many political elites, who began to disavow their long-standing allegiance to communist principles. Boris Yeltsin, who had been a candidate member of the CPSU Politburo in the early Gorbachev period before falling out with Gorbachev in October 1987, and who had returned to prominence in March 1989 by gaining election to the USSR Congress of People's Deputies, was inspired by the events in Eastern Europe to move more openly away from communist orthodoxy and to mount what soon became a direct challenge to the ideological legitimacy of the Soviet regime. In late 1989, shortly after communist rule in Eastern Europe disintegrated, Yeltsin argued that the demise of the "fraternal" parties "makes a mockery of the USSR's own . . . commitment to the victory of socialism":

---

[16] George Bush and Brent Scowcroft, *A World Transformed* (New York: Knopf, 1998), 367.

[17] Bush and Scowcroft, *A World Transformed*. See also S. F. Akhromeev and G. M. Kornienko, *Glazami marshala i diplomata: Kriticheskii vzglyad na vneshnyuyu politiku SSSR do i posle 1985 goda* (Moscow: Mezhdunarodnye otnosheniya, 1992), 214–216 for Akhromeev's own interesting account, written shortly before he committed suicide in August 1991, of his "overwhelming frustration" and "feelings of helplessness" as he "watched what was happening to the country" and saw "the socialist alliance being destroyed."

I am very happy that our neighbors in the socialist countries [of Eastern Europe] have experienced such profound changes. I am happy for them. But it seems to me that in light of these changes we must reassess what we proudly call perestroika. When we do this, we can quickly see that we are practically the only country on Earth that is trying to enter the 21st century with an outmoded ideology left over from the 19th century.[18]

In July 1990, Yeltsin demonstratively walked out of the 28th Soviet Party Congress and renounced his CPSU membership. He pledged to join with other prominent reformers who had left the Communist Party (notably Anatolii Sobchak and Gavriil Popov) in "offering the country a real program of transition to a new society."[19]

Aleksandr Yakovlev, one of the most influential aides to Gorbachev in the late 1980s, retained his CPSU membership after the upheavals in Eastern Europe, but he increasingly sensed that "the whole ideological and moral edifice" of the Soviet regime was a "sham" and a "lie."[20] At the July 1990 CPSU Congress, he warned the delegates that "when we see entire nations [in Eastern Europe] turning their backs on their communist parties [and] rejecting Marxism-Leninism," this "should spur us to rethink our own dogmas" and to "face up to the fact that the shift [away from communism] is irreversible."[21] By mid-1991, Yakovlev was working with Eduard Shevardnadze to set up an alternative, non-communist political party akin to those that had recently been established in Eastern Europe. (Shevardnadze himself had left the CPSU in protest soon after he resigned as Soviet foreign minister in December 1990.) On 15 August 1991, four days before the attempted coup in Moscow began, Yakovlev was expelled from the CPSU. Upon being removed, he told a Russian journalist that although socialism as an "idea of justice" was not finished, the Soviet Union "never had any real socialism anyway. All we had was a travesty and the purest kind of deceit."[22] Yakovlev later acknowledged

---

18 Boris Yeltsin, *Ispoved' na zadannuyu temu* (Moscow: PIK—Nezavisimoe izdatel'stvo, 1990), 183.

19 "Novosti," Soviet Central Television, 13 July 1990, videotape, Harvard University, Cold War Studies Archive, Soviet Television News Broadcast Collection, 1987–1991.

20 Aleksandr Yakovlev, *Sumerki* (Moscow: Materik, 2003), 373–375. Both here and elsewhere in *Sumerki*, Yakovlev vividly describes his growing ideological disillusionment in the 1980s and early 1990s.

21 *XXVIII s"ezd Kommunisticheskoi Partii Sovetskogo Soyuza 2-13 iyulya 1990 goda: Stenograficheskii otchet*, 7 vol. 1 (Moscow: Politizdat, 1991), 137, 139.

22 Vladimir Todres, "'Ya ne volnuyus', chto oni menya isklyuchili': Fragmenty iz interv'yu Aleksandra Yakovleva 'Nezavisimoi Gazete,'" *Nezavisimaya gazeta* (Moscow), 17 August 1991.

that his "gradual abandonment of Marxist conceptions" was an "arduous" process and that he initially felt "despondent" when he realized he "had been deluding [himself] for so long," but he said he could "no longer deny" what was "so blindingly obvious" in both Eastern Europe and the USSR.[23]

Gorbachev himself, despite proclaiming his continued fidelity to the CPSU and the "socialist idea," began moving further and further away from core Marxist-Leninist principles after the political transformation of Eastern Europe in 1989. In March 1990 he set up a state presidency as an alternative structure to the CPSU (reinforcing the new parliament) and revoked the provision in the Soviet constitution (Article 6) that had enshrined the "leading role" of the Communist Party in Soviet society. Although Gorbachev retained his post as CPSU General Secretary, he increasingly emphasized his role as president of the USSR. In addition, he brought his notion of the "socialist idea" more closely into line with the social-democratic thrust and "all-human values" of the "new political thinking," which earlier had been applied mostly in foreign policy. Even though Gorbachev continued to invoke Lenin and to insist that he "never felt ashamed to say that I am a Communist," his evolving conception of "socialism" was a far cry from the rigid ideology that had long guided the CPSU.[24] In late July 1991 he publicly lamented the "monstrous price we have had to pay for our blind adherence to ideological postulates and myths," and he called on the party to "learn from the experience" of Eastern Europe in "making a decisive break with outmoded ideological dogmas and stereotypes":

> In the past, the [CPSU] regarded Marxism-Leninism as the only source of its inspiration, and it adopted the most extreme and distorted form of this doctrine to suit the whims of the day, based on a smattering of orthodox texts. We must expand our ideological arsenal to encompass the rich heritage of socialist and democratic thought from our own country and from the rest of the world.[25]

- On the expulsion of Yakovlev from the CPSU, see "V Tsentral'noi Kontrol'noi Komissii KPSS: O publichnykh vystupleniyakh i deistviyakh chlena KPSS A. N. Yakovleva, nesovmestimykh s Ustavom KPSS," *Pravda* (Moscow), 16 August 1991.

[23] Yakovlev, *Sumerki*, p. 374.

[24] For an illuminating discussion of Gorbachev's ideological shift in the final two years of the Soviet Union, see Gregory Freidin, "How Communist Is Gorbachev's Communism?" in *Dilemmas of Transition in the Soviet Union and Eastern Europe,* ed. George W. Breslauer (Berkeley: Center for Slavic and East European Studies, University of California, 1991), 25–44.

[25] "Sokhranit' i obnovit' rodnuyu strany: Vystuplenie M. S. Gorbacheva v Belorussii," *Izvestiya* (Moscow), 1 March 1991, 1.

Gorbachev emphasized that "our country's experience and the events [in Eastern Europe] provide no reason to believe that communism is a practical goal," and he even raised the possibility that, "with a multiparty system now emerging in the Soviet Union," the CPSU should change its name to the Social Democratic Party.

At levels below the top leadership, the movement away from Marxism-Leninism was even more pronounced. Ideological cohesion had begun to erode in 1988 and early 1989 when glasnost led to a flood of revelations about "negative phenomena"—tragic episodes in Soviet history, deep-rooted social problems in the USSR, conflicts between Soviet nationalities, the appalling scale of environmental damage under Soviet rule, and numerous instances of high-level corruption and malfeasance—but the confusion within the CPSU was greatly magnified by the dramatic changes in Hungary and Poland in the spring and summer of 1989 and the subsequent collapse of communism throughout Eastern Europe. Ideological uniformity in the USSR was replaced by disarray and the emergence of rival political groups both inside and outside the party.

The rapid decline of ideological consensus in the Soviet Union was bound to pose a dire challenge for the regime. As Crane Brinton observed in his seminal study of revolution, the position of a ruling class is endangered "when numerous and influential members of such a class begin to believe that they hold power unjustly, [and] that the beliefs they were brought up on are silly."[26] The debunking of these long-cherished beliefs, Brinton argued, would inspire many elites to support those who were seeking to change the status quo. Nothing could better describe the ideological turmoil that pervaded the CPSU after communist rule in Eastern Europe disintegrated.

Consequences for the Soviet regime

The consequences of these developments for the fate of the Soviet Union were fourfold.

First, the growing demoralization and loss of purpose among influential members of the CPSU facilitated the rise of opposition movements that wanted to end communist rule. Diehard advocates of Marxism-Leninism were still around, but they were increasingly overshadowed by individuals and groups who were seeking a fundamentally different course. (Some of the new opposition groups supported liberal democracy and free markets,

---

[26] Crane Brinton, *The Anatomy of Revolution* (New York: Vintage Books, 1965), 51–52

whereas others, notably "Pamyat" and "Soyuz," embraced an ultranationalist or fascist agenda.) The new opportunities afforded by the USSR Congress of People's Deputies in the spring and summer of 1989—against the backdrop of momentous changes in Hungary and Poland—enabled radical politicians in the Soviet Union to form the Inter-Regional Group of Deputies (MDG, founded by Andrei Sakharov and Boris Yeltsin, among others) to push for a free-market economy, political decentralization and democratization, and wide-ranging autonomy for the union-republics.[27] The further precipitous decline of ideological cohesion in the Soviet Union after the demise of East European communism helped produce alternative centers of authority that could—and did—challenge the Soviet regime for political supremacy. In particular, Yeltsin, backed by the Democratic Russia movement (an outgrowth of the MDG), set up a government and popularly elected presidency in Russia that, he hoped, would enable him to eclipse Gorbachev and transform the Soviet Union into a loose confederation with Russia at its head.

Second, the demise of a unifying ideology in the USSR meant that Soviet elites had much less of a stake in the preservation of the Soviet regime. George Schöpflin has aptly noted that "an authoritarian elite sustains itself in power not just through force and the threat of force but, more importantly, because it has some vision of the future by which it can justify itself to itself."[28] As Marxism-Leninism lost its grip over the Soviet establishment in the late 1980s, especially after the upheavals in Eastern Europe, a huge exodus from the Soviet Communist Party began. In 1990 alone, according to official data, nearly five million out of nineteen million CPSU members formally renounced their status, and millions more ceased to pay their dues and eschewed all party activities.[29] At a CPSU Central Committee plenum in July 1991, Gorbachev acknowledged that "the party is experiencing a severe crisis, the most acute crisis in its history."[30]

---

[27] V. V. Zhuravlev et al., eds., *Vlast' i oppozitsiya: Rossiiskii politicheskii protsess XX stoletiya* (Moscow: ROSSPEN, 1995), 308–309.

[28] George Schöpflin, "The End of Communism in Eastern Europe," *International Affairs* 66, no. 1 (January 1990), 6.

[29] Data calculated from "Svodnye statisticheskie otchety o sostave partiinykh organizatsii za 1989," January 1990 (Secret), in RGANI, F. 77, Op.6, D. 10; "Svodnye statisticheskie otchety o sostave partiinykh organizatsii za 1990 god," January 1991 (Secret), in RGANI, F. 77, Op.6, D. 14; "Svodnye statisticheskie otchety o sostave partiinykh organizatsii na 1 yanvarya 1991 goda," January 1991 (Secret), in RGANI, F. 77, Op.6, D. 15; and "Spravochnik 'KPSS v tsifrakh,'" June 1991 (Secret), in RGANI, F. 77, Op.6, D. 22.

[30] "O proekte novoi programmy KPSS," 2.

Even worse were the problems afflicting the Communist Youth League *(Komsomol),* the organ responsible for preparing young people to join the CPSU. Membership in the Komsomol had been falling since the early 1980s because of demographic constraints, but this trend increased precipitously in 1989 and 1990, as ferment engulfed Eastern Europe and the USSR itself.[31] By mid-1990 the Komsomol had largely ceased to function.[32] Intellectuals and up-and-coming officials in Moscow (and in many of the union- republics) were ever more inclined to cast their lot with opposition groups and leaders like Yeltsin who wanted to end Soviet rule.[33] This shift of allegiances—whether motivated by a principled rejection of the old order or by a desire for personal enrichment and the acquisition of private property—was reminiscent of the process described by Crane Brinton whereby elites in authoritarian societies who "come to distrust or lose faith in the traditions and habits of their class" are wont to "desert the established order [and] become leaders in the crusade for a new order."[34]

Officials in Moscow who wanted to preserve the communist regime were alarmed by the growing number of Soviet elites who were leaving the CPSU and joining ranks with "anti-socialist forces." In February 1991 the head of the Soviet Committee on State Security (KGB), Vladimir Kryuchkov, informed Gorbachev that "the weakening of ideological work in defense of the socialist idea" had been "devastating for the unity of the USSR and of Soviet society."[35] Kryuchkov emphasized the "vital importance of maintaining state control over the mass media and of preventing the media from being watered down or, even worse, from becoming a propaganda organ for the anti-socialist forces." He warned that unless Gorbachev made a determined effort to reestablish ideological consensus immediately, "there is a real danger

---

[31] Annual data on Komsomol membership and on many other matters pertaining to the huge efflux of young people from the Komsomol in 1989–1990 can be found in "VLKSM: Statisticheskii i spravochnyi material," prepared by the Komsomol Central Committee apparatus, April 1990, in Rossiiskii Gosudarstvennyi Arkhiv Sotsial'no-Politicheskoi Istorii (RGASPI), F. 1M, Op.110, Dd. 483, 580.

[32] For a perceptive, well-documented account of the decline of the Komsomol, see Steven L. Solnick, *Stealing the State: Control and Collapse in Soviet Institutions* (Cambridge, MA: Harvard University Press, 1999), particularly 102–124, 285–291.

[33] See, for example, the testimony of the Belarusian writer Kastus Tarasov on why he left the CPSU, in "Pochemu ya vyshel iz partii," *Moskovskie novosti* (Moscow), no. 15, 15 April 1990.

[34] Brinton, *Anatomy of Revolution*, 252.

[35] "Dokladnaya zapiska: O politicheskoi obstanovke v strane," Memorandum No. 219-k (Top Secret—Special Dossier), from V. A. Kryuchkov to M. S. Gorbachev, 18 February 1991, in Lietuvos Ypatingasis Archyvas (LYA), Fondas (F.) K-1, Apyrašas (Apy.) 49, Byla (B.) 87, Lapai (La.) 14–19.

that the USSR will break apart and that its whole sociopolitical and economic system will be destroyed."[36]

Third, the breakdown of ideological controls accentuated rifts that emerged in the late 1980s within the organizations responsible for defending Soviet rule: the army, the KGB, and the Internal Affairs Ministry (MVD). Throughout the Soviet era, these bodies (and their predecessors) had been under the control of the CPSU. Senior military, KGB, and MVD officials were all members of the party, and their primary task was to uphold Soviet rule. The abrupt decline of Marxism-Leninism after 1989, and the splits that ensued within the Communist Party, steadily reduced the party's control over the military and internal security agencies. The political indoctrination programs that had cemented the CPSU's "leading role" in these organizations were undercut by the downfall of communism in Eastern Europe. Even some of the most orthodox KGB officials said that, in the wake of the upheavals in Eastern Europe, they had "begun to look at life more realistically and had come to realize that communism is just a utopian illusion and that the CPSU in its current form has no future."[37] Sensing this change of mood, Soviet leaders worried that the erosion of party control would enable "anti-Soviet forces" to make inroads into the army and security apparatus. The chairman of the KGB, Vladimir Kryuchkov, warned Gorbachev in February 1991 that opposition groups "are taking persistent measures to extend their influence over the army and are striving to neutralize it as one of the guarantors of the unity of the USSR."[38] Yeltsin's efforts to win support from key personnel in the military and security forces—efforts that proved crucial during the August 1991 coup attempt—would have been much less feasible if Soviet ideology had not been so gravely weakened by the collapse of communism in Eastern Europe.

Fourth, ideological disarray at the elite level helped spur, and was reflected in, a shift in public sentiment that facilitated the demise of the Soviet regime. In the pre-Gorbachev era, public opinion in the Soviet Union was of little importance, but in the late 1980s the introduction of glasnost and competitive elections gave the public a much more prominent role. Despite an initial groundswell of enthusiasm for the changes implemented by Gorbachev, public support for the reform program and for Gorbachev himself plummeted in 1990. A series of opinion polls in 1989 and 1990 revealed

---

[36] "Dokladnaya zapiska: O politicheskoi obstanovke v strane," La. 15.

[37] "Tainyi agent: 'A ya gorzhus,'" *Literaturnaya gazeta* (Moscow), no. 46, 14 November 1990.

[38] "Dokladnaya zapiska: O politicheskoi obstanovke v strane," La. 17.

that, in the spring of 1990, Gorbachev's standing as the most "authoritative" and "respected" politician in the Soviet Union dropped from roughly 45–50 percent to less than 20 percent, whereas Yeltsin's favorable ratings rose steadily, especially after he left the CPSU in July 1990.[39] (The precise figures varied slightly depending on the specific survey, but the pattern was the same in all the polls. Yeltsin's favorable rating surpassed Gorbachev's in mid-1990, and the disparity widened thereafter.) Public esteem for Soviet political institutions, including the CPSU and the Council of Ministers, was still at relatively high levels in 1989 but fell to remarkably low levels (into the single digits) in 1990, in most cases dropping by more than 90 percent.[40] During this same period, public support within Russia for the Russian republic government (headed by Yeltsin) increased sharply, soaring above 75 percent. This latter trend, as the surveys made clear, was attributable to the perception that the Russian government was opposed to the Communist Party and to the Soviet regime.[41]

Several factors, including the steep decline of the Soviet economy and the failure of the USSR Congress of People's Deputies to meet high public expectations, accounted for these changes of mood, but clearly one of the most important contributors was the impact of the East European upheavals on the Soviet regime's ideological raison d'être. The deputy head of the CPSU International Department, Valerii Musatov, acknowledged as much in March 1991:

> The turn of events in Eastern Europe has had a powerful negative impact on the broadest strata of Soviet society.... The collapse of the post-Stalinist model of socialism in the countries of Eastern Europe has been perceived at the level of ordinary consciousness and among the broad masses [in the Soviet Union] as the collapse of socialism more generally after it reached a historical dead-end.[42]

---

[39] All-Russian Center for the Study of Public Opinion, *Reitingi Borisa El'tsina i Mikhaila Gorbacheva po 10-bal'noi shkale* (Moscow: VTsIOM, 1993).

[40] Data compiled by the All-Union Center for Public Opinion, presented in "Sovetskii chelovek—eskiz portreta: Vsesoyuznyi opros obshchestvennogo mneniya," *Moskovskie novosti* (Moscow), no. 11, 16 March 1990. See also A. Grazhdankin, "Obshchestvo i armiya," *Izvestiya* (Moscow), 15 June 1990.

[41] Data compiled by the All-Union Center for Public Opinion based on surveys in 1989, 1990, and 1991, summarized in Aleksei Levinson, "Opros: Poleznye sovety sovetam," *Izvestiya* (Moscow), 19 April 1991.

[42] Valerii Musatov, "Vostochnaya Evropa: 'Taifun' peremen," *Pravda* (Moscow), 13 March 1991.

Musatov warned that the situation was apt to deteriorate even further "now that societal changes in the [East European] countries are increasingly taking the form of a repudiation of old values and a rejection of everything connected with socialism." This process, he argued, would continue to buffet the Soviet Union, fueling "ever greater public disillusion with the Communist Party and with the socialist way of life."[43] The steady erosion of the CPSU's legitimacy after 1989, and the deepening fissures within the Soviet political elite, ensured that by 1991 the Soviet public had even less of a stake in the continued survival of the Soviet regime.

The dissipation of Marxist-Leninist ideology, once begun, took on a life of its own. Ideological reassessments had begun soon after Gorbachev took office, and they were moving rapidly ahead by 1989. Nonetheless, the changes in Eastern Europe in 1989 and 1990 were so monumental that they raised doubts not only about orthodox communist ideology but also about the feasibility of Gorbachev's attempt to define a new "socialist idea." A memorandum prepared for the Soviet Politburo by the CPSU International Department in June 1991 conceded that "the socialist idea is extremely difficult to promote [in the USSR and elsewhere] now that it has fallen into such disrepute in Eastern Europe."[44] If, as Gorbachev originally hoped, reform-minded communist leaders had come to power in Eastern Europe to replace the old hardline regimes (as occurred for a brief while in Bulgaria and Romania), the blow to Soviet ideology would have been less severe. Some core principles probably would have survived. But the outright dissolution of communism in Eastern Europe, combined with the surge of political ferment and instability in the USSR itself, deprived the ideology of whatever cachet it still had, leaving an ideological vacuum in its wake.

Conclusion

The millenarian nature of Marxist-Leninist ideology facilitated the rise of Stalin and provided justification for the mass violent repression that transformed Soviet Russia into the USSR. The rampant violence was not adscititious; it was an inherent feature of the transformative process, given

---

[43] Musatov, "Vostochnaya Evropa."

[44] "TsK KPSS: O prodolzhenii politicheskogo dialoga KPSS s zarubezhnymi partiyami i ikh mezhdunarodnymi ob"edineniyami," Report No. 04605 (Secret), from V. S. Rykin, deputy head of the CPSU International Department, 7 June 1991, in RGANI, F. 89, Op.11, D. 95, Ll. 1–5.

the Bolsheviks' goals and their ruthless determination to achieve them at all costs. After Stalin's death, Soviet ideology moderated but continued to serve as the foundation and justification for an autocratic Soviet regime. In that context, the number of Soviet citizens who came to subscribe to liberal democratic thought was minuscule. Even many of the Soviet dissidents who pushed for human rights in the 1960s and 1970s did not truly espouse liberal democratic principles. Only a very small number of the dissidents genuinely came to see liberal democracy as the necessary goal for the USSR.

Because of the hegemonic nature of Marxist-Leninist ideology in the Soviet Union, the demise of the ideology in the late 1980s and early 1990s left an ideological abyss in early post-Soviet Russia. Most of the "democrats" in early post-Soviet Russia, especially those who served in Yeltsin's administration, had not actually given much thought to liberal democratic principles or the constraints those principles would impose on state power. Hence, when Yeltsin confronted obstruction on the part of a freely elected (albeit unsavory) parliament, he ultimately relied on extralegal violence in October 1993 to bring the parliament to heel. In the wake of that showdown, Yeltsin was able to push through a constitution in a hastily arranged referendum in December 1993 that invested him with immense power. The consequences were vividly evident a year later, when he launched a highly destructive war in Chechnya without even the pretense of consulting with the parliament.

Moreover, Yeltsin relied on dubious means to ensure his reelection as president in June 1996. The June 1991 election that elevated Yeltsin to the Russian presidency was the first time that Russians were ever able to take part in a free and fair election, but it also proved to be the last. The June 1996 election was largely free but not at all fair, with state ties to powerful media outlets invoked in turning the election around in Yeltsin's favor. The undemocratic precedent that was set in June 1996 paved the way for Putin's abandonment of even the pretense of free and fair national elections. The elimination of this central feature of liberal democracy underscored the shallowness of the "democracy" that replaced the Soviet Union after 1991. It was a democracy based less on liberal democratic thinking than on the political expediency of elites who aimed to marginalize and dislodge the Soviet regime.

The basic problem was that an ideological vacuum had been left by the collapse of Soviet Marxist-Leninist ideology—a vacuum stemming from the autocratic nature of the ideology and its incompatibility with liberal democratic thinking. Amid this vacuum, the rhetoric of "democracy" became fashionable for those in power. But without a much more solid foundation in the thinking of leading elites, the democratic rhetoric, far from bolstering the appeal of liberal democracy, severely damaged it. The economic upheavals of the 1990s, brought on by a combination of the ongoing disintegration of the Soviet economy and the ill-advised policies adopted by Yeltsin's administration, became associated with "democracy" as seen by many ordinary Russians. Opinion polls taken by the Levada Center over the past twenty years have revealed widespread public sentiment associating "democracy" with economic hardship and political instability.[45] Public opinion therefore did not constrain Putin as he steadily abolished even the most rudimentary features of democratization set up by Yeltsin.

Under these circumstances, the obstacles to the rise of liberal democratic thinking in Russia proved to be too formidable. Even though Russians seemed ready to embrace democracy in 1991–1992, they were equally ready to abandon it once they came to see it through the prism of economic deprivation and political instability. In that sense, Putin's authoritarian retrenchment took root on fertile ground. The autocratic nature of Soviet ideology had precluded the emergence of wide, deep-rooted liberal democratic thought and instead facilitated the rise of a shallow facsimile that proved evanescent.

The inimical effect of Soviet ideology on liberal democratic thinking in Russia does not bode well for the fate of democratic principles under Putin and his successors. Even as Putin systematically eliminated the last vestiges of democratization in Russia after returning to the presidency in 2012, his popularity reached stratospheric levels. Although "Putinism" cannot really be characterized as an ideology—Putin's authoritarian rule has been highly personalistic rather than based on a way of thinking—his neutralization of democratic institutions, emphasis on untrammeled state power, and opportunistic championing of "traditional values" (above all, homophobia) have bolstered his support. Liberal democratic alternatives to Putinism have been undermined, with scant likelihood that they can be revived, much less gain wide public acceptance. With Putin in control of Russia at least until 2024 (and probably until 2036 under new constitutional amendments), his autocratic outlook and disdain for liberal democracy pose grave obstacles to

---

[45] See, for example, Analiticheskii Tsentr Yuriya Levady, *Obshchestvennoe mnenie—2010: Ezhegodnik* (Moscow: ATsYuL, 2011), particularly 34–41.

the emergence of democratic thought in Russia. Even if Putin steps down for good in 2024, the damage his rule has done to the prospects for democracy in Russia will be long-lasting. Proponents of liberal democratic thinking in Russia face daunting odds for the indefinite future.

PART TWO

Economics

THE COMPARATIVE ASSESSMENT OF COMMUNIST AND POST-COMMUNIST SYSTEM PERFORMANCE AND HUMAN WELLBEING

Challenges and Insights from In-depth Case Study Approaches

Paul Dragos Aligica and Vlad Tarko

Introduction

The existing evidence suggests that life in post-communism should be considered an improvement over life under communism. It is not only a matter of individual liberty, but also of economic performance and wellbeing, of basic patterns of consumption, welfare, and quality of life. Yet, despite this, opinion polls also reveal surprising nostalgia for communism. This chapter takes a closer look at the conditions, factors, and characteristics of such judgments in order to further our understanding of the communist experiment and its aftermath. Such investigations also have a broader relevance for deciding which key criteria to use for the comparative evaluation of economic and political systems.

We now have a particularly fruitful window of opportunity for the study of the communist experiment. We now have access to data series that were not available 20 or even 15 years ago and also have more or less direct access to the subjective views of several generations of Eastern Europeans who experienced both communism and post-communism. Our study takes advantage of this window of opportunity and hopes to inspire similar case studies in other countries. We start with the puzzling phenomenon of Romanian positive perceptions of communism, as revealed by national surveys, and continue by building a composite framework for analysis of the relevant phenomena, with a special focuses on an innovative integration of insights from "happiness studies."

The use of the "happiness studies" literature is our main methodological innovation. The key idea is that, although unfortunately we don't have direct self-reported data on the subjective well-being of people for the entire period of interest, we can nonetheless engage in an indirect assessment of the population's subjective well-being by proxy with the help of developments in the field of "happiness studies." These developments give us a relatively comprehensive picture of the factors that have the biggest impact on subjective well-being.[1] Once we identify the most significant predictors of one's subjective well-being, we can use them as proxies for assessing their likely subjective well-being in the past. Although we cannot go back in time and ask those living in communist Romania about their self-assessed psychological well-being, we can get measure various factors that are known to be good predictors of one's subjective well-being. In this roundabout manner one is able to inquire into the likely state of subjective well-being in past periods and conjecture conclusions relevant for comparative purposes. Using this method, alongside more traditional criteria and data, we obtain a comprehensive picture of Romania's socio-economic development in a manner that is well suited to piecing together objective economic facts and subjective perceptions.

Challenges of interpretation and assessment

The findings of a number of national surveys in Eastern Europe, as well as of media reports and anecdotal evidence, reveal a puzzling and confusing attitude toward the communist past. In Romania, repeated surveys have revealed that about half or more of those surveyed say that life was better during communist times and that communism was a good idea improperly applied.[2]

We explore two main hypotheses: (1) The reported perceptions and views accurately reflect the deeper underlying reality. It may indeed be the case that

---

[1] Richard Layard, *Happiness: Lessons from a New Science* (London: Penguin, 2005); Bruno Frey, *Happiness: A Revolution in Economics* (Cambridge: MIT Press, 2008). Ed Diener and Robert-Biswas Diener, *Happiness: Unlocking the Mysteries of Psychological Wealth* (Hoboken, NJ: Blackwell, 2008).

[2] Centrul de Sondare a Opiniei si Pietei (CSOP), Institutul de Investigare a Crimelor Comunismului si Memoria Exilului Romanesc (IICCMER), 2010. Perception of Communism in Romania. Centrul de Sondare a Opiniei si Pietei (CSOP), Institutul de Investigare a Crimelor Comunismului si Memoria Exilului Romanesc (IICCMER), 2011. Romanians' perception of Communism. Institutul Roman pentru Evaluare si Strategie (IRES), 2010. Nostalgia for the past, present sacrifices.

a significant fraction of the population was better off during communism; (2) Even if life during communism was worse off according to many objective indicators, perhaps these indicators fail to capture what people find truly important. Perhaps at least some of the things that increase people's state of subjective well-being were better during communism, while many objective indicators are relatively unimportant for improving one's subjective well-being. Surveys might reflect this subjective reality.

The most thorough and careful survey so far has been CADI, IRT & IRES (2010),[3] which we cite below, but many of its results are similar to other surveys taken before and after. In order to gauge opinion about communism and post-communism, two questions were asked: "To what extent do you agree with the statement: 'During Ceauşescu's time, communism was a good idea badly applied?'" and "To what extent do you agree with the statement: 'In our times, capitalism is a good idea badly applied?'" The results were startling: 68% agreed to a large or very large extent with the statement about communism, but, also, 76% agreed to a large or very large extent with the statement about capitalism.

The survey also revealed apparent inconsistencies in understanding the basic elements of communism and capitalist models. For example, 83% of total number of interviewees agreed to a large or very large extent with the statement "The state should guarantee a job for everyone" (It should be pointed out that 35% of the respondents are employed by the state, 43% are employed by the private sector and 22% did not answer). Also, when asked "Who do you think should bear most of the responsibility for each person's welfare?" 53% answered "the state" and only 43% answered "the individuals themselves." Yet, at the same time, their answers to other questions reveal a reluctance to embrace statist solutions. For instance, 49% also answered that private property should be expanded, as opposed to only 33% who answered that state property should be expanded. Moreover, 82% agreed to a large or very large extent with the statement "You are better off struggling by yourself, than being helped by the state," and 90% agreed to a large or very large extent with the statement "What the state gives you with one hand, it takes back with two." Last but not least, 85% agreed to a large or very large extent with the statement: "Differences of income, resulting from skills and effort, are normal."

---

3   Centrul de Analiza si Dezvoltare Institutionala (CADI), Institutul Roman de Training (IRT), Institutul Roman pentru Evaluare si Strategie (IRES), 2010, Romanians: some attitudes and views on life, work, capitalism and the state.

How inconsistent are these answers? One can make some sense of them by noting the difference between idealized normative opinions, pragmatic normative opinions, and descriptive opinions. Considering this threefold distinction, we see that the Romanian respondents may think that *in a hypothetical ideal world*, state-lead communism would have delivered its promised results and the state would have promoted general welfare. Nonetheless, they may have a rather disparaging view of how *the state actually behaves in the real world*. Hence, there was a tendency among respondents to (hesitantly) endorse capitalism, private property, and individualism. If people think that life was better during communism, when property was nationalized, why are they in favor of moving further away from it (more private property)? One possible explanation seems to be that while they don't believe in the possibility of a properly functioning communist system, they nonetheless believe in the possibility of making capitalism work better (more people hold the view that capitalism is a good idea improperly applied than those who believe that communism has been a good idea improperly applied).

To sum up, the answers received in public opinion surveys are actually quite nuanced, at least if one tries to interpret them more charitably. Even so, the fact that people have a strikingly good opinion of communism appears to be a clear finding.

A comparative analysis of two systems (either two subjects geographically separated or one subject temporally separated in different time periods) can be framed based on a variety of criteria. The comparison can use either *aggregate system-level indicators* that convey a global and unified perspective on the economic and social life or *individual-focused indicators* that describe the life of an average member of society. Alternatively, the comparison can focus on *subjective perceptions of well-being* or on *objective estimations*. Combining these two criteria, four different types of approaches to comparative analysis emerge, illustrated in Table 1.

Table 1. Approaches to comparative analyses

	Subjective perceptions	Objective estimations
Aggregate, system-level	Narrative depictions	Efficiency Equality Freedom Safety & welfare
Individual-focused	Happiness studies indicators: - "Satisfaction with Life" - "Gross National Happiness" - "Happy Life Expectancy"	"Quality of life" "Standard of living" "Human development"

We now proceed by focusing on the Romanian case using a combination of the objective aggregate estimation perspectives and both types of individual-focused approaches.

Systemic indicators attempting objective assessment

This is the domain of the standard set of measures: efficiency (GDP per capita; labor productivity), equality (Gini index), freedom (Freedom House's *Freedom in the World*, Heritage Foundation's *Index of Economic Freedom*, Fraser Institute's *Economic Freedom of the World Index*), safety and welfare (social expenditure indicators), etc. They provide a background for understanding not only the context of the survey responses, but also the complexity of such assessments.

GDP per capita gives a picture of the **efficiency** of the Romanian economy. According to the official statistics, the economy grew at about 4% a year from 1950 to the early 1970s. Then growth declined in the 1970s, and the economy stagnated by the 1980s. Economic efficiency, both in terms of GDP per capita and labor productivity, plunged in 1990, and it then took 15 years for the economy to recover the official levels of 1980s.[4]

These statistics are likely misleading. The critique of using GDP as an indicator of prosperity (van den Bergh, 2009) is particularly relevant in the context of the discussion of a communist system. GDP takes into account all production and transactions without consideration of the consumer demand for the produced items or of the causes behind the transactions. Thus, large

---

[4]   World Bank, *World Development Indicators*, 2018.

misallocations of capital, which generally characterize communist economies, are counted as positive developments. Consequently, at least some of the post-1989 decline in GDP is probably due to the fact that a large part of the communist production has stopped.[5] This however, should count as a *positive* development, rather than a negative one, given that the communist production was in many cases effectively destroying valuable resources due to large misallocations of capital. Looking at the structure of the Romanian economy as it develops in time, one could see the rise of the services sector from about 25% of GDP in the 1980s to almost 70% in 2009. This highlights the restructuring process of the Romanian economy.

Equality can be assessed in several ways. The standard approach is to consider the income inequality Gini index. After 1989, we see a clear increase in income inequality, from about 23% in 1989 to a peak of 32% in 2007. This degree of inequality, similar to that of Austria or Germany, is still significantly lower than that of other European countries such as France or Denmark.

We should also point out that the basic methodology behind calculating the Gini index can be misleading when applied to communist countries. In a communist regime much of the existing property is state property. As such, it might appear there is a considerable amount of equality, as everybody privately owns a relatively equivalent amount of things. However, people did not have equal *access* to the state properties. It would thus be a mistake to assume that all state property was available equally to all citizens. Thus, when assessing equality under a communist regime one needs to consider *access rights*, rather than *ownership*.[6] This is very difficult to assess explicitly and quantitatively because communist regimes, due to their hierarchical organization, are generally managed by authority rather than by rules, i.e. an individual's access rights to a piece of state property are the result of *privileges* granted to him or her by another person with some form of higher authority within the communist state, rather than being the result of a clear-cut set of access-granting *rules*.

From this perspective, one can see that it is quite plausible that equality might have actually increased in the aftermath of 1989 revolution, as the system of communist privileges collapsed. Many pieces of state property that used

---

5   Vlad Tarko, "Understanding Post-Communist Transitions," *Review of Austrian Economics* 33, no 1 (2020): 163–186.

6   G. M. Anderson, and Peter J. Boettke, "Soviet Venality: A Rent-seeking Model of the Communist State," *Public Choice* 93, no. 1 (1997): 37–53.

to have very restricted access were transformed into public goods (and some of them were privatized). Access to these public goods was not equal either, but it is a reasonable conjecture that they were somewhat more egalitarian than it was during communist times. Consequently, the increase in the Gini index should be assessed in parallel to the decrease in state property, as this latter decrease also meant a decrease in the arbitrariness of access. In short, it is very difficult to objectively assess what really happened to equality in the 1980–2000 period.

When it comes to an assessment of **freedom,** one has to consider at least two types: political freedom and economic freedom. Political freedom is usually assessed by means of the Freedom House index, while we look at economic freedom as measured by two of the available indices, from Heritage Foundation and from Fraser Institute.

Unsurprisingly, we see that prior to 1989 Romania is classified by Freedom House as "not free," between 1990 and 1995 as "partially free" and post 1996 as "free." The increase in economic freedom has been sustained after 2004, and made a clear jump between 1996 and 2000. In the 1997–2003 period the two indices paint a contradictory picture of Romania, Heritage describes a decline in economic freedom, while Fraser an increase. Such situations remind us that such exercises are far from straightforward and their results may differ in function of apparently minor variations of method.

The issue of **safety and welfare** is a more sensitive one. We assess the amount of government aid to citizens by means of World Bank's government final consumption expenditure index. One of the first surprises is that in the 1990–1995 period and after 2005, the government consumption expenditure was actually *higher* than during communist times in the early 1980s. This contradicts the view that communist regimes traded growth for more generous government help. In fact, post-communist Romania has generally delivered both higher growth rates *and* larger government handouts to citizens. The average in the 1990s was over 13%, and from 2000 to the present, the average grew above 15%.

Consider a comparison with Austria. Austria delivered much higher levels of government aid (as percentage of GDP) than both communist and post-communist Romania, while at the same time maintaining a much higher rate of economic growth. We can explain this as a consequence of the differences in *both* political and economic freedom. The higher economic freedom generated higher levels of economic growth, while the higher political freedom forced the Austrian government to allocate a larger amount its expenditures to social goals. By comparison, Romania's communist government, lacking democratic constraints, allocated a much larger amount of its expenditures to various investment purposes (many of which proved to be quite misguided, as we have already noted above).

Beyond macro and aggregate data: individual-focused estimates

A methodical comparative assessment strategy needs to go beyond merely considering system-level data. Various estimations of individual welfare are important for the overall picture. Such statistics describe the life and situation of an "average individual," who is defined either relative to the entire population or relative to various sub-groups from the population. These individual-focused estimations don't merely duplicate the aggregate estimation from a different perspective, but also provide additional pieces of information. The main assessments one can reconsider from an individual-based perspective are those of economic freedom and equality. Additional angles include "Quality of life," "Standard of living," and "Human development."

Let us start with **economic freedom**. The main individual-based measure of economic freedom is buying power. The evolution of buying power, measured by the real earnings index (Anuarul Statistic, 1991, 2000, 2009), tells the same story as the GDP per capita data. There was an explosive increase in buying power up from 1950 until the early 1980s (real earnings were more than 4 times larger in 1980 compared to 1950), followed by stagnation until 1990. Surprisingly, in the years following the 1989 revolution, it looks like the buying power of an average person has *decreased*, with real earnings falling back to 1970s levels. After a decade of stagnation, real earning started to grow, reaching back to 1980s levels in 2005, and rising to 7 times the 1950 level by 2008.

However, the meaning of this apparent post-1989 decrease is tricky. While it is true that buying power decreased in the first 15 years compared to the previous ten years, the number of products and services available for purchase has increased. In other words, during the 1980s people had plenty of money, but nothing to buy with it! To see that this is indeed the case we can look at the evolution of the household final consumption expenditure as percentage of GDP. We see that in the early 1990s consumption skyrocketed.

COMMUNIST AND POST-COMMUNIST SYSTEM PERFORMANCE AND HUMAN WELLBEING **105**

What happened was a collapse of the communist-era industry and, to a smaller extent, agriculture, combined with the growth of the services sector and of consumer spending. To a large extent this consumer spending was fueled by runaway inflation during the 1990s (the average annual money growth was over 100%, reaching a peak of 170% in 1993). In the 2000s, inflation diminished, and, to a considerable extent, the communist era inefficient industries closed. This has led to more sustainable investment, to the development of the banking sector, and to a subsequent diminishing of consumer spending as percentage of GDP. This decrease is due to the increase in investment and does not reflect an *absolute* decrease in consumer spending, as evidenced by the continued increase in real earnings.

In other words, the 1990s can be seen as a readjustment period. In many respects one may understand it as a *Keynesian transition*: fueled by inflation and government handouts, almost the entire economy became a consumption economy, designed to ease the shock created by the elimination of communist era malinvestments. Even so, this shock was considerable.

Table 2. Consumption of three social groups[7]

	1960	1970	1980	1985	1990	1998	2005
Wage earners							
- foodstuffs	53	48.9	45.6	50.1	49.4	50.9	39.2
- clothes	17.7	18.7	17.2	16.6	17.3	8.5	7.5
- housing & durable goods	14.1	17.4	19	17.4	15.3	17.6	19.7
- healthcare	1.1	1	0.8	1.2	1	1.9	2.3
- transport & communications	3.9	4.6	8.6	6	6.9	10.4	13.9
- culture and education	7	6.7	5.4	4.6	5.3	4.9	6.4
- other	3.2	2.7	3.4	4.1	4.8	5.8	11
Farmers							
- foodstuffs	74.4	65.8	63.7	66.9	67	58.8	57.8
- clothes	9.4	13.7	12.6	11.8	11.9	6	6
- housing & durable goods	10.9	12.9	14.2	13.1	12.7	26.2	14.6
- healthcare	0.8	0.9	0.8	1	0.9	8	2.4
- transport & communications	1.4	2.2	3.7	2.5	2.9	4.2	6.6
- culture and education	1.5	2.8	2.9	2.3	2.1	1.5	2.6
- other	1.6	1.7	2.1	2.4	2.5	2.5	10

---

[7] Institutul National de Statistica (INS), *Anuarul Statistic*, 1991, 2000, 2009.

	1960	1970	1980	1985	1990	1998	2005
Retirees							
- foodstuffs		59.5	58	59.6	58.2	58.9	47.7
- clothes		10.8	9.3	7.9	8.6	5.2	4.6
- housing & durable goods		16.1	18	17.6	15.8	23.3	20.3
- healthcare		2.8	2.8	3.6	3.5	3.2	6.6
- transport & communications		3.4	5.1	4.9	5.9	4.4	8.7
- culture and education		5	4.1	3.4	4.6	2.2	3.8
- other		2.4	2.7	3	3.4	2.8	8.3

A different approach to **equality** is to consider the differences at individual level between different social groups, and to consider the difference in *consumption* rather than *income*. We consider the difference between wage earners (a proxy for the younger urban population), farmers, and pensioners in regard to the percentage of their income spent on food. This is an important measure, because the less one spends on food, the more one can spend on other, less pressing matters. This comparison is thus an indicator of the amount of equality in terms of economic independence between people from different social groups. Similar analyses can be made, with similar results, based on other factors such as housing, clothes, healthcare, etc. In Table 2 we present the data for other such analyses.

The data show a slight increase in equality between farmers and wage earners from the 1960s to the 1970s, and then, a very large increase in equality in the middle 1990s. However, this equality did not last, as inequality between wage earners and farmers returned in 2005 to the 1970s-1990s level. It is important however to understand why it didn't last: The increase in equality happened because farmers started spending less on food than they used to (from 67% in 1990 to 59% in 1998), while wage earners' situation remained unchanged (~50%).[8] However, in the 2000s the wage earners' situation improved dramatically (the amount spent on food changed from 51% in 1998 to 39% in 2005), while the farmers' situation remained unchanged (~58%). By late 2000s the urban population returned to the 1990 percentage, but many people from the countryside had left Romania for work in the EU rather than moving to Romanian cities. The situation of retired people also improved to some extent in the same period: after three decades of stagnation at about 58% it changed to 48% by 2005.

---

[8] It is also interesting to point out that in the period from 1990–2002 the Romanian urban population decreased by 1 percent, meaning about two hundred thousand people moved back to the countryside.

The analysis of **labor productivity** is very similar to the analysis done above in regard to GDP per capita and buying power. Labor productivity increased from about $3,000 USD in 1990 to about $9,000 in the late 1970s, remained stagnant during 1980s, took a sharp dive to about $5,000 in early 1990s, after which it increased to almost 12,000 by the late 2000s. As with the GDP data, we have the problem of misallocation of capital during communism, and thus the somewhat illusory nature of high productivity in the 1980s—the 1990 dive is best seen as revealing an underlining truth, rather than an actual change in labor productivity. In other words, *the communist regime misallocated not just physical capital, but also human capital.*

Once again, we can ask the counterfactual "What would have happened if communism wouldn't have happened?" By comparing the evolution of labor productivity in Romania to that in Austria, we get a very clear picture: the increase in labor productivity in the non-communist state was much higher. Labor productivity in Austria increased from below $10,000 USD in the 1950s to almost $50,000 in the late 2000s. The productivity of the average Romanian worker has thus gradually slipped further behind, rather than catching up.

In terms of **health**, out of the many possible proxies, we consider the following: life expectancy at birth, infant mortality, deaths due to disease, and physicians per thousand people.

Life expectancy increased by about 5 years in Romania during the 1950s and early 1960s, but, afterwards, from 1965 to 1990, it increased by only one year to about 70. After the revolution, by 1997, it *decreased* by almost one year, but this was only a temporary setback: in the following decade it increased by 5 years. By comparison, life expectancy in Austria has increased constantly for the entire period totaling an increase of more than 10 years since 1965. This comparison is quite striking. It shows that the Romanian communist state was not even capable of adopting and using the medical developments from the West.

In the long term, infant mortality in Romania shows gradual improvement. There is one notorious exception to the trend—the abortion ban in the mid 1960s caused a setback of almost a decade. Moreover, during the 1980s the progress in curbing child mortality stopped.

The leading disease-related causes of death in Romania are heart disease, cancer, and respiratory disease. In case of women, the main cause of death is by far pregnancy related. There has been a significant decline in respiratory diseases, and an increase in cancer (Table 3). Paradoxically, the increase in deaths from cancer is not necessarily such bad news: The main predictor of cancer is old age (rather than any environmental factors), and thus the increase in cancer rates simply reflects the fact that people live longer. The fact that cancer rates are relatively stationary since 2003, despite the increase in life expectancy, probably reflects that cancer treatment in Romania delivers better results than it used to.

Table 3. Main causes of death[9]

	1980	1985	1990	2003	2004	2005	2006	2007	2008
Female									
Cerebrovascular diseases	177	198	212	270	264.5	276.5	271	254	240
Ischaemic heart disease				237	234	240	240	233	231
Digestive system diseases	39	46	46	53	52	51	50	53	56
Respiratory system diseases	137	123	92	47	46	45.5	44	43	40
Neoplasm (cancer)	132	133	140	163	164	168	170	169	170
External causes (injury, poisoning etc.)	39	38	45	30	28	29	27.5	26	26
Pregnancy, childbirth and puerperium	527	493	293						
Male									
Cerebrovascular diseases	142	164	176	240	233	240	234	219	211
Ischaemic heart disease				271	264	266	266	260	258
Digestive system diseases				90.8	88	86	82.3	83.1	89
Respiratory system diseases	166	166	134	83	81	79	74.5	75.5	75
Neoplasm (cancer)	168	177	190	241	244	249	253	255	264
External causes (injury, poisoning etc.)	110	116	132	102	98	93.1	92.5	89	95

[9]   Institutul National de Statistica (INS), *Anuarul Statistic*, 1991, 2000, 2009.

Economic performance, wellbeing and "happiness studies"

We have analyzed so far our case from the perspective of estimations based on objective criteria, either aggregate, macro-oriented, or individual-focused. Another possibility is to consider well-being, trying to capture the subjective side as much as possible. This is also an individual-focused perspective. As mentioned in the introduction, our methodology involves using "happiness studies" in a novel way.

Among the relevant studies of interest are those relating to the connection between happiness and income,[10] health,[11] leisure,[12] and those about the importance of institutions,[13] unemployment, inflation, and the general sense of control over one's circumstances.[14] Moreover, particularly striking are the discoveries of the fact that people are generally optimistic and happiness tends to be quite robust, the importance of unfortunate events fading surprisingly fast.[15]

---

[10] Richard Easterlin, "Does Economic Growth Improve the Human Lot? Some Empirical Evidence," in Paul David and Melvin Reder, eds., *Nations and Households in Economic Growth* (Cambridge: Academic Press, 1974). Daniel Kahneman, Alan Krueger, David Schkade, Norbert Schwarz, Arthur Stone, "Would You Be Happier If You Were Richer? A Focusing Illusion." *Science* 312, no. 5782 (Jun. 2006): 1908–10. Betsey Stevenson and Justin Wolfers, "Economic Growth and Subjective Well-Being: Reassessing the Easterlin Paradox," *Brookings Papers on Economic Activity*, Economic Studies Program, The Brookings Institution, vol. 39 (August 2008), 1–102.

[11] Alex C. Michalos, "Social Indicators Research and Health-Related Quality of Life Research," *Social Indicators Research* 65, no. 1 (2004): 27–72. Carol Graham, "Happiness and Health: Lessons—and Questions—for Public Policy," *Health Affairs* 27, no. 1 (2008): 72–87

[12] Lina Eriksson, James Rice, Robert E. Goodin, "Temporal Aspects of Life Satisfaction," *Social Indicators Research* 80, no. 3 (2007): 511–33.

[13] Bruno S. Frey and Alois Stutzer, "Happiness, Economy, and Institutions," *Economic Journal* 110, no. 466 (2000): 918–938; Bruno S. Frey and Alois Stutzer, "Direct Democracy: Designing a Living Constitution," in *Democratic Constitutional Design and Public Policy: Analysis and Evidence*, eds. Roger D. Congleton and Birgitta Swedenborg (Cambridge, MA and London, U.K.: MIT Press, 2006), 39–80; Bruno S. Frey and Alois Stutzer, "Political Participation and Procedural Utility: An Empirical Study," *European Journal of Political Research* 45, no. 3 (2006): 391–418.

[14] Ruut Veenhoven, "Wellbeing in the Welfare State," *Journal for Comparative Policy Analysis* 2 (2000): 91–125; Andrew Oswald, Rafael Di Tella, Robert MacCulloch, "Preferences over Inflation and Unemployment: Evidence from Surveys of Happiness," *American Economic Review* 91, no. 1 (2001): 335–341. Piet Ouweneel, "Social Security and Well-being of the Unemployed in 42 countries," *Journal of Happiness Studies* 3, no. 2 (2002): 167–92.

[15] Philip Brickman, Donald Campbell, "Hedonic Relativism and Planning the Good Society," in *Adaptation Level Theory*, ed. M.H. Apley (Cambridge: Academic Press, 1971), 287–302; Philip Brickman, Dan Coates, Ronnie Janoff-Bulman, "Lottery Winners and Accident Victims: Is Happiness Relative?" *Journal of Personality and Social Psychology* 36, no. 8 (1978): 917–27; Ed Diener, R.E. Lucas, C.N. Scollon, "Beyond the Hedonic Treadmill," *American Psychologist* 61, no. 4 (2006): 305–314.

In order to create a series of relevant proxies for inferring subjective well-being, we need to distill this literature into a series of essential points. In this respect, the overview of the literature indicates that the following aspects *matter most* to improving subjective well-being: relationships, apparent control over one's circumstances, leisure, and purpose in life (the sense of being part of something important). The main economic effect of the "purpose in life" factor is that unemployment is an important source of unhappiness. Moreover, this factor combined with the general robustness of happiness generates an important socio-political effect: regret due to inaction is more important than regret due to mistaken action. Consequently, freedom of opportunity matters for promoting happiness. Thus, while safety matters, promoting safety by means of limiting opportunities can actually lead to a decrease in happiness.

It is also important to point out what *matters less*. Some of these factors are quite surprising. They include health, pain and suffering, freedom of choice, actual control (the illusion of control, even transparent falsities, often suffices). Perhaps pain and suffering are the most surprising and they are clearly relevant for understanding people's subjective well-being under repressive regimes such as communist Romania. It turns out that the impact of pain and suffering upon happiness is smaller than one would expect, especially when they happen under predictable situations and/or are justified by something valuable/important. Moreover, even severe pain and suffering are not lasting (people underestimate their own psychological robustness). It is clear that communism was promoted under the banner of utopia[16] and thus believers were probably willing to endure a certain amount of suffering and hardship in exchange for being part of what they perceived as a historic project. As Tismaneanu points out, to a significant extent, communism was doomed when its legitimacy by means of appealing to utopianism declined, and the regime continued to maintain itself mainly by force. Furthermore, by noting the importance of transparently illusory control and the relative lack of importance of actual control, we can perhaps understand why the communist regime preserved some democratic forms, such as elections, albeit emptied of any actual meaning.

Considering all these factors, we are now in the position to develop a tentative list of operational proxies for well-being, making use of the available empiric data to assess the predicted factors of subjective well-being. We

---

[16] Vladimir Tismaneanu, *Despre 1989: Naufragiul Utopiei* [*On 1989: The Shipwreck of Utopia*] (Bucharest: Humanitas, 2009).

consider the following: *relationships*—assessed through marriages, divorces, and communication technology; *control over circumstances*—assessed through number of cars owned, mother's age when first child is born, and freedom; *predictability*—assessed through employment, inflation, and security (external causes of death); *leisure*—assed through hours worked, number of TVs, and tourism.

Let us start with **relationships**. The data reveal a constant overall downtrend of marriages since the 1930s, from 10 marriages per thousand people in 1930 to 6 per thousand in late 2000s.[17] Considering the importance of relationships to subjective well-being, the decline in marriages is one factor that can contribute to the positive perception of the communist period relative to the present one. The rate of divorce has been constant, at below 2 per thousand, with a notable exception in the 1967–1975 period, when divorces temporarily dropped to below 1 per thousand, following the abortion ban. The importance of marriage for happiness is perhaps revealed by the fact that marriages increased above the trend during the late 1980s when the standard of living declined steadily. In other words, people might have compensated the loss in material conditions with personal relationships.

While marriages declined, other types of relationships probably increased. The post-2000 explosion of mobile phones (from zero in 1996 to over 25 million in late 2000s) and the growth of internet connectivity (from zero in 1993 to over 30 users per hundred people in late 2000s) reveal the dramatic increase in the ease of communicating and a newfound ability to organize.

Our next proxy is **control over circumstances**. We have already considered freedom, political and economic, from an aggregate perspective and from an individual-focused perspective. The importance of this factor for subjective well-being is attenuated by the fact that the number of choices doesn't seem to matter that much, illusory forms of control can be as good as true autonomy, and the utopia-focused communist propaganda might have provided more or less believable excuses.

We consider two more factors that reveal a great deal about the control over circumstances of an average person. One such factor is the means of transportation. While in the 1950 about 90% of the population traveled by train, by 1980 48% used automobiles.[18] It is worth noting that this number

[17] *Anuarul Statistic*, 1991, 2000, 2009.

[18] Bogdan Murgescu, *Romania si Europa. Acumularea decalajelor economice (1500–2010)* [Romania and Europe: the accumulation of economic gaps (1500–2010)] (Bucharest: Polirom, 2010).

seems very large, if we consider that in 1989 only 50 people per thousand had a car (Anuarul Statistic, 1991). One possible explanation is that during communism most people did not travel at all outside their own locality. The number of personal cars continued to grow in the 1990s and doubled by the end of the century, raising to 125 in 1999 and to almost 300 cars per thousand people in late 2000s (Anuarul Statistic, 1991, 2000, 2009). There is no question that post-communist Romania witnessed a tremendous increase in freedom to travel. This further increased once Romania became a member of the European Union.

Another important indicator of control over circumstances is the age of the mother when the first child is born. An increase in the number of older mothers reveal the fact that women have more independence. During communism, most newborns had mothers between 20 and 24 years old. In other words, despite the communist talk about gender equality and despite their employment, the reality was that women's traditional role did not change so much. This, however, changed abruptly after 1990. In 2003 the mothers between 25 and 29 years old had more children than the younger women for the first time in Romanian history. After 1989, we also see a decline in the number of newborns with mothers between 15 and 19 years old, and, after 1997, an increase in the number of newborns (not necessarily firstborns) by mothers between 30 and 35 years old. These trends thus show a significant increase in women independence after the fall of communism.

To sum up, overall data indicates that individual control over one's circumstances has clearly increased in the post-communist period.

Predictability, our next proxy, is quite important for subjective well-being and it is the main factor responsible for the most surprising findings in happiness studies. For example, if hardship is predictable, people's well-being is less affected by it. And while communism created plenty of hardship, in most instances it *was* predictable.

We can consider the way in which predictability impacts income, consumption, and security. In regard to income we consider unemployment. In regard to consumption we consider inflation—or, broadly speaking, the devaluation of currency. In regard to security we consider the number of violent deaths.

We start with *unemployment*. When asked why they think life was better during communist times, 62% of survey takers point to job security.[19] While

---

[19]   CADI, IRT & IRES, 2010

during communism there was virtually full employment, in the post-1989 period unemployment zigzagged between 5.5% and 8.5%, with the highest levels in the early 1990s and in 2003. Moreover, at one point or another, job security was an issue for many people. According to the CADI, IRT & IRES (2010) national survey, 43% of respondents have searching for work in the last 5 years.

In regards to *inflation*, we have already mentioned the very high rates of monetary expansion in the 1990s. By contrast, the monetary growth during communism was small, at one time (in 1983) it was even negative.

Last but not least is *security* (Table 3, external causes of death). Despite the totalitarian regime, private violence in society seems to have increased to some extent during the 1980s. The violence increased even more in the early 1990s, but has decreased significantly since 2000. Since 2010, it has been considerably lower than it used to be during communism. In case of women, it is about 50% lower than it used to be during communism. This improvement might be due to an improvement in police work, but also due to the fact that less people opt for using violent means in the first place, as a satisfactory level of welfare is easier to obtain by cooperative means.

Leisure is next on our list of proxies. The post-1989 development in regard to leisure is very interesting and revealing. On one hand, we see a *decline* in the total annual hours worked. On the other hand, we see an *increase* in the annual hours worked per worker. In other words, there has been an increase in the amount of leisure in society, but a decrease in the number of workers. The burden of productivity is placed on the shoulders of a smaller percentage of the population. Indeed, the number of retired people relative to workers skyrocketed, as the ratio of pensioners to wage earners going from 1:3 in 1990 to less than 1:1 in 2010.[20]

Thus, when we are assessing the developments in regard to leisure we need to consider two different social categories, the retired and the wage earners. The leisure of those retired increased, fueled by, as we have seen above, their increased economic freedom: in the last decade or so, the amount spent on food has decreased from 59% in 1998 to 48% in 2005, a historic improvement. On the other hand, the leisure of wage earners diminished significantly: compared to the early 1990s, by the late 2000s the amount of

---

[20] Asociatia pentru Pensiile Administrate Privat din Romania (APAPR), "Reforma pensiilor. De ce este nevoie de pensiile private?" ["Pension reform: why are private pensions necessary?"], 2012.

annual hours worked increased by almost 20%. The decline in leisure is also reflected in the sudden post-1989 drop in tourism (internal tourism halved, from 10–12 million in the 1980s to 4–6 million in last 20 years, a decline that was not compensated by travel to foreign countries—of only 0.9 millions).

Nonetheless, the news with respect to leisure is not all bad, as we also see an increase in TVs. We can understand TVs and radios as ultra-cheap forms of leisure. During communism, the number of TVs and radios exploded during the 1960s and 1970s, from about 25 TVs per thousand people in 1965 to over 200 in 1980. During the 1980s the number of TVs slightly declined (probably due to highly restricted programs), while the increase in radios continued at a smaller pace. The increase in TVs picked up pace again after the 1989 revolution (fueled by the appearance of many Romanian TV stations and cable TV), reaching about 350 TVs per thousand in late 2000s, while radios declined in the 2000s compared to the 1990s. In conclusion, it seems that people had more leisure during communism, and tourism was much more popular, but, nonetheless, the day-to-day leisure during communism did not include access to high entertainment value daily services like modern television or internet.

Tentative "happiness" comparison

Based on the above data we are now in the position to draw some tentative conclusions about the inferred subjective well-being level during communism as compared to current levels. As one can see, the record is mixed (Table 4) and does not permit an overwhelmingly strong conclusion, especially as weighting the different factors is not clear. Nonetheless, the very fact that it is a mixed record, rather than one favoring post-communism in an overwhelming manner (the way intuition and mass media analysts would expect) is significant and it hints toward a possible explanation of the surprisingly positive popular perception of communism.

Table 4. Happiness proxies: Communism/post-communism comparison

	Relationships	Control over circumstances	Predictability	Leisure
Communism	- Marriages ↑ - Divorces ↔ - Communication ↓	- Cars owned ↓ - Women's independence ↓ - Opportunities ↓	- Employment ↑ - Inflation ↑ - Safety from violence ↓	- TVs ↓ - Tourism ↑ - Wage-earners ↑ - Pensioners ↓
Post-communism	- Marriages ↓ - Divorces ↔ - Communication ↑	- Cars owned ↑ - Women's independence ↑ - Opportunities ↑	- Employment ↓ - Inflation ↓ - Safety from violence ↑	- TVs ↑ - Tourism ↓ - Wage-earners ↓ - Pensioners ↓

The positive aspects of life under communism, from the perspective of the predictors for subjective well-being, include: a larger amount of *predictability* about both one's income and one's consumption (and we should note again that the limited menu of available choices, the major downside of communism from an objective economic point of view, seems to matter less as a predictor of subjective well-being); and a larger amount of *leisure for wage earners*, which they have spent on within-country tourism. The number of marriages was also larger.

The positive aspects of life in the past two decades, from the perspective of the predictors for subjective well-being, include: more *freedom of movement*, more *opportunities* (for work and otherwise), *access to better communication technologies*, more *independence for women*, *less violence* (both private and from the state), and *more comfortable life for pensioners* in the past decade (although this may change due to the serious problems of the state pensions system).

In a nutshell, focusing on the predictors for subjective well-being, during communism, one may argue that life was more predictable and more leisurely, but people had less control over their own circumstances than today. Perhaps personal relationships were also somewhat better, although this is less clear. Thus, it is not utterly inconceivable that many people were actually happier during communism. Whether or not this is indeed the case depends on the relative importance of "control over circumstances" compared to the other factors. In fact, one may understand the development during communism as a gradual decline in happiness as freedom declined in the 1980s compared to the previous decade, while the other factors remained relatively constant. We thus see that the popular discontent with communism in 1989 makes sense from the point of view of "happiness studies," and, furthermore, it is in no contradiction with the favorable popular perceptions of communism as compared to the current period.

Conclusions

Once we have given up the notion that one set of data (be it based on responses given to a comprehensive national survey or based on time series of national statistics) may be sufficient for our comparative purposes, and once we adopt a more complex assessment strategy, perceptions about communism are no longer as puzzling as they seem at first. At the same time, we gain a more nuanced and substantive understanding of the very nature of the exercise of engaging in the comparative assessment of communist and post-communist performance in the same society, and what such exercise may assume, entail and imply.

If one adopts a purely "happiness studies" approach, two components of human development (health and education) will not be included. Nonetheless, one can argue that they are still important and should not be ignored even if they don't contribute very much as predictors of subjective well-being. One can of course, also turn the table on human development perspective, and argue for the inclusion of more factors such as relationships, leisure and general predictability of life. The bottom line is that our assessment is strongly determined by the different normative (social) philosophies that inspire our criteria and methods.

Even considering "happiness studies" factors, the record of communism is mixed at best—which explains people's ambivalence toward it. The fact that many people say that life was better during communism but nonetheless have a disparaging view of the state and favor pro-capitalist measures such the expansion of private property no longer looks as puzzling. As we have seen, it is somewhat plausible that people were subjectively happier towards the mid-point of the communist period, but it is also probable that subjective well-being gradually decreased during the 1980s. This of course is a likely contributing factor that fueled the popular revolt against the regime in

1989, and also shapes people's discontent about communism as a realistic alternative. At the same time, if we move from the subjective perspective to an objective point of view, the conclusion becomes firmer: Life seems significantly better during post-communism and it is getting better.

There are also implications for the larger research agenda. All these insights, gained from an in-depth focus on a specific country case, need to be expanded to other cases in order to consolidate our understanding of the complex factors and interpretive strategy that one needs to consider when engaging in comparative assessment of communist and post-communist wellbeing and performance. This paper should thus be seen as an initial contribution to this larger research agenda aiming at a step by step, country case study based approach, which aims at a more in-depth reappraisal of our understanding of economic performance and wellbeing in communism and post-communist systems as well as of our methods and approaches to that task.

COMMUNIST ECONOMY

The Verdict of History

Steven Rosefielde

If you're not a communist at the age of 20, you haven't got a heart.
If you're still a communist at the age of 30, you haven't got a brain.
(Various attributions)

The prophecy

Communism for many nineteenth and twentieth century activists was synonymous with Karl Marx and Friedrich Engels' concept of a liberated, tolerant, fully abundant, harmonious, peaceful, classless, stateless, democratic and global society where every individual freely and cooperatively maximizes his and her human potential without religious, family, or sexual constraint. It is superlative. Paradise is perfect harmony and bliss.[1]

Twentieth century communist leaders like Vladimir Lenin, Joseph Stalin, Kim Il-sung, Mao Zedong, Ho Chi Minh, and Pol Pot construed Marx and Engels' scattered musings to mean that criminalizing private property, markets and class distinctions would automatically bring the communist dream to fruition without significant collateral damage.[2] They contended that the liberated masses would be equal, and harmoniously cooperate for mutual benefit. They appeared confident that egalitarian cooperation and communist planning would outperform capitalism.[3] They expected fierce bourgeois resistance, but were convinced that the class struggle would save the day. Marx prophesized

---

[1] Karl Marx and Friedrich Engels never wrote a coherent blueprint for communism, leaving Marxists and everyone else at sea in trying to definitively reconstruct their vision.

[2] Steven Rosefielde, *Red Holocaust* (New York: Routledge, 2010). Limitations of space preclude consideration of Josef Bronz Tito and other East European communist leaders, but the nuances they introduced do not alter the fundamentals. Communist Yugoslavia, Czechoslovakia, Hungary, and Poland no longer exist.

[3] Eric Hoffer, *The True Believer* (New York: Harper, 1951).

that the proletariat would sweep capitalists into the dustbin of history and communism would rise full-fledged like Athena from Zeus's head.

The verdict of history

Marx and Engels' dialectical materialist prophecy failed.[4] The industrial workers of the world did not inherit the earth. One hundred and seventy years after the "worldly philosophers" predicted the proletariat's ineluctable victory,[5] the power of the working class has vanished almost everywhere. Marx and Engels had prophesized a peaceful transition from capitalism to communism, but communist party-led armed insurrectionaries seized power instead. Lenin, Kim, Mao, Ho Chi Minh and Pol Pot's systems were authoritarian, anti-religious, anti-family, and anti-democratic. Their systems were civically, socially, politically, religiously and intellectually tyrannical. Their systems did not create liberated, prosperous, harmonious, peaceful, classless, socially just, stateless, democratic societies where every individual freely and cooperatively maximized his and her human potential in one country and across the globe without religious, family or sexual constraint.

The Soviet Union, North Korea, China, Vietnam, and Cambodia were anything but humanitarian. They terrorized large segments of their populations, built vast Gulag Archipelagos,[6] and were responsible for no less than 50 million excess deaths.[7]

The Soviet Union, North Korea, China, Vietnam, and Cambodia until the start of the market communist era were structurally militarized authoritarian martial police states.[8]

Lenin, Kim, Mao, Ho, and Pol Pot's successors have all repudiated their twentieth century communist heritages.[9] Mikhail Gorbachev dissolved the

---

[4]   Karl Popper, *The Poverty of Historicism* (London: Routledge, 1957).

[5]   See Robert Heilbroner, *The Worldly Philosophers: The Lives, Times and Ideas of The Great Economic Thinkers* (New York: Simon and Schuster, 1999).

[6]   Aleksandr Solzhenitsyn, *Arkhipelag GULAG*, Vol 1 (Paris: YMCA-PRESS, 1973).

[7]   Rosefielde, *Red Holocaust*.

[8]   Vitaly Shlykov, "The Economics of Defense in Russia and the Legacy of Structural Militarization," in *The Russian Military: Power and Policy*, eds. Steven Miller and Dmitri Trenin (Cambridge: MIT Press, 2004), 157–177.

[9]   This holds for North Korea too. The word socialist has been substituted for communist in North Korean official documents, and Marx and Engels are all but forgotten. See Nicholas Eberstadt, "The Method in North Korea's Madness," *Commentary*, January 16, 2018, https://www.commentarymagazine.com/articles/method-north-koreas-madness/.

Soviet Union. Boris Yeltsin renounced the Soviet Communist Party. The Baltic States (Estonia, Latvia, and Lithuania), the Visegrad Four (Poland, Hungary, Czechia, and Slovakia), and some of the successor states of Yugoslavia all joined the European Union.[10] Xi Jinping distanced China's Communist Party from Mao's command and the Red Guard models. Vietnam and Cambodia followed Xi's lead.

The verdict of history is unequivocal. Marxists were wrong about dialectical materialism. Communists did not come to power peacefully. Lenin, Kim, Mao, Ho, and Pol Pot were wrong about the vanguard of the proletariat's ability to hothouse a communist utopia. They were wrong about the vanguard's fastidious humanitarianism. They were wrong about its commitments to democracy, civil rights, justice, peace, anti-imperialism, and social wellbeing. They were wrong to attribute civilization's discontents wholly to private ownership and free markets. They were wrong to claim that state social control was better than open societies.[11] They were wrong to contend that planning was better than free enterprise. They were wrong to suppose the Yugoslavian worker managed market system was a viable alternative to central planning,[12] and they were wrong to crow as Nikita Khrushchev did that, "We will bury you!"[13] The twentieth century buried Soviet and East European communism,[14] despite eyes wide shut denials.[15]

It is important to appreciate that the failure of twentieth Marxist-Leninist-Stalinist-Maoist communism does not settle the further issue of Xi Jinping's market communism.[16] Chinese market communism is ideologically imperfect, but Xi promises to make Marx and Engel's communist dream come true by 2049.[17] We shall see.[18]

---

[10] Serbia, Macedonia, and Montenegro are all candidates for EU membership.

[11] Karl Popper, *The Open Society and Its Enemies*, vol. 1, 5th ed. (Princeton: Princeton University Press, 1966); Karl Popper, *In Search of a Better World* (London: Routledge, 1994).

[12] Jaroslav Vanek, *The Participatory Economy: An Evolutionary Hypothesis and a Strategy for Development* (New York: Taylor & Francis, 1973).

[13] For an analysis of what Khrushchev said or did not say, and what he meant, see "Khrushchev's 'We Will Bury You,'" CIA, last modified February 7, 1962. https://www.cia.gov/library/readingroom/docs/CIA-RDP73B00296R000200040087-1.pdf

[14] László Csaba, "Comparative Economics and the Mainstream," *Economics and Business Review* 3, no. 3 (2017): 90–109; János Kornai, *The Socialist System: The Political Economy of Communism* (Oxford and England: Clarendon Press, 1992).

[15] Stanley Kubrick, *Eyes Wide Shut*, movie, 1999.

[16] Csaba, "Comparative Economics and the Mainstream," 90–109.

[17] Steven Rosefielde and Jonathan Leightner, *China's Market Communism: Challenges, Solutions and Prospects* (London: Routledge, 2017).

[18] Karl Popper, *In Search of a Better World* (London: Routledge, 1994).

What went wrong?

Twentieth century communism from 1917 to 1990 failed because Marx and Engels' conceptual musings in the *Economic and Philosophical Manuscripts of 1844* and the *Communist Manifesto* were puerile.[19] Communism as they formulated it in their youth was a soufflé of fanciful musings. The premises of Marx and Engels' communist utopia were internally contradictory. Individuals could not actualize their "full" human potential as Marx and Engels promised because communist doctrine abridged their freedom. Individuals could not fully maximize their quality of existence because communism prevented them from thinking sacred thoughts,[20] spurning "free love,"[21] nurturing family relations, doubting dialectical materialism, owning assets, bartering services, founding businesses, innovating, acting as entrepreneurs, borrowing and lending, and shopping to their hearts content.[22] Communism could not create full abundance because it penalized people for being productive and devotion to the communist cause proved to be an inadequate substitute for competitive individual utility seeking. Communists could not actualize their full human potential because communist taboos overrode their personal liberty.

Marx and Engels were devout nineteenth century "social romantics," apostles of a heroic struggle for the liberation of the downtrodden.[23] Like puppy love, their communist infatuation was much to do about nothing.

Twentieth century communism went wrong because the vanguard of the proletariat was ruthless and imposed its commands on the people. Party leaders refused to recognize that the utopias they created were dystopic.

Twentieth century communism went wrong because communism became the opiate of the intellectuals.[24] Marx and Engels' social romantic fantasy mesmerized activists, zealots and scholars, who allowed the chimera of social liberation to override their critical reason.

---

[19] Karl Marx, *Economic and Philosophical Manuscripts of 1844* (Moscow: Progress Publishers, 1932), and the *Communist Manifesto* (London 1848).

[20] Karl Marx, *A Contribution to the Critique of Hegel's Philosophy of Right* (Deutsch-Französische Jahrbücher, February, 1844); Sabrina Petra Ramet, ed., *Religious Policy in the Soviet Union* (New York: Cambridge University Press, 1993).

[21] Richard Weikart, "Marx, Engels and the Abolition of the Family," *History of European Ideas* 18, no. 5 (1994): 657–672.

[22] Steven Rosefielde and Jonathan Leightner, *China's Market Communism: Challenges, Solutions and Prospects* (London: Routledge, 2017).

[23] Alexander Gray, *The Socialist Tradition: Moses to Lenin* (London: Longmans, Green and Col, 1946).

[24] Raymond Aron, *The Opium of the Intellectuals* (Paris: Calmann-Lévy, 1955).

Twentieth century communism went awry because many intellectuals mistakenly believed that historical determinism was the arbiter of communism's success; that rational choice economics did not matter, and communist setbacks were only bumps in the road.

Twentieth century communism went wrong because direct worker cooperation (communal economy) restricted the scope of rational choice, and planning pre-empted consumer sovereignty. Central planning put planners in command with toxic consequences for social wellbeing. Communist nations were repressive economies of shortage, producing shoddy goods, in the wrong assortments, mal-distributed through forced substitution, offering no hope for brighter futures.

Twentieth century communism went astray because economists conflated computopic pipedreams about the possibilities of optimal mathematical planning with the realities of top-down command planning.[25] Western theorists pretended that the performance potential of imperfect planning and workably competitive market economies were broadly the same, even though they knew better.[26]

Twentieth century communism went wrong because false statistics, rosy Western estimates,[27] and freely invented communist propaganda allowed callous leaders to ignore the human cost of Bolshevism.[28]

Twentieth century communism went wrong because pundits facilely treated exaggerated GDP growth statistics and other measures of development as reliable indicators of the quality of existence. The Wagnerian soap opera of communist modernization enabled wishful thinkers to embrace the revolutionary aura and disregard the bleak truth.

Many scholars remain bewitched.[29]

---

[25] Egon Neuberger, "Libermanism, Computopia, and Visible Hand: The Question of Informational Efficiency," *The American Economic Review* 56, no. 1/2 (Mar. 1, 1966): 131–144.

[26] János Kornai, *Anti-equilibrium: On Economic Systems* (Amsterdam: North Holland, 1971).

[27] Steven Rosefielde, "Tea Leaves and Productivity: Bergsonian Norms for Gauging the Soviet Future," *Comparative Economic Studies* 47, no. 2 (June 2005): 259–273; Abram Bergson, "The USSR Before the Fall: How Poor and Why?" *Journal of Economic Perspectives* 5, no. 4 (Fall, 1991): 29–44; Abram Bergson, "The Communist Efficiency Gap: Alternative Measures," *Comparative Economic Studies* 36, no. 1 (Spring 1994): 1–12.

[28] Walter Duranty, *Duranty Reports Russia* (New York: The Viking Press, 1934); John Reed, *Ten Days that Shook the World* (New York: Boni and Liveright, 1919); Cf. Emma Goldman, *My Disillusionment with Russia* (New York: Doubleday, Page & Company, 1923).

[29] Sheila Fitzpatrick, *The Cultural Front: Power and Culture in Revolutionary Russia* (Ithaca NY: Cornell University Press, 1992).

Communist economic theory

Communist economy for Marx and Engels was simple. Communities of workers would assemble in collectively owned factories and retail outlets to discuss production and rationing. Members would make their decisions on a consensus basis, obviating the need for private property and competitive exchange. Consensus (harmonious cooperation) replaced individual utility seeking competition. Results would be optimal because communards were supposed to take account of everyone's quality of existence.

Harmonious cooperation, however, can only work satisfactorily in situations where it is practical for communists to assemble and discuss possibilities. It is impractical for inter-communal production and distribution.[30] Marx and Engels solved this problem to their own satisfaction by invoking the concept of central planning to bridge the gap between independent communal producers and distributors. Central planning, they insisted allowed communist economies to capture the opportunities afforded by Adam Smith's division of labor without recourse to private property and markets.[31] Marx and Engels believed that arms-length central planning was "scientific," undistorted by profiteering and therefore ipso facto better than capitalist competition.

Their production and distribution schemes are logical. If consensus building is inclusive, cooperative, harmonious, and efficient, good results are achievable. If planning has the same virtues, it should be beneficial. These however are big ifs. Private ownership and markets provide satisfactory results not because cooperators are supposed to behave selflessly, but because competition under the rule of law spurs initiative and limits the ability of some individuals to benefit at the expense of others. The same principle does not apply to central planning. There is no competitive mechanism to prevent the state from disregarding people's preferences or to prevent "red directors" (enterprise managers and rationing authorities) from acting on their own behalf. Marx and Engels endorsed consensus building, harmonious cooperation, and planning to eliminate the risk of market exploitation,[32]

---

[30] Cf. George Douglas Howard Cole, *Guild Socialism: A Plan for Economic Democracy* (New York: Frederick A. Stokes, 1921).

[31] Associationist planning is discussed in *The Civil War in France*, 1871; Paul Burkett, "Marx's Vision of Sustainable Human Development," *Monthly Review* 57, no. 5 (October 2005). https://www.marxists.org/archive/marx/works/1871/civil-war-france/

[32] Moral hazards may not be important for self-policing small communes, but the danger of insider privilege increases with the separation of insider commune managers from members in large communes.

but failed to appreciate that proscribing the invisible hand let the wolf in undetected via the back door. Without Adam Smith's invisible hand, there are no trustworthy whistle blowers. Factors can be inter-communally misallocated and workers can shirk their duties. Communes can satisfice with obsolete technology and shun innovation. Shoddy goods can be fobbed off as luxuries, commune members can be forced to consume products that they do not want, and planners can flagrantly miss manage inter-communal relations. Communal consensus building, harmonious cooperation, and central planning sound charming, but their consequences are malign. Inter-communal planning institutions cannot cope satisfactorily with moral hazard, and planners cannot do more than primitively satisfice.

Communist economic reality

Scale matters. It is easy to imagine how a small band of communist enthusiasts could live together harmoniously in Tao Yuanming's "Peach Blossom Spring." Likewise, central planners might be able to coordinate production and distribution among a few tight knit communes, but this will not work in modern industrial societies. Soviet statisticians report that the USSR produced between 25 and 30 million different products,[33] each with its own nomenclature number and engineering specifications to assure that they possessed prescribed characteristics. How could Soviet central planners have gathered all the information on consumer demand and producer supply possibilities in real time to compute a competitive equilibrium for all technologies, factors, goods, and services? The answer is that Gosplan (the Soviet State Central Planning Agency) could not and did not do so. Central planners did not even try. They took the easy way out, labelling aggregate aspirational production targets "scientific plans" to avoid acknowledging that satisfactory inter-communal micro-planning on a par with imperfectly competitive market alternatives was improbable.

---

[33] Steven Rosefielde, *Soviet Economy from Lenin to Putin* (New York: Wiley, 2007).

Top-down command planning

Gosplan prepared plans for 120 composite goods (automobiles, petroleum, chemicals, etc.), not 27.5 million goods. Plans were determined with linear extrapolation techniques that ignored opportunity costs, consumer preferences and rational choice. Gosplan had no real time information. It worked with historical data prepared by Goskomstat (the State Statistical Committee), input-output tables, and consolidated information compiled by ministries from draft enterprise *tekhpromfinplans* (technical industrial financial plans). Gosplan juggled production goals relying on party directives (Stalin's commands) and a crude technique called "material balances" that identified potential gaps in intermediate goods supply and demand plans, and tried to remedy the imbalances through rationing. No one made rational choices based on real scarcities and technological possibilities—not Stalin, not central planners, not ministerial lobbyists. Soviet planning from above was an exercise designed solely to provide primitive "rule-of-thumb" directive guidance to economic ministries, main departments (*glavks*) and red directors (enterprise managers),[34] lofty claims to the contrary notwithstanding.

The Soviet top-down planning process was analogous to American federal budgeting. The White House, Senate, Congress, departments and myriad lobbyists assisted by the Congressional Budget Office, the Office of Management and Budget, and the Treasury hammer out America's annual federal budget, financed by taxes and borrowing. The document provides funding for all federally approved programs and subprojects. Federal agencies have broad discretion in implementing subprograms and have the right to request supplementary money. The government at its discretion can sequester appropriations.

Soviet top-down central planning worked the same way, but rationed physical resources instead of money, supplemented by state bank (Gosbank) credit controls. Both the American and Soviet top-down command programming mechanisms function effectively in the sense that they provide agencies with the resources needed for their missions (in the Soviet case including enterprises). Consumers (recipients of public goods and services), however have to take it or leave it. Decisions are made about the assortment and quantities of public services produced and delivered on an ad hoc patchwork basis without global optimization. There is no competitive test,

---

[34] Igor Birman, "From the Achieved Level," *Soviet Studies* 30, no. 2 (April 1978): 153–72.

only fulsome declarations by public officials that they do their job right, even though they disregard the people's demands.

The Soviet version of federal budget management (top-down planning), however, was especially detrimental because it was inclusive and unaccountable to the electorate. Kremlin top-down central planning penetrated beneath the perimeter of public goods into the production of goods for private consumption. Soviet authorities fixed wages and prices. They selected technologies, designed goods, rationed inputs and outputs, micro-planned products, set goals, established managerial bonuses and worker incentives, and used motivational campaigns and stern discipline, including terror tactics to strengthen managerial and worker compliance with plan directives. America over-regulates the production of goods for private consumption too, but Soviet directive control was more intrusive.

Command and incentives

The Bolsheviks feared that "those who live by the sword would die by the sword." The vanguard of the proletariat, which claimed to have seized state power from the "capitalist class," feared that capitalist wolves in red sheep's clothing might launch a counter-insurrection, and designed the top-down command system to deter this from happening.[35] The state strictly subordinated red directors to main sub-departments, ministries, Communist Party organs and the secret police (NKVD). It ordered red directors to obey legally binding micro-plan directives prepared by *glavks* from the red directors' own draft production plans and Gosplan aggregates.[36] Punishments for non-compliance during Stalin's reign were draconian,[37] and might have been effective, if strict obedience had been costless, but it was not.

Tekhpromfinplans were imperfect and therefore misrepresented the system's true potentials. They sometimes were too lax, more often too taut. When they were slack, compliant red directors would under produce. When plans were overly ambitious, red directors also were inclined to under produce knowing that they would be punished whether they under fulfilled the plan by a small or large margin.[38]

---

[35] Gregory Grossman, "Notes for a Theory of the Command Economy," *Soviet Studies* 15, no. 2 (1963): 101–123.

[36] Steven Rosefielde, *Russian Economy from Lenin to Putin* (New York: Wiley, 2007).

[37] Under fulfilment of plan directives raised suspicions of counter-revolutionary sabotage.

[38] Steven Rosefielde and Ralph W. Pfouts, "Economic Optimization and Technical Efficiency in

The Bolsheviks could have stood on principle, but chose to hedge. Moscow decided to supplement compulsory *tekhpromfinplans* with managerial bonuses, rewarding red directors for fulfilling and over-fulfilling plan assignments.[39] If there were idle reserves, red directors always would be motivated to employ them, and if they could not produce as much as the Kremlin commanded, they would still produce as much as they could. Bonus incentives in this way transformed top-down planning from a command economy that required red directors to obey, into a resource mobilization system that exhorted everyone to work tirelessly for the revolution and rewarded them for maximizing employment and output. Effort, not results became paramount.

Resource mobilization had some obvious merits, but it was not a panacea. The Kremlin lost control over input and output assortments, the production of new products, and aspects of the modernization of enterprise technology.

When red directors received bonuses for maximizing output measured in tons, they produced one giant nail instead of the planned assortment.[40]

When red directors earned bonuses for maximizing quantities, they produced millions of tiny nails.

When profits determined rewards, red directors optimized at "false prices" giving the illusion, but not the reality, of competitive optimality.[41]

When the Kremlin decided to encourage red directors to introduce new products at high initial prices, managers enriched themselves by selling old wine in new bottles with extra "stars" on the label.[42] "Improved" 5-star cognac was the same old 1-star cognac, sold at five times the price. This spurious innovation not only allowed red directors to be over compensated, it distorted official GDP growth statistics by treating fake value added falsely attributed to better quality (hidden inflation) as real national income.[43]

Soviet Enterprises Jointly Regulated by Plans and Incentives," *European Economic Review* 32, no. 6 (1988): 1285–99.

[39] For a complete discussion of Soviet bonus incentives see Steven Rosefielde, *Russian Economy from Lenin to Putin* (New York: Wiley, 2007).

[40] Alec Nove, *The Soviet Economic System* (London: George Allen and Unwin, 1977).

[41] Steven Rosefielde and Ralph W. Pfouts, "Economic Optimization and Technical Efficiency in Soviet Enterprises Jointly Regulated by Plans and Incentives," *European Economic Review* 32, no. 6 (1988): 1285–99.

[42] Steven Rosefielde, *Russian Economy from Lenin to Putin* (New York: Wiley, 2007).

[43] Grigorii Khanin, "Ekonomicheskii Rost: Alternativnaia Otsenka: *Kommunist* 17 (1988): 83–90. Steven Rosefielde, "A Comment on David Howard's Estimate of Hidden Inflation in the Soviet Retail Sales Sector," *Soviet Studies* 32, no. 3 (July 1980): 423–27; Steven Rosefielde, "The Riddle

The same problem bedeviled the development and introduction of new production technologies.[44]

When the material technical supply system (*Gossnabsbyt'*) refused to accept delivery of surplus ball bearing, red directors resorted to "pre-cycling." They sent unsaleable ball bearings to smelters, melted them down into ingots, and produced more ball bearing.[45] Soviet national income accounts recorded the output at every stage of this Rube Goldberg operation as real GDP.

The sum and substance of these and other myriad distortions was what Ludwig von Mises called "planned chaos."[46] Soviet top-down planning displayed a façade of comprehensive scientific directive control, but was chaotic. Planners could not coordinate enterprise demand and supply on rational choice principles, and hidden inflation gave false assurances of success that blinded the Kremlin to the anarchy in its midst.

Structural militarization

The military industrial complex (VPK) was the exception that proved the rule. It alone was economically successful. Soviet top-down planning rationed resources on a priority basis, and defense was priority number one. The former co-chairman of the Russian Defense Council, Vitaly Shlykov captured this reality best by coining the term "structural militarization" to suggest that excessive defense spending was an institutionalized aspect of the Soviet economic system.[47] The VPK, Genstab, Ministry of Defense and the Politburo concurred that there could never be too much defense. They felt duty bound to prepare for worst-case military scenarios, and then added resources to deal with the unthinkable. Their obsession was "structural." It was not a whim, or a reflection of the external threat. The Soviet economy was defense intensive because this is what the leadership and the VPK

of Postwar Russian Economic Growth: Statistics Lied and Were Misconstrued," *Europe-Asia Studies* 55, no. 3 (2003): 469–481; Steven Rosefielde, "Tea Leaves and Productivity: Bergsonian Norms for Gauging the Soviet Future," *Comparative Economic Studies* 47, no. 2 (June 2005): 259–273.

44 Joseph Berliner, *The Innovation Decision in Soviet Industry* (Cambridge MA: MIT Press, 1978).

45 Information provided to the author by a Soviet ball bearing red director at a CIA conference held in the late 1980s at Airlie House.

46 Ludwig von Mises, *Planned Chaos* (Auburn Alabama: Ludwig von Mises Institute, 2014).

47 Vitaly Shlykov, "Chto Pogubilo Sovetskii Soiuz? Amerikanskaia Razvedka ili Sovetskikh Voennykh Raskhodakh" (What Destroyed the Soviet Union? American Intelligence Estimates of Soviet Military Expenditures), *Voenny Vestnik*, no. 8 (2001).

desired. The supply mechanism was complementary. The VPK had priority access to inputs. It had first dibs on both the quantity and quality of available supplies including high-skilled labor. It received the lion's share of RDT&E services, and new capital formation, and was self-sufficient. It had the production capacities to assure that the economy served the needs of the armed forces first, leaving the civilian sector with a Spartan residual. Shlykov and Academician Yuri Yaremenko, contended that the military machine building was the USSR's most dynamic sector and that military production accounted for 30 percent of Soviet GDP,[48] a figure supported by the research of the Office of the Secretary of Defense.[49]

Top-down planning worked in the military sector for another important reason. The Ministry of Defense's demand rationally governed weapons supply. Military planners acquired state of the arts foreign military technologies by hook-or-by-crook, and determined the weapons systems needed to win anticipated wars. They did not passively accept whatever weapons central planners foisted on them. MOD purchasers and VPK producers worked hand in glove in the national interest with superior results.

The Soviet Union consequently was what Henry Rowan and Charles Wolf, Jr. aptly dubbed an "impoverished superpower,"[50] a dual economy with a comparatively efficient military industrial complex and dysfunctional consumer sector.

Marxists accept the claim that the Soviet Union was a military superpower, and applaud communism's prowess in defending the revolution against the forces of Western imperialism, but avoid acknowledging that permanent peacetime structural militarization made a mockery of Marx and Engel's communist dream.

---

[48] Steven Rosefielde, *False Science: Underestimating the Soviet Arms Buildup*, 2nd ed. (Piscataway, NJ: Transaction, [1982] 1987); Steven Rosefielde, *Russia in the 21st Century: The Prodigal Superpower* (Cambridge: Cambridge University Press, 2005).

[49] David Epstein, "The Economic Cost of Soviet Security and Empire," in Charles Wolf, Jr., and Henry Rowan, eds., *The Impoverished Superpower: Perestroika and the Soviet Military Burden* (San Francisco: Institute of Contemporary Studies, 1990): 155–84.

[50] Charles Wolf, Jr. and Henry Rowan, eds., *The Impoverished Superpower: Perestroika and the Soviet Military Burden* (San Francisco: Institute of Contemporary Studies, 1990).

Full employment, price stability and growth

The Soviet economic system had other merits beyond its military industrial prowess. It displayed some positive macroeconomic characteristics. *Narodnoe Khoziaistvo*, the official Goskomstat statistical handbook boasted in the 70th anniversary edition (1917–87) that the USSR had eradicated unemployment by 1930, and limited inflation to less than one percent per annum in the postwar era. The same source reports that peacetime Soviet GDP grew faster than the Western norm.[51] CIA and independent scholars dispute Goskomstat's national income growth statistics on a variety of grounds,[52] but the USSR's solid anti-inflation and full employments records are incontestable. Both were artefacts of communist central planning and the Kremlin's resource mobilization strategy. The State Price Committee (Goskomtsen) set prices and kept them stable (except for new, improved and special order goods) to prevent red directors from padding their production reports. The Kremlin wanted real increases in production, not inflationary illusions.

The Communist Party institutionalized overfull employment by rewarding red directors for producing as much as they could instead of limiting production to the profit maximizing equilibrium ideal. Over-full employment was the USSR's anti-equilibrium norm.[53]

Anti-parasite laws provided additional support for resource mobilization. All able-bodied Soviets were required to work where they chose, or be assigned to the Gulag.[54] It was a criminal offense for non-penal workers to choose leisure over labor, a rule confirmed by comparative employment data. The share of workers in the Soviet population was sixteen percent higher than in America.[55] Soviet workers toiled more hours during the normal workweek for pay and additionally for free on weekends (*subbotniki*).

[51] *Narodnoe Khoziaistvo SSSR za 70 Let* (Moscow: Finansy I Statistika, 1987), 11–13, 480.

[52] *Measures of Soviet Gross National Product in 1982 Prices*, Joint Economic Committee of Congress (Washington, DC, 1990); Steven Rosefielde, "Tea Leaves and Productivity: Bergsonian Norms for Gauging the Soviet Future," *Comparative Economic Studies* 47, no. 2 (June 2005): 259–273.

[53] János Kornai, *Anti-equilibrium: On Economic Systems* (Amsterdam: North-Holland Publishing Company, 1972).

[54] There were ten to twelve million inmates incarcerated in Gulag when Stalin died in 1953. Two to four million were reported released in 1954–55, and another four million shortly after Khrushchev's secret speech to the Twentieth Party Congress. This left approximately four million inmates in 1959. CIA studies using national technical means counted and estimated that there were roughly four million prisoners in 1977, about half in the Gulag. Steven Rosefielde, *Red Holocaust* (New York: Routledge, 2010).

[55] Warren Eason, "Comparisons of the United States and Soviet Economies: The Labor Force," in *Comparisons of the United States and Soviet Economies*, Joint Economic Committee of Congress (Washington DC, 1960): Table 2, 79.

Marxists claim that these macro-economic accomplishments prove communism's superiority. They acknowledge that unpaid "Saturday" work was compulsory; that forced labor in Gulag was inhumane, that Soviet price fixing prevented consumers from maximizing their utility, and that Soviet growth did not translate into prosperity, but consider these flaws minor in the bigger picture. Supporters point out that communism spared Soviet workers the traumas of capitalist unemployment and inflation, and predicted that rapid economic development would soon overcome communism's micro-economic blemishes. This never happened.

Treadmill of reform

Marxists placed their hopes for communism's triumphal microeconomic forward march on the shoulders of reform. The Soviets tried everything. Everything failed.[56] Evsei Liberman devised[57] and Alexei Kosygin implemented a bonus incentive scheme that rewarded red directors for maximizing "profitability" instead of the physical volume of output in 1965.[58] The Soviet Union began computerizing in earnest during the mid-1950s.[59] The main thrust was toward the creation of a state system of computer centers. Late in 1963, a special commission of the Chief Administration on the Introduction of Computer Technology into the National Economy of the State Committee on Coordinating Scientific Research Work of the USSR reported that the purpose would be to perform computations related to formulating optimal national economic plans, re-computations of state prices, operational control,

---

[56] Gertrude Schroeder, "The Soviet Economy on a Treadmill of 'Reforms,'" in *Soviet Economy in a Time of Change*, Joint Economic Committee of Congress (Washington, DC, October 10, 1979): 312–66; Gertrude Schroeder, "Soviet Economic 'Reform' Decrees: More Steps on the Treadmill," *Soviet Economy in the 1980s: Problems and Prospects*, vol. 1, Joint Economic Committee of Congress (Washington, DC, 1982); Schroeder Gertrude, "Organizations and Hierarchies: The Perennial Search for Solutions," *Comparative Economic Studies* (Winter 1987): 7–28.

[57] Evsei Liberman, *Ekonomicheskie metody povysheniya effektivnosti proizvodstva*, 1970 (Economic Methods and the Effectiveness of Production) (New York, 1972); Martin Weitzman, "The New Soviet Incentive Model," in *Bell Journal of Economics* 7, no. 1 (1976): 251–57.

[58] Alexi Kosygyin, "Ob uluchshenii upravleniia promyshlennostiu sovershenstvovanii planirovania i usilennia ekonomicheskovo stimulirovanii promyshlennovo proizvodstva" (On Improving Industrial Management, Perfecting Planning, and Increasing Economic Incentives for Industrial Production), *Pravda* (September 28, 1965).

[59] Richard Judy, "Information, Control, and Soviet Economic Management," in *Mathematics and Computers in Soviet Economic Planning*, eds. John Hardt et al. (New Haven, CT: Yale University Press, 1967): 1–67.

banking, finance and statistics. The Soviet computer development strategy featured the construction of a national computer pyramid. The capstone was the main computing center of Gosplan, which would connect every module of the central planning hierarchy from head to toe in a comprehensive network that would enable 42 full-time employees to perform 600,000 computational operations involving 30,000–40,000 *tekhpromfinplan* data items in the Moscow Ball-bearing Works No. 1.[60] Full connectivity would assure that every red director could electronically report his *tekhpromfinplan*, coordinate with contractors, and receive centrally approved assignments. V. F. Pugachev estimated that a quadratic program using five million equations and constraints would suffice to plan the entire national economy.[61] For a moment, it seemed as if Vladimir Lenin's vision of the Bolshevik natural economy in *State and Revolution* might actually come true.[62] Reality, however, quickly set in. Although information was acquired, processed, distributed, stored, and retrieved for central planning, it soon became embarrassingly clear that the center did not have a clue what to do with its newfound computer capabilities. Soviet leaders remained opposed to consumer sovereignty, and displayed little interest in household satisfaction. The computer pyramid did nothing to change this. Nor was it much help in micro-controlling production for state purchase. Communist authorities were unable to choose preferred output mixes for more than a few hundred composite goods, and the prevailing administrative control structures continued to use traditional material balance procedures.

A succession of administrative overhauls, decentralization experiments and cybernetic efforts to regulate decentralized economic relationships did not fare any better. An algorithm was needed to cut through the maze of possibilities separating Soviet planning practice from the optimum. Management-system design, planning, and operations all had to be connected, and coordinated by key bits of information reflecting supplies and demands. A vast research and reform program called the automatic system of management and planning (ASUP) emerged from this humble origin during

---

[60] Gavril Popov, *Elektronnye mashiny I upravlenie ekonomikoi* (Moscow, 1963), 142.

[61] Vladimir Lenin, *State and Revolution* (Moscow, 1917); V.F Pugachev, "Voprosy optimalnovo planirovaniia narodnovo khoziaistvo s pomoshchiu edinoi gosudarstvennoi seti vchislitelnykh tsentrov," *Voprosy ekonomiki* 7 (1964), 103.

[62] Nikolay Fedorenko, "Optimal Functioning System for a Socialist Economy," *Progress* (Moscow, 1974); Martin Weitzman, "Iterative Multi-Level Planning with Production Targets," *Econometrica* (1970): 50–65.

the 1960s.[63] It focused on the construction of standardized management and planning indicators decision-making aids for utilizing them, mechanisms for distribution, coordination, and supervision. The endeavor was supposed to be cybernetic, but the feedback dimension was feeble. Algorithms made little inroads into displacing people, and the entire operation was a charade because it disregarded the sovereign preferences of the leadership and consumers.

Communist central planning did not fail for want of trying. It failed because the dream was unachievable.

The illusion of progress

The Kremlin leadership concealed its disillusionment with the bitter fruits of thirty years of futile central planning reform behind a mask of triumphalism. It confidently proclaimed at the Plenum of the Communist Party Central Committee, January 27–29, 1987 that: "Our achievements have been immense and indisputable, and the Soviet people are justifiably proud of their successes. They are the true guarantee of the realization of the current plan, and our future dreams."[64] Official Goskomstat statistics supported the party's jubilation, as did CIA estimates and those of Soviet economists who adjusted Goskomstat data for hidden inflation. Table 1 reports that Soviet national income grew 5.3 percent according to Kremlin and 2.9 percent according to the CIA 1966–1985.

Numbers however belied the reality of impoverished superpower. The *siloviki* (power services) were content, but a large Communist Party faction depressed by the meagerness of their existence, as they perceived it began pressing for radical change behind closed doors.[65] They successfully persuaded Mikhail Gorbachev to rescue the Soviet people from stagnation (*zastoi*),[66] by abandoning central planning in favor of radical market economic reform (*perestroika*).[67]

---

63 S.A. Kuznetsov, V.L. Makarov, and V.D. Marshak, *Informatsionnaia Baza, Perspektivnovo Planirovaniia v OASU*, Ekonomika (Moscow, 1982).

64 *Materials from the Plenum of the Communist Party Central Committee, January 27–29, 1987*, Politizdat, (1987): 6–7. Author's translation.

65 Archie Brown, *The Rise & Fall of Communism* (London: Bodley Head, 2009); Philip Hanson, *The Rise and Fall of the Soviet Economy: An Economic History of the USSR from 1945* (London: Pearson Education, 2003).

66 Abel Aganbegyan, *Inside Perestroika: The Future of the Soviet Economy* (New York: Harper and Row, 1989).

67 Mikhail Gorbachev, *Perestroika: New Thinking for Our Country and the World* (New York: HarperCollins, 1987).

The great Bolshevik experiment to construct a Marxist centrally planned paradise ended almost unnoticed with a whimper rather than a bang in 1987 when Gorbachev introduced the "New Law on the Enterprise," relieving red directors of their plan obligations.[68] This action transformed the Soviet economy virtually overnight without adequate preparation or warning into an inchoate market system, doomed to collapse in the early 1990s, either by Gorbachev's design or by his fecklessness.[69]

Table 14. USSR Comparison of CIA Estimates of Overall Growth With Official and Unofficial Soviet Estimates, 1961-87

	Percent average annual rates					
	CIA Estimates		National Income Produced		National Income Used	
	GNP a	NMP b	Official c	Selyunin and Khanin d	Official e	Aganbegyan f
1951-60	5.2	6.7	10.3	7.2	NA	NA
1961-65	4.8	4.9	6.5	4.4	5.7	NA
1966-70	4.9	5.2	7.8	4.1	7.2	5.5
1971-75	3.0	3.3	5.7	3.2	5.1	3.9
1976-80	1.9	1.8	4.3	1.0	3.8	2.1
1981-85	1.8	1.6	3.6	0.6	3.1	0.3
1986-87	2.7	2.4	3.2	2.0	2.4	NA
1951-85	3.8	4.3	6.9	3.9	NA	NA
1966-85	2.9	3.0	5.3	2.2	4.8	2.9

a) Based on value added at 1982 factor cost.
b) GNP excluding services that do not contribute directly to material

*Percent average **annual** rates*

Measures of Soviet Gross National Product in 1982 Prices, Joint Economic Committee of Congress, Washington, DC, 1990.

---

[68]   CIA, "'Restructuring' the Workplace: The New State Enterprise Law," SOV 87-10931, May 1987. (Confidential, but later declassified).

[69]   Steven Rosefielde and Stefan Hedlund, *Russia Since 1980* (Cambridge: Cambridge University Press, 2009); Steven Rosefielde, *The Kremlin Strikes Back: Russia and the West after Crimea's Annexation* (Cambridge: Cambridge University Press, 2016).

The verdict of history

Communist central planning is dead everywhere, except North Korea, where Kim Jong Un appears devoted to Stalin's impoverished superpower paradigm.[70] The verdict of history for those who prefer affluence, democracy, civil liberties, justice, and social wellbeing however is decisively negative. Top-down command communism, contrary to Marx and Engels' steadfast conviction, failed to prove its mettle. It turned out to be an oppressive economic system capable of producing guns, but little butter at immense human cost, despite its positive macro-economic characteristics: overfull employment, price stability, modest growth, and a Spartan social safety net.

The verdict of history is clear on other contentious issues too. Historical dialectic did not culminate in the ineluctable worldwide victory of communism. The class struggle did not enthrone the proletariat, and the working class does not appear poised to sweep capitalism into the ash heap of history. Marx and Engels had prophesized that communism would be a liberating, tolerant, prosperous, harmonious, peaceful, classless. stateless, democratic, and global society, where every individual freely and cooperatively maximizes his and her human potential. It was supposed to be heaven on earth. Twentieth century communist rulers tried mightily to create their versions of communist paradise, but their effort was in vain. Communism's meager economic, social and humanistic achievements did not compensate the losses caused by the Bolsheviks anti-democratic seizure of power, its criminalization of private property, markets and entrepreneurship, its repression of civil liberties, suppression of religion,[71] promotion of the anti-family "free love" movement,[72] Gulag forced labor, mass terror killings and structural militarization. Social romantic idealism and the ardent pursuit of communist justice proved to be profoundly counter-productive. The ends achieved in the final analysis did not justify the means. They were dystopic.

---

[70] Nicholas Eberstadt however recently argued that North Korea is moving to phase out central planning. See Nicholas Eberstadt, "The Method in North Korea's Madness," *Commentary*, January 16, 2018. https://www.commentarymagazine.com/articles/method-north-koreas-madness/.

[71] Daniel Peris, *Storming the Heavens: The Soviet League of the Militant Godless* (Ithaca, NY: Cornell University Press, 1998).

[72] Petr Svab, "The Failed Soviet Experiment With 'Free Love': Communists Made a Disastrous Attempt at Replacing Family with the State," *Epoch Times*, April 14, 2017. https://www.theepochtimes.com/the-failed-communist-experiment-with-free-love_2242535.html.

This dismal result was more than bad luck. Marx and Engels' utopia was always impossible. Lenin, Kim, Mao, Ho and Pol Pot obeyed their masters' voices, but Marx and Engels' fairy tale could not happen. It did not happen and it will never happen, yet the "best and the brightest" still refuse to accept this severe verdict.[73]

This time will be different

Marx and Engel's communism was a flop. Militant leftists however still are not discouraged. They insist that critics overstate the grimness of top-down command planned communism and understate it compensating virtues,[74] contending that it was better, warts and all, than open societies with democratic free enterprise.[75] Apparently, there is an inexhaustible supply of rationalizations for trying anew to construct a bright shining Marxism-Leninism-Stalinism future in the vain hope that next time will be different.[76]

Conclusion

Karl Marx and Friedrich Engel had an impossible communist dream. It was a soufflé of fanciful musings. The Soviets tried to apply its contradictory principles during "War Communism" 1917–21 with catastrophic results.[77] Stalin sought to achieve better outcomes with terror assisted communist central planning. Khrushchev eliminated terror and launched a treadmill of economic reforms that ended in disaster. Gorbachev dissolved the Soviet Union on December 25, 1991 bringing the Bolshevik revolution to an inglorious conclusion.

---

[73] David Halberstam, *The Best and the Brightest* (New York: Ballantine Books, 1993).

[74] Members of the Communist Party and the siloviki did enjoy compensatory benefits, and many Russians appreciated the benefits of full employment, price stability, and highly subsidized necessities.

[75] Kristen Ghodsee, *Red Hangover: Legacies of Twentieth-Century Communism* (Durham NC: Duke University Press, 2017).

[76] Leon Aron, "Kingdom Come: Millenarianism's Deadly Allure, from Lenin to ISIS Europe and Eurasia, Foreign and Defense Policy," *New York Review of Books*, February 13, 2018; John Rose, "Lenin's 'Left-Wing' Communism: An Infantile Disorder revisited," *International Socialism*, no. 138 (April 2013), http://isj.org.uk/lenins-left-wing-communism-an-infantile-disorder-revisited/.

[77] Steven Rosefielde, *Russian Economy from Lenin to Putin* (New York: Wiley, 2007).

Hostile foreign powers did not defeat Soviet communism. Party leaders terminated the experiment. It was a "mercy" killing. Their judgment however is not binding on others. There is no universally agreed standard of merit. People assess outcomes as they please. Dystopia may be just someone's cup of tea, and it is not surprising that a majority of Russians today are nostalgic for the security that they enjoyed under beggar communism. Humans appear capable of talking themselves into just about anything. No one should be shocked when a new generation of idealists tries again to succeed where Marxist-Leninist-Stalinist top-down command planning failed.

Appendix: Impossibility of perfect planning

Eminent economists like Lord Lionel Robbin contended as early as the 1920s that central planning was impossible because planners could not obtain all the information needed to compute general equilibrium prices and quantities.[78] Their critics did not deny this, but changed the subject. Oskar Lange diverted attention from the impossibility of efficient central planning to the possibility of "market" communism (central planning assisted with an inventory price adjustment mechanism), contending that the impossibility of efficient planning did not matter because "market assisted" centrally planned socialism based on state ownership of the means of production held more promise than capitalism.[79] The modern version of the communist economic calculation debate re-examines the core issues, but goes further taking account of advances in "big data" programming, and the previously excluded problem of communist "externalities." The key points in dispute are:

1. Can central planners use "big data" modern programming methods to compute a **consumer sovereign** competitive equilibrium?
2. Can central planners use "big data" modern programming methods to compute a consumer sovereign competitive equilibrium assisted with an Oscar Lange pricing algorithm?
3. Can central planners use modern programming methods to compute a **Communist Party sovereign** competitive equilibrium and compel managers and distributors to comply with commands and directives?

---

[78] Lionel Robbins, *Economic Planning and the International Order* (London: Macmillan, 1937). Ludwig von Mises, "Economic Calculation in the Socialist Commonwealth," in *Collectivist Economic Planning*, ed. Friedrich A. Hayek (Clifton, NJ: Kelley Publishing, 1975): 87–130.
[79] Oskar Lange, "On the Economic Theory of Socialism: Part One," *The Review of Economic Studies* 4, no. 1 (Oct. 1936): 53–71.

4. Can central planners use modern programming methods to compute a Communist Party or consumer sovereign competitive equilibrium and achieve **compliance** by allowing managers and distributors to profit maximize?

5. Can central planners take into account **externalities**?[80]

6. Can central planners apply the concept of **bounded rationality** to achieve **satisfactory communist outcomes** from the consumers, central planners or Communist Party standpoint? [81]

The answer to all six questions is no for two closely related reasons. First, central planners cannot compute optimal or even satisfactory economic outcomes from the Communist Party, planners or consumers viewpoints. Second, even if they could optimally compute them, irresolvable principal-agent dilemmas would preclude satisfactory results unless principals are content with a pittance.[82]

Let us consider these issues case-by-case:

7. Central planners cannot use "big data" modern programming methods to compute a **consumer sovereign** competitive equilibrium because they cannot ascertain real time consumer utility preference functions. This means that planners cannot serve as perfect consumer agents.[83]

8. Central planners cannot use "big data" modern programming methods to compute a consumer sovereign competitive equilibrium assisted with a Lange's pricing algorithm because Lange's algorithm imposes restrictions on factor pricing, is cumbersome in real time applications and is subject to severe moral hazard.[84]

9. Central planners cannot use "big data" modern programming methods to compute **a Communist Party sovereign** competitive equilibrium because they cannot ascertain real time Communist Party utility preference functions and cannot compel managers to comply ideally with plan directives.

---

[80] Ronald Coase, "The New Institutional Economics," *American Economic Review* 88, no. 2 (May 1998): 72–74.

[81] Herbert Simon, *Models of Man: Social and Rational Mathematical Essays on Rational Human Behavior in a Social Setting* (New York: Wiley, 1957).

[82] Jean Jacques Laffont and Jean Tirole, *A Theory of Incentives in Procurement and Regulation* (Cambridge MA: MIT Press, 1993).

[83] Steven Rosefielde and Ralph W. Pfouts, *Inclusive Economic Theory* (Singapore: World Scientific Publishers, 2014).

[84] Steven Rosefielde, "Competitive Market Socialism Revisited: Impediments to Efficient Price-Fixing," *Comparative Economic Studies* 28, no. 3 (Fall 1986): 17–23.

10. Central planners cannot adequately incentivize managers to comply with bonuses including tying rewards to profits because wages and prices are arbitrarily fixed.

11. Central planners cannot take account of externalities ideally because they lack the requisite real time information on the determinants of individual, central planners and Communist Party wellbeing.

Central planners cannot apply the concept of bounded rationality to achieve satisfactory communist outcomes from the consumer, central planners, and Communist Party standpoints. Imperfect American plenty is better than Soviet shortage.

LOOKING BACK AT THE SOVIET ECONOMIC EXPERIENCE

Peter Rutland

Introduction

More than 25 years after the Soviet collapse, views on the communist experiment are still sharply polarized. For the Right, the trajectory of Russia, China, and their satellite states stands as a sober warning of the dangers of utopian socialist thinking. Many on the Left, even if they now almost all concede that the Soviet experiment was a failure, still believe that the promise of the Bolshevik Revolution, the possibility of a socialist alternative, was nevertheless a worthy aspiration. Many intellectuals remain fascinated by the achievements in art, architecture, film, and science that came out of the Bolshevik drive for modernity.[1]

Some personal history

In 1984 I published a book, *The Myth of the Plan: Lessons of Soviet Planning Experience*, that mounted a Hayekian critique of central planning.[2] At the time I was a graduate student at the University of York, and Britain was deeply polarized over the radical market reforms introduced by Margaret Thatcher, who took power in 1979. I had joined the Labour Party at the age of 16, but the endless political warfare of the 1970s and the opportunity to visit Eastern Europe and the Soviet Union had made me skeptical of the socialist project. Thatcherism represented a revolutionary change of a different sort, and I saw its utility as an intellectual framework to explore the underlying reasons for the Soviet Union's economic stagnation.

---

[1] Owen Hatherley, *Landscapes of Communism* (London: New Press, 2016); Francis Spufford, *Red Plenty* (London: Faber, 2010).

[2] Peter Rutland, *The Myth of the Plan: Lessons of Soviet Planning Experience* (London: Hutchinson, 1984).

The Myth of the Plan was based primarily on secondary literature, leavened by a four-month stint in 1982 as a graduate student at the Georgii Plekhanov Institute of National Economy in Moscow on a British Council fellowship. I was there in November 1982 when Leonid Brezhnev died and was replaced by the former KGB head Yuri Andropov, who responded to the Reagan challenge by raising US-Soviet relations to a new level of confrontation.

At the Plekhanov Institute, where Western scholars were a rarity, I was attached to the department of labor economics, since the ostensible topic of my University of York PhD thesis was labor incentives—chosen in part because it was something for which the Soviet foreign ministry would approve an exchange student from a capitalist country. At that time *kapstrany* students were treated differently than *sotstrany* students: we paid more for museum tickets, but got to shop in the Beriozka dollar stores. Initially I was put in a language class with other foreign students—all Vietnamese. After one day it was decided that my presence was too politically sensitive, so I was removed and given a personal tutor. Later on, my faculty advisor at the Institute explained that he was forbidden from inviting me to his home, but he did introduce me to a couple of "dissident" sociologists, one of whom had been fired from the Academy of Sciences and was then working in the Ministry of Agricultural Machinery Production.

Despite the political neutrality of my topic, I was never allowed to set foot inside a Soviet factory. In previous years, through the Quaker-run International Voluntary Service I had spent my summers working in student labor camps in Eastern Europe, which gave me hands-on experience in a Polish factory, a Hungarian pig farm, a Czech archaeological dig, and a Bulgarian construction site. Those experiences at least gave me some sense of how socialism worked at ground level. Unfortunately, the Soviet Union did not take accept foreigners onto its student work brigades through the exchange, though there were Soviet students on the "Georgi Dimitrov brigade" in Bulgaria, an elite squad from the Higher Komsomol School in Moscow.

The problem with central planning

The main argument of *The Myth of the Plan* was that as a system of economic management central planning was fundamentally flawed, but as a political system, it had considerable advantages. Planning served to consolidate the power of the ruling elite and could achieve certain objectives that were important to the state (industrialization, militarization, modernization), albeit at tremendous cost. Most of the Western scholars writing about the Soviet economy were economists, and their debates revolved around technical issues of savings and growth rates. However, Hayek saw that planning was essentially a *political* process before it was an economic process, involving the stripping of property rights (along with all other rights) from the population.[3] Hayek framed this in purely negative terms, as *The Road to Serfdom*, the title of his 1944 book, whereas my approach was to recognize that it also had some positive features, especially from the point of view of the ruling elite.[4] Those features would enable the Soviet Union to survive for 75 years, and mount a serious challenge to the US for global hegemony.[5]

Planning was a way of dealing with the uncertainties of a market economy, by creating a political hierarchy under a unifying ideology that could discipline and control both the masses and the ruling elite. The plan was a "myth," but it was a necessary and useful myth: it provided an institutional structure for coordinated collective activity, and a legitimating framework for the ruling class. It was also a way for a country's leaders to lengthen the time horizon of decision makers, to ensure the reproduction of the ruling elite beyond the founding generation, and to enable investment in long-term projects that would strengthen the nation. This approach was consonant with the influential 1965 text by Harvard's Samuel Huntington, *Political Order in Changing Societies*.[6] Huntington admired the way that Communist Party rule seemed to stabilize societies undergoing the throes of modernization, when social expectations ran ahead of the economy's capacity to deliver the consumer goods and rewarding jobs that educated people were coming to expect and demand. I was also influenced by the work of Murray Edelman on US policy-making, whose argument is summarized by his book's title: *Political Language: Words That Succeed and Policies That Fail*.[7] Edelman argues that in

[3] On the reception of Hayek in Russia, see Rostislav Kapeliushnikov, "Filosofiia rynka F.A. Khaieka" [F.A. Hayek's market philosophy], *Mirovaia ekonomika i mezhdunarodnye otnosheniia* 12 (1989).

[4] Friedrich Hayek, *The Road to Serfdom* (London: Routledge, 1944).

[5] Peter Rutland and Jeremy Friedman, "Anti-imperialism. The Leninist Legacy and the Fate of World Revolution," *Slavic Review* 76, no. 3 (2017): 591–99.

[6] Samuel Huntington, *Political Order in Changing Societies* (Cambridge, MA: Harvard University Press, 1965).

[7] Murray Edelman, *Political Language: Words That Succeed and Policies That Fail* (New York: Academic Press, 1977).

the United States the rhetoric needed to win elections may not be conducive to the effectiveness of public policy. A similar disconnect between political utility and economic efficiency was present in Soviet communism.

Another important argument in the book was that the Soviet system of political and economic management was so tightly coupled, and so vertically integrated, that the *logic* of the system resisted reform: that it was, essentially, unreformable. In this I parted company with the mainstream of both liberal and socialist critics of Soviet communism, who advocated for "market socialism," whereby some elements of market economics would be grafted onto state ownership of the bulk of the economy. This was the position of my former undergraduate tutor, Włodzimierz Brus.[8] The Hungarian reform economist János Kornai was the most widely-read author on the subject in the 1980s.[9] Kornai identified the problem of the "soft budget constraint" facing the socialist enterprise as key to understanding the dysfunctionality of the planned economy. In *The Myth of the Plan* I argued that Hungary was uniquely placed as an entrepot between West and East, and hence it was unlikely that the (limited) success of market socialism in that country could be extended to the Soviet Union (which was among other things had a population 30 times larger than Hungary).

Many socialists did not want to hear the argument that Soviet planning was failing, or that it was primarily a tool of political control. They were so keen to critique the flaws of capitalism in the developed West and the evils that imperialism had wrought on the Third World that they refused to believe that socialism could be worse. They needed to believe that socialism could be better. In theory of course every system is perfect. The challenge is to look at how the systems work in practice, what East Germany proudly called "actually existing socialism." And the Soviet Union was the most important model of how socialism works. Castro's Cuba, Mao's China and even Pol Pot's Kampuchea all had their adherents in the West, but it was unclear how the lessons of anti-imperialist revolutions in peasant societies could be transferred to the West. My own illusions about Mao's China were dissolved by reading *The Chairman's New Clothes* by Simon Leys, published in English

---

[8]   As an undergraduate at Oxford I was tutored in socialist planning by the distinguished Polish economist Włodzimierz Brus, who was forced to step down from his post as a professor at Warsaw University in 1968 because he was Jewish. See Włodzimierz Brus, *The Market in a Socialist Economy* (London: Routledge Kegan Paul, 1972).

[9]   János Kornai, *Economics of Shortage* (Amsterdam: North Holland, 1980).

in 1977.[10] I had a similar revelatory experience for Stalinism when I read *I Chose Freedom* by Viktor Kravchenko, first published in 1946.[11] Kravchenko was a Soviet official who defected in the middle of World War II while he was on a trip to the US arranging for arms shipments. Kravchenko revealed the mechanics and the magnitude of the 1932 famine in Ukraine. He was denounced by the Left as a liar: he fought (and won) a libel case against the Communist Party newspaper in France.

Many Western intellectuals turned to Yugoslavia's self-management system as a model—about half of all the social science dissertations written on Eastern Europe between 1975 and 1985 were focused on Yugoslavia. Tito's Yugoslavia combined elements of market competition and worker self-management, and was free from the burden of Soviet occupation. (Unfortunately, because of Tito's desire to contain "bourgeois nationalism" it had the highest number of political prisoners in Europe.) It is a bitter irony that this socialist flagship did not survive long beyond the death of its founding father in 1980, and collapsed into a brutal civil war in 1991 that left more than 100,000 dead.

The Myth of the Plan was welcomed by libertarians. The libertarian Open Court Press bought the US rights and printed 3,000 copies, which greatly pleased my UK publisher, Hutchinson. However, it was dismissed as Thatcherite propaganda by socialists, including in a review published by *Soviet Studies*, the premier area studies journal of the time.[12] It is easy to forget the extent to which the Soviet Union still had its advocates, including in Britain, right up until its collapse. When I was defending my PhD thesis at the University of York in 1987, one of the external examiners instructed me to remove all references to "totalitarianism" from the manuscript, since it was not a "scientific" concept. I duly did so, and put them back in when the dissertation was published as a book.[13]

My thesis was an examination of the role played by the Communist Party in supervising economic activity. The prevailing model at the time was Jerry Hough's book *The Soviet Prefects* (1969), in which he argued that

[10]   Simon Leys [Pierre Ryckmans], *The Chairman's New Clothes: Mao and the Cultural Revolution* (New York: St. Martin's Press, 1977).

[11]   Viktor Kravchenko, *I Chose Freedom* (New York: Scribner, 1946).

[12]   László Csaba, "Review of *The Myth of the Plan*," *Soviet Studies* 39, no. 1 (1984): 143–146.

[13]   Peter Rutland, *The Politics of Economic Stagnation in the Soviet Union* (Cambridge, UK: Cambridge University Press, 1992).

the Soviet Union was becoming a technocracy and hence converging on Western corporatism. In contrast, I argued that ideology continued to play an important role in the recruitment and operations of the Soviet elite, based on a data base I compiled of biographies of regional Communist Party officials 1975–85 and a close reading of party journals and newspapers during that period. There were just as many "reds" as "experts" being promoted up the Communist Party hierarchy, and the party continued to spend a lot of time on ideological work. Moreover, I argued based on detailed case studies of agriculture, construction, and other sectors that party interventions were having a negative long-term impact on economic development. By the time the book came out (1992) the argument was moot, since both the Communist Party of the Soviet Union and the central planning system that it operated had disappeared from the face of the earth. It would be an object of study for future historians, not contemporary political scientists. (Fortunately, I received tenure in 1992.)

The Soviet system went from stagnation to collapse in a breathtakingly short period of time, from 1985 to 1991. This was unprecedented and unexpected, but with the benefit of hindsight there is no great mystery about why it happened. Mikhail Gorbachev's efforts to reform the economic system ran into opposition from conservative bureaucrats, but were sufficient to destabilize the central planning machinery. His political reforms—the introduction of limited press freedom and competitive elections—undermined the legitimacy of the Communist Party, which played an essential role in keeping the plan running. This argument is convincingly laid out by Michael Ellman and Vladimir Kontorovich in their 1998 book, *The Destruction of the Soviet Economic System*.[14] Of course, exogenous factors also played an important role: the collapse in the international oil price, the worker unrest in Poland, the military impasse in Afghanistan, and the new arms race triggered by Reagan's Star Wars initiative.

The disappearance of the Soviet Union and communist China's embrace of elements of market capitalism did not convince most Western intellectuals of the advantages of capitalism. Even today, Reaganism and Thatcherism are synonyms for evil on the Left, who believe that their ideas have become globally hegemonic since the collapse of the Soviet alternative and the rise of

---

[14] Michael Ellman and Vladimir Kontorovich, *The Destruction of the Soviet Economic System* (Armonk, NY: M.E. Sharpe, 1998).

"neoliberalism."[15] But for mainstream thinkers, "The discussion has moved away from 'more' or 'less' government towards the relative efficiency and effectiveness of different governments in providing public goods, from law and order to health and education and forms of social insurance."[16]

Critiques of the Hayekian critique

Re-reading (and occasionally teaching) *The Myth of the Plan* 35 years later, I still find myself agreeing with most of its arguments. Not that much new scholarship on the Soviet economy appeared in the 1990s and 2000s: most scholars of comparative economic systems shifted their attention to the challenge of transition economics, or to China, and left the Soviet past for the next generation of historians. The new scholarship, based on archival research and interviews with former Soviet officials, mostly confirms that the free market critique of Soviet planning was correct, for example Paul Gregory's *The Political Economy of Stalinism: Evidence from the Soviet Secret Archives* (2003), or Martin Kragh's 2013 article, "The Soviet Enterprise: What Have We Learned from the Archives?"[17] Recent years have seen a modest upsurge of interest in researching the Soviet economy. The new findings add nuance and depth, but do not fundamentally alter the picture. For example, Christopher Miller argues that opposition from conservative bureaucrats doomed Mikhail Gorbachev's reform efforts, while Joachim Zwejnert stresses the deep anti-market thinking of Soviet academic economists.[18] Benjamin Peters explains that efforts to introduce a computer network to automate decision making collapsed in the face of a policy process that was informal and conflict-ridden.[19] It was blocked by military bureaucrats who saw it as

---

[15] David Harvey, *A Brief History of Neoliberalism* (Oxford, UK: Oxford University Press, 2007); Naomi Klein, *The Shock Doctrine: The Rise of Disaster Capitalism* (Toronto: Vintage Books, 2007).

[16] Erik Berglof and Gerard Roland, *The Economics of Transition* (London: Palgrave Macmillan, 2006), 9.

[17] Paul R. Gregory, *The Political Economy of Stalinism: Evidence from the Soviet Secret Archives* (Cambridge, UK: Cambridge University Press, 2004); Martin Kragh, "The Soviet Enterprise: What Have We Learned from the Archives?" *Enterprise & Society* 14, no. 2 (2013): 360–394.

[18] Christopher Miller, *The Struggle to Save the Soviet Economy* (Chapel Hill: University of North Carolina Press, 2016); Joachim Zwejnert, *When Ideas Fail: Economic Thought, the Failure of Transition and the Rise of Institutional Instability in Post-Soviet Russia* (New York: Routledge, 2017).

[19] Benjamin Peters, *How Not to Network a Nation: The Uneasy Experience of the Soviet Internet* (Cambridge, MA: MIT Press, 2017).

a power-grab by the civilian sectors,[20] by civilian administrators who saw it as a threat to their discretionary power,[21] and by rivalry between the two main research institutes in Kyiv and Moscow.[22]

Four lines of argument have emerged that question some of the analysis in *The Myth of the Plan*. First, Vladimir Kontorovich castigates the established literature on the Soviet command economy for mostly ignoring the military sector—despite the fact that the military was a top priority of the state and probably accounted for 25% of Soviet GDP (and 75% of R&D).[23] Kontorovich systematically examines all the Western textbooks on the Soviet economy from the 1960s through 1980s and, astonishingly, finds very little coverage of the military-industrial complex. His critique holds true for *The Myth of the Plan*: there is no chapter or section on the military economy, and it is not in the index. Kontorovich does not accept the counter-argument that there was insufficient material available on Soviet defense plants to conduct an analysis. Information about all sectors of the Soviet economy was tightly controlled, and one could have tried to develop an analysis of the defense sector based on the same techniques of reading between the lines of official publications that we used to study any other aspect of Soviet society. That said, I take Kontorovich's critique as a friendly amendment, in that including the military sector would merely reinforce my central argument about the way that the planning system served the state's goals rather than general welfare.

Second, there is the argument advanced by Simon Kordonski and others that the Soviet economy was really a market economy all along.[24] The pervasiveness of *blat* (connections) and *tolkachi* (fixers) meant that there was an entire parallel economy fused with the official economy, and the latter cannot be understood without the former. Alena Ledeneva has developed this argument from a sociological perspective, in a series of books tracking the evolution of the informal economy from Soviet planning to Putinism.[25]

---

[20]   Peters, *How Not to Network a Nation*, 144.

[21]   Peters, *How Not to Network a Nation*, 154.

[22]   Peters, *How Not to Network a Nation*, 140.

[23]   Vladimir Kontorovich, *Reluctant Cold Warriors: Economists and National Security* (New York: Oxford University Press, 2019).

[24]   Simon Kordonski, *Rynki vlasti: administrativnye rynki SSSR i Rossii* [Markets of power: Administrative markets of the USSR and Russia] (Moscow: OGI, 2000); Vitalii Naiishul', *Drugaia zhizn'* [Another life] (Moscow: 1985), https://www.e-reading.club/bookreader.php/40881/Naiishul%27_-_Drugaya_zhizn%27.html.

[25]   Alena Ledeneva, *Russia's Economy of Favours: Blat, Networking and Informal Exchange* (Cambridge, UK: Cambridge University Press, 2006).

These points are valid and interesting, but not new. Classic texts on the Soviet economy from the 1950s and 1960s by scholars such as Joseph Berliner, Alec Nove, and Michael Kaser all drew attention to this phenomenon. Informal networks complemented the planned economy and were essential to its functioning, but they did not mean that it was a market economy.

Shifting the emphasis from planning to informal networks is a new twist on the old "convergence hypothesis": the argument that the spread of large bureaucratic institutions (an expanding welfare state, huge multinational corporations, etc.) meant that even the developed capitalist economies were coming to resemble centrally-planned economies. Thatcherism, we are told, was not so much about shrinking the size and influence of the state sector but as about changing the character of the state-business interaction. The agenda was not deregulation but re-regulation, aimed to improve the functioning of the nation's firms and workers in the global market economy, but not displace the logic of the market.[26]

This leads on to a third argument, that the Soviet economy was globally integrated and is best seen as a state capitalist economy, one that was responding to the overarching logic of global capital. While I would not deny that it is useful to think about the world as a single integrated system, it is also important to develop a taxonomy that differentiates between its constituent parts. In his book *Red Globalization* Oscar Sanchez-Sibony correctly notes that Soviet leaders did seek out trading partners and were heavily dependent on Western technology imports.[27] However, this does not alter the fact that the bulk of Soviet economic activity took place under rules of operation very different from those of a market economy. Also, most Soviet foreign trade took place with its East European satellites and was subject to a political rather than market logic. The same is true of Soviet arms sales to states like Vietnam, Iraq, Syria, and even India (where accounts were cleared in barter counter-trade: tea and flip flops for MiG fighters).

Finally, there is the argument that Russia's disastrous economic performance of the 1990s puts the deficiencies of central planning into perspective. The relevant comparison, some would argue, is not between Soviet central

---

[26]   Philip G. Cerny, "The Competition State Today: From *Raison d'etat* to *Raison du Monde*," *Policy Studies* 31, no. 1 (2010): 5–21.

[27]   Oscar Sanchez-Sibony, *Red Globalization: The Political Economy of the Soviet Cold War from Stalin to Khrushchev* (Cambridge, UK: Cambridge University Press, 2015). See also Kragh, "The Soviet Enterprise," 369.

planning and US capitalism, but between Soviet planning and Russia's "wild capitalism" of the Yeltsin years and crony capitalism of the Putin era. Certainly, many Russians have developed a sense of nostalgia for the Soviet past: as of 2018, 66% said they regretted the collapse of the USSR (and 25% did not).[28] There is a widespread sense among the Russian public that the Soviet economy performed better than its capitalist successor in terms of providing the basic necessities of life and protecting the population from the vicissitudes of market risk. Some Western scholars have picked up this theme, developing a harsh critique of the evils of "shock therapy."[29] It is indeed true that the Soviet model performed better than post-soviet capitalism in a broad range of indicators, from gender equality to mortality rate.

Be that as it may, one cannot re-run history. Certainly it is possible to imagine a world in which the Soviet Union did not collapse, where communist rule continued into the twenty-first century, as in China, Cuba and North Korea. Dimitry Shlapentokh dubbed this the "Andropov's kidney" theory, since it was kidney disease that removed Andropov from this world in 1984 at the age of 69, after serving just 16 months as General Secretary.[30] However, in the real world the Soviet system did disintegrate, and as Putin himself said: "those who do not regret the collapse of the Soviet Union have no heart, and those that want to bring it back have no head."[31] There is little point speculating about a counter-factual parallel universe in which perestroika worked, or Russia became Sweden overnight.

As for the lessons of Russia's unfortunate experience with "shock therapy," it is important to remember that in the early 1990s, there were no easy choices facing the new Russian government, and it is by no means the case that they mindlessly implemented a neoliberal agenda forced on them by international lenders. The political economy of the Russian transition repeated one of the central themes of *The Myth of the Plan*: the priority of politics over economics.[32] As Matthew May put it, "the urgency to divest the state of major industrial

---

[28] "Nostal'giya po SSSR, [Nostalgia for the USSR]," Levada Center, 19 December 2018. https://www.levada.ru/2018/12/19/nostalgiya-po-sssr-2/.

[29] Harvey, *Neoliberalism*; Klein, *Shock Doctrine*.

[30] Cited in Kontorovich, *Reluctant Cold Warriors*.

[31] The English language version of this quote on the Kremlin website mistranslates the Russian original. Vladimir Putin, "Interview with German television channels ARD and ZTF," *Kremlin.ru*, 5 May 2005. http://en.kremlin.ru/events/president/transcripts/22948.

[32] Peter Rutland, "Neoliberalism in Russia," *Review of International Political Economy* 20, no. 2 (2013): 332–362.

sectors was political (to make change irreversible) not economic (to make things work better)."[33] Academics at the time assumed that "politics" merely meant forestalling worker unrest and winning elections. They overlooked the need to forge a consolidated ruling elite, which in the Russian case was accomplished through corrupt self-dealing: using the privatization of state assets to secure the loyalty of the rising entrepreneurial class, while buying off bureaucratic holdovers from the ancient regime who could have derailed the reform program.

Lessons of the post-soviet transition

This final section turns from the past to the present and the future. The fall of the Soviet Union took the wind out of the sails of advocates for hyper-centralized planning, which is a good thing. However, as I wrote in *The Myth of the Plan*, the myth of the plan should not be replaced by the myth of the market. The market economy has its own set of negative externalities that demand redress through active political interventions by state and society. The corruption of political elites and rising social inequality within countries (even as inequalities across countries decline) means that the risks of state capture by self-serving elites are present even in mature market societies with democratic political institutions. Neoliberalism is a somewhat vague and contradictory set of policy prescriptions—it advocates the retreat of the state at the same time as the state is expected to guarantee property rights and the smooth functioning of competitive capitalism (not to mention social stability).[34]

Take the case of Britain itself, the birthplace of Thatcherism. In June 2017 fire broke out in the 24-story Grenfell Tower, an apartment block housing poor council tenants in Kensington and Chelsea, the richest borough of London and home to some of the world's wealthiest people.[35] Residents had been instructed to stay put in their apartments in the event of a fire, but the fire brigade was unable to contain the blaze and 71 people died. The

---

[33] Personal communication from Matthew May, Canberra.

[34] Melinda Cooper, "Complexity Theory after the Financial Crisis: The Death of Neoliberalism or the Triumph of Hayek?" *Journal of Cultural Economy* 4, no. 4 (2011): 371–85; Matthew Eagleton-Pierce, *Neoliberalism: The Key Concepts* (London: Routledge, 2016).

[35] "Grenfell Tower enquiry," *The Guardian*, September 2020. https://www.theguardian.com/uk-news/grenfell-tower-inquiry.

fire spread so quickly due to the flammable aluminum cladding which had been installed the previous year, despite warnings that it was unsafe. The inflammable version had been rejected because it cost $3 more per square meter. Building safety regulations had been weakened by successive British governments, including Tony Blair's Labour Government. Apart from the flammable cladding, which is banned in the US and Germany in high-rise buildings, the tower had only one fire escape, and no sprinklers (both illegal in buildings of that type in New York City, for example). There are dozens of towers with flammable cladding across the UK.

Housing is not the only example of the perils of deregulation. The British railway system, privatized under Thatcher, is in chaos.[36] On the one hand, train traffic has increased by 135% since privatization, but it still requires state subsidies (5 pence per passenger kilometer), and successive private operators of major routes have gone bankrupt due to excessively optimistic profit projections.

The most striking example of the need to constantly reassess the relationship between the state and the market is the remarkable success of China, which has enjoyed more than three decades of rapid growth, raising more than 400 million people out of poverty. It has done this by preserving many features of state planning while carefully opening the economy to market forces, producing an uneasy if not baffling hybrid held together by a hard authoritarian regime. By plunging into the international division of labor China was able to take advantage of the technological innovations and productivity surge that accompanied the wave of globalization of the 1980s and 1990s. They succeeded despite lacking some of the core features of a traditional market economy—such as rule of law and secure property rights. The China case shows that smart state dirigisme can still work.

Why did China succeed while the Soviet Union failed?[37] In part it was because Beijing was able to learn from the mistakes (as they saw them) of the Soviet leadership. First, they concluded that allowing political reform to run ahead of economic reform was dangerous to social stability. Second, they saw the dangers of over-centralization and the importance of deconcentration,

---

[36] Josh Spero, "Spending Watchdog Hits Out at 'Broken' Rail Franchise System," *Financial Times*, April 26, 2018. https://www.ft.com/content/ecd57816-493a-11e8-8ae9-4b5ddcca99b3.

[37] I tried to tackle this question in Peter Rutland, "Post-socialist States and the Evolution of a New Development Model: Russia and China Compared," in *Post-Communist Transformations*, eds. Tadayuki Hayashi and Atsushi Ogushi (Sapporo: Slavic Research Center, 2009): 49–72.

allowing experiments at regional level. Structural factors also came into play of course—the fact that Russia's comparative advantage in the global economy seems to lie in resource extraction, while China's lay in a vast pool of cheap labor (a pool which has now run dry, raising questions over whether China can smoothly transition to a high value-added economy).

Concluding thoughts

Debates about planning did not end with the collapse of the Soviet Union. However, in light of the Soviet experience, it is now much harder to argue that the state can be trusted to step in and provide public goods that are under-supplied due to collective action dilemmas and other reasons. The globalization of recent decades has produced great prosperity and remarkable technological innovations, but it has also increased the level of risk and uncertainty for many layers of society, in all the countries of the world. Generally speaking, few people now believe that we can plan our way out of these existential uncertainties by creating powerful, centralized political hierarchies. Rather, we are looking for solutions that are based on more information, transparency and responsiveness: horizontal networking rather than vertical obedience. Even China, which has turned its back on press freedom and electoral democracy, recognizes the importance of responsiveness to citizen demands.[38]

The failure of the Soviet Union and the success of China underlines the importance of the particularities of culture, history, and location: universal rules for either a planned or a market economy must be customized to suit local conditions. In this process, the quality of political leadership remains a key variable. It is the luck of the draw whether one's country ends up with Nelson Mandela or Robert Mugabe, Kemal Atatürk or Saddam Hussein. The interesting thing about the cases of Russia and China is that they defy these simplistic binaries. Mikhail Gorbachev was not a bloodthirsty tyrant, but he did bring about the destruction of the state that he was trying to protect. Deng Xiaoping oversaw the massacre on Tiananmen Square, but he also made China great again. There is much for historians to ponder in these paradoxes.

---

[38] Chris Heurlin, *Responsive Authoritarianism in China* (Cambridge, UK: Cambridge University Press, 2016).

INCENTIVES, COERCION, AND REDISTRIBUTION

Why Industrial Central Plan Economies Performed Worse Than Western Market Economies and Better Than Less Developed Economies

Michael S. Bernstam

1. Introduction: The tripartite ranking of economic performance

The title of this paper answers the question raised in the subtitle. It explores the hierarchical performance of nations in the twentieth century. The cross-national data assembled in Figures 1 and 2 and Table 1 exhibit the tripartite ranking of economic performance. Western market economies including Japan and the Asian Tigers generated high long-run economic growth. Industrial central plan economies of the Soviet Union and Eastern Europe including Yugoslavia had high medium-run growth in the 1950s-60s and moderate long-run economic growth. Less developed economies and non-industrial central plan economies such as Mao's China lagged behind with low economic growth. These clusters make up Rank 1, Rank 2, and Rank 3, respectively.

The second rank was not transient, nor a stage in economic development. It was a secular fact. Table 1 and Figure 2 show that the income gap between industrial central plan economies and Western market economies had been widening over time. Figures 3, 4, and 5 demonstrate the efficiency gap of industrial central planning. Human capital, fixed capital, technological development, and incentives for technological inventions in industrial central-plan economies were converging with Western market economies, while these two clusters of countries were diverging in economic growth and productivity.

To account for the tripartite ranking, this paper combines two literatures, on incentives and on economic growth. Incentives for technological inventions include intellectual property rights and public subsidies for human capital and R&D. Industrial central plan economies were not deficient on these scores (Figures 3 and 4). Yet even the greatest inventions cannot by themselves feed, clothe, shelter, heat, transport, cure, and otherwise provide for people. Technologies apply to and complement the material production of value-added goods and services through labor, investment, and innovation, including engineering and entrepreneurial innovation. Lagging productivity reveals deficient productive incentives to apply globally available and locally developed technologies to production. This deficiency unites all central plan economies and less developed economies.

Subsidies, bailouts, exactions, non-competitive suppressed and subsidized prices, wages, and profits, and other redistribution of income disable productive incentives. At the margin, some agents receive income without adding value at the expense of other agents who add value without adding income. In biological terms, redistribution is intraspecific kleptoparasitism. Stealing livelihood from members of the same species is widespread in the animalia. For humans, it matters. Income transfer from producers to non-producers impedes production because it creates costs for producers and opportunity costs of production for non-producers and would-be producers. Following Bernier, Smith, and Sah and Stiglitz,[1] Figure 6 shows the high extent of income redistribution in less developed economies, the USSR, and in post-central plan Russia through the channel of factor income transfer. Western market economies and post-central plan China exhibit minimal factor income transfer, which is consistent with their high long-run economic growth. Minimization of income redistribution is necessary for productive incentives.

Industrial central planning is unique. Central planning is shorthand for state-forced production, that is, output quotas and delivery quotas. It includes forced labor, forced investment, and, in the case of industrial central planning, forced engineering innovation, meaning the forced application of technological inventions to the production of material goods and services. Coercion, in short. Coercion can partially substitute for deficient productive incentives. Coercive substitution for productive incentives is partial, never complete. Stiglitz found that this is the principal reason why central planning could never achieve productive efficiency and converge with Western market

---

[1] Francois Bernier, *Travels in the Mogul Empire A.D. 1656–1668* (Westminster: Archibald Constable & Co., [1670] 1891), 238; Adam Smith, *An Inquiry Into the Nature and Causes of the Wealth of Nations*, vol. 1 (Oxford: Claredon Press, [1776] 1976), 111, 91; Raaj Kumar Sah and Joseph E. Stiglitz, "The Economics of the Price Scissors," *American Economic Review* 74, no. 1 (March 1984): 125–38.

economies.[2] Schumpeterian creative destruction from within[3] and entrepreneurial innovation derive from incentives. They cannot be coerced.

Coercion has a negative feedback creating perverse incentives. Firms maximize costs in order to minimize output quotas and to maximize profits under the cost-plus pricing. Ultimately, coercion cannot indemnify the disincentive effect of income transfer.

In the trichotomy of incentives, coercion, and redistribution, countries of the first rank combined technological and productive incentives. Post-central plan China is moving in this direction. Countries of the second rank combined technological incentives and coercion. Coercion partially substituted for productive incentives. Countries of the third rank lacked both technological and productive incentives in which case coercion was ineffective. It could not help non-industrial central plan economies break out of the less developed rank. Post-central plan Russia is moving in this direction.

The next section presents data on economic growth, productivity, technological development, labor, human capital, and fixed capital, by ranks of countries. The third section discusses incentives and application of technology to production across ranks of countries. The concluding section summarizes why central plan economies could never converge with the West.

2. Economic growth, productivity, technology, and factor inputs across ranks

This section documents the tripartite ranking and the efficiency gap of industrial central planning. The USSR and Eastern Europe were converging with Western market economies in technological inventions, human capital, and fixed capital and diverging in economic growth and productivity.

2.1. The data

The data in this paper covers a cross-section of 133 countries in 1988 to 164 countries in 1990, circa the end of industrial central planning in the USSR and Eastern Europe. To widen the sample, I use as separate countries in 1990 the republics of the soon-to-be-former Soviet Union, Yugoslavia, and

---

[2]   Joseph E. Stiglitz, "Incentives, Information, and Organizational Design," *Empirica* 16, no. 1: 3–29, Joseph E. Stiglitz, *Whither Socialism?* (Cambridge: The MIT Press, 1994).

[3]   Joseph A. Schumpeter, *Capitalism, Socialism and Democracy* (New York and London: Harper & Brothers, 1942), 82–83.

Czechoslovakia while retaining the former East Germany. The data also covers the time series for groups of countries and individual large countries for one hundred years, 1900–1999.

The data derives from several standard sources independent from one another. These are the Penn World Table, the Maddison Project, and the U.N. Division of Statistics. Specific versions and series are cited in Figures 1 through 6 and Table 1. The data on human and fixed capital draw on the series assembled by Hall and Jones.[4] The novel addition is the database on technological incentives and technological development across 140 countries compiled from the World Bank, UNESCO, the National Science Foundation, and other sources by the Rand Corporation.[5] I modified it for Figure 3.

The independent cross-national databases and time-series are consistent with one another. Specific observations for some countries, e.g., Czechoslovakia and Poland, differ between sources but the clusters of central plan economies are consistent.

2.2. *The taxonomy and definitions*

Figure 1 compares 164 countries at the end of central planning in 1990. The horizontal axis shows income levels approximated by GDP per capita. The vertical axis records productivity approximated by GDP per worker. Both are natural logarithms of actual values in 2000 dollars.

The rationale for a hierarchical taxonomy beyond income levels is the difference between income levels and economic development. The hydrocarbon economies such as Brunei, Saudi Arabia, and Qatar are rich not from their own economic growth and development. They are the satellites of Western market economies without internal engines of high income. Industrial central plan economies of the Soviet Union and Eastern Europe advanced in terms of technological development, human capital, and fixed capital, but their income levels lagged behind developed Western economies.

To explore economic growth when income and development levels are mismatched, the following taxonomy combines income levels, development levels, and economic systems. All countries are subdivided as developed vs.

4   Robert E. Hall and Charles I. Jones, "The Productivity of Nations," NBER Working Paper 5812 (Cambridge, MA: NBER, 1996).
5   Caroline S. Wagner, Irene T. Brahmakulam, Brian A. Jackson, Anny Wong, and Tatsuro Yoda. *Science and Technology Collaboration: Building Capacity in Developing Counties* (Santa Monica, CA: The Rand Corporation, 2001).

less developed and as market vs. central plan economies. This exercise yields four substantive classes of developed Western market economies, industrial central plan economies, non-industrial central plan economies, and less developed market economies.

Developed economies		Less developed economies	
Western developed	Industrial	Non-industrial	Less developed
Market economies	Central-plan economies		Market economies

In addition, there is a fifth, auxiliary class of satellite hydrocarbon economies. The five classes are marked by different symbols and colors in Figure 1 and thereafter. This taxonomy captures the real world. The five classes form five distinct empirical clusters in Figure 1 and thereafter.

Western market economies and less developed economies, to shorten both designations, separate by income levels matching their development levels. The income benchmark is empirical. It is twice the world average per capita GDP at purchasing power parity. In 1990, it was 10,000 in 2000 dollars. This is $15,000 in 2020 dollars. Western market economies include all Western European countries, the US, Canada, Australia, New Zealand, Japan, the Asian Tigers, and Israel. All but one (South Korea) had achieved per capita GDP at least twice that of the benchmark.

The cluster of less developed economies consists of countries below the $10,000 benchmark, with no exceptions. Several upper-tier countries such as Mauritius, Argentina, South Africa, Chile, Uruguay, Turkey, and Malaysia were close to the benchmark, but still never converged with Western market economies. This empirical relationship continued into the twenty-first century.[6] The great divergence remains intact for 250 years since the onset of the Industrial Revolution.

The cluster of industrial central plan economies consists of the USSR and Eastern Europe, including their soon-to-be independent constituent parts. The cluster of non-industrial central plan economies covers China before 1977, Albania, Mongolia, Vietnam, Laos, Cambodia, Cuba, Nicaragua, Ethiopia, Angola, and Mozambique. The difference between these two classes pertains to the level of development rather than income. Less than 25 percent of GDP derives from agriculture in the industrial group and more than 25 percent in

---

[6]   World Bank, *World Development Indicators*, 1 July 2020, http://databank.worldbank.org/data/download/GNIPC.pdf.

the non-industrial group. By the level of GDP per capita, all non-industrial central plan economies were significantly below the $10,000 benchmark in 1990, on par with less developed economies. Industrial central plan economies were either above the $10,000 benchmark in 1990 or somewhat below.

The principal dichotomy is that of market versus central-plan economies. In contrast to central planning, one can define market economies as voluntary production for voluntary exchange across the supply chains. This class can range from complete laissez-faire (free markets) under limited government to regulated economies under restrictive government in conjunction with various extent of private and state property on productive assets of fixed capital and land. Its singular defining criterion is voluntary production for the market. Its economic growth depends on incentives, not coercion.

Central planning is enforced through output quotas and delivery quotas. It is defined as the state-forced production for the state-forced delivery across the supply chains. It includes forced labor, forced investment, and, at higher stages of development, forced engineering innovation and application of technological inventions to production. Its singular defining feature is enforcement and coercion instead of voluntary productive incentives.

Incentives convey the impetus of voluntary production for the market. Incentives can be defined as a rational response of agents to benefits and costs including the opportunity costs.

2.3. Income levels and productivity across ranks in 1990

Figure 1 shows that industrial central plan economies overlap with several lower-tier Western market economies such as Portugal and Greece and several upper-tier less developed economies such as Mauritius, Argentina, and South Africa. The high ratio of GDP per capita to GDP per worker in industrial central-plan economies implies their very high labor force participation rate. Yet, after decades of rapid development, they never caught up with advanced Western market economies. As a cluster, they scatter below the majority of Western market and above the majority of less developed economies.

2.4. The growth paths, 1900–99, and rates, 1950–89

Nations' income levels in 1990 in Figure 1 comprise their cumulative growth rates ab initio. Figure 2 shows that growth paths of income levels throughout the twentieth century differ by economic systems. It plots by major countries and groups the natural log values of annual per capita GDP in 1900–99 at purchasing power parity in 1990 dollars.

Western market economies demonstrate high long-run economic growth. The US was consistently the technological frontier. The twelve Western European countries were catching up after World War II. Japan's post-war convergence from the low level was especially rapid. The upper-tier less developed economies, the eight Latin American countries, exhibited moderate economic growth throughout the twentieth century. By the end of the century, their divergence from Western market economies widened. Of the lower-tier less developed countries, India grew slowly until 1980 and accelerated thereafter.

China was stagnant before central planning. It exhibited low economic growth as a non-industrial central plan economy in 1950–76, with the disaster of the Great Leap Forward in 1958–63 and another fall in 1966–71, during the first stage of the Cultural Revolution. After the end of central planning in 1977, China launched rapid economic growth outstripping India and many other less developing countries and greatly outpacing former industrial central plan economies.

Industrial central plan economies of the USSR and Eastern Europe generated high medium-run and moderate long-run economic growth. The USSR saw periods of high growth after the onset of industrialization in the 1930s and in the 1950s–60s. Yugoslavia embarked upon rapid economic growth in the 1950s–1970s. The income levels of both were below the upper-tier Latin American countries before and at the beginning of central planning and above since the mid-1950s in the USSR and since the mid-1970s in Yugoslavia. However, they never replicated Japan's feat of exceptionally high growth and were not on the convergence path with Western market economies. Under central planning, Czechoslovakia and Hungary accelerated economic growth in the medium term until the mid-1970s and slowed down thereafter. The USSR decelerated in the mid-1970s and Yugoslavia in the 1980s. By the end of central planning in 1989, the USSR and Eastern Europe widened their income gap with Western market economies. After the end of central planning, the former USSR and the former Yugoslavia contracted in the 1990s below the Latin American levels and the world average.

Table 1 enumerates the tripartite ranking of economic performance and the dynamics of convergence and divergence in 1950–89. To pinpoint the high medium-run and moderate long-run economic growth of industrial central plan economies, the table singles out the period 1950–73 from the entire 1950–89.

The data shows that both during the higher-growth years 1950–73 and the entire growth period 1950–89, Western European economies and especially Japan grew faster than the USSR and Eastern European economies. The US as the technological frontier had slower growth, close to the world average. Both Western market economies except the US and industrial central plan economies grew faster than the world average. Various groups of less developed economies such as the eight upper-tier Latin American countries, East Asian countries, India, and Africa grew slower than the world average and slower than industrial central plan economies. China also grew slower in 1950–73 but faster for the entire period 1950–89, due to rapid growth after ending central planning in 1977.

Table 1 shows increasing divergence of industrial central plan economies from Western market economies. In 1950–73, Eastern European countries grew almost as fast as Western European, but the gap significantly widened thereafter during the slowdown. Less developed and non-industrial central plan economies lagged further behind. The data in both Figure 2 and table 1 reinforce this tripartite ranking of economic performance over the long run. It is not a transient artefact of economic development but a systemic dynamic phenomenon.

2.5. Technological development and incentives for invention

In a survey of several decades of cross-national empirical studies of economic growth, Hsieh and Klenow summarized the following consensus.[7] The differences of hours worked and thus of labor input are small across countries. Differences in fixed capital account for 20 percent of income level differences. Differences in human capital account for 10–30 percent of country income differences. The residual multifactor productivity can explain as much as 50–70 percent of income level differences between countries.

Technology constitutes an essential part of multifactor productivity. It consists of technical progress, inventions, and technological development. Figure 3 juxtaposes the data on national productivity and technology for 140 countries for which the data is jointly available. The vertical axis is the

---

[7]   Chang-Tai Hsieh and Peter J. Klenow, "Development Accounting," *American Economic Journal: Macroeconomics* 2, no. 1 (January 2010): 207–23.

same natural log of GDP per worked as in Figure 1. The horizontal axis is the Modified Index of Science and Technology (MIST). It modifies the Rand Corporation's Index of Science and Technology Capacity (ISTC) prepared for the World Bank.[8] Both indexes are weighted measures of several variables. Each variable is measured as the number of standard deviations from the global mean. The resulting index is weighted by the contribution of each variable to the total in the US

MIST includes five variables: 1) the number of scientists and engineers in research and development per million population in 1997–2000 based on the data from the World Bank and UNESCO; 2) the number of science and technology articles published in 1995–97 based on the data from the US National Science Foundation and UNESCO; 3) expenditures on research and development as percent of GNP in various years in 1987–97 based on the World Bank data; 4) the number of scientific teaching and non-teaching research institutions per million population based on the data from the World Bank and the Gale Group before 2000; and 5) the total number of US patents filed in 1995–99 and the European Patent Office patents filed in 1992–94 by a given country's citizens, based on the data from US and European patent agencies.

MIST captures domestic inventions, the production of ideas rather than adoption of global technologies, a mere use of foreign ideas. MIST includes expenditures on R&D, the share of scientists and engineers in population, research institutions, and Western patents for non-Western nationals. These inputs embody the very incentives for technological inventions such as intellectual property rights and subsidies for R&D and human capital that constitute a necessary condition of high long-run economic growth.[9]

---

[8] Caroline S. Wagner, Irene T. Brahmakulam, Brian A. Jackson, Anny Wong, and Tatsuro Yoda. *Science and Technology Collaboration.* MIST excludes from ISTC two variables not applicable to closed central plan economies.

[9] Kenneth J. Arrow, "The Economic Implication of Learning by Doing," *Review of Economic Studies* 29, no. 3 (June 1962): 155–73; Kenneth J. Arrow, "Economic Welfare and the Allocation of Resources for Invention," in *The Rate and Direction of Inventive Activity: Economic and Socials Factors* (Princeton: Princeton University Press, 1962), 609–25; William D. Nordhaus, *Invention, Growth, and Welfare: A Theoretical Treatment of Technological Change* (Cambridge: The MIT Press, 1969); William D. Nordhaus, "Schumpeterian Profits in the American Economy: Theory and Measurement," NBER Working Paper 10433 (Cambridge, MA: NBER, 2004); Paul M. Romer, "Increasing Returns and Long-Run Growth," *Journal of Political Economy* 94, no. 5 (October 1986): 1002–37; Paul M. Romer, "Endogenous Technological Change," *Journal of Political Economy* 98, no. 5, part. 2 (October 1990): S71–S102; Paul M. Romer, "Two Strategies

The data in figure 3 shows consistent clusters. All Western market economies are above the weighted global mean, to the right from zero on the horizontal axis, except Greece and Hong Kong, which are slightly lower. All less developed economies except South Africa are below the weighted global mean within a narrow gap but their productivity is greatly scattered. This shows that Parente and Prescott are precise saying that their performance depends primarily on how deficient are their incentives to adopt globally available technologies, not so much on inventing their own new technologies.[10] All satellite hydrocarbon economies are below the mean, which demonstrates that their riches are foreign-made. All non-industrial central plan economies except Cuba are below the weighted global mean. China is almost at the mean after ten-to-twenty years since the end of the Cultural Revolution and must be above the mean by 2020.

Most industrial central plan economies are above the weighted global mean except Bosnia, Macedonia, Georgia, and Moldova. Figure 3 shows that in terms of technological development and its incentives, industrial central plan economies overlap with Western market countries except the most advanced. They were converging with Western market economies in technological development while diverging in productivity and income levels.

2.6. Human capital

Figure 4 examines the human capital data for 133 countries in 1988.[11] The vertical axis contains the same summary variable as previous figures, namely log GDP per worker. The horizontal axis reports a corresponding measure, log of human capital per worker. The US serves as the benchmark. The values of both variables are measured in terms of differences from the US.

---

for Economic Development: Using Ideas and Producing Ideas," in *Proceedings of the World Bank Annual Conference on Development Economics 1992* (Washington, D.C.: The World Bank, 1993): 63–91; Paul M. Romer, "Idea Gaps and Object Gaps in Economic Development," *Journal of Monetary Economics* 32, no. 3 (December 1993): 543–73; Paul M. Romer, "The Origins of Endogenous Growth," *Journal of Economic Perspectives* 8, no. 1 (Winter 1994): 3–22; Benjamin F. Jones and Lawrence H. Summers, "A Calculation of the Social Returns to Innovation," NBER Working Paper 27863 (Cambridge, MA: NBER, 2020).

10 Stephen L. Parente and Edward C. Prescott, *Barriers to Riches* (Cambridge: The MIT Press, 2000); Stephen L. Parente and Edward C. Prescott, "A Unified Theory of the Evolution of International Income Levels," in *Handbook of Economic Growth*, vol. 1B, eds. Philippe Aghion and Steven N. Durlauf (Amsterdam and Boston: Elsevier North-Holland, 2005), 1371–1416.

11 The data derives from Hall and Jones, "The Productivity of Nations," 45–47.

In human capital, industrial central plan economies of East Germany, the USSR, Yugoslavia, Hungary, Poland, and Czechoslovakia, with the only exception of Romania, overlap with the majority of Western market economies including the most advanced. They are on par with West Germany, Japan, the U.K., and Hong Kong and are more advanced than France and Spain. All less developed economies and non-industrial central plan economies exhibit lower values of human capital than industrial central plan economies. Figure 4 shows an accomplished convergence of industrial central plan economies with Western market economies in human capital and their sharp divergence in productivity.

2.7. Fixed capital and investment

Bergson calculated "the Communist efficiency gap" in 1975. Holding constant the stock of fixed capital per worker, GDP per worker in the USSR, Yugoslavia, Poland, and Hungary was 29.5–34.3 percent below the average of seven Western European countries.[12] Using independent databases and estimation procedures, Hall and Jones found a similar gap. Figure 5 reproduces their data for 1988 for 133 countries. The vertical axis is log of GDP per worker, the horizontal axis the log of capital stock per worker, both expressed as differences from the US.

East Germany, the USSR, Yugoslavia, Hungary, Poland, and Czechoslovakia converged in fixed capital stock with the lower-tier Western market economies including Greece, Portugal, Hong Kong, Taiwan, and South Korea, but diverged from them and especially from the more advanced Western market economies in GDP per worker.

2.8. Total divergence and the efficiency gap

This section documented two patterns within the tripartite ranking of economic performance. First, less developed economies diverged from Western market economies on total scores. They were deficient in technological incentives and development and in factor inputs of human and fixed capital and whence in the levels of productivity and income. As a cluster, they also lagged behind industrial central plan economies on all these scores.

---

[12]   Abram Bergson, "The Communist Efficiency Gap: Alternative Measures," *Comparative Economic Studies* 36, no. 1 (Spring 1994): 1–12.

Second, industrial central plan economies, to summarize by Romer's criteria, experienced neither idea gaps nor object gaps.[13] They were not deficient in technological incentives, technological development, human capital, and fixed capital and yet lagged behind Western market economies in productivity and income levels. This was not a total divergence but a residual efficiency gap after technology and capital were embodied. The next section tackles this problem.

3. Productive incentives, coercion, and income transfer across ranks

Einstein qualified Occam's razor: "The supreme goal of all theory is to make the irreducible basic elements as simple and as few as possible without having to surrender the adequate representation of a single datum of experience."[14] This is a tall order as the efficiency gap of industrial central plan economies testifies.

Parente and Prescott pointed out a stark fact. Over time, advanced global technologies have become available to all countries to adopt. Counter-productive policies in poor countries block technology adoption, catchup, and economic development.[15] Industrial central plan economies, however, were eager to adopt the most advanced global technological knowledge and tools, in addition to promoting and developing their own. Their policies were to maximize production, albeit by coercion, not by incentives. The broad explanation of the efficiency gap of industrial central plan economies is the failure of the government as the central manager of the economy. The term failure is ontological, not judgmental. It denotes what the government cannot do by the nature of things. The government makes inefficient production decisions on allocation of resources due to information asymmetries in the absence of market prices.[16] This is one part of accounting for the efficiency gap. Another part if deficient innovation and, generally, deficient application of technological inventions to production which the government cannot fully coerce and enforce.

---

[13] Paul M. Romer, "Idea Gaps."
[14] Albert Einstein, "On the Method of Theoretical Physics," Herbert Spencer Lecture, Oxford, June 10, 1933, *Philosophy of Science* 1, no. 2 (April 1934), 165.
[15] Parente and Prescott, *Barriers to Riches*.
[16] Friedrich A. Hayek, "The Use of Knowledge in Society," *American Economic Review* 35, no. 4 (September 1945): 519–30.

Schumpeter distinguished between inventions and innovation.[17] Inventions can be defined as new ideas, invention as the production of new ideas. Innovation can be defined as the engineering and entrepreneurial application of new ideas to the production of goods and services. Application is a broad process. It encompasses materialization of technological and managerial ideas into the production of goods and services through labor, investment in human and fixed capital, and innovation. Application is endogenous. Had it been not so, all countries would have been rich by technological adoption alone.

Be it adoption or domestic technological incentives and development, their application takes either productive incentives or coercion. Stiglitz concluded that central planning by its nature lacked productive incentives.[18] At the same time, coercion could not fully substitute for missing productive incentives. This section brings together the literatures on economic growth and incentives to address this efficiency gap. It singles out income transfer that impairs productive incentives.

3.1. Application of technological inventions to production

Human production is the material application of non-material knowledge. Table 2 offers a schematic summary of how growth models divide and subdivide growth determinants. These are ontological and functional dualities given by nature and the production process.

First is the duality of non-material ideas applied to the production of material goods and services through factor inputs and innovation. Jefferson anticipated it.[19] Romer extended Samuelson's ontological framework to found the endogenous growth theory.[20] For reasons described by Jefferson, non-material ideas are ontologically unlimited (non-rivalrous), that is, each can be simultaneously used as a whole by multiple agents; and they are incompletely excludable and thus generate knowledge spillovers. Their production requires

---

[17] Schumpeter, *Capitalism, Socialism*, 132.

[18] Stiglitz, "Incentives, Information"; Stiglitz, *Wither Socialism?*

[19] Thomas J. Jefferson, in *The Writings of Thomas Jefferson*, eds. Andrew A. Lipscomb and Albert E. Bergh, vol. 13 (Washington: Thomas Jefferson Memorial Association, [1813] 1905), 333–35.

[20] Paul A. Samuelson, "The Pure Theory of Public Expenditure," *Review of Economics and Statistics* 36, no. 4 (November 1954): 387–89; Paul A. Samuelson, "Diagrammatic Exposition of a Theory of Public Expenditure," *Review of Economics and Statistics* 37, no. 4 (November 1955): 350–56; Romer, "Endogenous Technological Change," Romer, "Two Strategies"; Romer, "Idea Gaps"; Romer, "The Origins."

specific incentives for technological invention and R&D. Material goods
and services are ontologically limited (rivalrous), that is, each unit can be
simultaneously used by a single agent only, and they are variably excludable,
meaning they can be used as common goods or as private goods, can be
confiscated or retained, directly or as returns in the form of income.

Production factors and innovation are, by their nature, material goods
and services. The above mentioned ontological duality makes them and
technological inventions complementary. Boskin and Lau and Lau modeled
and empirically demonstrated their complementarity in Western market
and less developed economies.[21] Their complementarity means that they are
non-substitutable and mutually reinforcing. Together, they exhibit increasing
returns. Separately, they run into diminishing returns. Even the greatest labor
effort, human capital accumulation, fixed capital stock, and innovation cannot
substitute for new inventions. Even the greatest ideas and inventions cannot
themselves provide food, clothing, shelter, heating, cure, transportation, and
other necessities and production factors. Only their application can. One
can immediately see why the Soviet Union could have superior science and
inferior consumption.

In the second duality, the neoclassical growth model of Solow and Swan
decomposes growth accounting into measurable factor inputs and the residual
multifactor productivity (total factor productivity).[22] The multifactor productivity is an unmeasured force that may add or, in the case of industrial central
plan economies, subtract from growth rates of factor inputs that add up to
GDP growth. It can estimate the feat of technological invention and it can
show the efficiency gap.

The third duality, by Parente and Prescott, subdivides total factor
productivity into the "pure knowledge or technology component" and "relative
efficiency" of countries.[23] This is a key subdivision for it brings together in

---

[21]   Michael J. Boskin and Lawrence J. Lau, "Post-War Economic Growth of the Group-of-Five
       Countries: A New Analysis," Center for Economic Policy Research Technical Paper no. 217
       (Stanford University, 1990); Laurence J. Lau, "The Sources of Long-Term Economic Growth:
       Observations from the Experience of Developed and Developing Countries," in *The Mosaic of
       Economic Growth*, eds. Ralph Landau, Timothy Taylor, and Gavin Wright (Stanford: Stanford
       University Press, 1996), 63–91.
[22]   Robert M. Solow, "A Contribution to the Theory of Economic Growth," *Quarterly Journal of
       Economics* 70, no. 1 (February 1956): 65–94; Robert M. Solow, "Technical Change and the
       Aggregate Production Function," *Review of Economics and Statistics* 39, no. 3 (August 1957):
       312–20; Trevor Swan, "Economic Growth and Capital Accumulation," *Economic Record* 32
       (November 1956): 334–61.
[23]   Parente and Prescott, *Barriers to Riche*; Parente and Prescott, "A Unified Theory."

Table 2 the two preceding dualities. The technology component of total factor productivity matches ideas, inventions, and incentives thereof. The relative efficiency component is ontologically part of material production and its factor inputs and innovation. It evaluates how efficiently technological inventions are applied to material production through factor inputs and innovation.

By implication, relative efficiency depends on specific incentives of its own or, in their absence, on coercion. The fourth duality derived from Stiglitz[24] further subdivides what the previous line in Table 2 called relative efficiency. The dividing line is between productive incentives in market economies and coercion in central plan economies. The dichotomy of coercible and non-coercible components of productive efficiency is mine but the emphasis on incentives and their non-substitutable components is Stiglitz's. The most productive, creative, and innovative processes are non-coercible by nature. Hard work is coercible, work ethic is not. Investment is coercible, managerial efficiency is not. Creative destruction from above, restructuring the industrial mix, e.g., replacing coal with nuclear power, is coercible. Creative destruction from within,[25] introducing new products and practices to replace the old ones and changing the shape of industries, is not coercible. Taking orders is coercible, risk-taking is not. Engineering innovation is coercible, entrepreneurial innovation is not. This is why substitution of coercion for productive incentives in industrial central plan economies can only be partial and is never complete. As such, they are long-run inferior to and could never converge with Western market economies.

The last line in Table 2 makes a synthesis of central points. By nature, technological ideas cannot substitute for material production factors and innovation, and vice versa. This is their exogenous complementarity. Agents and countries can apply, to a chosen extent, technological inventions to the production of material goods and services. This is their endogenous complementarity. Agents and countries choose application to various extent, either by incentives or by coercion. I treat coerced application as endogenous because the government chooses to practice it while agents in the market and central plan economies choose to respond to incentives. However, what is coercible is limited by nature, whence comes the efficiency gap of industrial central plan economies. The key findings are the centrality of application and

[24]   Stiglitz, "Incentives, Information"; Stiglitz, *Wither Socialism?*

[25]   Joseph A. Schumpeter, *The Theory of Economic Development* (New Brunswick, N.J.: Transaction Books, [1911] 1983); Schumpeter, *Socialism, Capitalism*, 82–83.

the duality of incentives. Incentives for technological invention and incentives for material production through labor, investment, and innovation are of a different nature.

3.2. The uniform calculus of technological and productive incentives

The wealth of nations grows from incentives that require retention of the fruits of one's industry. Bernier was first to say this.[26] Smith put it succinctly: "That security which the laws in Great Britain give to every man that he shall enjoy the fruits of his own labor, is alone sufficient to make any country flourish, notwithstanding these and twenty other absurd regulations of commerce."[27]

Pigou formulated the universal calculus that applies uniformly to material goods and services and to externalities including knowledge spillovers. For reasons of nature or human activity or both, the return to the economy and society from what agents produce and the return to the producers themselves can diverge and can converge.[28] In the language of subsequent research, it is either divergence or convergence between social returns and private returns. Returns need to converge to create incentives for producers of ideas and material goods and services alike. They reduce technological and productive incentives and create opportunity costs and other disincentives when diverge.

Given natural spillovers of knowledge, technological incentives require compensation of inventors for a feasible part of social returns from spillovers of their ideas. Practice was ahead of theory in this realm. Intellectual property rights in the forms of patents emerged in the Renaissance Florence and Venice and were codified in the proto-industrial England. Public subsidies for human capital and R&D came later.

Compensation of knowledge spillovers is minuscule in relation to their contribution to human progress. Nordhaus calculated that in the US in 1948–2001 inventors "are able to capture about 2.2 percent of the total social surplus" from their inventions.[29]

Divergence between social and private returns in the production of goods and services takes the form of income transfer. Income in money

---

[26]   Bernier, "Travels in the Mogul," 238.

[27]   Smith, "An Inquiry," vol. 1, 238.

[28]   Arthur C. Pigou, *The Economics of Welfare* (London: Macmillan and Co., [1912] 1929), 129–32, 135–45, 174–214, 223–27.

[29]   Nordhaus, "Schumpeterian Profits," 34. See also Jones and Summers, "A Calculations of the Social Returns."

and in kind is a comprehensive return on productive and non-productive activities of agents. Income can be defined as the purchasing power obtained during a given period from all activities and materialized in consumption and investment. The difference between the purchasing power of income of agents and the true value-added of their production evaluated at competitive market prices measures income transfer.

Income transfer and income redistribution are identical terms. Non-producers of the true marginal product for a given unit of income receive income for nothing. Producers of the true marginal product for this unit receive nothing for it. This transfer of income creates a direct cost to producers and an opportunity cost of production to non-producers and would-be producers. Labor is arduous, investment is costly, innovation is risky, and, as Jefferson, Clark, and Pareto saw it, neither will be supplied at the margin at which non-producers can obtain income otherwise.[30] This combination of the costs to producers and opportunity costs of non-producers reduces productive incentives of both parties for labor, investment, and innovation. It impairs application of technological inventions to production and impedes economic growth.

Income redistribution is familiar in taxes and subsidies of the modern welfare states but it encompasses hundreds of other channels from forced production under slavery and central planning to a panoply of subsidies, bailouts, and exactions[31] around the world through millennia.[32] These channels are governmental and private, violent and lawful. A short list includes rent seeking, suppressed agricultural prices in less developed economies, suppressed wages, financial repression, sectoral subsidies and price cross-subsidies,

---

[30] Thomas J. Jefferson, in *The Writings of Thomas Jefferson*, eds. Andrew A. Lipscomb and Albert E. Bergh, vol. 14 (Washington: Thomas Jefferson Memorial Association, [1816] 1905), 466; John Bates Clark, "Distribution as Determined by a Law of Rent," *Quarterly Journal of Economics 5*, no. 3 (April 1891): 289–318; Vilfredo Pareto *Manual of Political Economy* (New York: Augustus M. Kelley Publishers, [1906] 1971), 341.

[31] Alfred Marshall, *Principles of Economics* (London: Macmillan & Co., [1890] 1920), 411.

[32] For an empirical taxonomy and a detailed discussion see Michael S. Bernstam and Alvin Rabushka, *From Predation to Prosperity: How to Move from Socialism to Markets* (Stanford: The Hoover Institution, 2000–08), https://www.hoover.org/research/predation-prosperity-how-move-socialism-markets, especially Annex 3.1; Michael S. Bernstam, "Loot the Looters: Out of Revolutions With and Without Wealth, Health, Knowledge, Liberty, and Justice," in *Revolutions: Finished and Unfinished, From Primal to Final*, eds. Paul Caringella, Wayne Cristaudo, and Glenn Hughes (Newcastle upon Tyne, U.K.: Cambridge Scholars Publishing, 2012), 252–93, 372–77.

monopolies and monopsonies, oligopolies and oligopsonies, protectionism, abrogation of property rights and lawlessness, privileges and corruption, plunder and looting, and industrial, financial, and national bailouts. Akerlof and Romer equated the latter with looting the public purse.[33]

Jefferson wrote about "parasite institutions."[34] The modern literature analyzes parasite networks such as industrial-financial conglomerates[35] and parasite firms in less developed economies trapping them into poverty.[36] Income transfer is indeed a human specimen of a broad biological phenomenon of intraspecific kleptoparasitism. It means stealing livelihood from members of one's own species.

Pareto was right: income redistribution is a global rule "uniformly revealed by history."[37] Minimization of income redistribution is a unique exception of Western market economies. Friedman wrote that they follow the principle "to each according to what he and the instruments he owns produces."[38] This expresses in national income accounting terms Bernier's principle of "retention of the fruits of his industry (...) that forms the main foundation of everything excellent and beneficial in this sublunary state."[39] Minimization of income transfer is a necessary condition of high long-run economic growth achieved in Western market economies.

3.3. Income shares across ranks and factor income transfer

The extent of income redistribution in each economy is directly measurable. It is the weighted average of the rates of income transfer through various channels in all transactions in the flows of funds. Such direct measurement is superior to various expert indexes, but is not available now. This subsection discusses one major empirical example of income transfer where the data exists.

---

[33] George A. Akerlof, and Paul M. Romer, "Looting: The Economic Underworld of Bankruptcy for Profit," *Brookings Papers on Economic Activity*, no. 2 (1993), 1–73.

[34] Thomas J. Jefferson, in *The Writings of Thomas Jefferson*, eds. Andrew A. Lipscomb and Albert E. Bergh, vol. 19 (Washington: Thomas Jefferson Memorial Association, [1818] 1905), 263.

[35] Tarun Khanna and Yishay Yafeh, "Business Groups in Emerging Markets: Paragons or Parasites?" *Journal of Economic Literature* 45, no. 2 (June 2007): 331–72.

[36] Halvor Mehlum, Karl Molke, and Ragnar Torvik, "Parasites," in *Poverty Traps*, eds. Samuel Bowles, Steven N. Durlauf, and Karla Hoff (New York and Princeton: Russell Stage Foundation and Princeton University Press, 2006), 79–84.

[37] Pareto, *Manual of Political Economy*, 341.

[38] Milton Friedman, *Capitalism and Freedom* (Chicago: University of Chicago Press, 1962), 161–62.

[39] Bernier, *Travels in the Mogul*, 238.

A most widespread and consequential channel of income redistribution is factor income transfer from workers and rural smallholder farmers to owners of capital and land. Smith contrasted colonial India and America in this respect.[40]

Following the earlier Soviet debates, the literature uses the metaphor "the price scissors." Another familiar term is "urban bias." Both terms describe how the government in central plan and less developed economies procures agricultural foodstuffs from rural producers at suppressed prices and distributes them at subsidized prices to the low-wage urban dwellers for the sake of industrialization and economic development.

Sah and Stiglitz demonstrated how the weight of factor income transfer shifts.[41] Urbanization increases the number of industrial urban workers by decreasing the number of rural producers while suppressed prices depress agricultural productivity. The government then has to finance subsidized food and industrialization by suppressed industrial wages. Over time, suppressed wages assume a higher share of factor income transfer from labor and small farmers to owners of capital and land, which is often the government itself. This evolution increases factor income transfer from labor to capital. In central plan economies, this form of forced saving becomes the principal source of forced investment and innovation. Figure 6 finds the global contrast described by Smith in 1776 effective at the end of the twentieth century. The data shows income shares in GDP by the generation of income account. Compensation of employees and self-employment income including farm income sum up the category of labor and mixed income. The categories of net operating surplus and consumption of fixed capital together represent gross operating surplus, that is, capital income and income of landowners. The residual is indirect taxes on production and imports net of subsidies. The purpose of this table is to compare, roughly speaking, labor shares (labor and mixed income) and capital shares (gross operating surplus of capital owners and landowners) between economic systems.

Solow established the 150-year pattern in the US of the relative shares of labor and capital in GDP in the ranges about 2/3 and 1/3 respectively, abstracting from indirect taxes.[42] Figure 6 shows the same pattern prevailing in Western market economies of the US, U.K., Germany, Spain and Japan and

---

[40]   Smith, *An Inquiry*, vol. 1, 111, 91.

[41]   Sah and Stiglitz, "The Economics of the Price Scissors."

[42]   Solow, "Technical Change."

in post-central plan China. It means that Marshall's assertion that capital and labor receive their income shares according to their marginal productivity[43] holds in these countries. Clark stated that in competitive market economies "what a social class gets is (...) what it contributes to the general output of industry."[44] Friedman's principle "to which according to what he and the instruments he owns produces" holds. Income redistribution is minimal between providers of production factors.

The red line in Figure 6 separates Western market economies from the two other groups. The data for non-Western countries is limited; the selection here is merely by data availability. Less developed economies include Iran, Mexico, Argentina, and Egypt. Russia in 1989 as a constituent republic stands for the USSR as an industrial central plan economy. I added post-central plan Russia in 2000 to contrast it with post-central plan China the same year. All less developed economies in this figure, the industrial central plan Russia in 1989, and post-central plan Russia exhibit relatively low shares of labor income, below the 2/3 and relatively high shares of capital income, above the 1/3, excluding indirect taxes. The data indicates a high extent of factor income redistribution in these countries.

This transfer creates direct costs to suppliers of labor and opportunity costs of capital investment and innovation to capital owners and thwarts productive incentives of both parties. This contrast is consistent with high economic growth of Western market economies and China, superior to economic growth of other countries in Figure 6.

3.4. The negative value-added and income transfer

One more indication of the high extent of income transfer is the negative value added. It means that, in world market prices, the price of finished goods is lower than the cost of raw materials and intermediate and capital inputs went into their production. This is impossible to sustain without massive inter-sector subsidies and price cross-subsidies. They must cover not only the 100 percent of wages and profits of finished goods producers but also the difference between their output price and the cost of material inputs.

In Western market economies, under price competition and free trade, the negative value-added producers cannot survive. They are widespread in

---

[43] Marshall, *Principles of Economics*, 292–312.
[44] Clark, "Distribution as Determined," 313.

central plan economies. McKinnon showed this in detail.[45] Tan analyzed the negative value-added in protectionist less developed economies.[46]

In the study of input-output tables for Eastern European economies in 1986–87, Hughes and Hare found after adjusting for product quality that the negative value-added amounted to 34.8 percent of gross output in Czechoslovakia and 34.6 percent in Hungary. Poland and Bulgaria exhibited similar magnitudes.[47] This magnitude of the negative value-added can alone account for the bulk of the efficiency gap in industrial central plan economies. Massive subsidies downstream create the opportunity cost of innovation and efficiency and disable productive incentives.

3.5. Non-coercible application of inventions and the negative feedback of coercion

This section made three findings. First, high redistribution of income in industrial and non-industrial central plan economies and less developed economies rendered productive incentives deficient.

Second, even though industrial central plan promoted technological incentives, the latter were not sufficient to set industrial central plan economies on the path of high long-run economic growth. Application of technological inventions to production was partial because coercion could only partially substitute for missing productive incentives.

Third, by this partial application, coercion nevertheless enabled industrial central plan economies to outperform less developed economies. This did not happen in non-industrial central plan economies because of deficient technological development, forgoing even adoption of available global technologies.

The remaining question is why several key components of application are non-coercible. They include work ethic, managerial efficiency, creative

[45] Ronald I. McKinnon, *The Order of Economic Liberalization: Financial Control in the Transition to a Market Economy* (Baltimore and London: The Johns Hopkins University Press, 1991), 171–86.
[46] Augustine Tan, "Differential Tariffs, Negative Value-Added and the Theory of Effective Protection" *American Economic Review* 60, no. 1 (March 1970): 107–16.
[47] Gordon Hughes and Paul Hare, "Competitiveness and Industrial Restructuring in Czechoslovakia, Hungary, and Poland," *European Economy*, Special Edition, no. 2 (1991): 83–110; Gordon Hughes and Paul Hare, "Industrial Policy and Restructuring in Eastern Europe," *Oxford Review of Economic Policy* 8, no. 1 (1992): 82–104; Gordon Hughes and Paul Hare, "The International Competitiveness of Industries in Bulgaria, Czechoslovakia, Hungary, and Poland," *Oxford Economic Papers, New Series* 46, no. 2 (April 1994): 200–21.

destruction at the firm level, risk taking, and entrepreneurial innovation. Part of the problem is that the government, as the central manager of the economy, itself fails at these tasks even though it launches new industries, reallocates resources to new uses, and promotes managerial talent. Yet, it cannot coerce agents to maximize application of technological inventions to production. This is the ultimate problem.

Coercion engenders a negative feedback loop. Perverse incentives arise on top of deficient productive incentives and disincentives. The government imposes output quotas and delivery quotas on producer firms. Unlike government procurement in market economies, these are mandates, not privileges. In order to enforce the quotas, the government controls unit prices of producers, which enables the government to monitor the quantity of output. This enforcement mechanism converges with the cost-plus pricing method in government procurement contracts in market economies. The cost-plus pricing with profits proportional to costs emerges by default in the absence of market exchange for a given project, e.g., military procurement and infrastructure. Laffont and Tirole showed that firms would not minimize costs when their profit in such contracts is proportional to costs and proposed corrective regulations.[48] For a correction to work, market firms need to want to take the job, not be forced to undertake it like central plan firms.

Output quotas and delivery quotas across the supply chains exist for output maximization. This is the raison d'être of central planning. But this creates strategic interdependence of the government and producer firms. Firms need the government to exist and the government needs the firms to function. Furthermore, the government needs the firms for other firms to function. They are too interconnected to fail. Delivery failures over the supply chains create bottleneck externalities described by the proverbial "all for the want of a horseshoe nail (...) the kingdom was lost."

Government dependence on the firms unleashes the principal-agent problem. The government wants to maximize output quotas at fixed prices. Both are punishing. Firms want to minimize output quotas and raise supply prices. By default, to this end, firms maximize costs including resources and factor inputs.[49] The government softens the budget constraint so that output

---

[48] Jean-Jacques Laffont and Jean Tirole, *A Theory of Incentives in Procurement and Regulation* (Cambridge: The MIT Press, 1993).

[49] Michael S. Bernstam, "The Wealth of Nations and the Environment," in *Resources, Environment, and Population: Present Knowledge, Future Options*, eds. Kingsley Davis and Michael S. Bernstam (New York, Oxford: Oxford University Press, 1990), 355–63, 369–71.

reduction is less than price increases while firms thus maximize profits.[50] Cost maximization forms the perverse incentives of central plan firms.

Application of technological inventions to production in central plan economies was partial because coercion could only partially substitute for missing productive incentives. Even this partial application runs into disincentives and perverse incentives. Managerial and quasi-entrepreneurial talent is spent on maximizing costs and resisting innovation, or else output quotas would be raised and prices and profits lowered. Output maximization ends up in cost maximization. This is the negative feedback loop of coercion. It fosters the efficiency gap of industrial central planning.

4. Conclusion. Incentives, coercion, and redistribution across ranks

The second rank of industrial central plan economies in the tripartite ranking of economic performance relies on GDP per capita and per worker. It does not take into account the human costs. Income levels approximated by GDP per capita are a measure of production, not of consumption, living standards, and welfare. Productivity approximated by GDP per worker is not a measure of human progress. The central problem of central planning is enforcement and it often took violent forms. In fact, there has never been a central plan economy, industrial or non-industrial, which did not experience extensive periods of repressions, in many cases mass terror and policy-induced famines.

These incidences are usually interpreted as campaigns of political enforcement. I view them rather as episodes of enforcement of central planning. Observations are too few for statistical inferences but two major episodes stand out: the Great Terror of 1936–38 in the USSR and the Cultural Revolution of 1966–76 in China. Both occurred after major failures of accelerated industrial policies that ended in famines, viz., collectivization of agriculture and the first wave of industrialization in the USSR and the Great Leap Forward in China. The reason for collectivization of agriculture in both countries and elsewhere was, in my view, enforcement of central planning. Imposing agricultural output quotas on millions of small farms is unenforceable while requisitions reduce production to subsistence. Farmers had to be rounded up into large-scale plantations whose managers would enforce gang labor and

---

[50] János Kornai, "Resource-Constrained Versus Demand-Constraint Systems," *Econometrica* 47, no. 4 (July 1979): 801–819; János Kornai, *Contradictions and Dilemmas: Studies on the Socialist Economy and Society* (Cambridge: The MIT Press, 1986).

deliver output quotas, or else. The project failed, famines followed, the first industrial wave could not sustain, and the mass terror across-the-board, from ordinary people to top managers, shifted the blame from surviving leaders to everyone else. These are the human costs and opportunity costs of the second rank of economic performance of industrial central planning.

Table 3 summarizes the results found in this paper. The columns distribute three hierarchical ranks of economic performance among the four clusters of countries. The second row from the bottom says what path of long-run economic growth is associated with each hierarchical rank in the columns. Rank 1 with high long-run economic growth includes Western market economies, to which I added post-central plan China. Rank 2 with high medium-run, moderate long-run economic growth covers industrial central plan economies of the USSR and Eastern Europe. Rank 3 with low economic growth encompasses two clusters: non-industrial central plan economies and less developed economies, to which I added post-central plan Russia.

Each rank and each cluster answer to three systemic questions: 1) whether technological incentives are high or low; 2) whether productive incentives for the application of technological inventions are high and low, characterized by minimal income redistribution; and 3) whether they practiced state-forced production of central planning. The last row in Table 3 summarizes these systemic characteristics with pictorial symbols. The proverbial carrot and stick stand, respectively, for incentives and for coercion. The last cell depicts intraspecific kleptoparasitism, the two canines stealing a piece of food from one another, standing for income redistribution as a human specimen of this biological phenomenon. The stick of coercion encompasses also a high degree of income redistribution under central planning.

Western market economies combined high technological and productive incentives and no coercion. Their symbols are the two carrots, two complementary incentives. Industrial central plan economies combined high technological incentives and coercion of central planning to partially substitute for productive incentives in application of inventions to production. Their symbols are one carrot on the left for technological incentives and one stick on the right for coercion.

Non-industrial central plan economies combined low technological and low productive incentives. Their coercion correspondingly included only forced labor and forced investment in fixed capital, without forced innovation and forced application of technology to production. Their symbols are an empty space on the left implying absence of technological incentives and the stick of coercion on the right in lieu of productive incentives. Less developed economies combined low technological and low productive incentives and no coercion substitutes. Their symbols are an empty space on the left in the place of technological incentives and intraspecific kleptoparasitism of income redistribution on the right.

Coercive application of technological inventions to production in industrial central plan economies could not generate high long-run economic growth. Coercion could not compensate for disincentives of income redistribution. It engendered its own negative feedback loop of perverse incentives. Industrial central plan economies could never close the efficiency gap and converge with Western market economies. Even if they did not kill a single person for the sake of enforcement, their economic system was second-rate.

The advantage of the markets is that voluntary production for voluntary exchange can, under a specific condition, create productive incentives for the voluntary application of technological inventions. This condition is minimization of income redistribution. Call it "The Invisible Wrist" to support The Invisible Hand of the market. Incentives for technological invention and minimization of income redistribution are complementary conditions. Both conditions are necessary and jointly sufficient for high long-run economic growth. This finding is consistent with the global data and meets the above-mentioned Einstein rule.

Table 1. Annual Growth Rates of GDP per Capita, Western Market, Industrial Central Plan, and Less Developed Economies, World Regions and the World, 1950-73 and 1950-89 (in percent)

	US	Western Europe 12	Japan	USSR	Eastern Europe 7	Latin America 8	East Asia LDCs	India	Africa	China	World
1950-73	2.5	4.0	8.1	3.3	3.9	2.6	2.4	1.4	2.0	2.8	2.9
1950-89	2.3	3.2	5.9	2.4	2.7	1.9	1.6	1.9	1.3	3.7	2.3

Notes:

1. **Western Europe 12** includes Austria, Belgium, Denmark, Finland, France, Germany, Italy, The Netherlands, Norway, Sweden, Switzerland, and the UK.

2. **Eastern Europe 7** includes Albania, Bulgaria, Czechoslovakia, Hungary, Poland, Romania, and Yugoslavia.

3. **Latin America 8** includes Argentina, Brazil, Chile, Colombia, Mexico, Peru, Uruguay, and Venezuela.

4. **East Asia LDCs** include East Asian countries except Japan, China, the Asian Tigers, Malaysia, Indonesia, Thailand, and the Philippines.

Source: *The Maddison-Project*. 2013. http://www.ggdc.net/maddison/maddison-project/home.htm

Table 2. Ontological and Functional Dualities: A Schematic Representation of Compiled Growth Models

Romer; Boskin and Lau	Production of material goods and services through factor inputs and innovation: Complementarity of technological invention and production factors			Ideas and incentives for invention and R&D
Solow; Hall and Jones	Factor inputs: labor, human capital, physical capital	Total factor productivity		
Parente and Prescott	Factor inputs	Relative efficiency		Knowledge, technology
Stiglitz; Schumpeter	Factor inputs - coercible	Coercible	Non-coercible, incentives only	Technology
Synthesis	Endogenous complementarity: application of technological inventions to production Productive incentives: Minimization of income transfer			Exogenous complementarity, Technological incentives

Table 3. The Tripartite Ranking of Economic Performance

Rank of performance	1	2	3	4
Clusters	Western market economies and the post-central plan China	Industrial central plan economies	Non-industrial central plan economies	Less developed economies and the post-central plan Russia
Technological incentives: intellectual property rights, subsidies for invention, R&D, and human capital	High	High	Low	Low
Productive incentives for labor, investment, and innovation, for application of technological inventions to production; minimization of income redistribution	High	Low	Low	Low
State-forced production: forced labor, investment, and innovation, forced application of technological inventions to production	None	High	Forced labor and investment in fixed capital only	None
Economic growth	High long-run	High medium-run, moderate long-run	Low	Low
Symbols: Incentives, coercion, and redistribution				

Figure 1. THE WORLD AT THE END OF CENTRAL PLANNING:
NATURAL LOG OF GDP PER CAPITA AND PER WORKER AT PURCHASING POWER
PARITY IN 2000 DOLLARS, 164 COUNTRIES, 1990

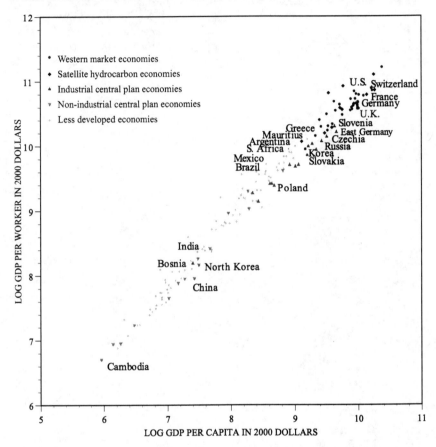

Note: The data for Bulgaria are for 1991, for Eritrea and Georgia for 1992, and for the former East Germany for 1988.

Source: 160 countries except the former East Germany, Yugoslavia, Angola, and Belarus: Heston, Alan, Robert Summers, and Bettina Aten. 2006. *Penn World Table Version 6.2.* Center for International Comparisons of Production, Income and Prices at the University of Pennsylvania. The former East Germany and Yugoslavia: Converted to 2000 dollars from *Penn World Table Version 5.6*; Angola and Belarus: *Penn World Table Version 6.1.*

Figure 2. GDP PER CAPITA, WESTERN MARKET, INDUSTRIAL CENTRAL PLAN, AND LESS DEVELOPED ECONOMIES, 1900-99

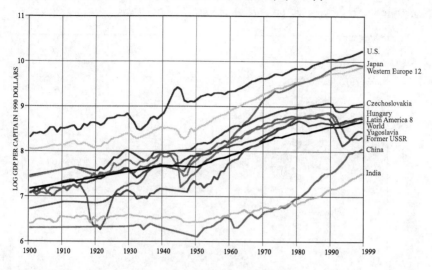

Notes:

1. Western Europe 12 includes Austria, Belgium, Denmark, Finland, France, Germany, Italy, The Netherlands, Norway, Sweden, Switzerland, and the U.K.

2. Latin America 8 includes Argentina, Brazil, Chile, Colombia, Mexico, Peru, Uruguay, and Venezuela.

3. The data is missing for some countries for the period of World War II and other years but is complete for the second half of the twentieth century.

Source: *The Maddison-Project*. 2013. http://www.ggdc.net/maddison/maddison-project/home.htm

Figure 3. THE WORLD AT THE END OF CENTRAL PLANNING:

MODIFIED INDEX OF SCIENCE AND TECHNOLOGY AND NATURAL LOG OF GDP PER

WORKER AT PURCHASING POWER PARITY IN 2000 DOLLARS, 140 COUNTRIES, 1990

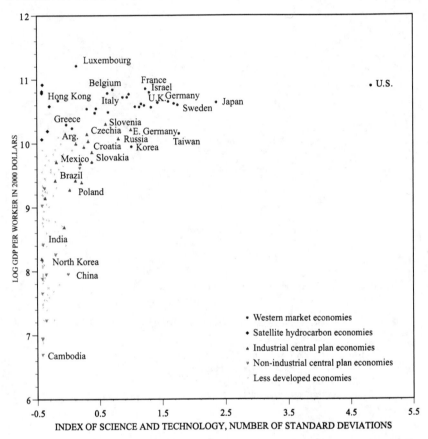

Note: The data on GDP per worker for Bulgaria are for 1991, for Eritrea and Georgia for 1992, and for the former East Germany for 1988.

Sources: 1. GDP per worker: 136 countries except the former East Germany, Yugoslavia, Angola, and Belarus: Heston, Alan, Robert Summers, and Bettina Aten. 2006. *Penn World Table Version 6.2.* Center for International Comparisons of Production, Income and Prices at the University of Pennsylvania; The former East Germany and Yugoslavia: Converted to 2000 dollars from *Penn World Table Version 5.6*; Angola and Belarus: *Penn World Table Version 6.1.*

2. Index of Science and Technology Capacity: Wagner, Caroline S., Irene T. Brahmakulam, Brian A. Jackson, Anny Wong, and Tatsuro Yoda. 2001. *Science and Technology Collaboration: Building Capacity in Developing Countries?* Santa Monica, CA: The Rand Corporation: 67-69.

Figure 4. THE WORLD AT THE END OF CENTRAL PLANNING:
NATURAL LOG OF HUMAN CAPITAL PER WORKER AND OF GDP PER WORKER
AT PURCHASING POWER PARITY, DEPARTURE BELOW THE U.S. LEVELS, 133
COUNTRIES, 1988

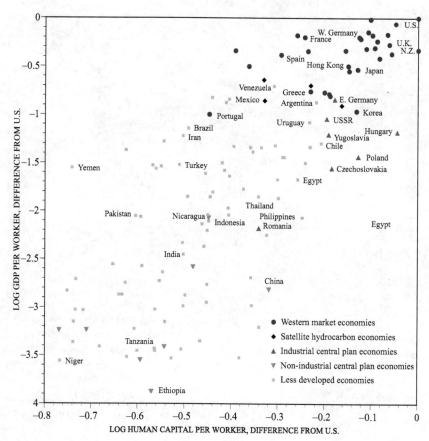

Source: Hall, Robert E., and Charles I. Jones. 1996. "The Productivity of Nations." NBER Working
Paper 5812. Cambridge, MA: NBER: 45-47.

Figure 5. THE WORLD AT THE END OF CENTRAL PLANNING:
NATURAL LOG OF CAPITAL STOCK PER WORKER AND OF GDP PER WORKER AT
PURCHASING POWER PARITY, DEPARTURE BELOW THE U.S. LEVELS, 133 COUNTRIES,
1988

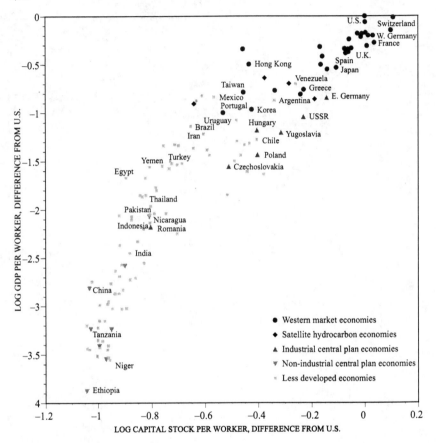

Source: Hall, Robert E., and Charles I. Jones. 1996. "The Productivity of Nations." NBER Working
Paper 5812. Cambridge, MA: NBER: 45-47.

Figure 6. INCOME SHARES OF GDP (IN PERCENT), ELEVEN ECONOMIES, CA. 2000, AND RUSSIA STANDING FOR THE USSR IN 1989

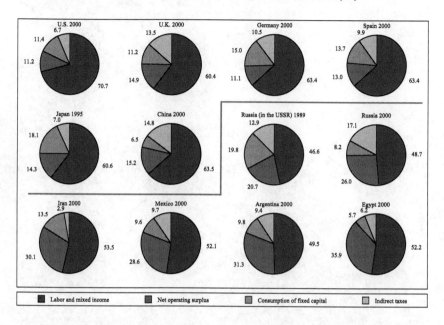

Note: The data on mixed income is missing for some countries including Russia. It is imputed from gross operating surplus following Douglas Gollin. 2002. "Getting Income Shares Right." *Journal of Political Economy* 110, no. 2 (April):458-74.

Sources: All countries except Russia in 1989 and Argentina and Germany in 2000: U.N. Division of Statistics. 2008. *National Accounts Statistics: Main Aggregates and Detailed Tables, 2006* (hereinafter *NAS:MADT* and year). New York: United Nation, pt. I: 675, 1015-16; pt. II: 284-85, 430-31, 824; pt. III: 375, 950, 996; Argentina and Germany, 2000: *NAS:MADT* 2009. New York: United Nations, pt. I: 54; pt. 2: 523-24. Russia, 1989: Russian State Committee on Statistics. 1994. *Rossiiskii Statisticheskii Ezhegodnik 1994*. Moscow:Russian State Committee on Statistics, 238.

THE RISE AND FALL OF THE PLANNED ECONOMY AND ITS LONG-LASTING EFFECTS ON TRANSITION

Serguey Braguinsky

In 1996, when I was an aspiring scholar interested in new institutional economics, Steven Cheung (of the "Private Property Rights and Share-cropping" article fame[1]) invited me to give a talk on the Russian transition to a market economy at the economics department of Hong Kong University, which he was chairing at the time. At the dinner party in his house after the talk, he mused out loud about why the Soviet Union implemented a planned economy, despite its obvious huge deadweight loss. He just could not understand why the communist dictatorship would not simply let the markets do their job and impose a revenue-maximizing tax making both the rulers and the people better off.

At the time, I was not yet that familiar with the "Chicago" way of thinking—that no one would ever leave money on the table unless there were good reasons to do so—but the question intrigued me. I had to admit to Steven that I did not have a good answer, but I promised that I would think about it. Seeking an answer led me to realize that established conceptions of the planned economy may have missed some important logic. Basically at that time there were two views. One was that the planned economy somehow represented a superior mode of organizing production compared to the market mechanism. The other (the one articulated by Cheung) was that it represented an irrational choice that could only be explained by ideology.[2] I felt that there should have been more to it—after all, even though the planned economy had existed for a much shorter historical period than Cheung's celebrated system of sharecropping in China, the impact that it had on the Russian society (and much of the world) made it hard to dismiss it as totally

---

[1] Steven Cheung, "Private Property Rights and Sharecropping," *Journal of Political Economy*, 76, no. 6 (1968): 1107–22.

[2] See for example Abraham Katz, *The Politics of Economic Reform in the Soviet Union* (New York: Praeger Publishers, 1972).

irrational. Most crucially, I felt that without understanding the *rational* logic behind the planned economy, it would be hard to grasp what was happening to the post-communist economy. If all that the planned economy amounted to was just one big set of irrational constraints, removing those should have been enough for a "normal" market economy to emerge. Indeed, that was how many (myself included) wishfully thought at the start of the "transition." But it very quickly became apparent (and is, of course, even more apparent today), that a "normal" market economy failed to materialize in Russia. My hope was that solving Cheung's puzzle would at the same time shed light on an even more burning puzzle—why were the one-time high hopes for Russia after it got rid of communism being dashed?

The view of the planned economy, the logic behind its creation and collapse, and how it continued to play out during the so-called "transition" presented in this chapter draws on ideas expressed in a book I coauthored with Grigory Yavlinsky.[3] Yavlinsky, whom I befriended back in 1989, also played a key role in making sure that I began seeing how things really were in the Russian "transition" earlier than many other Western-style economists. I want to use this opportunity to thank him for years of friendship and extremely stimulating intellectual exchange. Needless to say, he is in no way responsible for any errors of fact or judgment in this paper.

***

The answer to Steven Cheung's puzzle begins by correctly identifying the objectives of the communist principal. Since rationality simply means being efficient in achieving a given objective—be it a selfish consumer's objective to maximize own utility, or an altruistic nun's objective to bring maximum possible relief to the poor and the deprived, or a suicide bomber's objective to maximize the death toll from the bomb he detonates—the understanding of the nature of the objective is the starting point for any meaningful analysis.

The communist dictatorship was a totalitarian, not a tinpot dictatorship.[4] As noted below, Putin's dictatorship in today's Russia is a of a tinpot type, so it allows markets to operate while striving to maximize the revenue of the ruling elite by determining taxes (including occasional 100% tax

---

3   Serguey Braguinsky and Grigory Yavlinsky, *Incentives and Institutions: The Transition to a Market Economy in Russia* (Princeton: Princeton University Press, 2000).

4   Wintrobe, Ronald, "The Tinpot and the Totalitarian: An Economic Theory of Dictatorship," *American Political Science Review*, 84, no. 3 (1990): 849–72.

rates through expropriation). The logic and the deadweight loss of a tinpot dictatorship and its revenue-maximizing tax are well understood.[5] But a totalitarian communist dictatorship presents a more complicated picture.

The primary objective of the communist dictatorship was to maintain its *totalitarian* control. The communists understood that to achieve this goal, it was imperative to prevent the emergence of any independent resource base in the hands of individual economic agents.[6] The communist system thus had to eliminate markets in capital goods and labor, centralize property rights over means of production, and severely restrict the use of money.

The second objective of the communist dictatorship was to "overtake and outstrip the advanced technology of the developed capitalist countries."[7] This required generating and diffusing technological innovations. In capitalist economies the task is achieved through activities of independent Schumpeterian entrepreneurs, coordinated by the market, and motivated by "big prizes" for successful innovations.[8] Such a system obviously cannot function in the absence of markets for capital goods and labor. The communist system had to find a substitute. The planned economy, backed by institutionalized terror, was such a substitute.

---

[5] See for example Mancur Olson, "Dictatorship, Democracy, and Development," *American Political Science Review*, 87, no. 3 (1993): 567–76; Mancur Olson, *The Rise and Decline of Nations* (New Haven: Yale University Press, 1982).

[6] In 1918 Lenin wrote, "The petty bourgeois... wants to employ his thousands... in opposition to any kind of state control. And the sum total of these thousands, amounting to many thousands of millions..., undermines our socialist construction." Vladimir Lenin, "'Left-Wing' Childishness and the Petty-Bourgeois Mentality," *Collected Works*, 4th ed. (Moscow: Progress Publishers, 1972), 165–271, https://www.marxists.org/archive/lenin/works/1918/may/09.htm. Even in 1921, as he had to accept a temporary retreat from "war communism" to "new economic policy," Lenin still warned that "the unrestricted trade... means turning back towards capitalism.... [E]xchange and freedom of trade inevitably lead to... a revival of capitalist wage-slavery." Vladimir Lenin, "Report on The Substitution of a Tax in Kind for the Surplus Grain Appropriation System," *Collected Works*, 1st ed. (Moscow: Progress Publishers, 1965), 323–334, https://www.marxists.org/archive/lenin/works/1921/10thcong/ch03.htm.

[7] Joseph Stalin, "Industrialization of the Country and the Right Deviation in the C.P.S.U.(B.)," speech delivered at the Plenum of the Central Committee of the C.P.S.U.(B.), November 19, 1928, https://www.marxists.org/reference/archive/stalin/works/1928/11/19.htm. He continued: "We have overtaken and outstripped the advanced capitalist countries in the sense of establishing a new political system, the Soviet system. That is good. But it is not enough. In order to secure the final victory of socialism... we must also overtake and outstrip these countries technically and economically. Either we do this, or we shall be forced to the wall." Ibid.

[8] Joseph A. Schumpeter, *The Theory of Economic Development: An Inquiry into Profits, Capital, Credit, Interest, and the Business Cycle* (Cambridge, MA: Harvard University Press, 1934).

When thinking about incentives, economists normally think about *positive* incentives, that is, the promise of a personal reward in return for performance. The communist experiment, of course, did not completely lack its own system of positive incentives—promotion to a higher rank in the hierarchy carried with it not just more power but also very clearly defined consumption benefits not available to ordinary people. But the impact of such incentives on technical and economic advancements was limited as promotion mostly rewarded loyalty to the party line and to the immediate superiors, not necessarily good economic or technical performance. To achieve some degree of economic "efficiency" (in the sense of moving towards the objective of overtaking and outstripping developed capitalist countries), the communist system had to rely largely on *negative* incentives, that is, a credible threat of punishment.[9]

Once the communist party (Stalin) had set the goals, the system had to ensure that all the productive resources were devoted to meeting those. Since the goals would have nothing to do with consumers' welfare, the market mechanism (even if it could be allowed) would not work. Assigning productive resources to meet Stalin's goals required giving state-owned enterprises and "collective" farms direct orders in terms of physical units of production and severely punishing non-compliance. To keep the threat of punishment credible, real or imaginary non-compliers had to be regularly exposed and executed. Hereby lies an explanation for the otherwise mind-boggling reality that Stalin's mass purges were not limited to potential political rivals but also engulfed millions of innocent ordinary people—managers, engineers, workers, peasants—who had no political aspirations and certainly did not pose any threat to the regime. The explanation, from the logic of the planned economy is simple: picking up and executing people at random instilled mortal fear in everyone else, and this mortal fear made sure that everybody worked as hard as they could to pursue the goals set out by Stalin.[10, 11]

---

[9]   Consumer welfare was never considered to be an independent objective, so the whole meaning of the term "efficiency" must be redefined in the context of communism. This is discussed in more detail in Chapter 1 in Braguinsky and Yavlinsky, *Incentives and Institutions*.

[10] This is somewhat of a simplification in the following sense. The planning mechanism was not entirely top-down even during Stalin's years. Bargaining took place at various levels, encompassing the relationships between workshops within a particular state-owned enterprise (SOE) and its management; between the management of SOEs and their supervising body; and, ultimately, between the highest authority (Stalin) and major industry leaders. However, during the Stalin years the limits for this bureaucratic bargaining (and the inevitable corruption

Thus, from Lenin's and Stalin's vantage point (theirs, of course, being the only ones that mattered), the planned economy, far from being irrational, represented the best possible choice given their goals and constraints. The goal, once again, was growth in industrial and military production at the highest possible speed, while the constraint was the need to keep productive resources out of private hands. The production plan, which was enforced through existential fear from the very top to the very bottom of the social pyramid with no exception, replaced market incentives, while the elimination of markets for capital, labor, and intermediate goods (also enforced by the police state) made sure that no economic agent could accumulate an independent resource base. Of course, a market economy with a revenue-maximizing tax would have delivered much more in terms of economic welfare, but the communist dictatorship was not interested. Welfare and the very lives of millions of people were all sacrificed on the altar of the communist *religion*, promising heaven on earth, but for some future generation.

***

Stalin died on March 5, 1953. Several years later, his successor, Nikita Khrushchev, declared that by 1970 the Soviet Union would overtake the United States of America in terms of per capita output, and that by 1980, "the construction of the communist society would be finished in the main."[12] He

---

it entailed) were very strict. Stalin employed an all-pervasive network of secret police agents, independent from both the industrial and party hierarchy and answering only to Stalin himself. This furnished him with a powerful system of monitoring and punishing those agents who tried to pursue their own goals. The small amount of slack that this system allowed came only from "a conscious awareness that cracking down too hard on the unlawful practices of management would cause the system to be so rigid that it would freeze up and stop producing." Joseph A. Berliner, *Factory and Manager in the USSR* (Cambridge, MA: Harvard University Press, 1957), 293.

[11] Regular mass purges also served another "rational" purpose—that of ensuring constant supply of new prisoners to replace those who died working in labor camps. Big infrastructure projects and mining in harsh Siberian conditions appear to have been the two main areas where the planned economy relied on outright slave labor. The situation in agriculture was less harsh but otherwise similar; "collective farm" workers were not issued national identification documents and thus could not leave their villages. In effect, this re-introduced rural serfdom, abolished back in 1861.

[12] Khrushchev, Nikita, "On the Program of the Communist Party of the Soviet Union," Speech to the 22nd Communist Party Congress, Oct. 18 1961 (in Russian), http://www.historyru. com/doc/persons/xr/docorg/doc10c.html. An explanation is in order here for a reader unfamiliar with the Marxist-Leninist dogma. Even though it is common in the West to refer to the USSR and other similar countries as "communist," in their own ideology they were still going through the initial stage of transition to communism, called "socialism." Under this first, "socialist" phase, the remaining scarcity requires measuring workers' productive

also introduced big changes to the way the planned economy and the political system operated. By doing so Khrushchev, unintentionally of course, set in motion the process that led the whole system to collapse, just 10 years after what was supposed to be the country's triumphant arrival in the promised land.

The changes implemented by Khrushchev were two-fold. First, he lifted the state of terror. To be sure, the police state did not disappear, and the dissidents continued to be harassed and persecuted. But mass purges became the thing of the past, and an average law-abiding Soviet citizen could now sleep in his bed without (the previously very real) fear of being dragged out of it and executed in the wee hours of the morning. Slave labor was also largely abolished, both in the prison system and in rural areas. The power of the secret police was reigned in and put under the control of the communist party. The positive effect this had on the society cannot be overestimated.[13] But without the non-discriminating terror, the incentive system that was based on it, and kept the planned economy functioning, started crumbling. Khrushchev's and subsequent reforms tried to introduce positive incentives in the form of bonuses for achieving and overachieving the plan targets in lieu of terror. But with the fundamental constraint that prevented the communist system from utilizing the full power of market forces still in place, this could not have a serious effect on preventing the system from working less and less effectively.

Apart from the incentives issue, the planned economy was also running into diminishing returns, in particular due to increased complexity resulting from growth. In the years preceding Khrushchev's rise to power, economic planning had been coping with a huge proliferation in the number of items in which plans had to be formulated. By 1953, the production and materials-allocation sections of the Soviet national economic plan contained twice as

---

contributions to allocate consumption goods. The state (which is the mechanism for class dominance) also survives at this stage because despite the abolition of the exploiting capitalist class, class differences remain, in particular between (industrial) workers (the dominant class) and peasants (a friendly, but subordinate class). The society freed from capitalist exploitation, however, eventually attains unprecedented technological and economic prosperity, leading to the elimination of scarcity and allowing consumption to be allocated in accordance with individuals' needs. (Basically, anyone can take as much as he/she needs, still leaving plenty for everybody else.) The elimination of scarcity ushers in communism. At this point, the remaining class distinctions also disappear, resulting in "withering away" of the state.

[13] Growing up in the late years of the Soviet Union I could only imagine what my mother went through when the police came for her father one night in 1938. He never came back and died several years later in a labor camp--his wife and daughter only learned about his fate after Khrushchev initiated, in the late 1950s, the posthumous exoneration of the wrongfully convicted.

many specific items as in 1940. Khrushchev decided to reverse this trend, and reduced the number of targets contained in the annual plan by 46%, leaving the rest to lower-level bodies, such as local leadership and the management of SOEs. The number of parameters of performance to be reported to the state and to the ministries by SOEs (which in effect performed the functions of centralized monitoring) was also reduced by 67%.[14]

In response to mounting incentives and information problems, the communist dictatorship also relaxed the rigidity of the top-down planning with respect to each individual SOE. The planning of more specific targets was relegated to the management of SOEs in the 1960s, and the authorities also gave up the practice of assigning the SOEs plans itemized by individual workshops in physical units of output. Instead, they tried to control the industrial activity by more indirect means, employing volume of sales and profits targets. With centralized prices, this did not introduce fundamental changes from the point of view of conventional economic efficiency. However, the consequences of these changes in terms of incentives proved to be of first-order importance, although not in the way they were intended.

As mentioned, bonuses and penalties under Stalin's planned economy were linked to success or failure in achieving very detailed output targets and in implementing specific technical goals assigned by the authorities. As the plans became less detailed and technology-specific, the control over the most essential aspect of economic planning was lost. Instead, the system was leaning more and more heavily toward planning on the margin, or, as it was called in the Soviet Union, "from the achieved level." The changes opened the way to the practice of *ex post* "corrections" of the plans. As a 5-year plan period drew to an end, the SOEs would present the supervising bodies with the prospect of having to report to the central authorities that the original plan could not be fulfilled (of course, due to some insurmountable, "objective" difficulties). This would undermine those bodies' positions vis-à-vis the central planning authorities and jeopardize their own bonuses and career prospects. Those bodies (industrial ministries and/or all-union industrial associations introduced by the 1973 Brezhnev reform) would thus align themselves with the SOEs and lobby for *ex post* adjustment of the plan. Deprived of reliable information about what was going on inside each individual SOE, the planning authorities found it increasingly difficult to push back against such requests,

---

[14]   Ivan Gladkov, ed., *Istoriya Sotsialisticheskoi Ekonomiki v SSSR* (The History of the Socialist Economy of the USSR) (Moscow: Nauka, 1980), 286.

especially when they came jointly from major enterprises in the industry backed by its ministry. Moreover, the top of the hierarchy was increasingly concerned not so much with the actual fulfillment of the plan as with the semblance thereof, which allowed them to propagate the myth of an ever-growing socialist economy.[15] But once the plan can be adjusted in such a way, bonuses can be obtained and penalties avoided by means other than striving to fulfill the assigned tasks. The whole incentive scheme of planning breaks down.

While the SOEs were thus spending less resources and effort on the tasks assigned to them by the plan, they also found they had much more slack than before, that is, extra resources they could now deploy at the discretion of their management and higher officials complicit in the malfeasance. Reallocating resources to private use was made easier by Kosygin's 1965 reform which introduced "planning according to orders (direct contacts)."[16] This allowed SOEs, for the first time, to make transactions directly among themselves and put those bilateral and multilateral exchange links into the plan. The (unintended) consequence was that it opened the window for even more elaborate slack schemes, and greatly expanded the "creative" ways in which resources "saved" in the process of plan adjustments could be diverted to private benefit. The reform also gave the management more freedom with regard to labor allocation. The only indicator to be handed down under the new system was the total wage fund, while the indicators of labor productivity, average wages, and the number of personnel were left to the SOE management's discretion. Not surprisingly, whole workshops soon sprang up inside SOEs, working with unreported resources and labor on producing unreported output to be sold in the "parallel" market, the revenues from which would be pocketed by the management and parallel market dealers (with some going also to workers).

At this point, the planned economy was already basically dead. A very small slack in SOE-controlled resources, implicitly tolerated under Stalin as a precaution against the total failure of rigid planning, had developed into a full-scale "parallel economy," which flourished by making and selling goods outside of the planning system and was protected by an ever-increasing

---

[15] The Soviet Union, especially under Brezhnev, became a repository of self-deprecating jokes. In one of them Stalin, Khrushchev, and Brezhnev are all riding a train. All of a sudden, the train comes to a halt. Stalin immediately orders the train operator to be shot. The train is not moving. After a while, Khrushchev posthumously exonerates the operator. With the train still not moving, Brezhnev, with a deep sigh, draws the window curtain and says, "All right, let's pretend that we are moving."

[16] Katz, *The Politics of Economic Reform.*

body of various lobbying groups (industrial ministries, all-union industrial associations, local communist party authorities, and so on). Private accumulation of wealth was in full swing, and, just as Lenin anticipated back in 1918, individually obtained thousands of rubles quickly became "thousands of millions" putting the parallel economy at the helm.

Nothing illustrates the newly found power of the parallel economy better than the following story told by the investigative journalist, Arkady Vaksberg in his book, "The Soviet Mafia."[17] In 1980, he was assigned to write an article about the work of the Railways Ministry. As it happened, soon after the assignment began, there were not enough railway carriages near wheat fields in Kazakhstan to ship the harvest to grain elevators in Central Russia. Rainy season was starting, and it was urgently required to find the carriages to accomplish the task. The ministry did find 34 spare carriages in the northern Caucasus and ordered a train to be formed to move to the Kazakhstan region as a matter of highest priority. The following is the narrative of the Minister of Railways at the time, Ivan Pavlovsky, as reported by Vaksberg:

> The whole operation [of moving the carriages] was monitored by Leonid Ilyich [General Secretary Brezhnev]. We set up a military-style HQ. ... I have been on the phone around the clock. We battled to get this additional freight train through, having reports about its progress on an hourly basis. ... Passenger trains had to wait to let our wagons through. Brezhnev's office was in regular touch... Finally, they got beyond the Urals and all the problems were sorted out. ... An hour ago I was informed that there are no wagons. None at all. There never were any. They were not making their way from anywhere and were not being sent through to anywhere. The whole thing is a mirage, the fruit of a vivid imagination, a deception which I swallowed like an idiot.[18]

Later, together with a colleague, Vaksberg found out what actually happened:

> The fact of the matter was that the wagons were there and there was the desire and intention to carry out the instruction from the minister. However, at the very last minute, ... the wagons were requisitioned by local mafia, because they needed urgently to get off some fruit which was already beginning to spoil to the rich northern markets. This much-sought-after commodity, always in short supply, and the production cost of which is ten times less than

---

17   Arkady Vaksberg, *The Soviet Mafia* (New York: St. Martin's Press, 1991).
18   Vaksberg, *The Soviet Mafia*, 78.

its market value 'up there' where a peach or a bunch of grapes is an almost unattainable dream, brings in a profit of millions. ... So, when the question arose of who should get priority, the answer was a forgone conclusion.... The false telegrams ... were needed in order to play for time ... In the end, the winners [the mafia] were infinitely more powerful than the people whose job it was to check railway movements.[19]

Rich evidence about the extent of such practices was uncovered by the Soviet press and prosecution reports during the years of "*glasnost*" and "*perestroyka*" under the last Soviet leader, Mikhail Gorbachev. Cases such as the above, with the mafia often involving the highest levels of the hierarchy were reported in the republics of Central Asia and Caucasus, Moldavia, Krasnodar region, Moscow, and various other places. In an infamous *Okean* affair, the USSR Ministry of Fisheries obtained permission to open its own network of seafood shops. The short-in-supply delicacies that were supposed to be sold there were instead "swallowed by underground dealers at five or six times the official price. Roughly a third of the money would be appropriated by those immediately involved in the operation; the rest would go in bribes to those capable of guaranteeing complete protection of the criminals—not only their job security but also their future careers."[20] The last act of this drama unfolded in front of my own eyes—during the short-lived "anti-corruption campaign" after Brezhnev died in 1982, the father of a high-school classmate of mine (the manager of one of the shops involved in the scheme) was arrested and quickly executed, presumably to silence him and to protect those above him in the hierarchy.

Hoping to revive the socialist system, Gorbachev introduced a limited private sector into the economy and embarked on a far-reaching political reform which ushered in free press, ideological tolerance, and reasonably free and democratic elections in the Soviet Union for the first time in its history. This only precipitated the collapse. Once a legal private sector came into existence, it became sufficient just to establish a private company under the auspices of SOE to assume full control over its activity. Money began to flow in the open, and the parallel economy further dramatically increased its grip on resources. The clash between it and the remnants of the hierarchical order became imminent, and finally crystallizing in the dramatic events of August 1991 that swept away the communist regime almost overnight.

---

[19]   Vaksberg, *The Soviet Mafia*, 79–80.
[20]   Vaksberg, *The Soviet Mafia*, 5–6.

***

The planned economy formally collapsed, together with the Soviet Union, in 1991. Since the communist ideology and the planned economy were widely viewed as the greatest obstacles to normal economic development based on private property and market mechanism, economists saw good reasons to predict a smooth transition to a market economy followed by sustained economic growth.[21] As should be clear from the exposition above, this view did not pay enough attention to the fact that the planned economy had been largely supplanted by the parallel economy long before its formal collapse. Thus, in order to understand the true nature of the transition that took place in Russia after 1991, it is important to understand the key features of the parallel economy that destroyed the planned economy and completely took over after its collapse.

The parallel economy did have some features in common with a market economy. In particular, it was free from government intervention (but for the need to bribe or harass government officials). In this sense, it was much "freer" than market economies in developed countries. However, even as the parallel economy helped to correct some of the inefficiencies of the planned economy, it was the source of other inefficiencies, and those took the central stage in the 1990s.

The first inefficiency is linked to the absence of an institutional arrangement defining and enforcing property rights. In the planned economy, property rights were strictly delineated and enforced. In the parallel economy, each agent had to defend his property rights by himself and, moreover, do it while avoiding detection. This required hiring an expensive private enforcement team, or paying off a gang.

The resulting permanent state of feud between various "mini-states" surrounding clusters of the parallel economy involved large deadweight losses, including those from high degree of market segmentation.[22] Although the formation of prices in the parallel economy was (more or less) governed by "supply and demand," a great variety of prices resulted. The fact that the parallel economy was based on personal trust relationships, not impersonal rules, strictly limited the number of participants in each market segment.

---

[21] Gerard Roland, *Transition and Economics: Politics, Markets and Firms* (Cambridge: The MIT Press, 2000), 3.

[22] Serguey Braguinsky, "Enforcement of Property Rights During the Russian Transition," *Journal of Legal Studies*, 28, no. 2 (1999): 515–44.

The flows of goods, capital, labor, and information were severely disrupted. High transaction costs also made it impossible to attain an optimal scale of production. The planned economy may have erred on the side of creating too many excessively large firms (in part, to keep under control the costs of economic planning), but the parallel economy erred on the opposite side. And the opaque and illicit nature of the parallel economy made it no less hostile to competition than the planned economy.

The parallel economy was by its nature also oriented towards extremely short-term profit maximization. This is explained both by the insecure nature of property rights, and by the natural absence of a financial market enabling risk-sharing. Hence, it could not provide either the funds or the motivation for long-term investment. Instead, it had a natural inclination for directly unproductive, rent-seeking activities, with detrimental implications for the allocation of human talent.[23] In Braguinsky (2009), I examined the census of Russian "oligarchs" from the 1990s and documented that almost half of them were "old" oligarchs deriving their status from a privileged *nomenklatura* background dating back to the previous regime. Even more significantly, the rest ("new" oligarchs who did not have such background and were essentially self-made) prospered by developing their own special relationship with the government and/or the mafia. Hence, instead of changing the rules of the socioeconomic game (which they appeared to be positioned to do due to their relative youth, superior human capital, and sources of initial success in the consumer-oriented sectors neglected by the planned economy), the new oligarchs readily adopted the existing rules inherited from the parallel economy.[24]

The nature of the parallel economy described above determined the direction the transition took in the 1990s. Post-communist reforms only strengthened the grip on resources by parallel economy dealers and corrupt bureaucrats, politicians, and bosses of organized crime affiliated with them. The starkest example is presented by the privatization program, at the time touted as one of the most "successful" among post-communist economies.

By now it is widely acknowledged that the so-called "voucher" privatization of 1993, despite its proclaimed target of "peoples' privatization," in effect simply

---

[23] See for example Kevin M. Murphy, Andrei Shleifer, and Robert Vishny, "The Allocation of Talent: Implications for Growth," *Quarterly Journal of Economics*, 106, no. 2 (1991): 503–30.

[24] Serguey Braguinsky, "Postcommunist Oligarchs in Russia: Quantitative Analysis," *Journal of Law and Economics*, 52, no. 2 (2009): 307–49.

handed over the assets formerly owned by the state to insiders. However, the notion of "insider" ownership is sometimes misunderstood in this context. Under the privatization program adopted in Russia, most of the assets were formally given out basically for free to members of "workers' collectives." But ordinary workers never had any say in managing the assets, and, at the time, they often even did not receive their meager wages for months. The real "insider owners" were the top management, in conjunction with other agents formally outside the firm. The latter could be key suppliers or customers, export-import intermediaries, offshore companies that brought financing, and so on. Members of regional and/or local governments as well as outright gangsters would also be involved. Over time, those opaque "structures" (as the Russians called them) acquired full control over most productive assets through elaborate schemes designed to hide the real owners.

It is thus hardly surprising that privatization did not produce new incentives for increased efficiency of former SOEs. Segmented markets, short-term planning horizon and other features of the post-communist economy incentivized insider owners to continue to divert revenue flows to their own separate business and non-business interests (now often located outside of the country). That is, the management of privatized firms continued to derive benefits from their control rights not through dividends or increased market valuation, but from the parallel-economy-type malfeasance, illicit operations, and rent-seeking activities.

The outcome of the ill-designed initial privatization scheme was further exacerbated by the outright giveaway of most valuable state-owned assets, especially in oil and gas industry, to politically-connected "oligarchs" through the "loans for shares" and other similar shams.[25] To protect their newly acquired wealth, the major "oligarchs" temporarily joined hands to subvert the young Russian democracy, securing Yeltsin's reelection in 1996. Once the election was over, however, their infighting resumed with a vengeance.

In the late 1990s, as it became apparent that Boris Yeltsin could not remain in power for much longer, one of the most powerful oligarchic groups led by Boris Berezovsky, together with members of Yeltsin's immediate family, designed and implemented the "successor plan," which eventually brought Vladimir Putin to power. Little did they know that by doing so, they

---

[25] See for example Sergei Guriev and Andrey Rachinsky, "The Role of Oligarchs in Russian Capitalism," *Journal of Economic Perspectives*, 19, no. 1 (2005): 131–50.

also ushered in an entirely new stage in the "transition" process. Once in power, Putin quickly moved to establish his own power base, expropriating or otherwise putting shifting control of most of the oligarchs' assets to his cronies, while jailing or kicking out of the country those who tried to resist.[26] The segmented "parallel economy" system, which as mentioned basically ignored the government machine (apart from paying off bureaucrats and politicians), was reigned in and had to cede to the reasserted powers of the Putin government. But the new system of government control was very different from the totalitarian control of the planned economy. Today's Russian government led by Vladimir Putin does not care that much about ideological control over its citizens (although it has recently started using some elements of it to tighten its grip on power). It cares even less about catching up with, let alone "outstripping" developed countries in terms of technology and productivity. Instead, its overarching goal is continued concentration of wealth in the hands of Putin and his inner circle, and the preservation of control over the economy's rents.

Today, the "transition process" is indeed complete, just not the transition to western-style market economy. The actual transition that took place was from a totalitarian to a tinpot dictatorship. Steven Cheung's view of the world has finally been vindicated; with totalitarian objectives gone, the tinpot dictator reigns over a (quasi-)market economy and utilizes a revenue-maximizing tax (including occasional expropriation).

***

So, what comes next? Having served two 4-year terms and consolidated power, Putin heeded the constitutional limit by appointing a crony to serve as president from 2008–2012, but never relinquished actual power. He then decided to return to presidency himself in 2012, with an extended 6-year term, and was crowned for another 6-year term in 2018. As the process of con-centration of power and wealth in Putin's hands reached its peak, in a de-

---

[26] Berezovsky, the "Godfather of the Kremlin," was one of the first to be kicked out. He fled to the U.K. in late 2000 and later reportedly took part in anti-Putin demonstrations in London, carrying a sign that read "I gave birth to you, and I will kill you too." Instead, in March 2013 he was found dead in his home in England. The circumstances of his death remain unclear. Mikhail Khodorkovsky, once the richest man in Russia, was arrested in 2003, convicted (twice; the second time already in jail, as his first sentence was about to expire) on tax evasion charges, and had spent nine years in jail before being sent into exile. Paul Klebnikov, *Godfather of the Kremlin: The Decline of Russia in the Age of Gangster Capitalism* (Orlando: Harcourt, 2000).

velopment typical of tinpot dictatorships, he embarked on several ill-advised adventures—among them, annexing Crimea, unleashing a bloody conflict in eastern Ukraine, and escalating Russian subversive activity against Western democracies in Europe and the United States. While his regime of personal power seems to be in no immediate jeopardy, we know from history that tinpot dictatorships are prone to destabilization at a moment's notice, triggered by an unexpected crisis. This is also what makes it so hard to predict when and what exactly is going to happen that will put an end to Putin's regime, or what sort of a new system is going to replace it. It looks like we haven't seen the end of the communist experiment yet; what Russia appears to be going through is its new and, hopefully, final phase.

PART THREE
Politics

ROMANCING A MILLENARIAN STATE

From Petrograd to Raqqa[1]

Leon Aron

In his memoir of Lenin, Maxim Gorky confesses that in 1917, after Lenin called for a socialist revolution in his "April Theses," he, Gorky, thought it a hopeless and dangerous endeavor: "Lenin was sacrificing the tiny army of politically advanced workers and the entire revolutionary intelligentsia," by "throwing them, like a handful of salt, into the swamp of the [Russian] village to dissolve there, changing nothing in the spirit, day-to-day existence and the history of the Russian people."[2]

Gorky was far from alone in his wariness. Attempting to seize power from the Provisional Government before the Constituent Assembly was elected looked like a reckless adventure not just to most of the other Russian Social-Democrats, especially the Mensheviks, who at the time dominated the soviets, but the majority of the Bolsheviks were opposed to it as well. Among the doubters was Lev Kamenev, one of Lenin's oldest and closest associates, the future chairman of the Central Executive Committee of the All-Russian Congress of Soviets, the Politburo member and Chairman of the Moscow Soviet. Shortly before Lenin's arrival from Switzerland, Kamenev argued at a closed meeting of the Petrograd Bolshevik Committee that while the "bourgeois" Provisional Government was destined to be overthrown, "the important thing is not to take power: it is to hold on to it."[3]

[1] A version of this chapter was first published in the *New York Review of Books* on February 13, 2018 (https://www.nybooks.com/daily/2018/02/13/kingdom-come-millenarianisms-deadly-allure-from-lenin-to-isis/).

[2] Maksim Gorky, "V.I. Lenin," http://www.tov.lenin.ru/titan/about/gorky.htm.

[3] Richard Pipes, *The Russian Revolution* (New York: Knopf, 1990), 338. Along with another of Lenin's closest associates, Grigory Zinoviev, Kamenev persisted in opposing the planned coup, voting against it in the Central Committee on October 10 and publishing an open letter decrying a week before the uprising. Throughout I draw on Richard Pipes's *The Russian Revolution* and *Russia Under the Bolshevik Regime* (New York: Knopf, 1994).

Kamenev had a point. There were 23,000–24,000 Bolsheviks in a country of 150 million.[4] As for the class that according to Marxist historical materialism was supposed to accomplish the revolution, industrial workers numbered no more than three million (or two percent of the country's population), and among them the Bolsheviks had far fewer adherents than their moderate ex-comrades, the Mensheviks.[5]

The story of how, barely five months after the "April Theses," the Bolsheviks seized power, held on to it, and (no less astonishingly) continued to increase in number and extend and solidify their reach over an enormous country is a story that continues to mystify and fascinate despite having been told many times.

It has also proven a usable history. For, *pace* Marx, History does not always repeat itself as a farce. Sometimes, perhaps more often than not, it returns as a tragedy. Most recently, we saw another initially miniscule extremist movement accomplish a similarly improbable feat of suddenly attracting tens of thousands of followers from all over the world, creating a state, and proceeding to conquer and hold major cities and vast tracts of land.

The Islamic State "set a new standard for extremist groups," wrote a leading student of Islamism, "proving it possible to capture and hold large swathes of territory… without the benefit of widespread popular support."[6] Not quite. Lenin and the Bolsheviks set that "standard" almost a century before.

***

The similarity in the outcomes matches the consonance in the context and in the traits of both movements, which seems to account for their triumphs. These similarities bear dwelling on even at the risk of repetition, so they remain fresh in our minds should History produce another version of the same tragedy.

To begin, both the Bolsheviks and ISIS capitalized on the strains and brutalization from seemingly endless slaughter: World War I and the Syrian civil and sectarian war. Daily hardships multiplied, civilizing institutions collapsed, savagery ensued.

---

[4]   Pipes, *The Russian Revolution*, 511; A. James McAdams, *Vanguard of the Revolution: The Global Idea of the Communist Party* (Princeton: Princeton University Press, 2017), 90.

[5]   Pipes, *The Russian Revolution*, 387; Pipes, *Russia Under*, 494.

[6]   Shadi Hamid, *Islamic Exceptionalism: How the Struggle Over Islam Is Reshaping the World* (New York: St. Martin's Press, 2016), 232.

It one of his most beautiful poems, written in 1917, Osip Mandelstam captured these surroundings:

Everything's in disarray. And no one's there
To say, as cold sets in, that disarray
Is everywhere. And how sweet it becomes the prayer:
Rossiya, Lethe, Lorelei.[7]

As a body drained of life, the country is growing "cold." Its soul, like those of the Greek dead, was drinking of the Lethe, the river of forgetting, that runs through the Hades. Memory is addled, and history can caution no more. Russia is also under the spell of Lorelei, the Rhine mermaid, who, like the sirens of the *Odyssey*, lures ships to their death with enchanting songs.

Lenin described the same context with characteristic flippancy and matter-of-factness "The power was lying under our feet in the street; all we had to do is pick it up." Toppling the Provisional Government, he added, was like "lifting a feather."[8]

Mass terror has helped as well. In both cases, violence was not contingent but relentless and central to the ideology, targeting groups, or "classes," rather than individuals. Stigmatizing, demonizing, and, eventually, de-humanizing the "enemy,"[9] was a common trait as well. Guilt or innocence mattered little so long as it belonged to a category judged guilty of class enmity or apostasy: the "bourgeoisie" or Shiites, "counterrevolutionary agitators"[10] or Sufis, the kulaks or the Yazidi.

Indulging, indeed reveling, in grotesque brutality advanced these causes as well. A prominent historian of the Russian Revolution wrote that Lenin displayed "militarized politics": "He treated politics as warfare, the objective

---

[7]   The in-text English translation is my own, see the original below transliterated from Cyrillic.
      "Vsyo pereputalos'. E nyekomu skazat'
      Chto, postepenno kholodeya,
      Vsyo pereputalos'. E sladko povtoryat'
      Rossiya, Lyeta, Loreleya."
      Osip Mandelstam, "Dekabrist (Decembrist)," in *O.E. Mandelshtam, Sobranie sochineniy v chetyryokh tomakh* (O.E. Mandelstam; collected works in four volumes), vol. 1, ed. G.P. Struve (Moscow: Terra, 1991), 66.

[8]   Pipes, *Russia Under*, 498.

[9]   In calling for attacks on "the rich, swindlers, and parasites," Lenin elucidate the objective as "cleansing of Russia's soil of all harmful insects, of scoundrel fleas, bedbugs... ISIS taxonomies of hatred include, for example, flies and dogs with Jews and Shiites." Pipes, *Russian Revolution*, 790–91.

[10] Lenin ordered in his February 21, 1918 decree "The Socialist Fatherland in Danger!" that the said "agitators" were to be "executed on the spot." Pipes, *Russian Revolution*, 794.

of which was not to compel the enemy to submit but to annihilate him."[11] One of the founders of the Cheka, Iosif Unshlikht, recalled how Lenin "mercilessly made short shrift of philistine Party members who complained of the mercilessness of the Cheka, how he laughed at and mocked the 'humanness' of the capitalist world."[12]

As one of Lenin's top lieutenants and personal friends, the St. Petersburg party chief Grigory Zinoviev put it, "We must carry with us 90 million of the 100 million of Soviet Russia's inhabitants. As for the rest, we have nothing to say to them. They must be annihilated."[13] With appropriate substitution of the victimized category, what ISIS commander would not heartily welcome this call to action from the Red Army's newspaper: "Without mercy, without sparing, we will kill our enemies by the scores of hundreds, let them be thousands, let them drown in their own blood.... [L]et there be floods of blood of the bourgeoisie—more blood, as much as possible."[14] The founder of ISIS, Abu Musab al-Zarqawi, "pushed... brutality to unprecedented levels," which shocked even the al-Qaeda founders, bin Ladin and Zawahiri, who reportedly pleaded with Zarqawi to "restrain himself" at least in his massacres of Iraqi Shiite civilians.[15]

The Bolsheviks and the jihadists were also alike in their rationalization of the violence. Both believed they had been given absolution by History or by God.[16] They killed humans to rescue humanity, whether from capitalist "exploitation" or "idolatry." They felt supremely lucky, nay, chosen and privileged to be instruments of the inexorable deliverance. In a recent book on the Soviet collectivization, Anne Applebaum quotes a communist activist: "I firmly believed that the ends justified the means. Our great goal was the universal triumph of communism, and for the sake of the goal everything was permissible—to lie, to steal, to destroy hundreds of thousands and even millions of people, all those who were hindering our work or could hinder it, everyone who stood in the way."[17]

---

[11]   Pipes, *Russia Under,* 499.

[12]   Pipes, *Russia Under,* 507–8.

[13]   Pipes, *The Russian Revolution,* 820.

[14]   Pipes, *The Russian Revolution,* 820.

[15]   Graeme Wood, "True Believers," *Foreign Affairs* (September–October 2017), https://www.foreignaffairs.com/reviews/review-essay/2017-08-15/true-believers.

[16]   Wood, "True Believers,"

[17]   Anna Reid, "Rule by Starvation," *The Wall Street Journal,* October 6, 2017, https://www.wsj.com/articles/rule-by-starvation-1507319629.

This belief in predestination animated both groups: the inexorability of the future, and thus of victory, as foretold in the sacred prophesies of Marx or Mohammad. They could not fail. Alive or dead, they won. Napoleon used to say that a battle is won or lost in the minds of the combatants before the first shot was fired. Is there an energy more powerful, a cause more mesmerizing and irresistible, a confidence in the inevitability of victory greater than the one generated by the ecstatic hope of liberating humanity from the miseries of daily life and ushering it into a conflictless Eden?

Hence the shared obsession with eschatology: winning meant the end of the world as it was known and the advent of another, made exactly to the prophesied specifications. Those who forged the Islamic State were said to be "millenarians," their strategy shaped by "when they thought the Mahdi was going to arrive." For the followers of the Islamic State, the "millenarian vein," into which ISIS tapped, was a key source of the inspiration.[18] Zarkawi was reported to "inject the apocalyptic message into jihad" and ISIS made the apocalypse the central element of its ideology.[19] (Hailing mostly from elite Sunni families, the al-Qaeda founders, bin Laden and Zawahiri, were said to "look down" at the eschatological content of Islam, which they considered "something that the masses engage in.")[20]

Of course in the Bolshevik eschatology the sun was not to rise in the West, nor was the Mahdi to reveal himself, nor Issa (Jesus), Islam's prophet second only to Mohammad, to lead the troops of the faithful into the final battle. Yet theirs, too, was a self-imposed mission to bring about the end of "pre-history," and forge nothing short of a new civilization, conveying humanity, as Engels put it, from the realm of necessity to the realm of freedom." Marx called the proletariat "the messiah-class": with History acting as God, the proletariat was a "universal redeemer," and the revolution meant "ultimate salvation."[21] Labelled by Raymond Aron "Christian heresy" and a "modern form of millenarianism," Marxism, Aron wrote, "places the kingdom of God on Earth following the apocalyptic revolution in which the Old World will be swallowed up."[22]

---

[18] Graeme Wood, *The Way of the Strangers: Encounters with the Islamic State* (New York: Random House, 2017), 252, 268.

[19] Wood, *The Way of the Strangers*, 246.

[20] Wood, *The Way of the Strangers*, 252.

[21] Vladimir Tismaneanu, *The Devil in History* (Berkeley: University of California Press, 2012), 87, 227.

[22] Raymond Aron, *The Dawn of Universal History: Selected Essays from a Witness to the Twentieth Century* (New York: Basic Books, 2002), 203.

To be sure, once through death's door, ISIS fighters and the Bolsheviks parted ways: the former believed themselves to be headed to Paradise, while the militantly atheistic latter thought that service to the world proletarian revolution and the gratitude of future generations would be their only reward. Yet the glorification of death for the cause was central to the ideology of both movements. Islamic State fighters are reported to be not only willing to die: "in a blaze of religious ecstasy," they even welcome death.[23] "Being killed … is a victory," the Islamic State's spokesman Abu Muhammed al-Aldani declared,[24] while Lenin confessed to Karl Radek that he had "sought to reconcile Marx with the Narodnaya Volya (People's Will)," a member of which, Ignaty Grinevitzky, killed Tsar Alexander II and was likely the world's first suicide bomber. (The father of Russian Social Democracy and Lenin's mentor, Georgy Plekhanov, had begun his revolutionary career as a leader of an earlier version of People's Will: *Chyornyi Peredel*, or Black Repartition.)

In the words of one historian, People's Will was "animated by the faith that makes heroes and martyrs."[25] The cause of the group's key organizer, Alexander Mikhailov, hanged for the killing of Alexander II, was said to be "his religion… inseparable from his belief in God."[26] Knowing full well that he was doomed, Mikhailov considered himself "fortunate" to be part of the movement: "A lucky star has shown over my head," Mikhailov wrote, "Who does not fear…death is almost omnipotent."[27]

A member of the "Terrorist Section" of the People's Will, Lenin's elder and much beloved brother, Alexander Ulyanov, was "a man… who calmly accepted the prospect of self-immolation in the service of the cause."[28] Sentenced to be hanged for conspiring to kill Alexander III, he told the court that terror was "the only weapon at the disposal of a small minority," which relied solely on their "spiritual strength and the consciousness that [they were] fighting for justice" and who "will not consider it a sacrifice to lay down their lives for the cause."[29]

***

---

[23] Hamid, *Islamic Exceptionalism*, 9.

[24] Hamid, *Islamic Exceptionalism*, 9.

[25] Avrahm Yarmolinsky, *Road to Revolution* (Toronto: Collier-Macmillan, 1969), 227.

[26] Yarmolinsky, *Road to Revolution*, 228.

[27] Yarmolinsky, *Road to Revolution*, 228.

[28] Yarmolinsky, *Road to Revolution*, 318.

[29] Yarmolinsky, *Road to Revolution*, 319.

It could be argued that, *mutatis mutandis*, many, perhaps most, extremist chiliastic sects have been in thrall of similarly rigid ideologies and pursued them with a comparable zeal. Still, very few succeeded as spectacularly *and* as quickly.

It appears that in both cases a key, if not *the* key, catalyst of success, the weightiest final component, was the anchoring of their movements in a physical space, translating ideology into state power, crystallizing doctrines into tangible real estate. Lenin called it "the state of the dictatorship of the proletariat." The proponents of "political Islam"—for instance, Abu Ala Maudidi, a key modern Islamic philosopher and the founder of Jamaat-e-Islami, the largest mass religious organization of South Asia—called it *hakimiyya*, the "securing of political sovereignty for God."[30]

To recall the title of Irving Loius Horowitz's brilliant essay on Hegel, "Romancing an Organic State,"[31] Lenin and al Bagdhadi "romanced" a millenarian state.

Romancing is one thing but, again in both cases, consummation, let alone marriage of ideology to state was not merely problematic from an operational point of view, as pointed out by Kamenev. It was at a rather significant variance with doctrinal foundations of both movements. For both Lenin and Baghdadi declaring the "state of the dictatorship of the proletariat" and the Islamic State and, especially, the Caliphate, was a doctrinal leap.

The notion of such a state belongs to "a minority interpretation of Islamic scripture," and this version of Islam was said to bear only passing resemblance to the Islam practiced or espoused today by most Muslims.[32] Indeed, the "original" jihadists, al Qaeda and, certainly, Osama bin Laden personally, were said to have had an "aversion to state building" and to declaring a caliphate on its territory.[33] Declaring a Caliphate was "controversial" even among many militant Salafis, who were the majority of the ISIS fighters.[34]

Lenin's doctrinal predicament was more complicated still. To the extent that Engels (it was almost exclusively Engels, not Marx) had dwelled on what happens after a socialist revolution—and he wrote precious little on the

---

[30] Shiraz Maher, *Salafi-Jihadism* (New York: Oxford University Press, 2016), 170.
[31] Irving Loius Horowitz, "Romancing the Organic State," in *Behemoth*, I.L. Horowitz (New Brunswick, New Jersey: Transaction Publishers, 1999).
[32] Wood, *The Way*, xxvii.
[33] Wood, "True Believers."
[34] Maher, *Salafi-Jihadism*, 4.

matter—the state, as "a special agent of suppression" of the proletariat by the "bourgeoisie," would not be needed any longer after the proletariat takes power. In a classless society, the state would be either "extirpated" once and for all by the revolution, "wither away," or "sink into a slumber." Socialism ultimately meant the absence of a state. Hiding in a Finnish forest after an unsuccessful Bolshevik insurrection in July 1917, in what was to become his key political testament, *State and Revolution*, Lenin argued that far from being versions of the same phenomenon, the state's "extirpation" and its "withering away" were two *distinct* and *sequential* processes. First the proletariat "smashes" the bourgeois state (as Marx wished the Paris Commune had done) and establishes the state of the dictatorship of the proletariat. Then, and only then, after such a state is well established, it begins to gradually "wither away."[35] Stretching Engels still further, Lenin claimed that "repression," that key and most hated attribute of the class-based state, too, will be preserved: "A special apparatus, a special machine of repression," the state would still be necessary.[36]

Another hurdle rose from among the core tenets of historical materialism. As was the case with all the "modes of productions" that had come before it, capitalism was to collapse from the unresolvable contradiction between the economic "basis" and the political "superstructure" *when* it reaches its highest stage of maturity. It followed that capitalism must be well established in a country before the conditions are ripe for a socialist revolution.

Twisting Marxism, as was his wont, to justify immediate political objectives, Lenin argued in *Imperialism: The Highest Stage of Capitalism* that the uneven development of capitalism during its final "imperialist stage" made it possible for less developed countries, as imperialism's "weakest links," to take shortcuts in the process. And so immediately upon his arrival in Russia from exile, he declared in his "April Theses" that, far from entering an open-ended period of capitalist "bourgeois-democratic republic," Russia's "bourgeois" stage was already over and the country was ripe for a socialist revolution.[37]

---

[35]   "...[H]ere Engels talks about the "annihilation" of the bourgeois state by a proletarian revolution, whereas the words about the withering [of the state] refer to the remnants of the proletarian state after a socialist revolution. According to Engels, the bourgeois state does not "wither," but is annihilated by proletariat in the course of a revolution. It is the state or half-state of the proletariat which withers after this revolution.")." V. I. Lenin, "Gosudarstvo i revolyutsita. Konspekt (The State and Revolution: Notes)," BezFormata, electronically published September 12, 2011, https://engels.bezformata.com/listnews/lenin-gosudarstvo-i-revolyutciya-konspekt/1223404/.

[36]   Ibid.; See also Pipes, *The Russian Revolution*, 469.

[37]   McAdams, *Vanguard*, 87; Pipes, *The Russian Revolution*, 393.

Still, for both Lenin and Al Baghdadi, there remained one more, and perhaps the largest, ideological obstacle: the obsolescence, indeed anathematization, of the key attributes of a state: nationality, national cultures, national sovereignty, national borders. Both circumvented the hindrance similarly by emphasizing the purely temporal, instrumental nature of their creations: the sole mission of the state of the dictatorship of the proletariat and the Islamic State was to serve as the base, the catalyst of and a magnet for a "world revolution" and a global Caliphate, respectively. As Trotsky put it, "[the Bolshevik Party] set itself the task of overthrowing the world."[38] Once masters of the Russian state, Aron wrote, "Lenin and his comrades began by awaiting the European or world revolution in the same way as the early Christians awaited the Second Coming of Christ."[39] The Islamic State, too, "craved an all-out civilizational war."[40] Like the state of the dictatorship of the proletariat, the Caliphate "served a dualistic purpose between temporal and cosmic ends," the latter being served by "hastening the day of resurrection."[41]

In the end, it was the "cosmic" attribute of the dictatorship of the proletariat and the Caliphate that became the weightiest components of their legitimacy in the eyes of the faithful. A "home of a religion of temporal salvation," in Raymond Aron's words, the sway of the Soviet state ranged from the "peasants of Asia" to "atomic scientists" in the West.[42] Jihadists, too, did not regard the "seizure of Mosul as a local victory... Instead, first as murmur and soon as a roar, they insisted that ISIS's ascendance was an event of world-historical import. Indeed to call it world-historical would diminish it, because the entire cosmos was in play."[43]

***

Doctrinal daring[44] paid off spectacularly. After a Bolshevik state was in place, the party's membership grew from under 24,000 in February 1917 to

---

[38] Pipes, *The Russian Revolution*, 339.

[39] Aron, *The Dawn*, 207.

[40] Aron, *The Dawn*, 246.

[41] Maher, *Salafi-Jihadism*, 4.

[42] Aron, *The Dawn*, 203.

[43] Wood, *The Way*, xx.

[44] "The Bolsheviks must take power!" Lenin implored the Central Committee in September 1917. V.I. Lenin, "Bol'sheviki dolzhniy vzyat' vlast' (The Bolsheviks must take power)!" Marxists Internet Archive, last modified electronically February 19, 2004, https://www.marxists.org/russkij/lenin/works/lenin004.htm#topp; "Waiting was for the weak," concluded the leaders of the Islamic State Hamid, *Islamic Exceptionalism*, 216.

250,000 in 1919 and 730,000 in 1921.[45] Following the establishment of the Islamic State in northern Syria with the capital of Raqqa in 2013 and al Baghdadi's declaration of a Caliphate a year later, the ranks of the movement swelled from an estimated 1,000–2,500 in 2012 to between 20,000–31,500 in 2014.[46]

Much of the upswell, undoubtedly, was due to the anticipated rewards for loyalty as well as sanctions for defiance associated with state power. As a historian of early Soviet Russia put it, "they joined because membership [in the Party] offered privileges and security in a society in which extreme poverty and insecurity were the rule."[47]

Yet the early Soviet state and the Islamic State were hardly ordinary states and the growth of their support cannot be explained solely, or perhaps even primarily, by the lures of steady employment. There is an abundance of evidence in memoirs as well as journalistic accounts (and, in the Russian case, some brilliant fiction as well[48]) that for many converts the etatization, as it were, of a millenarian dream spawned an appeal for a different and, at least for a time, far more powerful kind of dream. As described by a student of the Islamic State, the motives of its acolytes would ring true for many, perhaps most, of the early recruits of the Bolshevik state:

> ISIS asked its followers to join not because it was fighting US troops—an orthodox bin Ladenist goal—but because it had established the world's only Islamic state, with no law but God's and with a purity of purpose that even the Taliban had not envisioned [....] "The breadth of the appeal of the Islamic State was as shocking as its depth...Tens of thousands ... had all drunk their inspiration from the same fountains. In addition to the physical caliphate, with its territory and war and economy to run, there was a caliphate of the

---

45 Pipes, *The Russian Revolution*, 511.

46 Bill Roggio, "Al Qaeda in Iraq suicide bomber kills 31 at Iraqi Army base in Taji," *Long War Journal*, November 6, 2012, https://web.archive.org/web/20141110183855/http://www.longwarjournal.org/threat-matrix/archives/2012/11/al_qaeda_in_iraq_suicide_bombe.php; Jim Sciutto, Jamie Crawford, and Chelsea J. Carter, "ISIS can 'muster' between 20,000 and 31,500 fighters, CIA says," *CNN*, September 12, 2014, http://edition.cnn.com/2014/09/11/world/meast/isis-syria-iraq/; Jim Michaels, "New U.S. intelligence estimate sees 20–25K ISIL fighters," *USA Today*, February 3, 2016, https://www.usatoday.com/story/news/world/2016/02/03/isil-fighters-new-estimate-25000-iraq-syria/79775676/.

47 Pipes, *Russia Under*, 138.

48 See for example, Vasily Grossman, *V gorode Berdicheve* (In the town of Berdichev), *LibRu*, last modified November 14, 2004, http://lib.ru/PROZA/GROSSMAN/r_berdichew.txt. For an English translation, see Vasily Grossman, *The Road* (New York: New York Review of Books, 2010).

imagination [to which all these people had already emigrated long before they slipped across the Turkish border]...They believed the state that awaited them would purify their lives by forbidding vice and promoting virtue. Its leader, Abu Bakr al Baghdadi, would unify the world's Muslims, restore their honor, and allow them to reside in the only truly just society...[where they would] enjoy perfect equality..."[49]

***

Resplendent in military garb as he addressed in the Kremlin on March 2, 1919 in what was to become the founding session of the Third International, Lev Trotsky remarked that the "mole of history" had not done badly under the Kremlin walls.[50]

An apparently rather whimsical animal, this mole can also connect seemingly distant passages. At its height, ISIS is estimated to have had 9,000 citizens from the former Soviet Union—by far the single largest national contingent. Of these fighters, 4,000 were from Russia itself and 5,000 from Central Asia,[51] the latter mostly Russian-speaking, radicalized and recruited on Russian construction sites. Second only to Arabic by the number of fighters speaking it, the language of the Bolshevik state became a language of the Caliphate.

[49] Wood, "True Believers"; Wood, *The Way*, xxiv.
[50] McAdams, *Vanguard*, 102.
[51] See for example, Vladimir Putin, "Interview to Mir broadcasting company," interviewed by Radik Batyrshin, *Mir*, April 12, 2017, http://en.kremlin.ru/events/president/news/54271.

STALIN, TITO, DJILAS, AND THE DIALECTICAL QUARRELS OF POST-WAR EUROPE

Tito's Leninism

Marius Stan

Introduction

In the aftermath of WWII, many European communist leaders have culti-vated what historian Alfred Rieber has described as "the illusion of popular democracy."[1] Some of them truly believed in "the original path toward socialism" (Władysław Gomułka in Poland, and Lucrețiu Pătrășcanu in Romania). Notwithstanding Stalin's true intentions, there was no "acknowl-edged international communist center to coordinate the activities of local communist parties" between 1943 (the dissolution of the Comintern) and 1947 (the establishment of the Cominform). The Soviet picture of the world has been "one of trial and error informed by a Marxist perception of the world."[2]

But speaking in Moscow, on the occasion of the 30th anniversary of the October Revolution, in November 1947, Vyacheslav Molotov (then Politburo member and minister of foreign affairs) referred to the old adage "All roads lead to Rome" by saying that, in our age, all roads lead to communism. Obviously, for the ultra-dogmatic Stalinist that meant all roads lead to a Soviet-style regime (with a one-party system, terror, and the rest). At that moment, one could argue, the national roads temptation ceased to be a viable choice. Although the Georgian Affair of 1922, that "mild case of premature Titoism,"[3] should have been—at least with hindsight—enough evidence of Stalin's true

---

[1] Alfred J. Rieber, "Popular Democracy: An Illusion?" in *Stalinism Revisited: The Establishment of Communist Regimes in East-Central Europe*, ed. Vladimir Tismaneanu (Budapest: CEU Press, 2009), 72–95.

[2] Rieber, "Popular Democracy: An Illusion?" 72–73.

[3] Adam Ulam, he BUlam,ty policies. for Stalin'ould have been reason enough for a to the Soviet-style regime ()scribed *The Bolsheviks: The Intellectual and Political History of the Triumph of Communism in Russia* (Cambridge, MA: Harvard University Press, 1998), 565.

intentions and nationality policies. Gomułka and Pătrăşcanu were doomed. Such strategic choices were the opposite of Stalin's vision of internationalism (which meant unconditional support for the USSR) and suggested to the hyper-suspicious despot that nationalism needed to be weeded out as an unforgivable heresy. It took Tito and his team some time to realize that they had been designated the new fifth column and that what Stalin required was total obedience, sycophantic admiration, and renunciation to any claim to autonomy.[4]

A few months after that Moscow event, Stalin and Molotov wrote to Tito and his comrades lamenting the "anti-Soviet" attitudes among the "Yugoslav comrades."[5] Tito's "national path" became the symbol of treason. The Titoists (real or imagined) were ruthlessly denounced as "deviators," "objective enemies," and so on. The original paths to socialism were a short-lived experiment that had come to an abrupt end. Stalin had made up his mind: zero tolerance for "national communism." Instead, full regimentation, *Gleichschaltung*, uniformity. But to achieve such a goal, the Soviets needed a subtler, even if seemingly self-contradictory plan: "the partial undoing of the *Gleichschaltung*. [...] Further, the potential appeal of Titoism to semi-autonomous Soviet dependencies in Eastern Europe had to be neutralized, and this, it seemed, could best be done by making friends with Tito, or at least making it appear that friendship was restored. Then Titoism could cease being a symbol of anti-Sovietism and its disruptive force would be negated."[6] How could anyone explain such a puzzling behavior? How could anyone be able to anticipate the Kremlin's moves, or for that matter Stalin's thoughts? Let's also remember that one of the forefathers of what we now call *the theory of totalitarianism*, Franz Borkenau, had warned us that "the Russians believed in two contradictory conceptions at the same time and with equal vigor: in the constant approach of revolution, and in the constant betrayal by all and everybody."[7]

---

[4] See the illuminating discussion of the Tito-Stalin "divorce" in Zbigniew Brzezinski, *The Soviet Bloc: Unity and Conflict* (Cambridge, MA and London: Harvard University Press, 1967), 185–209.

[5] See G.F.H., "The Stalin-Tito Correspondence: Roots of the Cominform Dispute," *The World Today* 4, no. 12 (Dec. 1948), 530–541.

[6] See Robert C. Tucker, *The Soviet Political Mind: Stalinism and Post-Stalin Change* (New York: W.W. Norton, 1971), 238–239.

[7] See Franz Borkenau, *World Communism: A History of the Communist International* (Ann Arbor: The University of Michigan Press, 1971), 265.

All pervasive Stalinism

For Stalin, the fact that Tito had instigated a number of international actions without consulting him beforehand was an utterly unacceptable, centrifugal risk. The Kremlin despot had been most disturbed by the 1947 attempt to establish a Danubian Confederation which would include Yugoslavia, Bulgaria, and Romania (with joining prospects for Albania and Hungary). He was suspicious of the idea put forth by Tito and Georgi Dimitrov. Presumably, the warning against the Bulgarian leader in a *Pravda* article hastened his death. When it comes to the Soviet domination over the new bloc, there was no room for any original experiments. Stalin was supposed to set the tune and other satellites would follow. In the words of a Czechoslovak adage of the Stalinist epoch: "Together with the Soviet Union for Eternity!" Mention should be made that the Czechoslovak little Stalin, Klement Gottwald, had flirted with the national road idea, but abandoned it earlier than other prominent communist figures.

However, the ideas expressed by Tito and Dimitrov were familiar to some of their close contacts from other Sovietized countries. Today, we know from Petre Pandrea's memoirs (1904–1964; Romanian lawyer and publicist, who deserves a separate discussion) that he had talks with the Bulgarian leader on the "Helvetization" of some of the neighboring states during one of the latter's visits to Bucharest. Pandrea was Lucrețiu Pătrășcanu's brother-in-law and his friendship with Dimitrov dated back to their common Berlin days, well before the Nazi takeover. Stalin simply simulated initial support for the confederation plan, then bent Dimitrov to his will in the most brutal way.

We also know from Milovan Djilas's memoirs, the Yugoslav vice-president turned dissident, that the Soviet potentates were indignant at any form of parallel authority within the communist world. For Stalin, the Soviet bloc had to abide by the logic of a besieged fortress, especially after the March 1947 formulation of the Truman Doctrine. While they landed on the Cominform's desk as vital imperatives, closing ranks around the CPSU and intensifying the struggle for the exposure of "opportunists, liquidators, and double-dealers" were, for the Soviets, just means to the same end. Baptized by Stalin himself, *For a Lasting Peace, for People's Democracy* (*Za prochny mir, za narodnuyu demokratiyu*), the Information Bureau weekly had been the propaganda mouthpiece for a discourse of both panic and vigilance. After 1949, "cosmopolitanism" was added to the list of mortal sins, the evil-twin of "bourgeois nationalism." The various deviations had to have names and faces: Gomułka's chauvinism, the Titoism of Traicho Kostov in Bulgaria, of László Rajk in Hungary, of Lucrețiu Pătrășcanu in Romania.

In Bucharest, the Romanian communist zealots gathered around Gheorghiu-Dej—Ana Pauker group arduously played the Stalinist card. In 1947, they received Tito with a warm welcome and gave loud encomia on the historical role played by the Yugoslav Marshal. A few months later, the same Gheorghiu-Dej, Vasile Luca, Miron Constantinescu, Iosif Chișinevschi, and Leonte Răutu lambasted the "the gangster" Judas-Tito. During the first Cominform meeting in the fall of 1947 in Poland, the Yugoslav delegates were more Stalinist than any of the representatives of any other party. Tito was also the main supporter of the Greek communist army led by the "Odysseus" of the Greek Left, Markos Vafiadis.[8] In brief, Yugoslav domesticism could not be tolerated by the Soviets any longer.

In a May 1948 ultimatum, Stalin and Molotov riled against the Yugoslav leadership. At this point, the risk of excommunication had become real. From the Kremlin's point of view, during his days, Trotsky had also been useful to the revolution cause, but this did not mean that the CPSU could ever close its eyes on his later "crass" and "opportunistic" errors, which made him an enemy of the Soviet Union. The obsession with the "Trojan Horse," with "the Fifth Column," i.e., with the infiltrated enemy, defined the Stalinist mental universe. It was rooted in Lenin's pamphlet *What Is to Be Done?* (1902) and grew bigger with the constructed mythology of the "new vanguard party" made of "professional revolutionaries."

Simply put, in 1945 not all decisions had yet been made. Obviously, as Stalin declared to Milovan Djilas[9]: "In this war, whomever sets foot first establishes the political system!" This was a strategic goal. The tactics however, at least until 1947, could still be different. That explains why Lucrețiu Pătrășcanu

---

[8] In the archives of the Central Committee of the Romanian Communist Party there are numerous documents regarding Yugoslav and Greek emigration to Romania. To the best of my knowledge, this is an unvisited chapter in the history of the anti-Tito campaigns. The person in charge with the Yugoslav and Greek communist refugees was Romanian Workers' Party International Department instructor, RCP veteran and later, a neo-Marxist critic of the Stalinist system, Pavel Câmpeanu (his books were published by M. E. Sharpe under the pseudonym "Pablo Garcia Casals"). The émigrés continued to be politically active in the 1960s and 1970s, less in Romania, mostly in the USSR and Belgium. The Cominformist threat, real or imagined, persisted as a major theme in the Titoist propaganda.

[9] See Milovan Djilas, *Conversations with Stalin* (San Diego: Harcourt Brace, 1963).

proclaimed in 1946 that he was first Romanian and second communist. Once the Cominform was created, one might assume, this stage of tactical permissiveness came to an end, and the Soviet model became mandatory. Afterward, even minor variations were treated as major deviations.

After the Yugoslav excommunication in June 1948, a couple of significant things happened. In Hungary, László Rajk (1909–1949) was arrested, tried, and convicted for Titoism, nationalism, and treason. In Romania, under house arrest, Lucrețiu Pătrășcanu was pressured to admit to nationalist mistakes and connections to Western intelligence agencies. And things did not stop there, for at the last Cominform meeting in 1949, in Budapest, Gheorghe Gheorghiu-Dej delivered a vicious attack (one penned by the Soviets, to be sure), denouncing Rajk, Kostov (1897—1949), and Pătrășcanu as imperialist spies who had infiltrated the workers' movement. In the words of Vladimir Tismaneanu, "international communism was entering the age of universal suspicion, diabolical conspiracies, and mass terror."[10]

Titoism vs. Cominform

The Cominform had merely been a Soviet weapon designed to impose a better (and bitter) grip over satellite communists. However, this political structure did not come into being in order to discipline the Yugoslavs, although this happened (indeed) along the way. Of course, Tito's strategies after 1945 had been a distressing factor for Stalin, and the former's intentions to acquire parts of Austrian Carinthia and Trieste were complicating Koba's dealings with the Western Allies. In the same vein, Tito's support for the Greek communists was deemed unacceptable by the Soviets since Greece had fallen under Western influence. And as there were clear ambitions for a Balkan Federation (including Bulgaria and Albania), they collided with Stalin's preference for tight control over such states.[11] But most importantly, the fact that Tito's partisans took power without any need for alliances with "friendly" parties, and the fact that they became more radical in their policies than other East-European "comrades," represented a threat in the Kremlin (not to mention the idea that this political model could eventually overshadow the

---

[10] See Vladimir Tismaneanu, *Stalinism for All Seasons* (Berkeley & L.A.: University of California Press, 2003), 106.

[11] See Tony Judt, "Why the Cold War Worked," in *When the Facts Change: Essays 1995—2010* (London: Vintage, 2015), 124–158.

Soviet pattern of thought and action). As Tony Judt accurately pointed out, "in matters of revolution Tito was becoming more Catholic than the Soviet pope."[12]

The Cominform represented an attempt to institutionalize the Soviet domination over communist parties in Central and Eastern Europe, as well as over the other two most important parties in the West (the French and Italian). At the Cominform founding conference, held in great secrecy in Poland, there were communist leaders from the Soviet Union, Yugoslavia, Romania, Poland, Bulgaria, Hungary, Czechoslovakia, France, and Italy. Stalin's special emissaries were Andrei Zhdanov, Georgi Malenkov,[13] and Mikhail Suslov. It had been envisaged as a limited organization, contained to the European region, but the absence of the KKE (the Communist Party of Greece), as well as the Spanish and East German communists was striking. The Yugoslav delegates, however, Milovan Djilas, Edvard Kardelj, and Aleksandar Ranković, complied with the Soviet behests and lambasted the Italian and French communists for "capitulation" and "lack of revolutionary zeal." It was, in fact, Stalin's concocted game that was meant to isolate the Yugoslavs from potential allies in the event of a break between Moscow and Belgrade. Imbued with a sense of hyper-activism, the Yugoslavs took the bait and played into Stalin's trap.

Stalin's main issue with Tito was not his lack of orthodox Leninism, but his ambition to become the leader of the newly Sovietized states, especially in the Balkans. The Yugoslavs' sin had to do with their firm belief in the right to decide their own priorities, since they had been the only communists in Europe to take power by themselves without military and political support from the Kremlin. Initially flat, the conflict between Tito and Stalin gained momentum in the spring of 1948 when the two dictators started exchanging increasingly irritated letters. The CPSU's Politburo gave Tito a tongue-lashing for not taking seriously the "hints" of various Soviet advisers. Stalin also criticized Tito's "adventurism" in foreign politics and his "liquidatorism" regarding the central role of the communist party. Stalin's critique was in fact an ultimatum. In turn, Tito offered an acerbic, tongue-in-cheek reply,

---

[12] Judt, "Why the Cold War Worked," 136.

[13] It was Georgi Malenkov's words (according to Tito's biographer, Vladimir Dedijer) to the other delegates at the first Cominform meeting that gave a vague "flavor of the immediate postwar atmosphere in Russia, that interlude of comparative calm and popular hopefulness between the great war that had just ended and the great cold war that was about to begin." See Robert C. Tucker, *The Soviet Political Mind*, 87–88.

professing endless love for Stalin and USSR. But the reality was different, and the Yugoslav leader did not want to abide by Stalin's humiliating demands. Until mid-1948, the Cominform weekly's headquarters was located in Belgrade—with Pavel Yudin, one of the most vocal Soviet propagandists, as editor-in-chief. The situation eventually became untenable and Stalin decided to move the head office to Bucharest.

A major implication of the Yugoslav break was the understanding of the very definition of *internationalism*. For Stalin, to be an internationalist meant to have demonstrated unconditional support for the USSR, i.e., for him. He proclaimed this attitude "the touchstone of proletarian internationalism."[14] In fact, the Brezhnev doctrine of "limited sovereignty" was a slightly updated version of Stalin's notion of the requirement of indefectible support for the Soviet positions regarding crucial issues such as the one-party system, rejection of any revisionist temptation, and the *Kremlinocentric* revolutionary cosmology in general.

However, for Tito and his comrades, this was an already obsolete understanding, belonging to an era when the Soviet Union was the only socialist country in the world (Mongolia, being, of course, a Soviet colony in everything but name). This conflict of visions would continue to haunt global communism for decades and helps explain the Soviet reactions to other heresies, such as Imre Nagy's in 1956, Alexander Dubček's in 1968, Mao Zedong's rejection of the Kremlin's hegemonic claims, and Eurocommunism (starting in fact with the condemnation by the French, Italian, and Spanish communist parties of the Soviet suppression of the Prague Spring).

Tito embraced Bolshevism[15] as a prisoner of war in Russia near Kazan

---

[14] Tismaneanu rightly notes that "what these countries experienced was not merely institutional import or imperial expansion," and that talking about the main features of Stalinism means also to acknowledge how "they went through what one could label, using Stephen Kotkin's wording, a 'civilizational' transfer that transplanted a secular eschatology (Marxism–Leninism), a radical vision of the world (…), and, ultimately, an alternative idea of modernity (…) self-identified as infallibly righteous." See Vladimir Tismaneanu, ed., *Stalinism Revisited: The Establishment of Communist Regimes in East-Central Europe* (Budapest: CEU Press, 2009), 3–4; for a discussion of Soviet policies and Stalin's aggrandizement in post-war Europe see Mark Kramer's chapter in the same volume "Stalin, Soviet Policy, and the Consolidation of a Communist Bloc in Eastern Europe, 1944–53."

[15] For details on Tito's formative experience as a prisoner and traces of future *Weltanschauung*, see Katerina Clark and Karl Schlögel, "Mutual Perceptions and Projections: Stalin's Russia in Nazi Germany—Nazi Germany in the Soviet Union," in *Beyond Totalitarianism: Stalinism and Nazism Compared*, eds. Michael Geyer and Sheila Fitzpatrick (Cambridge: Cambridge University Press, 2009), 413–414: "The war in the eastern lands was the central experience of an entire generation of young and not so young men. The war made thousands of young men pacifists and revolutionaries, not by theory but by disillusionment. An entire generation of

(in March 1915, seriously wounded, he spent 13 months in the hospital). He took part in the Bolshevization of the Yugoslav Communist Party in the 1930s and the formation of the International Brigades. He saw himself (and rightly so) as Stalin's most prominent Balkan disciple, equal only to Georgi Dimitrov. For him, the Leninist dogmas as codified by Stalin were infallible, truly sacrosanct. As such, he was perplexed when Stalin accused him of heresy and treason. It is only logical to conclude that "the Tito-Stalin confrontation destroyed the ideological uniformity of Stalinism," and what followed was that "Yugoslavs, eager to prove their Communist credentials, felt compelled to conceptualise and publicise their interpretation of 'authentic' Marxism. They revived Marx's early theses, which Stalin had buried in order to create a monstrous hybrid of a system."[16] In other words, "the Yugoslavs offered their 'road to socialism' as an alternative to Stalin's dogma."[17]

Slowly and hesitantly, Tito, Kardelj, and other Yugoslav communist lumi-naries came to the conclusion that the ossified structure of the Soviet-type vanguard party needed to be revamped. This happened more consistently in 1958 with the Program of the Communist League of Yugoslavia. Even renouncing the identification as a "Party" meant distancing from the enshrined model. The reaction within world communism was particularly aggressive—both the Soviet and the Chinese parties lambasted the Yugoslav revisionism. An international campaign was waged to denounce Tito and Titoism. It was Edvard Kardelj who became Tito's main theoretical spokes-man, including in defense of workers' self-management as a challenge to bureaucratic centralism. But the limit of this defiance was Tito's adamant refusal of political pluralism, i.e., the acceptance of free elections and a multi-party system. In the words of Milovan Djilas himself, "Decentralization in the economy does not mean a change in ownership, but only gives greater rights to the lower strata of the bureaucracy or of the new class. If the so-called liberalization and decentralization meant anything else, that would be mani-fest in the political right of at least part of the people to exercise some

---

leading central European communists developed in Russian POW camps—Karel Čapek, Ernst Reuter (the mayor of West Berlin after World War II), Josip Broz Tito, Béla Kun, and many, many others. The Eastern Front and the Russian Civil War became a school of radicalization and military education on both sides: for communists and sympathizers with Soviet Russia and for hard-core White Russian and Freikorps members, for the 'Baltikumer' and others."

[16] See Svetozar Rajak, "The Cold War in the Balkans, 1945–1956," in *The Cambridge History of the Cold War*, vol. 1, eds. Melvyn P. Leffler and Odd Arne Westad (Cambridge, UK: Cambridge University Press, 2010), 215.

[17] Rajak, "The Cold War in the Balkans."

influence in the management of material goods. At least, the people would have the right to criticize the arbitrariness of the oligarchy. This would lead to the creation of a new political movement, even though it were only a loyal opposition. However, this is not even mentioned, just as democracy in the party is not mentioned."[18]

This was the main difference between Tito and Imre Nagy and explains the Yugoslav leader's condemnation of the second stage of the Hungarian Revolution.

Why Djilas matters

One can rightly consider Milovan Djilas a paradigmatic apostate—a former adamant Stalinist turned into the brain behind the Yugoslav break-up with the Kremlin in 1948, the most visible and articulate ideologue of Titoism, until his second apostasy. During those three years after the war, the "blood brothers" of Yugoslavia had eliminated internal and external enemies and become very nervous regarding Soviet attempts to infiltrate into their party. This is precisely the moment when Djilas denounced Sovietism as "state capitalism" and sought to turn his party toward "workers' management." However, the break with Moscow triggered divisions within the Yugoslav party, too. The main outcome was the prison on Goli Otok, the island in the Adriatic where most pro-Stalin Yugoslav communists found their ending, and, as Stéphane Courtois and Mark Kramer remind us: "the persecution of Communists ['Stalinists,' or 'Cominformists'] in Yugoslavia that began in 1948–49 was probably one of the most massive persecution movements that Europe had witnessed, including those of the Soviet Union from the 1920s and the 1940s, Germany in the 1930s, and the repression of communists during the Nazi occupation. What happened in Yugoslavia was a truly immense phenomenon considering the number of inhabitants and the number of communists."[19] That was Tito's main purge in the aftermath of the war. Both Tito and Djilas had feared a Soviet invasion, but they eventually dealt with this "nightmare" through a partisan logic. The latter would later assume that the break with the Soviet Union initiated an "epochal" disintegration of world communism into national parts. In a way, not only did the Yugoslav "dissidence" within the

---

[18] Milovan Djilas, *The New Class* (London: Thames and Hudson, 1957), 63.

[19] Stéphane Courtois and Mark Kramer, trans., *The Black Book of Communism: Crimes, Terror, Repression*, (Cambridge, MA: Harvard University Press, 1999), 425.

communist camp anticipate Eurocommunism but Tito's stance deliberately defied the Stalinist theory of proletarian internationalism. Djilas was yet again right: The East German revolt of 1951, the Hungarian uprising of 1956 (which Tito would condemn), and even Gomułka's reforms in Poland were all, to one degree or another, made possible by the Yugoslav break of 1948.

Another major issue with Titoism was that by the time Stalin passed away in 1953, Tito had already developed a personality cult, which seemed rather outrageous to a heretic like Djilas. Moreover, Ranković was running the secret police, while Kardelj was dealing with Party affairs. Djilas was left to run the party newspaper, *Borba*. For him, the contrast between partisan conditions, equally shared with his "blood brothers" (who had lived in caves during the war, experienced shortages, illness, etc.), and Yugoslav communist conditions (with villas and summer houses on the Adriatic) was nothing but obscene—a true priviligentsia for which he coined the term "new class." Of all the old revolutionaries, Djilas was the only one to realize and publicly acknowledge that the old Marxist ideals were crumbling into pieces. As a consequence, he started to write his inside critique in the party daily *Borba* in 1953, accusing his former comrades of "intrigues, mutual scheming and trap laying, pursuit of posts, careerism, favoritism, and advancement of one's own followers, relatives—all of it under the mask of high morality and ideology."[20] He, of course, went first to Tito for support, but the Marshal decided that the time was not ripe for democracy, that dictatorship must continue. The major difference between the apostate and his comrades was that the former believed no party has the monopoly of truth. Djilas was expelled from the Yugoslav Communist Party in 1954. When Kardelj and Ranković asked him to repent, he refused. Kardelj, the one who led the attack against Djilas, would later claim that this episode had been the most difficult in his life. Given what they all did together during and after WWII, this statement comes with a reader's smirk of surprise...

But Djilas's role was far more complex. As one of Tito's closest collaborators during the anti-Nazi resistance and one of the most influential Yugoslav communist leaders in the aftermath of the war, he had remained true to his social justice ideals of equality and equity. He took the critique of Stalinism to its highest form in his writings; *The New Class* remains one of the most devastating attacks against the bureaucratization of a revolution since

---

[20] Duncan Wilson, *Tito's Yugoslavia* (Cambridge: Cambridge University Press, 1979), 92.

Trotsky's. Djilas was the only person after Leon Trotsky to challenge the party monopoly from the inside, but also the very first to apply Marxist categories to the sociology of his own autocracy and the first to risk his own political life by telling the truth and publishing abroad.

After the Stalin–Tito break, Djilas asked for the formulation of a real democratic alternative, the establishment of a political model opposed to Soviet-type bureaucratic totalitarianism. Without hesitating or fearing the reactions of his comrades in the Yugoslav Politburo, he questioned the dogma of infallibility of the supreme leader. He put together *The New Class* between 1955–1956 (published in 1957), challenging all power and material privileges of the communist nomenklatura. From that moment on, he would become a pariah within the universe that he had cherished so much. For Djilas, breaking with Titoist authoritarianism would be complete only in jail, where he realized that the communist system, even in its milder, less oppressive forms, remains essentially an authoritarian-bureaucratic dictatorship.

Milovan Djilas's ideas have played a crucial role in the political radicalization of the East European intelligentsia. The emancipatory movements in Poland, Hungary, and Czechoslovakia, where the democratic opposition never ceased to stigmatize the prevalent bureaucracy's abuses, owe him a great deal.

But apostasy cannot be tolerated within the choking atmosphere of the Leninist sects. Nothing exasperates and scares the ideological commissars more than protesting in the name of that very cause they all claim to serve. By attacking Marxism in the name of revolutionary hope, Djilas became an arch-rival of the communist magnates in Belgrade. Of course, Tito had denounced *some* of the Stalinist crimes and abuses. However, he could not tolerate the courage of one who pretended that the rotten apple is the system *per se*, that Leninism is a recipe for the asphyxiation of any form of democratic thought and action. And we should not forget that at the height of Tito–Stalin dispute, the Yugoslav leader did his utmost to preserve his image as a genuine, committed, and untainted Marxist. Another lesson of the Yugoslav story is that any form of sentimentalism vanishes when it comes to political survival. Regardless of Tito's personal previous friendships and attachments, he pursued in his anti-Stalinist campaigns the Leninist logic of mutual exclusion: Who will get rid of whom? (*Kto kogo?*) In this respect (and not only in this one), the Yugoslav dictator consciously and unwaveringly applied the lessons learned from Stalin: no compromise with those considered enemies, no concessions to "bourgeois" elements, and extensive powers granted to the secret police (UDBA) to dismantle any possible plot against the regime and its supreme leader.

Instead of conclusions

During High Stalinism, especially in the late 1940s, Eastern Europe experienced heavy Stalinist terror instituted by each national secret police under close monitoring by Soviet counselors and agents.[21] The 1948 conflict between the former Yugoslavia and the Soviet Union contributed to turning the heat on European politics in this part of the world. According to the Stalinist political demonology, the malignant "class enemy" had infiltrated all communist parties.

For Stalin, as well as for all his cohorts in Central and Eastern Europe, no one was fully trustable. Mátyás Rákosi, Jakub Berman, Klement Gottwald, Gheorghe Gheorghiu-Dej, and Ana Pauker, they could all be suspected of treason and each of them was a potential candidate for a show trial. In other words, if Tito with all his Comintern and anti-Nazi record could be a "duplicitous renegade," anyone could be. The purges were initiated in order to crush all "hidden conspirators" in the egg.[22]

The Stalinist political philosophy was an absurd expression of an absolute whole prevailing over its parts,[23] and therefore of a "false" totality

---

[21] There has been enough material published during the Prague Spring describing the repressive system run by secret police and confirming the involvement of the Soviet secret police in the Czechoslovak show-trials. See Eugen Loebl, *My Mind on Trial* (New York: Harcourt Brace Jovanovich, 1978). Loebl himself had survived the Slánský trial in 1952 and emigrated to the US in 1968, after the Soviet invasion of Czechoslovakia. Jiří Pelikán, ed., *The Czechoslovak Political Trials, 1950—1954: The Suppressed Report of the Dubcek Government's Commission of Inquiry 1968* (Stanford: Stanford University Press, 1971). In Romania, the Soviet agents had played an even bigger part as both members of the secret police and Gheorghe Gheorghiu Dej's entourage.

[22] Adam B. Ulam, *Titoism and the Cominform* (Cambridge, MA.: Harvard University Press, 1952); Zbigniew Brzezinski, *The Soviet Bloc: Unity and Conflict* (Cambridge, MA: Harvard University Press, 1967); Hélène Carrère d'Encausse, *Le Grand frère. L'Union soviétique et l'Europe soviétisée* (Paris: Flammarion, 1983).

[23] Djilas remarked in the 1940s that the Soviet leaders' rule was still "anchored in ideology, as was the divine right of kings in Christianity, and therefore their imperialism, too, has to be ideological or else it commands no legitimacy. This is why the men in the Kremlin can lose no territory once acquired, why they cannot abandon friends and allies no matter how objectively they may have become to them… or admit alternative interpretations of the true faith." See Milovan Djilas, "Christ and the Commissar," in *Stalinism: Its Impact on Russia and the World*, ed. George Urban (Aldershot: Wildwood, 1982), 197.

predominant over the actual Soviet Bloc.[24] And since "the Cominformists did not really constitute a movement, [and] they had no single leadership and no consistent program, it can fairly be concluded that they shared little common ground besides reliance on the USSR or—in some cases—on Soviet satellite states. This is [indeed] a clue to the larger question of the roots of Cominformism."[25]

---

[24] For a critical analysis of Stalinism, see G. R. Urban, ed., *op. cit.*, in particular Urban's interviews with Leszek Kołakowski, Milovan Djilas, Adam B. Ulam, and Robert C. Tucker; see also Leonard Shapiro's text in the same volume ("Epilogue: Some Reflections on Lenin, Stalin, and Russia,"). I recommend the entries on the Cominform, Djilas, Kardelj, and Tito in Silvio Pons and Robert Service, eds., *A Dictionary of the 20th Century Communism* (Princeton and Oxford: Princeton University Press, 2010).

[25] Ivo Banac, *With Stalin against Tito: Cominformist Splits in Yugoslav Communism* (Ithaca and London: Cornell University Press, 1988), 256.

CHINA'S ENDURING LENINIST TOOLKIT

Perspectives on CCP Organization and Ideology

Margaret M. Pearson

This volume's focus on the centenary of 1917—captured in the theme of "One Hundred Years of Communism"—finds a competitor in another centenary goal being sought in Xi Jinping's China: the centenary of the founding of the Chinese communist party in 2021. Indeed, Xi Jinping's ascendency in 2012/13 to the positions of Party General Secretary and PRC President brought into high gear the promotion of two centenary goals (事业单位). By 2021, China is to have achieved a full *xiaokang* (often translated as "moderately well-off") society.[1] "*Xiaokang*" (小康) carries echoes of both Confucianism and socialism, as it suggests the goal of creating a less unequal society but also one connected to conservative traditional—and importantly non-Western—values. 2049 will be the second centenary to mark the founding of the PRC, with the goal of becoming a "strong, democratic, civilized, harmonious, and modern socialist society." The two centenary goals have taken a prominent place among party slogans, often recited in news reports, at conferences, and training sessions for party officials. For our purposes, they tee up the need to explain why, in stark contrast to the trajectories of other Leninist states considered in this volume, China's communist party-state is in a position to think about moving to a second hundred years.

A complete explanation of the relative longevity of China's communist party-led regime would require us to consider many paths. Many accounts would no doubt point to the legitimacy created by the Maoist and, especially, the post-Mao regime's signature economic achievement: lifting millions out

---

[1] Quantitatively, the party has set the goal of doubling the 2010 per capita income level by 2021. Other goals also set for 2020, the year before the centenary, are achieving a 60 percent urbanization rate; completing construction on the Chinese space station, becoming an "Internet power"; capping coal use; and transitioning to clean energy.

of abject poverty, particularly in the post-Mao era.[2] Some might disparage this outcome as a reflection of the low bar set by the context a century of upheaval, or in light of the excesses and horrors of the Maoist regime, most notably (but not solely) in the Great Leap Forward and Cultural Revolution. Nevertheless, the achievement is legitimately heralded by the party as well as development-minded observers. According to the World Bank, "but for China there would have been no decline in the numbers of poor in the developing world over the last two decades of the 20th century."[3] We also could point to China's national security environment. Except for the Korean War, China has been spared from conflict with major powers. China's government has solved most border disputes with minimal conflict.[4] And the country has benefited from the relative lack of international conflict in the eras of US-Soviet bipolarism and, subsequently, US unipolarity. Once the decision was made to globalize the economy, China's leaders benefited from a favorable global environment for those export goods it could mobilize easily to produce. Prosperity and peace seemed to work to the benefit of party longevity. China has thus far avoided the curse of unmet rising expectations predicted by modernization theory. Social discontent definitely exists, as seen in the rise of social protest in the post-Mao era, a phenomenon that is seemingly of deep concern to the party-state.[5] Yet the sort of anti-regime sentiment that undermined communist dictators in Eastern Europe remains an anomaly. Indeed, the supposition that prosperity would ignite a civil society to rise up against the elite has proven faulty, and China's leadership remains robustly legitimate in the eyes of the citizenry.[6]

---

[2] Although Chinese poverty statistics are broadly thought to be too optimistic, even when brought into line with international standards the story is impressive. Particularly great reductions in poverty were made in the early reform era, before the mid-1980s, when 400 million people were brought out of poverty. Barry Naughton, *The Chinese Economy: Transitions and Growth* (Cambridge, MA: MIT Press, 2007), 214. The broader economic tale of the reforms is told ably in Arthur R. Kroeber, *China's Economy: What Everyone Needs to Know* (New York: Oxford University Press, 2016).

[3] World Bank, *China: From Poor Areas to Poor People* (Washington, DC: The World Bank, 2009), iii.

[4] M. Taylor Fravel, *Strong Borders Secure Nation: Cooperation and Conflict in China's Territorial Disputes* (Princeton, NJ: Princeton University Press, 2008).

[5] Yongshun Cai, *Collective Resistance in China: Why Popular Protests Succeed or Fail* (Stanford: Stanford University Press, 2010).

[6] See Bruce Dickson, *The Dictator's Dilemma: The Chinese Communist Party's Strategy for Survival* (New York: Oxford University Press, 2016); Margaret M. Pearson, "Entrepreneurs and Democratization in China," in *The New Entrepreneurs of Europe and Asia: Patterns of Business*

Performance legitimacy, based largely on economic successes, and a stable and largely welcoming international environment should not lead us to ignore the very political reasons for the staying-power of China's communist regime. These political reasons, I will argue here, are three-fold: the continued utilization of the Leninist party toolkit, the adaptive capacity of the party, and—evident most recently under Xi—the willingness to employ coercive tools to undermine potential ideological and domestic security threats. Contradictions exist amongst these three, certainly, and one could be emphasized at some junctures, others at separate junctures. All three, however, are important to understanding China's communist party-based politics today.

The persistence of China's Leninist toolkit: organization and ideology

Put simply, the Leninist organization that Mao adopted in 1949 for the CCP has remained largely in-tact. Small differences with the imported Soviet model exist, such as the CCP's expansive use of a United Front organization to manage relations with overseas Chinese. And, as I discuss in more detail below, the CCP permits more autonomy for local governments. Nevertheless, the basic parallel party-state structure forms the core institutions of governance.[7] Enormous attention is paid to recruitment and placement of the *right* people in the important positions, with the powerful Organization Department of the party overseeing a *nomenklatura* system as well as a complex personnel management system designed to reward cadres for demonstrated loyalty and competence. The quality of personnel recruited through this system has been upgraded, most notably in Deng Xiaoping's "four-caliber transformation" (四化) that aimed to identify and promote cadres around the age of 40 who were "revolutionary, younger, more educated, and more technically specialized"—with an emphasis on the latter three "calibers." Over time, the partial de-emphasis on "redness" as the key criteria for cadres has created a more meritocratic and technically competent bureaucracy, which Deng thought key to the economic modernization of the country. A technically

---

Development in Russia, Eastern Europe, and China, eds. Victoria Bonnell and Thomas Gold (Armonk, NY: M.E. Sharpe, 2002), 154–180; and Margaret M. Pearson, "Breaking the Bonds of 'Organized Dependence': Foreign Sector Managers in China," *Studies in Comparative Communism* 25, no. 1 (1992): 57–77.

[7] The classic work on China's Leninist organization is Franz Schurmann, *Ideology and Organization in Communist China* (Berkeley: University of California Press, 1968).

competent and carefully curated cadre corps has without a doubt helped create a stable meritocracy. Yet, counter to the meritocratic tendency, the cadre corps still must be ready for *ad hoc* mobilization in Maoist-style campaigns.[8] Campaigns are mobilized to promote policy implementation, such as routinely occurs with anti-corruption drives, or in times of crisis, as when facing the SARs health crisis in the early 1990s.[9] The use of mobilization tactics has endured longer in China than was the case in the USSR.

Looking beyond the corps of elite officials, the profile of rank-and-file party members has also been upgraded. Party membership stands at approximately 90 million people. Its membership is increasingly heterogeneous, and more elitist, compared to the worker-peasant base of the revolutionary-era party. Half of CCP members possess university degrees, and while the numbers of entrepreneurs and professionals remain relatively small, their numbers are increasing.[10] Party members who are employed outside of the party-state apparatus per se are intended to participate in the party cell of their unit. China's many so-called "public institutions" (事业单位, *shiye danwei*) continue to have leaders appointed through the party *nomenklatura* system, and have party cells to which any party member belongs and is, in theory, active.[11] (More on this below.) The party's presence has more recently been extended even into private enterprises as a means to maintain some control over the influential private sector. The means used include dispatching "party-building instructors" to private firms, rewarding private business people with party appointments, and being sure local party offices are primed to serve the needs of the private sector.[12] According to the party's

---

[8] The meritocracy-mobilization dilemma is discussed in more detail in Ciqi Mei and Margaret M. Pearson, "The Dilemma of "Managing for Results" in China: Won't Let Go," *Public Administration and Development* 37, no. 3 (2017): 203–16.

[9] On cadre management, see Melanie Manion, "The Cadre Management System, Post-Mao: The Appointment, Promotion, Transfer and Removal of Party and State Leaders," *China Quarterly* 102 (1985): 203–33. On mobilization see Elizabeth J. Perry, "Studying Chinese Politics: Farewell to Revolution?" *China Journal* 57 (2007): 1–22; and Patricia M. Thornton, "Crisis and Governance: SARS and the Resilience of the Chinese Body Politic," *China Journal* 61 (2009): 23–48.

[10] Lea Shih, "Centralized Leadership-Heterogeneous Party Base: Changes in the Membership Structure of the Chinese Communist Party," *MERICS China Monitor* (August 17, 2017). https://www.merics.org/sites/default/files/2017-09/China%20Monitor_40_FTZ_EN.pdf.

[11] Previously these "public institutions" often were part of the state hierarchy, but in downsizing moves, especially in the early 2000s, they were technically moved out of it to become self-funding.

[12] Xiaojun Yan and Jie Huang, "Navigating Unknown Waters: The Chinese Communist Party's New Presence in the Private Sector," *China Review* 17, no. 2 (2017): 37–63. For the party's role in foreign invested enterprises after the Tiananmen massacre see Margaret M. Pearson, "Party and Politics in Joint Ventures," *China Business Review* 17, no. 6 (Nov.-Dec., 1990): 38–40.

Organization Department, moreover, between 2006 and 2016, it increased the number of party cells in the private and foreign firm sector nine-fold (to 1.8 million).[13] Far from reducing its "manpower" presence in China, then, the party leadership is intent on reinvigorating it.

To be sure, in recent years leaders have promoted efforts to discover and publicize the "traditional" (meaning imperial and indigenous, in contrast to the Leninist import) roots to Chinese leadership norms and structure.[14] These efforts, which are in part (though not completely) state-driven, have extended to foreign relations; the aims of China's foreign policy should be not only to increase power vis á vis the US, but also to promote a model of "humane authority" or moral leadership in international affairs that is superior to American hegemony.[15] Yet despite the search to identify relevant traditional Confucian roots, the Leninist toolkit is the mainstay of the party's governance system.

Formal ideology also remains communist, sometimes shockingly so given the global eschewal of such language. Major party meetings, with lengthy work reports, are couched in terms depicting China's steady march to socialism "with Chinese characteristics." For example, the 2017 Party Congress resolution on the work report of the prior (18th) Central Committee declared:

> The report is a crystallization of the wisdom of the whole Party and the Chinese people of all ethnic groups. It is a political declaration and a program of action for the Party to unite the Chinese people and lead them in upholding and developing socialism with Chinese characteristics in the new era. It is a guiding Marxist document.... The Congress stresses that we must put the Party's political building first. All of us in the Party must strengthen our consciousness of the need to maintain political integrity, think in big-picture terms, follow the leadership core, and keep in alignment. We must uphold the authority and centralized, unified leadership of the Party Central Committee, closely follow the Party's political line, strictly observe its political discipline and rules, and closely align ourselves with the Central Committee in terms of political stance, direction, principle and path.[16]

---

[13] Cited in Shih, "Centralized Leadership-Heterogeneous Party Base," 7.

[14] See Ruiping Fan, ed., *The Renaissance of Confucianism in Contemporary China* (Amsterdam: Springer, 2011); and Daniel A. Bell, *China's New Confucianism: Politics and Everyday Life in a Changing Society* (Princeton: Princeton University Press, 2010).

[15] Xuetong Yan. *Ancient Chinese Thought, Modern Chinese Power* (Princeton University Press, 2011).

[16] Resolution of the 19th National Congress of the Communist Party of China on the Report of the 18th Central Committee, October 24, 2017. Note that "developing socialism with Chinese characteristics in the new era" is Xi Jinping's ideological contribution to Chinese Marxism, and was enshrined in the Party Constitution in 2017.

As this excerpt from the party congress resolution indicates, the "law" of democratic centralism remains a core tenet, and even appears to have been strengthened with the ban on internal party "factionalism" and, as explored further below, moves to centralize power and weaken the norm of collective leadership.

China's Leninist toolkit is also evident in the state's efforts to control the terms of discussion of history post-1949. These efforts are notable with regard to Mao. Indeed, Maoist influence remains symbolically potent. Mao's portrait and embalmed body sit in the middle of the symbolic center of the nation, Tiananmen Square, and Mao's image adorns the national currency. His name remains prominent in the Constitution. Once the official (meaning party) decision on how to understand Mao's contributions was announced in the 1981 "Resolution on Certain Questions in Our Party's History since the Founding of the PRC," which affirms his overall legacy despite acknowledgement of Mao's "mistakes" in his later years, further official consideration has remained essentially dormant.[17] This formulation allows Mao to retain his position as the architect of "Chinese Marxism." Maoist concepts have actually been quite central to the reform agenda. Deng Xiaoping resurrected Mao's directive to "seek truth from facts" (实事求是), encouraging experimentation rather than adherence to crusty dogma, to justify the "reform and opening" of the post-Mao era.[18] The regime that governs as much as possible by not "rocking the boat," preferring to allow Mao's legacy to remain in a grey area so that it can claim a direct link to the revolution, and refer to regime longevity as a source of legitimacy.[19]

It would be unexpected, admittedly, for a regime to erase its founder. State control of history also is perhaps unsurprising in light of the Chinese

---

[17] This long, and long debated, resolution states that "Comrade Mao Zedong was a great Marxist and a great proletarian revolutionary, strategist and theorist. It is true that he made gross mistakes during the 'cultural revolution,' but, if we judge his activities as a whole, his contributions to the Chinese revolution far outweigh his mistakes. His merits are primary and his errors secondary." An English translation is available at https://www.marxists.org/subject/ china/documents/cpc/history/01.htm. For an excellent analysis of the resolution's drafting see Robert L. Suettinger, *Negotiating History: The Chinese Communist Party's 1981 Resolution on Certain Questions in Our Party's History Since the Founding of the PRC* (Arlington, VA: Project 2049 Institute, June, 2017). http://www.project2049.net/documents/Negotiating%20 History%20CCP_Suettinger%202049%20Institute.pdf.

[18] An excellent discussion of the use of Mao thought in post-Mao discourse is discussed in Dirlik Arif, "Mao Zedong in Contemporary Chinese Official Discourse and History," *China Perspectives* 2 (2012): 17–27.

[19] Also on the importance to the regime of upholding Mao's legacy: Geremie R. Barmé, "Red Allure and the Crimson Blindfold," *China Perspectives* 2 (2012): 29–40.

dynastic tradition in which new dynasties wrote the history of the previous (vanquished) one. Yet in the contemporary world, it is surprising to see the regime fail to publicly confront the atrocities of the Cultural Revolution (1966–69) and Great Leap Forward (1958–61), and violence of the 1949 revolution itself. Calls to do so, such as Yang Jisheng's, the editor, public intellectual, and author of the Great Leap Forward account *Tombstone*, have been largely ignored.[20] (A partial exception was the brief acknowledgement in official media in 2016, the 50th anniversary of the Cultural Revolution, that it "could never happen again.") Intellectuals in China are well aware of these events, and discuss them in private or semi-private. Still there is no public *debate* about the meaning of these events. This silencing extends to the post-Mao era, moreover, as we see in the whitewashing of the events at Tiananmen in June, 1989. As Louisa Lim found when asking young people recognize iconic images from June 4, there is profound ignorance and/or avoidance.[21] The education system has broadened in recent years to emphasize not only science and engineering but also the social sciences and public administration. Yet political education remains a core of the curriculum, and unsurprisingly appears relatively effective, even if students may ignore or belittle it.[22] Students' exposure to political ideology deepens in secondary school to include compulsory courses on "Thought and Politics," designed to mold consciousness. Even in the grueling two-day National College Entrance Examination, commonly known as the *gaokao*, politics is highlighted. Much as the imperial examination system reinforced legitimacy of dynastic regimes, the current university examination system requires students in questions on politics to demonstrate fealty to the policies and ideas of the regime.

The CCPs's adaptive capacity

The CCP has kept intact the Leninist organization of the party-state and tended to Marxist-Leninist-Maoist (etc.) ideology. While these factors may

---

[20] Jisheng Yang, "A nation that cannot face its history has no future," (*Buneng miandui lishi de minzu shi meiyou weilai de*, 不能面对历史的民族是没有未来的), September 21, 2011, http://blog.sina.com.cn/s/blog_1455c7a270102vjy7.html on May 28, 2017.

[21] Louisa Lim, *The People's Republic of Amnesia: Tiananmen Revisited* (Oxford: Oxford University Press, 2015).

[22] Elizabeth J. Perry, "Higher Education and Authoritarian Resilience: The Case of China, Past and Present," *Harvard-Yenching Institute Working Paper Series* (Cambridge, MA: Harvard-Yenching Institute, 2015); Cantoni David E., Yuyu Chen, David Y. Yang, Noam Yuchtman, and Y. Jane Zhang, "Curriculum and Ideology," *NBER Research Paper* 20012 (2014).

seem quite old-school, many scholars of China would hasten to emphasize that the party's resilience must depend on something other than ideological purity and organizational coercive power. True enough. Two other sources of resilience have already been mentioned, namely, the increased capacity of the state to govern (meritocracy), and the delivery of economic growth. An extensive literature on China's authoritarian "resilience" highlights many additional features, including:

- willingness of the top leadership to bind its hands with seemingly institutionalized rules that limit terms of rule and centralization of power by a singular leader;
- incrementalism in rolling out new policies to avoid the shock and political alienation that often accompanies dramatic economic reform;
- use of consultative mechanisms to gain "buy-in" from constituent agents;
- formalization of popular input at the local level though direct local elections;
- willingness to experiment with "pragmatic" new policies, even if ideologically questionable;
- extensive autonomy for local governments; and
- willingness to rethink the role of social forces previously viewed by the regime as dangerous.[23]

In the third section of this essay I will discuss the first element listed above, Deng's institutionalization of rules to limit the scope of dictators' rule, and how this check on power appears to be being undermined by Xi Jinping. Here, I focus briefly on the last three inter-related elements in this list, namely, autonomy for local governments, experimentalism, and rethinking definitions of "dangerous" forces. All three factors—not coincidentally—are broadly seen to have contributed to China's economic success.

The essential nature of China's central-local political relations is very difficult to capture. As a unitary political system without formal rights for subnational units, Beijing in theory has not only authority over important personnel via the *nomenklatura* system but also absolute authority to direct

---

[23] Representative works include Andrew J. Nathan, "Authoritarian Resilience," *Journal of Democracy* 14, no. 1 (2003): 6–17; Keping Yu, "Ideological Change and Incremental Democracy in Reform Era China," in *China's Changing Political Landscape*, ed. Cheng Li (Washington: Brookings Institution Press, 2008), 44–58; and Tsang Steve, "Consultative Leninism: China's New Political Framework," *Journal of Contemporary China* 18, no. 62 (2009): 865–80.

and prohibit local actions. Yet top-down control is neither possible nor, in many instances, desirable. While central state and party organs in Beijing churn out regulations at a dizzying pace, they often are quite broad in order to leave room for local discretion. They should be seen more as a signal from the top, to which bureaucrats must demonstrate a response. Scholars inside and outside of China commonly attribute the success of China's economic reforms to the country's decentralized, authoritarian political system that creates incentives for local officials to promote market-oriented growth. In short, subnational officials—and increasingly firms—have the biggest hand in actually running the economy.[24] Many scholars point to the complementary tradition—also with imperial roots but legitimated by Mao—of local experimentalism. Whereas democratic centralism is crucial for intra-party matters, Mao's "mass line," as ensconced in the phrase "from the masses, to the masses," has continued apace in the economy. Efforts to deploy local resources and strengths in the service of market-oriented growth are allowed to flourish, and may even provide a feedback loop to the center, to demonstrate policy that might be beneficially disseminated more broadly. Localism has not always led to good governance, and much in the way of corruption and waste (and resulting social discontent) can be attributed to this model. But in the end it is hard to disagree that local initiative has been a potent driver of growth.

The CCP also has shown considerable flexibility in the post-Mao era with regard to how it assesses the reliability of societal forces. Most dramatically, in light of Mao's struggles against "capitalist roaders," the party opened its membership to capitalists at the 16th Party Congress in 2002. A 2004 amendment (Article 13) to the Party Constitution sanctions a degree of private ownership as beneficial and consistent with building socialism, declaring that citizens' lawful private property is "inviolable." Consistent with the effort to build a "moderately prosperous" society, moreover, the party-state has embarked on the task of "constructing"—engineering—a middle class. The Chinese Academy of Social Sciences has been directed to design categories for a middle class, and assess who and how many citizens fit which category.

---

[24] The center continues to set plans, provide a regulatory environment, and distribute resources, to localities. Contrary to what would be expected in a centralized Leninist system, though, much is decided locally. Xu Chengguang, "The Fundamental Institutions of China's Reforms and Development," *Journal of Economic Literature* 49, no. 4 (2011): 1076–1151; Pranab Bardhan, *Awakening Giants, Feet of Clay: Assessing the Economic Rise of China and India* (Princeton: Princeton University Press, 2011).

Interestingly, whereas the middle class constitutes probably no more than about 15% of the population, ambitious growth targets for the middle class have been set. To wit: "In 2005, it was announced that 40% of the workforce would be middle class by 2010; and in 2007 the target was raised to 55% of the population by 2020."[25] The idea is that a universalizing middle class will help further promote the ideal, and perhaps the reality, of social harmony. (The goal of increasing social harmony was promoted by Party Secretary and President Jiang Zemin [1989–2002] in the party-sanctioned guise of the "Three Represents," and has been highlighted as an aspiration ever since.) While many outside China, in the vein of "modernization theory" will expect the emergence of a robust middle class to lead to democratizing pressures, the CCP has rejected this as an acceptable path.[26]

The notion that China's Leninist state is in fact quite flexible and adaptable, especially with regard to economic policy, is quite well-established. Moreover, given the intra-class brutality of the revolution and, at times, the Maoist era, it can only be a relief that the social basis of governance has come to include the vast majority of Chinese citizens. Yet these important steps should not be taken to mean that "anything goes." The next section examines the continued, and importantly resurgent in some senses, deployment of Leninist tools in the service of the ideological straightjacketing of society.

The resurgent deployment of coercive ideological tools

Xi Jinping came to power in 2002 as a leader many Chinese citizens hoped would be strong enough to "get something done," as an antidote to the seeming inability of his predecessor, Hu Jintao, to combat corruption, fight vested interests in the economy, and raise China's status as a world power. Xi's signature campaign early on was the "Chinese Dream of National Rejuvenation," the idea (inherent in *re*juvenation) that China, wronged in the past, needed to claim its rightful place in the pantheon of great nations by recreating its superior civilization and building a strong, modern, disciplined

---

[25] David S.G Goodman, "Locating China's Middle Classes: Social Intermediaries and the Party-state," *Journal of Contemporary China* 25, 97 (2016): 1–13

[26] This modernization theory-consistent outcome has also been questioned by scholars of China. See for example Dickson, *The Dictator's Dilemma*; Kellee S. Tsai, *Capitalism Without Democracy: The Private Sector in Contemporary China* (Ithaca: Cornell University Press, 2007); and Margaret M. Pearson, "China's Emerging Business Class: Democracy's Harbinger?" *Current History* 97 (1998): 268–72.

state. While much about the "China Dream" has remained vague, what is clear is that building a strong civilized nation means, to Xi, the eradication of evil ideological weeds and anything that calls into question—and thereby undermining—the judgment of Xi's party. This orientation became clear in what has become widely known as "Document No. 9," the April 2013 Central Committee document titled "Communiqué on the Current State of the Ideological Sphere." The communiqué specified that in order to communicate General Secretary Xi Jinping's powerful and positive China Dream better, China should guard against seven "perils," mostly Western philosophical and political concepts, including "universal values," constitutional democracy, civil society, economic neo-liberalism, Western views of a free media, and questioning China's path of reform and opening. The document argued that "Western forces hostile to China and dissidents within the country are still constantly infiltrating the ideological sphere," and that opponents of one-party rule "have stirred up trouble... to provoke discontent with the party and government." Among the condemned topics, the communiqué included "historical nihilism" (*lishi xuwu zhuyi* 历史虚无主义), which it defined as "rejecting the accepted conclusions on historical events and figures, disparaging our Revolutionary precursors, and vilifying the Party's leaders." The upshot of this particular diktat is that the 1981 Resolution on Certain Questions of our Party's History would remain the final assessment of the party from 1921 to 1981, including Mao's role. Document 9 further called on Party members to resist "infiltration" by outside ideas, renew their commitment to work "in the ideological sphere," and handle with renewed vigilance all ideas, institutions, and people deemed threatening to one-Party rule.[27] In the months after it was issued, and responding to Xi's signal, the campaign for ideological orthodoxy led to publication of a torrent of commentaries in party-run publications, many of which invoked Maoist discussion of class warfare, and claimed that Western ideas were tools of Western subversion of the sort that had led to the collapse of the Soviet Union.[28]

Xi Jinping's unusually long and deep anti-corruption campaign, begun in 2013, has attracted much attention outside China. Less well-known is that

---

[27] A translation of the document is found in "Document 9: A ChinaFile Translation," *ChinaFile* (November 8, 2013), http://www.chinafile.com/document-9-chinafile-translation.

[28] Chris Buckley, "China Takes Aim at Western Ideas," *New York Times*, August 19, 2013, http://www.nytimes.com/2013/08/20/world/asia/chinas-new-leadership-takes-hard-line-in-secret-memo.html.

Xi Jinping's ascension and Document 9's publication have been followed by a harsh clampdown on human rights activists, lawyers for dissidents and civil society causes, and media outlets. A new law restricts severely the activities of foreign NGOs and in general the atmosphere has placed a chill on the work of many non-governmental civil society organizations. In July 2015 in particular, Beijing security units targeted 250 rights lawyers and activists, leading to many arrests, illegal detentions, and "disappearances"; reports of torture and Cultural Revolution-style public forced confessions surfaced in the Western media. While most detainees were released, some were put on trial for crimes such as "state subversion."[29] The founder of a law firm known to represent artist Ai Weiwei and adherents to the banned religious sect Falun Gong was sentenced to seven years in prison.[30] Another crackdown targeted ethnic Muslim Uyghurs in Northwest China. The PRC government identifies terrorism associated with Islam as a major threat to domestic security, and in 2016 took sweeping measures, including confiscating passports of Uyghurs in parts of the Xinjiang Autonomous Region and, more generally, an intensification of the domestic security apparatus in that region.[31]

Repression also has returned with renewed force to the intellectual community. Chinese scholars, in both in imperial and communist times, have had a long relationship with the state. Today, universities remain under the leadership of a party official, and universities maintain a curricular commitment to teachings of the regime, such as in departments and colleges of Marxism within universities (e.g., the School of Marxism at Peking University). Universities also are a major recruiting ground for party members and activists. Moreover, scholars commonly maintain that they feel the desire to help the country's modernization. Put differently, the PRC has no tradition of academic independence. In the communist party era, standard practice is that scholars attend mandatory and time-consuming political study meetings following major party meetings and decisions, and publication of

---

[29] See for example reports such as: Benjamin Haas, "China 'Eliminating Civil Society' by Targeting Human Rights Activists: Report," *The Guardian*, February 15, 2017, https://www.theguardian.com/world/2017/feb/16/china-eliminating-civil-society-by-targeting-human-rights-activists-report); and Tom Mitchell, "Xi's China: Smothering Dissent," *Financial Times*, July 27, 2016, https://next.ft.com/content/ccd94b46-4db5-11e6-88c5-db83e98a590a).

[30] Peter Humphrey, "China's Crackdown on Human Rights Lawyers has Ancient Roots," *Financial Times*, August 23, 2016, https://www.ft.com/content/22b8a356-6470-11e6-8310-ecf0bddad227.

[31] Edward Wong, "Police Confiscate Passports in Parts of Xinjiang, in Western China," *New York Times*, December 1, 2016, https://www.nytimes.com/2016/12/01/world/asia/passports-confiscated-xinjiang-china-uighur.html.

Document 9 has been followed by an ideological clampdown in universities. For example, scholars and staff are asked to report colleagues observed discussing forbidden topics. Important scholars are asked regularly to write academic articles that are explicitly supportive of the regime. The words of a well-known Chinese commentator summarize the general situation well, "Things that we could openly discuss before, such as the Cultural Revolution, are now considered sensitive or even forbidden. In the past there was some room for non-governmental organisations and rights lawyers. Now all of them have been suppressed."[32]

Scholars have for several years depended on virtual private networks (VPNs) to get around China's internet Great Firewall, to access research studies abroad—a behavior that could universally be justified as helping to build China's intellectual and scientific capacity. In 2017, the regime announced a crackdown on VPNs that are not controlled (and hence subject to monitoring) by the state. While such a move has potential to hit all academic disciplines hard, it is perhaps most problematic for the sciences, in which the norm of sharing cutting-edge research is crucial for progress, and restrictions can deeply harm research by Chinese scholars and institutions.[33] Science is being deployed in the service of the state in other ways as well. Nowhere is this more obvious than in plans to harness big data in a massive citizen monitoring project known as the "Social Credit System" (alternatively, "Social Rating System"). The system is designed, to monitor and guide the behavior of firms operating in the market in a more comprehensive way than done by traditional corporate ratings systems (such as Moody's). "Data" entered on behavior of corporate officers (awards, misconduct) and corporate compliance with regulations automatically generates and updates rating scores that then may influence business opportunities. A goal is to minimize the need for government monitoring (though exactly how monitoring will be minimized, given the need to input data, remains unclear), and to encourage firms to discipline themselves according to rules. Consistent with China's use of experimental sites to test policy initiatives, since 2015 dozens of cities have been tapped to run pilots of the system.[34]

---

[32] Quoted in Mitchell, "Xi's China."

[33] Dennis Normile, "Science in China Suffers as Internet Censors Plug Holes in Great Firewall," *Science Magazine,* August 30, 2019, http://www.sciencemag.org/news/2017/08/science-suffers-china-s-internet-censors-plug-holes-great-firewall.

[34] See Mirjam Meissner, "China's Social Credit System," *MERICS China Monitor* #39, May 24, 2017, https://www.merics.org/en/merics-analysis/china-monitor/merics-china-monitor-no-39/).

More Orwellian still is the effort, formally launched in June 2014, to use data gathered through monitoring to incentivize citizens to maintain "proper" behavior.[35] Here the party relies on the rapid advances, within China, of facial recognition technology, and concomitant development of tools to handle big data. Facial recognition technologies have become widespread (and are the source of considerable pride) among consumers—for example, facial recognition is widely used for smartphone logins and also, increasingly, in retail payment systems. Yet these technologies are also being broadly deployed by the party-state. One core system is dubbed "Sharp Eyes" (雪亮, *xue liang*), a name that hearkens back to Mao's observation that "the masses have sharp eyes" that can help the party monitor other citizens. Security bureaus have routinized the gathering of data citizen-by-citizen into an enormous database, a "police cloud" of data pieced together from security cameras, monitoring of social media, and integrating information from immigration and police databases, medical and education records, and travel patterns, among others. China's corporate technology behemoths, notably Tencent and Alibaba (equivalent to the West's Google and Facebook), have been contracted to provide data collected through their "normal" (in this day and age) data mining system on purchasing and bill-paying patterns, as well as online activity. The idea is to provide the state with the capacity to track social activities of citizens (and their associates), including dissidents and ethnic minorities deemed potentially harmful. Once gathered, moreover, the intention is to create a single "social score" for each citizen, a rating that reflects government priorities and, in turn, is to be used to incentivize behavior, e.g., by dictating the interest rate on mortgages and access to cash loans (which in turn can be used on Alibaba's e-commerce sites!). The government has touted the system, in which participation will be mandatory by 2020, as a way to measure and enhance "trust" and build a national culture of (echoing Confucian precepts) "sincerity."[36]

Underlying these moves in the social sphere has been the elevation of CCP General Secretary and PRC President Xi Jinping to a position of paramount

---

[35] The State Council document launching the program is "Planning Outline for the Construction of a Social Credit System." On data gathering, see Simon Denyer, "The All-seeing 'Sharp Eyes' of China's Security State," *Washington Post*, January 8, 2018.

[36] See Rachel Botsman, "Big Data Meets Big Brother as China Moves to Rate it Citizens," *Wired*, October 21, 2017, http://www.wired.co.uk/article/chinese-government-social-credit-score-privacy-invasion.

importance. Xi's original promotion came, as noted, with the hope that he would be strong enough to make breakthroughs on issues such as economic reform and corruption. Many observers were hopeful that the ensuing centralization of power would be effective. Xi went on to revamp the system of ad hoc committees designed to address urgent problems, the leading small groups (LSGs, 领导小组, *lingdao xiaozu*), and placed himself at the head of many of them. He created a new National Security Commission to centralize control of national and domestic security (a relatively uncontroversial move that had long been proposed by Chinese leaders). He launched the patriotic China Dream of National Rejuvenation, as noted. As the anti-corruption campaign carried on for longer than past such campaigns, and hence much longer than expected, and attacked both "tigers and flies" (major and minor political figures), concern spread that Xi was using the campaign to eliminate political enemies. While this intention has not been decisively proven, and attacking corruption is popular, the campaign also appeared a harbinger to subsequent moves to punish human rights activists and straightjacket ideological life. As the 19th Party Congress meetings surrounding Xi's "re-election" to a second term at top positions came and went in 2017–18, he also appeared to erode leadership rules and norms Deng had designed to check arbitrary power in the post-Mao era. Most notable in the rollback was the failure to name a successor at Xi's mid-point of the expected two terms, leading to speculation that Xi Jinping would himself attempt to break the norm of a two-term limit. Failure to name a successor, the consolidation of new points of power directly reporting to Xi, and the absence in the newly named Politburo Standing Committee of clear counterpoints who might check Xi all have spurred concerns about the centralization of power. In short, the concern is that Xi is undoing the move to collective leadership that Deng carefully constructed based on the lessons learned from Mao's cult of personality.[37]

---

[37] Scholars of China and of authoritarian rule more generally have tended to see, in the post-Mao era, an institutionalization of power, through a reiteration of norms to check an individual leader's power. See for example Alice L. Miller, "Institutionalization and the Changing Dynamics of Chinese Leadership Politics," in *China's Changing Political Landscape: Prospects for Democracy*, ed. Cheng Li (Washington: Brookings Institution Press, 2008): 61–79; and Milan W. Svolik, *The Politics of Authoritarian Rule* (New York: Cambridge University Press, 2012). For a counterpoint view that such "institutionalization" was much weaker than often argued, see Christopher K. Johnson, "Chinese Politics Has No Rules, But it May Be Good if Xi Jinping Breaks Them," (Washington DC: Center for Strategic and International Studies, August 9, 2017). https://www.csis.org/analysis/chinese-politics-has-no-rules-it-may-be-good-if-xi-jinping-breaks-them.

Concluding observations

Mao, although he massaged Leninism to fit China's circumstances, nevertheless adopted the core elements of the governance toolkit, from organization, to party rules (democratic centralism), to campaign politics, to intolerance of civil society. It is obvious that China has changed tremendously in the more than four decades since Mao's death in 1976, and these changes are particularly noteworthy now that the post-Mao period is substantially longer than the Mao era itself. With the post-Mao, era China's leaders brought prosperity, and also opened a much wider zone of personal (especially consumer) freedom that was not possible in a poverty-stricken and politically restricted society. Yet these changes have not upended the Leninist core. Nor has the move to greater freedom been expanded and institutionalized or shown itself to be impervious to setbacks. The use of digital tools to enhance the powers of a core leader suggests new tools to mobilize society in a way that Mao could never have imagined. It appears to be the Xi regime's hope that these tools will allow it to avoid what it condemns as the failed path of the Soviet Union.

REDUCTIO AD REAGANUM

Reflections on Communism's Enduring Ideological Invulnerability

Venelin I. Ganev

The most effective way to justify murder and oppression is to argue that political regimes that kill and subjugate also embody higher moral principles and promote progressive policies. If the validity of this proposition is accepted, then a simple conclusion ensues. The central fact about the "red century" that began with the successful Bolshevik coup in October 1917 is that communism—the set of ideas formulated by Karl Marx as interpreted and implemented by Lenin and the Bolsheviks—is the most effective justification for mass murder in the history of the modern world.

In the course of that history, many other vicious types of government followed the "rise and fall" trajectory that also characterized the historical fate of Soviet-type dictatorships—Nazism, Jim Crow, and apartheid come to mind. But communism is the only ideology that survived the demise of the exemplary regimes that embodied it. While the political defeat of other despotic systems of rule resulted in the death of the ideologies that sustained and legitimated them, the collapse of Marxist autocracies in Eastern Europe and the Soviet Union did not lead to the discrediting of the ideology that reigned supreme there before 1989. And this is the single most important lesson to be learned about communism—despite the fact that it is undeniably implicated in appalling crimes, colossal economic failures, and massive human suffering, it continues to enjoy the support of influential admirers. Its ideological invulnerability endures.

In the 1990s it did appear that—to refer to the title of François Furet's well-known book—communism was "an illusion" whose time had "passed."[1] But even then perspicacious observers pointed out that the writing of communism's

---

[1] François Furet, *The Passing of an Illusion: The Idea of Communism in the Twentieth Century* (Chicago: University of Chicago Press, 1999).

obituary might be a premature intellectual endeavor. As Michael Ignatieff put it in an insightful review of Furet's *magnum opus*, the main fact about "the illusion" in question is not that it had vanished, but that it "refuses to die."[2] With the benefit of hindsight, we can unambiguously state that it was Ignatieff and not Furet who got it right. That communism as an ideology that legitimated Soviet political practices survived the extinction of one-party regimes in Europe is a contention easy to substantiate. A glimpse at the intellectual controversies that have recently attracted attention will quickly reveal that such controversies revolve around books with titles such as "The Communist Hypothesis," "Lenin Reloaded," or "Communism for Kids"—all published by very prestigious presses.[3] These titles capture perfectly well the main messages the books in question seek to convey: the political practices associated with Leninism should inspire any effort to resolve these problems, and it is imperative that the "truths" that inspired communist revolutionaries shape the thinking of future generations. And since it is simply unthinkable that Verso, Duke University Press, or MIT Press will publish books entitled "The Afrikaaner Hypothesis," "Hitler Reloaded" and "Segregation for Kids," the important conclusion we should draw is that among academic elites around the world the conversation about the desirability of communism is still going on—in a way in which conversations linked to other ideologies that legitimated government-inflicted human suffering are not.

How can communism's ideological survival be explained? I will focus on one particular factor, the resilience of anti-anti-communism. While in the mainstream media's op-ed pages radical critics of twentieth century systems of government, including liberal democracy, are celebrated and acclaimed, radical opponents of communism are constantly under attack. Their motives are questioned, their analyses are treated with disdain, and their arguments are summarily dismissed. The vilification of anti-communists is one of the main reasons why communism's aura survives. When everything is said and done, Marxist regimes are still depicted as a redemptive force unjustifiably defamed by rabid adversaries. Anti-anti-communism shapes a climate of opinion where various aspects of the Soviet experiment are glorified and

---

2   Michael Ignatieff, "The Era of Error," *The New Republic*, August 9, 1999.

3   Alain Badiou, *The Communist Hypothesis* (London: Verso, 2015); Sebastian Budgen, Stathis Koulevakis, and Slavoj Zizek, eds., *Lenin Reloaded: Toward a Politics of Truth* (Durham: Duke University Press, 2007); Bini Adamczak, *Communism for Kids* (Cambridge, MA: MIT Press, 2017).

canonized, while condemnations of that project are derided as prejudices that stand in the way of progress.

The *Reductio ad Reaganum*, or the permanent structure of anti-anti-communist thinking

The systematic assault on anti-communism is grounded in a mode of reasoning that I would like to call *Reductio ad Reaganum*. The logic underpinning is fairly straightforward. Its point of departure is the proposition that the ruling political class in the West—as personified by Ronald Reagan—has been, and continues to be, deeply involved in a malign brinksmanship whose objective is to stymie the global advances of various anti-capitalist movements in the developing world, and to discredit the Left in Western democracies. Reagan's statement that the Soviet Union is "an evil empire" allegedly demonstrates how an inflammatory rhetoric is deployed to legitimate this brinksmanship. The sole purpose discussions of Soviet-regimes' failures serve is to occlude the various ways in which such regimes actively promote progressive causes abroad and to negate Marxist experiments' numerous achievements at home. Radical, "Reaganite" critiques of communism are devoid of analytical insight and interpretative substance: anti-communism is just an incendiary sentiment that routinely fuels "right-wing" backlashes against leftist ideas. The conclusion that follows is that any argument against communism should be dismissed if it can be demonstrated that it is compatible with the views of someone like Ronald Reagan.

The anti-anti-communist way of thinking is not particularly flexible: it revolves around an enduring matrix consisting of a very few but tightly interwoven themes. Anti-anti-communists openly pour scorn on the alleged motives of anyone who dares to subject communism to radical criticism. They also assert that the proper way to judge communist regimes is from a historical-global perspective that takes into account the contributions that such regimes allegedly have made to the ascent of progressive movements and policies around the world. And they insist that insofar as the domestic policies of the dictatorships of the proletariat are concerned, mass murder and economic deprivation are outweighed by social, cultural, and industrial successes. To be sure, the anti-anti-communist narrative goes, Leninist regimes were not perfect—but their flaws ought to be examined in a tentative manner.

Attempts to judge such regimes based on their misdeeds and shortcomings would be reminiscent of Reagan's "evil empire" statement and therefore ipso facto illegitimate.

If the proposition that communism has been invidiously stigmatized is the point of departure of the *Reductio ad Reaganum*, its logical endpoint is the following imperative: "Anti-communism has to be fought." We owe this crisp formula to Ralph Miliband and Marcel Liebman, two of the most influential academic luminaries of the last century. It appears in an essay entitled "Reflections on Anti-Communism," which was published in 1984.[4] This essay makes it easy to grasp the permanent structure of anti-anti-communist thinking: it reveals the arsenal of rhetorical tropes and substantive claims deployed to neutralize analyses unsympathetic to communism.

What exactly is wrong with anti-communism? The general attitude that underpins it. In their programmatic text Miliband and Liebman raise the following question: is it conceivable that denunciations of communism might be considered "an article of political intelligence, decency, morality, etc." In other words, would it be possible to attribute anti-communism to ethical concerns and the determination to uphold the same universal, normative principles that inspire critiques of racism, colonialism, and Nazism? Of course not, is their answer: what invariably lurks behind such denunciations is dastardly motives. Emphatic renunciations of the grand experiment launched by Lenin and the Bolsheviks are driven solely by the hateful fanaticism of "the primitive [members] of the John Birch Society and other ultra-right organizations in the United States and other capitalist countries" and by "ex-Stalinists, ex-Maoists and former ultra-left revolutionaries." Anti-communism also reflects the narrow-minded parochialism of "Soviet and East European emigres"—individuals blinded by their "bitterness and hatred." Miliband and Liebman charitably describe such individuals' feelings as "understandable," but then use the recognition of their pain as a pretext to dismiss their views. The problem with the "understandable" arguments articulated by communism's victims is that they rely on personal experiences and not on a theoretical-philosophical understanding of the essence of the capitalist era. The "emigres" are simply unable to see how in the larger scheme of things the very existence of the regimes that terrorized them made

---

[4] Ralph Miliband and Marcel Liebman, "Reflections on Anti-Communism," *Socialist Register*, Vol. 21 (1984): 22.

the world a better place. It is because of this lack of sophistication that East Europeans are likely to express negative views about the dictatorship of the proletariat and lend "valuable support" to "the anti-communist camp."[5]

In my view, this facet of anti-anti-communism, namely the notion that East European testimonies regarding sufferings and humiliations should be politely or firmly disparaged, is particularly important to note. After all, it is demonstrably true that Reagan's views about the "evil empire" coincided with the opinions of tens of millions of people who actually lived under Marxist regimes. According to the political logic underpinning the *Reductio ad Reaganum*, what follows from this simple truth is most definitely *not* that Reagan's interpretation of Soviet realities would appear to be validated by individuals with some expertise in the subject matter. What follows, instead, is that the individuals in question should be treated as prejudiced witnesses whose suffering renders them incapable of comprehending the historical mission of the millenarian forces to which Lenin and the Bolsheviks belonged.

With regards to "the larger scheme of things," what Miliband and Liebman complain about is that anti-communists focus too much on developments that transpired in the "second world" and not enough on how the Cold War affected the "first" and the "third." The champions of anti-anti-communism insist that the proper way to construe the geopolitical confrontation between the Marxist East and the capitalist West is as a series of blameworthy, US-led geopolitical machinations and repressive practices that pursue a two-pronged objective. On the one hand, they are driven by "the determination of the Western powers to contain revolutionary movements everywhere and even for that matter reformist movements, a purpose to which the Soviet Union… is something of an obstacle."[6] A corollary of this interpretation of the Cold War is that the Soviet Union is an ally of progressive constituencies in the third world. Anti-communist efforts to scrutinize Leninist regimes' failures in a systematic manner might demoralize such constituencies—which is why the anti-imperialist credentials of Marxist dictatorships should be reaffirmed.

On the other hand, Western Cold Warriors try to turn anti-communism into "a dominant theme" in a domestic "political warfare waged by conservative forces against the entire left… social democracy included." The realities of this warfare are such that radical critiques of communism might provide

---

5   Miliband and Liebman, "Reflections," 18.
6   Miliband and Liebman, "Reflections," 12.

ammunition for "right wing" forces—and this circumstance matters much more than any questions related to the accuracy or moral thrust of anti-communists' claims. From a certain narrow perspective, such criticisms might appear to be justified insofar as they provide victimized groups and individuals with the opportunity to air their grievances. But from the broader politically sophisticated and philosophically informed perspective of anti-anti-communists negative depictions of Soviet-type regimes are nothing but a rhetorical weapon which is wielded by "conservative forces" and should therefore be neutralized.[7] Thus an important pillar of anti-anti-communist thinking is that any exploration of patterns of repression and subjugation in the contemporary world should focus not on Eastern Europe but on the problems of third world movements and how the Soviet Union alleviated such problems. Such investigations must also provide detailed accounts of how and why anti-communist revelations make life more difficult for Western leftists.

Finally, according to Miliband and Liebman, radical critics of the Soviet Union are wrong because they present a distorted picture of actually existing Marxist regimes. "Anti-communism," the professors assert, "has always relied on, and has itself produced, much false and tendentious information about the Soviet Union." Communism has "a positive side": "alongside massive repression and murder, there was also great contribution and advance," as well as remarkable "economic, social and cultural accomplishments." Soviet institution builders created "elaborate mechanisms of participation and consultation which make possible the expression of multitude of demands, promptings, grievances and discontents at the grassroots."[8] Anti-communism must be rejected because factual evidence exists that contradicts its empirical claims.[9]

A more general implication of the *Reductio ad Reaganum* is that there are right and wrong ways to criticize communism. Certainly communism was not flawless, anti-anti-communists acknowledge. There were things like

---

[7]   Miliband and Liebman, "Reflections," 1, 11–12; 19.

[8]   Miliband and Liebman, "Reflections," 2–4; 6–7.

[9]   Ralph Miliband's positive impressions of the Soviet Union were formed when he took a trip to that country in the early 1960s. During his travels, he stayed in luxurious hotels, was chauffeured around in a special car, and was accompanied everywhere by an interpreter whom he described as "a most fluent and pleasant young man from the Russian Foreign Office." In fact, the interpreter—whose name was Mikhail Lyubimov—was a KGB officer. See Michael Newman, *Ralph Miliband and the Politics of the New Left* (London: The Merlin Press, 2002), 81.

mass murder during Stalinism, and also shortages of consumer goods in the post-Stalinist era. Nonetheless, the anti-anti-communist gospel goes, critical assessments of Marxist dictatorships should be restrained. Jean-François Revel was among the first to notice that labels such as "obsessive," "vicious," and "Neanderthal" were routinely used to convey the message that radical "anti-communism … is never the result of historical observation, only of evil predisposition."[10] No other opponent of a modern system of governance would be facing a similar problem: it is impossible to imagine that a decrier of racism will be described as "obsessive," that an adversary of colonialism will be referred to as "vicious," and that a critic of the West will be labeled a "Neanderthal." Anti-communists are the only critics whose arguments are dismissed on account of going "too far." Such dismissals would perhaps be understandable if analytical interpretations of the shortcomings of contemporary political regimes were dominated by balanced and evenhanded views. But that is not the case at all: as Aurelian Craiutu has demonstrated in a brilliant book, scholars who proffer non-radical views "pay a certain price:" the lines of inquiry they pursue are considered "tangential" as opposed to "essential," and their moderation is regarded "a weak and insignificant virtue, incapable of quenching [the] thirst for absolutes, authenticity and adventure."[11] Indeed, over the last few decades the globalized academic community has generated unquenchable demand for radical analyses: of heteronormativity, of patriarchy, and, most importantly and most insatiably, of liberal democracy and capitalism. Only anti-communists are treated differently: as Miliband and Liebman made it clear, opponents of Soviet-type regimes are expected to spend as much time (if not even more) on the positives aspects of communism as they do on its negative features.

The reason why I devote so much time on the text coauthored by Miliband and Liebman is because it offers an interpretation of the political history of the last century which had, by the late 1980s, attained a hegemonic status in Western academia and the mainstream press.[12] Their work exemplifies

---

[10] Jean-Francois Revel, *The Totalitarian Temptation* (New York: Penguin Books, 1977), 70.

[11] Aurelian Craiutu, *Faces of Moderation: The Art of Balance in an Age of Extremes* (Philadelphia: University of Pennsylvania Press, 2017): 17.

[12] On the origins of anti-anti-communism in the 1920s and the 1930s, see Ludmila Stern, *Western Intellectuals and the Soviet Union, 1920–40* (London: Routledge, 2006); on how and why "the French radical intelligentsia fed itself on a steady diet of anti-anti-communism" in the 1940s and 1950s see Tony Judt, *Past Imperfect* (Berkeley: The University of California Press, 1992), 179; on anti-anti-communists' rise to prominence in the 1960s and 1970s, see Paul Hollander,

the effort to impose a certain "a priori" on any discussion of communism and eliminate certain kinds of knowledge as irrelevant. In Kant's approach to the "a priori" what gets eliminated is knowledge based on experience; in the case of anti-anti-communism the objective is to banish any testimony that suggests that the Soviet experiment was irredeemably flawed. Unlike Kant's analysis of pure reason, the anti-anti-communist effort to establish an "a priori" that would structure any conversation about Marxist regimes is definitely grounded in experiential knowledge. This effort is propelled by the very empirical fear that radical rejections of the Soviet experiment might diminish the prospect that exploited humankind might take advantage of the historical opportunity which Lenin's successes opened up. Still, I would argue that one fragment of Kant's discussion of the notion of a priori might help us grasp the thrust of anti-anti-communism. Should we say "of a man who undermined the foundations of his house," Kant asks, "that he might have known a priori that it would fall?" His answer is no: this man, the philosopher pointed out, "had first to learn through experience that bodies are heavy, and therefore fall when their supports are withdrawn."[13] In my view, the anti-anti-communists resemble the man who knows for a fact that a structure bereft of support is destined to crumble. The ideological tenet that inspires them is that communism is a valuable construction—and radical critics should not be allowed to undermine it.

Here, then, is one of the main lessons of the twentieth century: while other ideologies implicated in mass murder were eventually perceived as a cause to be defeated, communism is treated as the house where the hopes and aspirations of capitalism's noble enemies reside. The foes of anti-communism do not deny the fact that the furniture is decrepit, the amenities subpar, the plumbing permanently clogged, the electricity supply subject to constant disruptions—or that there are corpses buried in the basement and blood stains on every wall. Still, for them communism is an edifice that should not be abandoned but constantly refurbished and beautified.

Political Pilgrims (New York: Oxford University Press, 1981); on why anti-communism was "still considered a damnable heresy" in the 1980s, see Furet, *The Passing*, 492; and on how "scholars who chose to focus on the crimes of communism" faced "the career-blocking danger of being labeled right-wingers" in the 1990s, see Jeffrey Herf, "Unjustifiable Means," *The Washington Post*, January 23, 2000, https://www.washingtonpost.com/archive/entertainment/books/2000/01/23/unjustifiable-means/d317baa8-4fe0-4caa-8442-850147bd23e3/?utm_term=.fa74629c2f8a.

13   Cf. Immanuel Kant, *Critique of Pure Reason* (New York: St. Martin's Press, 1965), 43.

Anti-anti-communism after the end of the Cold War

Miliband and Liebman wrote their essay during the Cold War, but their arguments survived the end of this geopolitical conflict. Insofar as anti-anti-communism is concerned, the collapse of Soviet-type regimes was a non-event: it continued to reproduce itself, unaltered and unmodified, in the writings and opinions of the leading academics and op-ed writers of the post-Cold War era. Its permanent structure was preserved: the bona fides of messengers conveying anti-communist opinions are still questioned, the view that the world as a whole benefited from the Soviet experiment is still defended, and historical narratives that accentuate the supposed accomplishments of one-party dictatorships are still enthusiastically disseminated.

A typical example of how the *Reductio ad Reaganum* is deployed to disparage condemnations of Soviet-type regimes is an op-ed entitled "The CIA's Fake News Campaign" authored by Kenneth Osgood.[14] Here is a sample of the kinds of statements Osgood considers "fake news": "Communism was awful;" Soviet-occupied Eastern Europe was "Communist-controlled hell-on-earth;" the lives in many East Europeans were wrecked by "communist repression." And how did Professor Osgood reach the conclusion that such statements are "fake"? His reasoning proceeds in the following manner: the above mentioned statements routinely featured in the broadcasts of Radio Free Europe, an organization partially financed by the CIA. The CIA, in this logic, is a tool reactionaries use unscrupulously in order to prop up American imperialism abroad and intimidate the Left in the United States. Therefore anything Radio Free Europe broadcast, by fact of being associated with the CIA, must be fake. In other words, Osgood dismisses negative depictions of communism not because they contradict verified facts or credible witness testimonies, but because of the *source* they come from, Radio Free Europe. Now, that the CIA sponsored Radio Free Europe—as well as other institutions such as the Congress for Cultural Freedom—is indisputably true. But this fact lends itself to multiple interpretations. As Martin Krygier pointed out, the funding of such projects might conceivably be characterized as "one of the few unarguably good things the CIA had done."[15] But anti-anti-communists

---

[14]   Kenneth Osgood, "The CIA's Fake News," *The New York Times*, October 13, 2017, https://www. nytimes.com/2017/10/13/opinion/cia-fake-news-russia.html.

[15]   Martin Krygier, "An Intimate and Foreign Affair," in *What Did You Do in the Cold War, Daddy? Personal Stories from a Troubled Time*, eds. Ann Curthoys and Joy Damousi (Sydney: New South Publishing, 2014), 38.

are unwilling to pay due heed to such unorthodox opinions. The simple syllogisms of the *Reductio ad Reaganum* quickly lead Professor Osgaard to the conclusion that if a US agency or official announced that "communism was awful," then it should be taken as a given that communism must have been anything but awful.

An interesting question to ask is whether having unmasked the fake news of one of the protagonists entangled in the Cold War Professor Osgood would be willing to apply his inquisitive mind to the other. After all, it is demonstrably true that statements such as "the American working class is subject to economic exploitation," "American society is racist," "the gap between rich and poor is growing," "American capitalism debases all cultural values," "US foreign policy is imperialistic" were all aggressively pushed by Radio Moscow. Given the source, should we dismiss them as "fake"? Must the *Reductio ad Reaganum* be paralleled by a *Reductio ad Kremlinum*? This tantalizing question remains open.

The second leitmotif integrated into the permanent structure of anti-anti-communist thought—namely that from a global perspective the Bolshevik project had a consistently positive impact that its critics fail to appreciate—also survived the end of the Cold War. The views of two of the most powerful and influential professors in the world are quite representative in that regard. For Frederic Jameson, during the Cold War the Soviet Union's "foreign policy … generally supported the right causes." The urgent issue, he adds, that has to be raised in the aftermath of 1989, then, is: "who will support them now?"[16] In other words, to the anti-communist argument that in 1989 Eastern Europeans regained their freedom the anti-anti-communists respond that from the point of view of the totality of human experiences the end of the Cold War as a particularly disturbing turn of events because "the right causes" that inspired activists in the developing world lost a well-armed protector.

According to Eric Hobsbawm, something similar happened in the "first" world: "Whatever Stalin did to the Russians, he was good for the common people of the West. It is no accident that the Keynes-Roosevelt way of saving capitalism concentrated on welfare and social security, on giving the poor money to spend, and on that central tenet of postwar Western policies… full employment."[17] Would the acclaimed historian approve of a cost-benefit

---

[16] Frederic Jameson, "Conversations on the New World Order," in *After the Fall: The Failure of Communism and the Future of Socialism,* ed. Robin Blackburn (London: Verso, 1991), 256.

[17] Eric Hobsbawm, "Goodbye to All That," in *After the Fall,* 122.

analysis that reaches the conclusion that "whatever Southern plantation owners did to the slaves, they were good to the common people who needed cheap cotton"? That we do not know. What we do know is that he readily applies such analysis to the Cold War: since all costs were inflicted on "the Russians" and all the benefits accrued to "the common people of the West," communism ought to be perceived as a profoundly positive force. To be sure, an anti-communist might ask the question "what exactly happened to the Russians?" But anti-anti-communists like Hobsbawm would be quick with a rejoinder: The Soviet experiment opened up exciting new opportunities for the exploited masses, and that is all that matters.

Finally, the glorification of Soviet achievements continued unabated in the post-Cold War era. To critics of the Soviet Union who might opine that life there was "bad" and that Soviet citizens were ensnared in "webs of immorality" Berkeley anthropologist Alexei Yurchak responds in the following way: "for great numbers of Soviet citizens many of the fundamental values, ideals and realities of socialist life (such as equality, community, selflessness, altruism, friendship, ethical relations, safety, education, work, creativity and concern for the future) were of genuine importance."[18] (Parenthetically, it is worth underscoring that even though Yurchak refers to "great numbers of Soviet citizens," his fieldwork focused on two dozen Komsomol activists, i.e. on the regime's reliably indoctrinated youthful enforcers). The proper way to think about the Soviet experiment is as the historical moment when practically every normatively appealing principle was realized in practice; with the Soviet Union's passing, such principles no longer structure "the realities" of everyday life.

More generally, the recent literature on twentieth century political experiences is still dominated by a two-pronged fear: that the misdeeds of non-communist regimes might remain unanalyzed, and that the achievements of communist regimes might remain unacknowledged. A recently published essay praises a book authored by Domenico Lasurdo whose main claim is that that "the history of the West [is] the history of a 'master race democracy'" and that the gas chambers in Auschwitz only came about because certain "intellectual traditions" persisted in the United States.[19] Isn't blaming America for the

---

[18] Alexei Yurchak, *Everything Was Forever, Until It Was No More* (Princeton: Princeton University Press, 2006), 8.

[19] Domenico Lasurdo, *War and Revolution: Rethinking the Twentieth Century* (London: Verso, 2015), 8, 288.

Holocaust a bit too radical? Not at all—this line of inquiry is applauded as a worthwhile effort to "rethink the twentieth century through a counter-history of liberalism that demolishes the privileged place of the West."[20] The same essay praises a different book, written by Kristen Ghodsee, which allegedly proves that communist Bulgaria became "a global model of women's rights and welfare."[21] Supposedly, such stunningly positive accounts are valuable because they counter a very disturbing tendency, namely the "blackwashing" of communism: in the aftermath of 1989 a "torrential stream of official revisions" was unleashed in Eastern Europe that led to the emergence of "a veritable industry of anti-Communism that includes... commemorations to the victims of Communism."[22] Thus efforts to causally link liberal democracy to the extermination of the European Jews are praised as an important contribution to our understanding of modern politics, while attempts to commemorate the victims of communism are depicted as particularly troubling because they might amount to "blackwashing" of communism. One can hardly think of a better example of how the anti-anti-communist principle that communism is the only type of regime exempt from radical criticism works in practice.

The most important piece of evidence confirming that positive accounts of Soviet communism are systematically encouraged and circulated is the *New York Times*'s series of op-eds entitled "Red Century" and devoted to the 100th anniversary of the Bolshevik coup in Russia.[23] Some of those op-eds are critical of the Soviet experiment,[24] but most are not, and this is the centrally important fact about the series. It would be hard to imagine that the newspaper's editors would tolerate a similarly "balanced" exchange about apartheid or a denial of full citizenship status to women. While anti-communist views are not completely eliminated, it is the anti-anti-communists that clearly dominate the discussion. The readers of the *New York Times* are duly informed that Lenin was a "strategic genius," that the communists set the standard for truly

---

[20] Ronald Suny, "The Left Side of History: The Embattled Pasts of Communism in the Twentieth Century," *Perspectives on Politics* 15, no. 2 (June 2017): 456.

[21] Suny, "The Left Side," 462. Cf. Kristen Ghodsee, *The Left Side of History: World War II and the Unfulfilled Promise of Communism in Central Europe* (Durham: Duke University Press, 2015).

[22] Suny, "The Left Side," 461–462.

[23] The op-eds can be found here: https://www.nytimes.com/column/red-century.

[24] See for example Jonathan Brent, "The Order of Lenin: 'Find Some Truly Hard People,'" *New York Times*, May 22, 2017.

idealistic political behavior, that the Bolshevik movement engendered the utopian energies that eventually made possible the creation of "Star Trek," that under communism the cause of gender equality advanced dramatically—and that East European women enjoyed great sex.[25] Perhaps the most revealing and important essay is the only one that offers an interpretation of the term "Lenin's legacy." What is Lenin's legacy? The bloody insurrection that triggered a devastating civil war? The creation of the GULAG? The fact that he became a dictator who "never showed generosity to a defeated opponent or performed a humanitarian act unless it was politically expedient?"[26] None of these things, the *New York Times* author asserts. Rather, in 1921 Lenin, "a longtime enthusiast for hiking and camping," signed a decree mandating that "significant areas of nature" be protected –*that*, apparently, is what his legacy consists of.[27] In other words, the proper way to construe Leninism is as a form of progressive environmental activism. Everything else he did should be consigned to the footnotes of history.

Discussions of the dark truths about communism should be avoided; conversations about communism's triumphs should be encouraged. This is the anti-anti-communist message eagerly disseminated by the most influential media outlets in the world more than a century after the beginning of the Soviet experiment.

---

[25] On Lenin as a strategic genius, see Tariq Ali, "What Was Lenin Thinking," *New York Times*, April 3, 2017; on communists as role models, see Vivian Gornick, "When Communism Inspired Americans," *New York Times*, April 29, 2017; on communism and Star Trek, see A.M.Gittlitz, "Make It So: Star Trek and Its Debt to Revolutionary Socialism," *New York Times*, July 24, 2017; on how "communism taught women to dream big," see Helen Gao, "How Did Women Fare in China's Communist Revolution," *New York Times*, September 25, 2017, and on sex under communism, see Kristen Ghodsee, "Why Women Had Better Sex Under Communism," *New York Times*, August 12, 2017.

[26] Cf. Victor Sebestyen, *Lenin the Dictator: An Intimate Portrait* (London: Weidenfeld and Nicolson, 2017), 3.

[27] Fred Strebeigh, "Lenin's Eco-Warriors," *New York Times*, August 7, 2017. On ecological truths about the catastrophic Soviet policies, see Murray Feshbach and Alfred Friendly, Jr., *Ecocide in the USSR: Health and Nature Under Siege* (New York: Basic Books, 1992) and Ryszard Kapuściński, "Central Asia: The Destruction of the Sea," in Ryszard Kapuściński, *Imperium* (New York: Vintage International, 1994), 254–64.

Annoying encounters: Western academics vs. East Europeans dissidents

As we already saw, one of the main objectives of anti-anti-communism during the Cold War was to create a climate of opinion in which anti-communists are treated as nothing more than staunch defenders of Western militarism and imperialism, and to make sure that radical criticisms of Soviet-type regimes are dismissed as unbefitting of a true scholar or ethical thinker. After the collapse of Marxist dictatorships in Eastern Europe this climate appeared to be endangered when former East European dissidents emerged from their relative obscurity and demanded to be considered full-fledged participants in the conversation about communism. Before 1989, these individuals were conveniently kept out of the West's sight by the communist governments that repressed them. Of course, occasionally their opinions were heard and, if deemed hostile to Marxism or "primitively" anti-communist, these opinions were duly repudiated.[28] But, for the most part, East European and Soviet voices were excluded from the conversation about the vices of anti-communism and the virtues of anti-anti-communism. After 1989–1991 that changed: some former dissidents began to publish texts in widely read journals and newspapers and to gain access to Western public and academic spheres. And the preponderant majority of them shared the view that there was something fundamentally evil in communism and something morally misguided in the effort to relativize its many crimes. Troublingly, East European voices questioned the anti-anti-communist credo. Western academic elites were forced to respond to this challenge: the dismantlement of Marxist autocracy in the former Soviet satellites was their "cue to fight," and they knew it "without a prompter."[29]

The responses varied. Undoubtedly, there were intellectuals who insisted that when Easterners speak about communism, Westerners should listen, learn—and try to revitalize a Left no longer beholden to the Leninist myths about revolutionary success and a reassuring Soviet "normalcy."[30] The typical

---

[28] A typical example of how a Western intellectual superstar lambasts an East European dissident is E.P.Thompson's hundred-page long "open letter" to Leszek Kołakowski. E.P.Thompson, "An Open Letter to Leszek Kołakowski," *The Socialist Register* (1973): 1–100. For Kołakowski's response, see "My Correct Views on Everything," *The Socialist Register* (1974): 1–20.

[29] Cf. William Shakespeare, *Othello*, Act I, Scene 2, 103–04 (New York: Simon and Schuster, 1993): 27.

[30] See for example Andrew Arato and Jean Cohen, *Civil Society and Political Theory* (Cambridge, MA: MIT Press, 1994), and Jeffrey Isaac, *Democracy in Dark Times* (Ithaca: Cornell University Press, 1998).

reaction to East European opinions, however, was along the lines "we should listen politely, but there is nothing we can learn." A characteristic example in that regard is Seyla Benhabib. On the one hand, she acknowledges that "we should all be seriously reflecting on the discourses of intellectuals like Vaclav Havel, Georg Konrad, Adam Michnik and Jacek Kuron." On the other hand, she quickly dismisses such discourses as "suspicious" because they seek to re-valorize things like "liberal parliamentary democracies, free-market capitalism, and tolerant societies open to individual ambition and self-unfolding." And the problem with that, Benhabib explains, is that old fashioned excitement about such aspects of contemporary politics have been superseded by exhilarating new orthodoxies and any effort to re-launch a conversation about their possible desirability should be resisted: "Let's face it: after two decades of poststructuralist, post-Foucauldian, psychoanalytic, feminist, post-colonial discourse" there is a "great resentment at being told that the world historical mission of 1989 is the restoration of liberal capitalism."[31] Put differently, East European messengers should be allowed to speak, but since their opinions reiterate the significance of precisely those normative principles that anti-communists routinely invoked in order to criticize communist practices, what they have to say about the potentialities and dangers inherent in modern politics must be firmly rejected.

Notably, Benhabib treats those who spent time in prison because of their ideas with respect and civility. This is not the case with other intellectual celebrities who zealously deployed the *Reductio ad Reaganum* in order to discredit dissident views emanating from Eastern Europe. In 1990 academic superstar Frederic Jameson flew to a seminar in Dubrovnik (then a part of Yugoslavia) expecting to engage East European participants in a dialogue about the incredible richness of Marxist thought. What he found out is that most of his interlocutors were not interested: they simply refused to get involved in a conversation about how humankind might be redeemed through radical Marxism-inspired activism. Instead, they launched a frontal assault on Jameson's beloved ideology. Appalled, he withdrew from the conference, left the hotel where he was staying—incidentally, the hotel was called "Imperial" and was the most expensive one in the city—and retreated to the safe waters of American academia where the probability

---

[31]   Seyla Benhabib, "The Strange Silence of Political Theory: Response," *Political Theory* 23, no. 4 (November 1995): 677.

that he would be inconvenienced by the kinds of heresies propagated by East Europeans was close to zero.[32] Reflecting on the annoying encounter, Jameson announced to the world that "arguments ... let alone dialogues, are difficult to sustain with our opposite numbers from the East" because there exists an "utter disparity or incommensurability of the explanatory terms in which each side seeks to stage its discourse."[33] He also made it clear which one of these "incommensurate" discourses is superior. Westerners like him were intellectually equipped to analyze "culture and commodification" and to dissect phenomena such as "the well-nigh Lacanian investment of fantasy in images of the collective Other."[34] In stark contrast, East Europeans were obsessed with "power and oppression" and blinded by a "banal anti-communism" that dulled their capacity to recognize "the fact that Stalinism was a success, fulfilling its modernizing mission, developing political and social subjects of a new type." Ultimately, Jameson concludes, the problem with East Europeans is that everything they have to say can be traced back to their "toilet training": whatever argument they have to offer is rooted in instinctual reactions and unthinkingly internalized shibboleths bereft of the analytical sophistication, theoretical insight and deep knowledge that informs the view of anti-anti-communists like Jameson himself.[35]

Once again, it is worth pausing for a moment in order to appreciate the uniqueness of dismissive attitudes towards anti-communism: attributing the ideas of a black intellectual critiquing racism, or of a woman inveighing against patriarchy, or of a radical activist condemning liberal democracy to their "toilet training" would be considered nothing short of scandalous. And yet Jameson's approach is judged to be perfectly acceptable way of discrediting the anti-communist ideas espoused by East Europeans.

But the best example of how the *Reductio ad Reaganum* is used to discredit East European dissidents is Noam Chomsky's character assassination of Václav Havel, occasioned by the Czech dissident's 1990 speech at a joint session of the US Congress.[36] According to Chomsky, the views expressed by Havel might be reduced to the following proposition: "the Cold War, now thankfully put

---

[32] The Dubrovnik incident is discussed in Miglena Nikolchina, *Lost Unicorns and Velvet Revolutions: Heterotopias of the Seminar* (New York: Fordham University Press, 2012), Chapter 2.

[33] Jameson, "Conversations," 261.

[34] Jameson, "Conversations," 265–66.

[35] Jameson, "Conversation," 262, 257.

[36] Havel's speech is included in his book *The Art of the Impossible* (New York: Fromm International, 1998), 10–20.

to rest, was a conflict between two superpowers, one a nightmare, the other, the defender of freedom." And Chomsky describes this proposition, which is clearly redolent of Reagan's "evil empire" oratory, as "embarrassingly silly and morally repugnant." Speculating about the motivation behind Havel's "shameful performance," the iconic American intellectual suggests that the Czech president might have been trying to "find a way to extort money from the American taxpayer for his (relatively rich) country." But irrespectively of what objectives exactly Havel was pursuing, his account of communism actually was a display of "supreme hypocrisy" because "in comparison to the conditions imposed by the US tyranny and violence, East Europe under Russian rule was practically a paradise." Hence, according to Chomsky, the former political prisoner's moral stature was lower than that of a "Stalinist hack."[37]

In sum, as the annoying encounters between anti-communist East Europeans and anti-anti-communist Western intellectuals became more frequent in the post-1989 era, the latter increasingly cast former in the role of "the other": instinctual, impulsive creatures with a primitive way of thinking, prone to believing in outlandish myths, to worship false gods, and to become preoccupied with imaginary demons. What such "others" have to say should be either ignored—or, as the examples of Jameson and Chomsky demonstrate, treated with contempt, "the feeling we have for those who have done what is shameful."[38] The self-described "victims of communist oppression" threatened to unsettle the consensus reigning in Western intellectual circles, namely that any conversation about suffering in the modern world should shun references to Soviet-type regimes, and any conversation about a Soviet-type regime should shun references to the suffering it inflicted. That is why these victims should under no circumstance be allowed to have the last word on communism.

Conclusion: The valorization of nostalgia

The only generalizable statement about communism is that in Western academic circles it will always be treated as something exceptional.

---

[37] Noam Chomsky, "On Vaclav Havel Speech," in Alexander Cockburn, *The Golden Age Is in Us* (London: Verso, 1995), 149–51.

[38] The definition of contempt I borrow from Kwame Anthony Appiah, *The Moral Code: How Moral Revolutions Happen* (New York: W.W.Norton, 2010), 17.

Soviet-style communism is the only type of repressive rule whose critics are deemed to be more dangerous than its active supporters. One of the disturbing "transformations" of the modern age, Albert Camus argued more than sixty years ago, is that "it is innocence that is called upon to justify itself."[39] A twenty-first century version of this phenomenon is that it is communism's opponents and not its cheerleaders that should explain their motivation: critics of Bolshevism are constantly pressured to elaborate on Soviet accomplishments, while its admirers readily dismiss negative depictions of Soviet realities as "Cold War clichés."

Anti-communists are the only intellectual constituency whose principal arguments are not assessed in terms of accuracy but refracted through unabashedly partisan considerations. Back in the 1990s Michael Scammell wrote that "the liberal *Le Monde* ... went so far as to call the appearance of *The Black Book* [*of Communism*] "inappropriate" because it would encourage the extreme right in France, led by the neo-fascist Jean-Marie Le Pen."[40] And this pattern is still observable today: even if accurate, an anti-communist view is dismissed because it might be abused by "the right wing." Even if persuasive, an anti-communist opinion is liable to be rejected because it might trigger a "reactionary backlash." Even if true, an anti-communist claim should be denounced for empowering opponents of "the Left." Criticisms of no other modern system of government are subject to such an opportunistic treatment.

Finally, the prevalent climate of anti-anti-communist opinion consistently and systematically privileges narratives that focus on socialism's winners and downplay the experiences of their victims. The unanimously embraced consensus in Western academia is that in discussions of such systems of rule as colonialism and Nazism the point of view of the colonized and the persecuted is much more relevant than the point of view of white settlers and Aryans. In discussions of communism, the exact opposite perspective prevails: when Soviet-type regimes are normatively assessed, the testimony of those who experienced "upward social mobility" counts for much more than the fact that "the Communist project ... was based precisely on the conviction that certain social groups were irretrievably alien and deservedly murdered."[41] Communism, just like any other type of regime, produced

---

[39]   Albert Camus, *The Rebel* (New York: Vintage Books, 1954), 4.

[40]   Michael Scammell, "The Price of an Idea," *The New Republic*, December 20, 1999, 33.

[41]   Vladimir Tismaneanu, *The Devil in History* (Berkeley: The University of California Press, 2012), 14.

certain "winners"—and this fact is used to silence everyone else. The Philo-Soviet argument that Soviet-type regimes: 1. ensured full employment; 2. provided free medical care; and 3. guaranteed free education, is still invoked to neutralize radically negative assessments of communism. In the dominant political discourse on the pre-1989 era, nostalgia is openly valorized: this sentiment is depicted not only as a set of fond memories, but also as normatively justified way of thinking about the dictatorships created by Lenin and his followers. Those who are nostalgic about communism display the virtuous sensitivity of ethically grounded individuals who can tell the difference between good and bad; those who focus on communism's failures are exposed as narrow-minded defamers prone to embrace the "Cold War rhetoric" championed by Western propagandists.

In his still-relevant book *The Opium of the Intellectuals* Raymond Aron pointed out that "far from being a science of working-class misfortune, Marxism is an intellectualist philosophy which seduced certain groups of the proletariat."[42] Today there are no proletarian groups entrapped in "working class misfortune" that are still seduced by Marxism—and neither are there Third World "revolutionary movements" of the type hailed by Miliband and Liebman. Marxism-inspired anti-anti-communism is entirely and solely "an intellectualist philosophy" that dominates academic campuses and media venues like the *New York Times*. Why and how this status quo coalesced is an issue open to debate. One thing is clear, however. Among the most intriguing lessons of the last century is that if the fate of the Berlin Wall were to be determined not be the peoples of Eastern Europe but by a random sample of Western academics, the only outcome compatible with the *Reductio ad Reaganum* would have transpired: the oppressive structure would still be standing.

---

[42] Raymond Aron, *The Opium of the Intellectuals* (New Brunswick: Transaction Publisher, [1957] 2001), 83.

IDEOLOGY AND VIOLENCE IN COMMUNIST VENEZUELA

Jordan Luber

"*I shall not pause to dwell on the singularly undialectical nature of this line of thought of an otherwise great dialectician. It is enough to note in passing the rigid contrast, the mechanical separation of the 'positive' and the 'negative,' of 'tearing down' and 'building up' directly contradicts the actuality of the Revolution. For in the revolutionary measures taken by the proletarian state, especially those taken directly after seizing power, the 'positive' cannot be separated from the 'negative' even conceptually, let alone in practice. The process of struggling against the bourgeoisie, of seizing from its hands the instruments of power in economic conflict coincides— especially at the beginning of the revolution—with the first steps towards organizing the economy. It is self-evident that these first attempts will need to be revised later on. Nevertheless, as long as the class struggle persists— that is to say, for a long time—even the later forms of organization will preserve the 'negative' quality of the struggle, i.e. the tendency to tear down and keep down.*"[1]

Here György Lukács attacks Rosa Luxemburg's opposition to Lenin, and defends Lenin's "negative" revolutionary measures, like disbanding the Russian legislature and creating the concentration camp universe. With this paragraph Lukács gives a direct justification for communist oppression: communists believe they are building freedom. To them the only ones oppressed are oppressors. Lukács reveals exactly why communists in rice fields, barrios, steppes, and the tropics silence, humiliate, and massacre.

From 1999 until his death in 2013, Hugo Chávez was the dictator of Venezuela. Since then Nicolás Maduro has ruled Venezuela. Examining Chávez's politics demonstrates ideological authoritarianism was intrinsic to them. Though the methods were slightly upgraded for the new century and

---

[1] György Lukács, *History and Class Consciousness: Studies in Marxist Dialectics*, trans. Rodney Livingstone (London: Merlin Press, 1968), 278.

his ideology was not explicitly dialectical Marxism, Chávez's political move-ment and rule were fundamentally communist. His politics, including the ones Maduro has maintained, though severely escalated, are only possible in a communist project: the same paranoid worldview and utopian passions are the exact—and the only—explanation for its tyranny and popularity. Simi-larly, evaluating Maduro and his politics show a clear communist identity. Yet Maduro's politics are distinctly Jacobin. As the Venezuelans can attest to, Jacobins are even more destructive than typical communist. Recognizing why Chávez is a communist and comparing communism with Jacobinism are necessary to understanding what is happening in Venezuela. And this provides a framework for thinking about communism overall, to move past the narrowest possible definition of Marxists alone, and about Jacobinism, the especially cruel and shocking attempt at liberation through total violence. Both examples also testify to the ease of national terror and worldwide shame in the shining twenty-first century.

Chávez

Communism does not seize power on the effects of mass deprivation—that is a simplified assumption which misses the point. Mass deprivation is the trigger, but the actual cause of oppression in the pursuit of eschatological utopia lies deeper.[2] Only philosophical motivations lead to political oppres-sion and social destruction in the name of social liberation.[3] Before Chávez took power, Venezuela's Punto Fijo democratic system stood for decades as an example to the world.[4] Eventually mass poverty developed, after the col-lapse of oil prices in 1982 and a currency devaluation in 1983 combined with

---

[2] Hannah Arendt, *On Revolution* (New York: Penguin Books, 2006), 99–105.

[3] "One of the distinguishing features of Communism was the conviction of the importance of philosophy in political life." This is also why "the Marxist doctrine was a good blueprint for converting human society into a giant concentration camp." Leszek Kołakowski, *The Main Currents of Marxism: The Founders, The Golden Age, The Breakdown*, trans. P. S. Falla (New York: W. W. Norton & Company, 2005), vi, 833.

[4] David J. Meyers, "Normalization of Punto Fijo Democracy," in *The Unraveling of Representative Democracy in Venezuela*, eds. Jennifer L. McCoy and David J. Meyers (Baltimore: The Johns Hopkins University Press, 2004), 11–29. During a visit to Venezuela in 1961, President Kennedy declared Venezuela a model, disproving "the view, which some now preach, that the only way we can make economic progress is through dictatorship." John F. Kennedy, "Remarks at La Morita Resettlement Project Venezuela," December 16, 1961, John F. Kennedy Presidential Library and Museum. https://www.jfklibrary.org/Asset-Viewer/Archives/JFKPOF-036-034.aspx.

unreformed elitism and urbanization. Dependent on oil, scared of pushing the right on reform, and struggling to grasp the challenges presented by the suddenly urbanizing population, the elitist democracy quickly proved unwilling to solve dire problems. Destitution spread and intensified through a decade and a half of economic crisis. The conditions to spark ideological authoritarianism were present in Venezuela in the 90s, not because people were poor, but because they were justifiably angry.

The economic problems brought about the second requirement for communist revolution, a deeper social malaise. Its roots had been there throughout Punto Fijo. Punto Fijo's two dominant parties had always split the urban poor vote, muting them.[5] Outside of routine elections the parties ignored the people. Additionally, the urban poor were unable to participate because they lacked the resources necessary for political involvement. As Tocqueville wrote about the French Revolution, the political and social exclusion of the poor was precisely what caused the revolution to become so fanatic and violent. In France, "the separation of the classes was the crime of the old monarchy," as the people became "more divided than ever."[6] The middle classes competed with political elites for power, while the poor's only political lifeline was the radical intellectuals, who "ended up inflaming and arming... [the people's] rage and cupidity,"[7] while the government's endless promises of reform "threw public affairs into disorder and finally upset every citizen even in his private life."[8] This prophecy was fulfilled in Venezuela. Elitism, failure to address mass injustice, and then economic crisis caused a collapse in solidarity. This understandably transformed an imperfect system into a revolutionary society. Helpless and in need of change, the masses' pain arising from their material situation became rage toward their metaphysical one: suffering from extreme poverty, they grow angry at the democracy instead of their undemocratic rulers. Misery produced underlying malaise, creating a mob determined to achieve violent transformation of their experience of existence. This begins the saga of communism in Venezuela.

---

5   Damarys Canache, "Urban Poor and Political Order," in *The Unraveling of Representative Democracy in Venezuela*, eds. Jennifer L. McCoy, David J. Meyers (Baltimore: The Johns Hopkins University Press, 2004), 36.

6   Alexis Tocqueville, *The Ancien Regime and the Revolution*, trans. Gerald Bevan (London: Penguin Books, 2008), 89, 111–112.

7   Tocqueville, *The Ancien Regime and the Revolution*, 185.

8   Tocqueville, *The Ancien Regime and the Revolution*, 191.

Chávez, a military officer separate from the masses' lived suffering, was a fanatic of his own accord. After his unsuccessful coup in 1992, the urban poor fanatically supported him. Inspired by Chávez's proclamations, there was "such a meek response in defense of democratic rule" that it was clear the people no longer cared about democracy at all.[9] Through 1998 the urban poor coalesced around Chávez.[10] He talked incessantly about rescuing the poor from neoliberalism, which he said was colonizing the nation and forcing the masses into destitution.[11] Many voters were motivated by his strong position against businesses and the promise to end the corruption they so desperately despised.[12] They were fed up with the two parties and the democratic system.[13] A mass movement, Eric Hoffer explains in his classic book, is when people "rise not against the wickedness of the regime but its weakness."[14] They did not seek to just vote a different party into power, but specifically to destroy the democracy. Chávez frankly admitted that Punto Fijo had to end, because it was a "dictatorship."[15] Over the next few years, the masses came to agree with his ideological worldview: enemies inflict suffering, only revolution can bring progress.

From the beginning Chávez and his followers were an ideological mass movement. Chávez ceaselessly rallied the people to struggle for a righteous society. Chavismo was a new politics to forge a new society. "One of the most effective seductions of Evil is the call to struggle,"[16] and this explains Chávez's massive success in gaining support. Believing Chávez, suddenly people thought businesses, Punto Fijo democrats, and America were relentless enemies engineering the nation's oppression.[17] So obsessed with the alleged

---

[9] Jorge G. Castañeda, *Utopia Unarmed: The Latin American Left After the Cold War* (New York: Vintage Books, 1993), 331–34.

[10] Canache, *The Unraveling*, 38–39.

[11] Leslie C. Gates, *Electing Chávez: The Business of Anti-neoliberal Politics in Venezuela* (Pittsburg: University of Pittsburg Press, 2010), 3–13.

[12] Gates, *Electing Chávez*, 39–81.

[13] Gates, *Electing Chávez*, 14–36.

[14] Eric Hoffer, *True Believer: Thoughts on the Nature of Mass Movements* (New York: Perennial Classics, 2002), 42–43.

[15] Hugo Chávez, "El Pacto de Punto Fijo fue la verdadera traición al pueblo venezolano," January 23, 2011, Correo del Orinoco, http://www.correodelorinoco.gob.ve/presidente-Chávez-se-suma-a-concentracion-revolucionaria-conmemoracion-al-23-enero-1958/.

[16] Franz Kafka, *Aphorisms*, trans. Willa and Edwin Muir and Michael Hofmann (New York: Schocken Books, 2015), 9.

[17] "Yesterday, the Devil was here in this very place. The rostrum still smells like sulfur," Chávez said about Bush during his official speech to the UN General Assembly in 2006. In Venezuela,

exploiters, a revolutionary Marxist's hope is "the thought that one day soon he would exterminate the whole mass" of enemies of the people.[18] Believing in Chávez was not a political decision but a primordial seduction. During the neo- communist Corbyn's 2015 rise in Britain, Tony Blair realized "those in the bubble feel good about what they're doing."[19]

Seizing the opportunity produced by the people's anger at their political isolation, Chávez called for unity. In 2012 he said that "unity, unity, and more unity" is the answer to enemies trying to destroy the new Venezuela, that Venezuela must have "united popular forces" against "the enemies of the country."[20] This is a basic principle of any communist; just as the masses' rage comes from powerlessness, their hope lies in acting as *and being* one. Furthermore, unity is a correction, a return to nature which the artificial society of exploitation has ruined. Conformity is not a revolutionary means, but the utopian end.

For a communist movement it is critical that people believe the ideology. Ideology is the oxygen and blood of dictatorship in modernity.[21] Totalitarianism can be defined simply as "a dictatorship resting on popular enthusiasm."[22] Every word a leader says is for the purpose of achieving this popular support, of convincing people of the ideology. This is necessary for the regime to continue its revolution, and adherence to the truth is the entire point of the revolution at all. Chávez incessantly made public speeches. Citizens heard his voice for hours every day. The TV often just stayed on in homes, and

---

the rhetoric is even more bizarre—and totally constant. He used the speech to source himself in a Chomsky book, displaying the classic Stalinist tactic of pseudo-intellectualism. Hugo Chávez, "Statement at the 61st United Nations General Assembly," trans. Mission of the Bolivarian Republic of Venezuela, non-official translation (New York, September 20, 2006), United Nations, http://www.un.org/webcast/ga/61/pdfs/venezuela-e.pdf.

[18] Andrei Platonovich, *The Foundation Pit*, trans. Mirra Ginsburg (Evanston: Northwestern University Press, 1975), 61.

[19] Tony Blair, "Jeremy Corbyn's Politics are Fantasy just like Alice in Wonderland," *The Guardian*, August 29, 2015, https://www.theguardian.com/commentisfree/2015/aug/29/tony-blair-labour-leadership-jeremy-corbyn.

[20] CubaDebate, "Hugo Chávez: Unidad, unidad, y más unidad, esa debe ser nuestra divisa," CubaDebate, December 09, 2012,http://www.cubadebate.cu/especiales/2012/12/09/hugo-Chávez-unidad-unidad-y-mas-unidad-esa-debe-ser-nuestra-divisa/.

[21] Kate C. Langdon and Vladimir Tismaneanu, *Putin's Totalitarian Democracy: Ideology, Myth, and Violence in the Twenty-First Century* (Cham: Palgrave MacMillan, 2020), 88–90, 165–77, 225–44.

[22] J. L. Talmon, *The Origins of Totalitarian Democracy* (New York: W.W. Norton & Company Inc., 1970), 6.

people trusted it.[23] He would appear at random times doing quirky things, each time demonstrating his connection to the nation and superhuman ability to act. This had an effect: people did not just support Chávez's policies, they revered him. That is, Chavistas became ideological: they believed in him and his mission, rather than their own personal fortunes. Chávez did not drag Venezuela into the abyss, he was merely the people's representative to handle the leadership role required in fulfilling their wish to take them there. This has always been the case with Latin caudillos, since the Supremo and the Restaurador de los Leyes.[24]

Ideology rests on two simple beliefs: the justice of the cause and the vileness of the enemies. All measures taken and losses incurred are not only vindicated sacrifices but also required heroics. A conviction of how society should function drives the ideological. No crime committed in the revolutionary war can be appalling,[25] because everything is in service of the righteous cause against the monstrous evil. Besides, "democracy" and "human tights" are incomplete, exclusionary, and deceptive. Collectivism brings true joy. Plurality and diversity are divisive, unity is natural. This is why, for example, communist regimes are always as violently intolerant of ethnic and cultural minorities as the most fascist right-wing extremists. This particular philosophical outlook is the foundation of these politics. Do you support misery and exploitation or equality and joy? Only exploiters feel the need for "free speech," because all those who care about the people and know the truth would be in agreement. Freedom is a sham; civil society, a plot. Only totalitarian revolution can bring happiness.

When the masses feel "the worse, the better," they will likely turn to utopian ideology and tyrannical politics. This happened in Venezuela. The crazier Chávez was, the more people liked him. The more made-up his ideas, blatantly impossible his promises, ridiculous his conspiracy theories,

---

[23] Juan Carlos Chirinos, *Venezuela: Biografía de un suicidio* (Madrid: La Huerta Grande Editorial, 2017), 26, 28. Virtually all accounts of people who have been in Chávez's Venezuela terrifyingly confirm this.

[24] See for example Augusto Roa Bastos, *Yo El Supremo* (Caracas: Biblioteca Ayacucho, 1986); and Domingo Faustino Sarmiento, *Facundo* (Buenos Aires: Penguin, 2018).

[25] "War is harsh, and at a time when the enemy's aggressiveness is on the rise, it is not possible to tolerate even the presumption of treason." Many episodes throughout his book recount executions of those insufficiently loyal, with similarly unrepentant justifications. Che Guevara, *Reminiscences of the Cuban Revolutionary War*, trans. Victoria Ortiz (London: Penguin Books, 1970), 168.

Orwellian his musings on democracy as dictatorship and dictatorship as democracy, chaotic his efforts and greater his failures, and blatantly legitimate the criticisms of him, the more the masses adored him. An outlandish Chávez ruling would mean the old Venezuela could not endure him, which was people's goal. Impossibility is the entire point of the metaphysical revolt, because in their pessimistic view of the world, the impossible endeavor is the only justified one: everything already in existence in the world is corrupt. It became the narrative that under Punto Fijo, as during pre-revolution France, conditions were "a social crime," so the people were determined "to make themselves unrecognizable."[26] The wildly endorsed terror and propaganda because it was a clear break with the democracy they hated.

Chávez wasted no time in flexing the power such mass faith bestowed on him. As soon as he took power in 1999, the government adopted a new constitution. A referendum ratified it, "proving" Chávez's popularity. The new constitution provides—along with the ideology, the mass movement, and the rhetoric that connects them—the final cornerstone of Chávez's reign, extreme centralization. Frequently, especially in the second half of his reign, Chávez simply ruled by decree. From 2000 to his death in 2013, Chávez's rule was based on three things: 1) political oppression, 2) social kleptocracy, and 3) the ideological mass movement. Frequently referred to as a hybrid-regime, Venezuela under Chávez was a new sort of dictatorship, where the opposition was allowed to exist, but the government made it impossible for its opponents to ever take power, or even approach an ability to offer checks on the regime. Election-rigging, the arrests of opposition leaders, the fusing of regime and society, an entire propaganda universe, and all sorts of classic dictatorial tricks were used. It castrated the opposition without alarming the world.

The Chávez regime's censorship and crushing of civil society eliminated serious challenges to his rule. Through the "*use, abuse,* and *non-use*" of the rule of law, Chávez deployed all sorts of schemes to shut down independent voices one way or another.[27] The result was that "private media wither[ed]," and only pro-regime voices remained. The *New York Times* called it "stealth censorship:" "taking novel, more covert, forms," censorship in Venezuela is

---

26 Tocqueville wrote this about French society before the Revolution, and the same applied to Venezuela. Tocqueville, *The Ancien Regime*, 7.

27 Javier Corrales, "Autocratic Legalism in Venezuela," in *Authoritarianism Goes Global: The Challenge to Democracy*, eds. Larry Diamond, Marc F. Plattner, and Christopher Walker (Baltimore: Johns Hopkins University Press, 2016), 79, 78–95.

done through the guise of media companies 'restructuring'" their editorial content under direct but secret orders from the government.[28] Through pressure, business deals, and threats, all media became and has remained either overtly favorable to the government or self-censoring. Over time, it became merely the former, with the heroic exception of *El Nacional*. As *The New Republic* describes this climate of censorship:

> Welcome to the world of twenty-first century censorship: censorship without censors. The Chávez government operates nothing so crass and cumbersome as an old-fashioned censorship board. Instead, by keeping broadcast editors and station managers under the vague but constant threat of shutdown, it relies on them to silence their organizations. And it is wildly effective.[29]

Similarly, the regime's machine pressured civil society into powerlessness and virtual nonexistence. "Discrimination on political grounds has been a defining feature of the Chávez presidency," the result being that harassment, pressure, and isolation has crippled civil society.[30] Resources—almost all in the hands of the state, enabled by the oil-rush—were awarded through politics alone. The judiciary, controlled by Chávez,[31] was used to conclusively harass civil society. Finally, Chávez used his extensive propaganda tools to discredit any activists and organizations who advocate for human rights and democracy against his efforts.[32] Jailed, outlawed, defunded, harassed, and finally despised by the Chavista population, civil society became a ghost. Rather than murder it, the regime masterfully engineered civil society's starvation.

Robert C. Tucker wrote "the Soviet Union is most usefully viewed as an educational establishment. It is not a prison—that is a distortion."[33] Chávez

---

[28] Daniel Lansberg-Rodríguez, "Stealth Censorship in Venezuela," *New York Times*, August 06, 2014, online version, https://www.nytimes.com/2014/08/07/opinion/daniel-lansberg-rodriguez-stealth-censorship-in-venezuela.html.

[29] Francisco Toro, "Welcome to Censorship in the 21st Century," *The New Republic*, August 05, 2010, online version, https://newrepublic.com/article/76796/censorship-Chávez-venezuela.

[30] Human Rights Watch, *A Decade Under Chávez: Political Intolerance and Lost Opportunities for Advancing Human Rights in Venezuela*, Human Rights Watch, September 18, 2008, online edition, https://www.hrw.org/report/2008/09/18/decade-under-Chávez/political-intolerance-and-lost-opportunities-advancing-human.

[31] Juan Forero, "Venezuela's Chávez Tightens Grip on Judiciary," *NPR*, April 27, 2010, online edition, https://www.npr.org/templates/story/story.php?storyId=126304030.

[32] Human Rights Watch, *A Decade*.

[33] Robert C. Tucker, *The Soviet Political Mind: Stalinism and Post-Stalin Change*, revised edition (New York: Norton, 1972), 93.

understood his effort to build a new society in the same way. Along with severe but limited violence, Chávez simply used information to maintain the masses' support for him and contempt for all rival political opinions and efforts. This is all the better for him, since utopia requires that people have seen the truth. Honest press and diverse civil society were replaced through Chávez's own efforts, creating and working with the second and third pillars of his rule.

Chávez made Venezuela a social kleptocracy: the economy was destroyed, the state controlled everything, and all rules were arbitrary. Social kleptocracy was possible for a simple reason: the massive selling of oil.[34] Putin's kleptocracy robs Russia in order to fuel a compliant corporate elite, but Chávez's profits went to the mob (and him and his friends of course) further earning unshakable loyalty. Stolen treasures were given to mobilized regime forces, not only London bank accounts like typical rent-state tyrants. Chávez created "bases" and "colectivos." Hailed as "the most perfect politics that President Hugo Chávez could devise,"[35] these were locally-based organizations fanatically loyal to and directly controlled by the regime, like Bashaar's mukhabarat. They hand out food and are the primary instruments of triumphant bloodshed against protests. All social and political activities of communities were controlled by the regime. Receiving essentially all funds available in the state's coffers, these activities ensured many people's fantastic devotion,[36] both out of calculation and the genuine faith that only Chávez and his revolution could deliver such wondrous material results. Even more hypocritically, this statist chokehold was praised as people power. The spending did not just buy favor, it convincingly advocated the ideology. Educated, privileged, foreign observers particularly adored this de facto totalitarian system.

The "positive" is accompanied by the "negative."

---

[34] Enrique Krauze, "Hell of a Fiesta," *The New York Review of Books*, March 08, 2018, online edition, https://www.nybooks.com/articles/2018/03/08/venezuela-hell-fiesta/.

[35] Telesur, "Misiones socialies destacan como legado de Hugo Chávez en Venezuela," *Telesur*, June 04, 2014, online edition, https://www.telesurtv.net/news/Misiones-sociales-destacan-como-legado-de-Hugo-Chávez-en-Venezuela-20140604-0057.html.

[36] See Michael Penfold-Becerra, "Clientelism and Social Funds: Evidence from Chávez's Misiones," *Latin American Politics and Society* 49, no. 4 (Winter 2007): 63–84, online edition, https://www-jstor-org.proxy-um.researchport.umd.edu/stable/pdf/30130824.pdf?ab_segments=0%252Fbasic_SYC-4946%252Fcontrol&refreqid=excelsior%3A828e5b43a0babe 52773251fa7b9635b5.

Taking the space of transparent information and vigorous debate, Chávez filled the national public space with an advanced indoctrination industry. Unlike many other twentieth century communist regimes, Chávez's propaganda was not pathetic and monotonous that people knew were lies and so ignored, but instead energetic and compelling broadcasts that employed endlessly varied tactics. José Pedro Zúquete calls Chávez's rhetoric "missionary politics," as it "puts forward a narrative portraying a community that is besieged, threatened, and surrounded by powerful and conspiratorial forces. The rhetoric of threat and fear serves to maintain the group's mobilization and energy at high levels."[37] Crime and the economy were never discussed on TV or radio, but there was constant focus on Chávez's activities, his social projects' success stories, and plots of the people's enemies. "Charismatic hyperactivity [was] so critical to his populist government's survival since its beginnings," as seen in Chávez's hours-long ramblings on topics like imperialism or baseball on TV every Sunday.[38] Through oppression and social kleptocracy, Chávez maintained his ideological mass movement.

How could someone on the left support this? For them, the press is against the people, loyal only to business and imperialist interests, and civil society is elitist.[39] Logically, oppression is liberation in the eyes of the Venezuelan urban poor and North Atlantic leftists. For more thoughtful Chavistas who are not so naïve, they take the position of the Kaiser of Austria: "People tell a lot of lies... [and] they can find out the truth later."[40] That is, if something is a lie, if something is wrong with the regime, it will work out later. It is

---

[37] José Pedro Zúquete, "The Missionary Politics of Hugo Chávez," *Latin American Politics and Society* 50, no. 1 (Spring 2008): 104–05, online edition, http://onlinelibrary.wiley.com.proxyum.researchport.umd.edu/doi/10.1111/j.1548-2456.2008.00005.x/epdf.

[38] See Daniel Lansberg-Rodríguez, "Aló Presidente!—Venezuela's Reality Show Authoritarianism," in *The New Authoritarians: Ruling Through Disinformation*, Legatum Institute (June 2015), 7–14, online edition, https://lif.blob.core.windows.net/lif/docs/default-source/publications/the-new-authoritarians---ruling-through-disinformation-june-2015-pdf.pdf?sfvrsn=4.

[39] See Ion Iliescu and Vladimir Tismaneanu, *The Great Shock at the End of a Short Century: Ion Iliescu in Dialogue with Vladimir Tismaneanu on Communism, Post-communism and Democracy* (New York: Columbia University Press, 2004), 269–70. Iliescu discusses his firm belief that civil society activists and organizations were just a minority representing the interests of the rich, while the masses supported him—a populist dictatorship—and thus he was right to use force on them. He defends an infamous massacre of peaceful students by violent government-commanded thugs because the students represented special interests. That is, peace is violence and violence is peace, tyranny is democracy and democracy is tyranny.

[40] Joseph Roth, *The Radetzky March*, trans. Joachim Neugroschel (New York: Overlook Press, 2002), 9–10.

literally impossible for the regime to become the incorrect choice, no matter what happens, no matter what it does. To overcome the lies of the enemies, and to keep people motivated until victory has been achieved, information has to be controlled, the masses need direction. Besides, the propaganda is only education if the lie is true, and barbaric socialism[41] is based on the idea that the one true way forward has been discovered. Censorship only harms the agents of evil; all righteousness remains free. Ideology is so compelling it succeeds in "justifying or at least excusing arbitrary evil in the name of a higher truth."[42]

Throughout his reign, North Atlantic intellectuals cherished Chávez. Further proof of ideology is demonstrated by the fact that Chávez's first and strongest political act—to install extremely centralized executive power— was celebrated by the North Atlantic Left. Although the Leviathan state is the original enemy of the Left, they do not celebrate Chávez in spite of his centralization, they celebrate Chávez's centralization itself. There is no short-age of academic English-language books pumping this line.[43] Demonstrating how ideology mutates and controls someone's opinions, the North Atlantic Left saw Chávez's executive rule as the path toward social justice. According to them, the special interests which seek the marginalization of the masses are so strong that only a stronger movement *in the name of* (but not by) the people can overturn it. From *New York Times* articles to liberal politicians to Hollywood to social justice activists, Chávez created a nascent mob in North Atlantic society.

---

[41] As opposed to real socialism, demonstrated for instance by the opposition Voluntad Popular, the Venezuelan socialist party. Another example is the SDs of Weimar Germany; their electoral poster called their supporters to strike down monarchy, Nazism, and communism. The Radicales of Argentina are the sworn enemies of Peronismo. Many elders of the Syrian Revolution, like Yassin al-Haj Saleh, are former communists, because then and now they fight for equality and justice. No one fights communism and fascism—ideologically authoritarian socialism—more honorably and eternally than real socialists.

[42] Daniel Chirot, "The Power of Imaginative Analogy: Communism, Faith, and Leadership," in *World Order After Leninism*, eds. Vladimir Tismaneanu, Marc Morje Howard, and Rudra Sil (Seattle: University of Washington Press, 2006), 271–72.

[43] See for example Barry Cannon, *Hugo Chávez and the Bolivarian Revolution: Populism and Democracy in a Globalized Age* (Manchester, Manchester University Press, 2009); Chesa Boudin, Wilmer Rumbos, and Gabriel Gonzalez, *The Venezuelan Revolution: 100 Questions-100 Answers* (New York: Thunder's Mouth Press, 2006); Sujatha Fernandes, *Who Can Stop the Drums: Urban Asocial Movements in Chávez's Venezuela* (USA: Duke University Press: 2010).

The cultivation of fellow-travelers[44] was so thorough under Chávez that it lingers under Maduro's blatantly humiliating incompetence and violence. With the publication of Maduro's "call for peace" in 2014,[45] *The New York Times* leveled the same arguments decrying tastelessness and indecency levelled against the Freedom Marchers by moderate, treasonously self-declared anti-segregationists. Hypocrisy is the basic subatomic structure of the global Chavistas, just as it was in Stalinist anti-fascism. In 2018, the highest American leftist intellectuals called for mediation, not sanctions, concerned more by American "regime change" than Madurista terror.[46] Until the famine took effect in 2018, Hollywood actors continued to pay pilgrimage. Jeremy Corbyn condemned violence "by all sides" when peaceful mass demonstrations were mowed down by regime machine guns.[47] This argument is atrocious; condemned with incredulity and outrage when Trump used it to excuse neo-Nazi violence in America, yet the exact same thing said about a Leftist *dictador* meets hardly any protest, and absolutely no public relations crisis as it did for the right-wing extremist American president.

What precisely made Chávez a proto-communist, rather than just an authoritarian, beyond the calls for equality in his reign? Official declaring yourself a communist is hardly the definition of a communist. Rather, communism is whenever human dignity and equality are intentionally, systematically, urgently, they say, violated in the name of utopian freedom—when, as Hannah Arendt realized, the part of the population which exercises its human plurality is made superfluous for the revolutionary vision. Making citizens superfluous does not require mass murder, only mass exclusion and

---

[44]   An inaccurate term. A better way to describe those who *the god that failed* described as "worshippers from afar" is imperialists. As told in Richard Wolin, *The Wind from the East* (Princeton: Princeton University Press, 210), 124–25, leftists in a North Atlantic country support the communist "revolutionary" state of a developing world country because of their own domestic utopian fantasies, not because of the transformations actually happening in the affected country. If we take the definition of imperialism as sacrificing another population for the triumph, progress, and mental perseverance of your own civilization (Hannah Arendt, *The Origins of Totalitarianism*, Part II) this fits perfectly: Venezuelans are sacrificed in the name of the North Atlantic Left's utopian pride.

[45]   Ghostwriters of Nicolás Maduro, "Venezuela: A Call for Peace," *New York Times*, April 01, 2014, online edition, https://www.nytimes.com/2014/04/02/opinion/venezuela-a-call-for-peace.html.

[46]   Petition, "Open Letter in Support of Mediation in Venezuela, Not Sanctions," *WorldBeyondWar*, https://worldbeyondwar.org/open-letter-in-support-of-mediation-in-venezuela-not-sanctions/.

[47]   Rowena Mason, "Jeremy Corbyn condemns 'violence done by all sides' in Venezuela," *The Guardian*, August 07, 2017, online edition, https://www.theguardian.com/politics/2017/aug/07/no-10-reiterates-uk-condemnation-of-venezuelan-government-may.

humiliation, whether of a social or ethnic group, or a political group, in this case liberals and socialists who were not sufficiently revolutionary. Demonization of your people can be intangible. "It was not so much what Chávez did as what he said... Few realized then that there was a method to it all, that polarization was a strategy. A trap. Behind the big mouth there was a mind of cunning, foresight and subtlety."[48] Chávez intentionally said outrageous things to provoke the opposition to have to respond with equally ridiculous arguments—the well-known Trump strategy. In fact, it has been remarked how Trump mirrors Chávez's, and other Latin caudillos, rhetoric.[49] "He calculated that Venezuela's electoral arithmetic made polarisation a winning strategy," and "he sucked up all the oxygen" so every citizen could only pay attention to only him.[50] This successfully created an ideological society-state, when every individual in the population is either frenzied or cowed. Confrontation was not an electoral strategy but a social virtue, because the highest and only priority was a new collective people. Chávez was a neo-communist because he thought the answer to the poor's material deprivation was the entire population's mental deprivation.

Maduro

Ordained successor, Maduro claimed victory in the rehearsed presidential process he called "elections" less than a month after Chávez's death. Immediately, he intensified the rhetoric and power which Chávez had used. Maduro marked the transition from proto- to hyper-communism. To be precise, he is a Jacobin, and his ideological mass movement became so as well. Today he remains securely in power while Venezuela is in a state of unfathomable humanitarian collapse, a despotic inferno. Maduro fits Chávez's ideology perfectly, but he is more severe—just as Stalin's purges of the Party were not anti-communist paranoia but perfect Leninist logic.[51]

---

[48] Rory Carroll, *Comandante: Inside Hugo Chávez's Venezuela* (Edinburgh: Canongate, 2013), 60. This is the best book about Chavismo based on life in Venezuela rather than an Olympian political analysis.

[49] Gillian Brassil, "Donald Trump Tweets Like a Latin American Strongman," *Politico Magazine*, March 24, 2016, online edition, https://www.politico.com/magazine/story/2016/03/2016-donald-trump-latin-america-twitter-213759.

[50] Rory Carroll, "Insult, Provoke, Repeat: How Donald Trump Became America's Hugo Chávez," *The Guardian*, June 22, 2016, online edition, https://www.theguardian.com/us-news/2016/jun/22/donald-trump-hugo-chavez-political-similarities.

[51] Kołakowski explains that everything about Stalinism, including and especially the Purge, was

Maduro was a bus driver, so for the *relato* his roots are impeccable. A former union leader, he has the two crucial yet paradoxical components of a communist man of the people: someone who is one of the people but simultaneously leads them, from comfort. He joined Chávez's revolutionary movement in the early 90s and was a founding member of the movement which Chávez used to first get elected.[52] Maduro then served in a number of important posts. As foreign minister, before being appointed vice-president when Chávez's health deteriorated, Maduro was "wait[ing] in the wings." Chávez himself said "My firm opinion, as clear as the full moon—irrevocable, absolute, total—is... that you elect Nicolás Maduro as president. I ask this of you from my heart. He is one of the young leaders with the greatest ability to continue, if I cannot."[53]

Under Maduro, a corrupt rent-state became a controlled economy. Instead of the command economy's oppressive bureaucracy, a controlled economy is a state using chaotic domination. Everything is dependent on the delusional decisions of Maduro and his depraved army of little fuhrers. Their thought process is ideology, paranoia, megalomania, and idiocy. What businesses remained after Chávez were now decimated. Oil continued to be the only enabler. Coffers emptied for client networks and elite corruption: this maintained the masses' support, and wiped out, through starvation of funds, any organizations remaining outside the Chavista hierarchy. The intensity and amount of state violence, the ratio of information that was controlled, the fanaticism of the propaganda, and the failure of Chávez's economy all intensified. Smoothly but decisively, Maduro's Venezuela became a totalitarian camp.

---

perfect Leninism. It was the continuation of Leninism because it followed Lenin's instructions of grinding down everything not outside the one Leader's declared visions of Utopia. The Party was the final being scheduled to be destroyed. Lenin would have done the same if he lived, Kołakowski says. Kołakowski, *The Main Currents*, 851–860.

[52] Maduro's wife headed the legal team which got Chávez's early release in 1994. It's yet another point on which Chávez and his crew followed the path of Hitler, who also served a miniscule jail sentence for leading a pathetic coup and then became nationally popular from the platform he got. Virginia Lopez, "Nicolás Maduro: Hugo Chávez's Incendiary Heir," *The Guardian*, December 13, 2012, online edition, https://www.theguardian.com/world/2012/dec/12/hugo-Chávez-heir.

[53] Catherine E. Shoicet, "Venezuela: As Chávez Battles Cancer, Maduro Waits in the Wings," *CNN*, December 09, 2012, online edition, http://edition.cnn.com/2012/12/09/world/americas/venezuela-maduro/.

For a couple of months in 2014, protests rocked Venezuela. Focusing more on the economic than the political—the way most revolutions against totalitarianism typically start out—the protests ended months later after dozens were killed by regime rifle fire in the boulevards. As a Polish activist said in the early 80s, "'we must be aware of the reality of force.'"[54] The defeated Venezuelans stayed quiet, either seething in rage but hopeless, cynical and so obedient, or ideological and euphoric. Either way for Maduro, as long as the rebels stayed quiet, the mob supported him and the rebels were powerless. Totalitarianism survived.

Most Chavistas supported Maduro. Few left before the famine which began in 2017, and since then it has remained an honorable minority. Part of this is that a Chavista generation has been sown and reaped. Along with the constant propaganda and mobilization, as with all totalitarians, creating ideologically refined schools was one of Chávez's first and most intense projects.[55] Schools became militarized, and Chávez dared the schoolteachers demanding honesty and independence for children's education: "Come out to the street and look at me! The more dirt you throw at me the more I'll throw at you. That is who I am."[56] The result is that, similar to the Putin generation,[57] a generation of young Venezuelans has hardly ever heard a word besides exactly what Chávez meticulously calculated for them to hear. If everything from school and TV agree, a citizen will too.[58] In Hitler's education system, "evidence for the enthusiasm of the youth comes to us from all sides;" that generation was captured "by instilling within [the pupil] a sense of community."[59] Similarly, Chávez's Stalinist-type Bolivarian cult that celebrated the modern Venezuelan as continuing the revolutionary leader's fight meant that there was simple, concrete, heroic task for the citizen to fulfill by following the leader. Such romanticism succeeds if it monopolizes socialization.

[54] Lawrence Weschler, *The Passion of Poland: from Solidarity Through the State of War* (New York: Pantheon Books, 1984), 169.

[55] See Manuel Anselmi, *Chávez's Children: Ideology, Education, and Society in Latin America* (Lanham: Lexington Books, 2013).

[56] Carroll, *Comandante*, 60.

[57] Anton Troianovski, "The Putin Generation: Young Russians are Vladimir Putin's Biggest Fans," *Washington Post*, March 09, 2018, online edition, https://www.washingtonpost.com/news/world/wp/2018/03/09/feature/russias-young-people-are-putins-biggest-fans/.

[58] Kate C. Langdon and Vladimir Tismaneanu, *Putin's Totalitarian Democracy: Ideology, Myth, and Violence in the Twenty-First Century* (Cham: Palgrave MacMillan, 2020), 153–83.

[59] George Mosse, *Nazi Culture: Intellectual, Cultural, and Social Life in the Third Reich* (Madison: University of Wisconsin Press, 1966), 264–65.

Totalitarianism in the twenty-first century is a fundamentally different operation than it was in the twentieth. Mass murder can carry a higher price for the perpetrator now than it used to—though only sometimes, as Syria, China, Myanmar, Russia, and Sudan prove. Nevertheless, totalitarians today sometimes prioritize indoctrination over terror. Russia best demonstrates this, as Putin uses relatively less violence because most people willingly support his regime.[60]

Since December 2015, Maduro has used the full capabilities of the ideological mass movement in power to ensure that it is literally impossible for anyone but his Party to wield power, influence, or even existence. 2016 was marked by Maduro stripping away much of Congress' powers, for example by declaring (and of course the leader's spontaneous word is an iron law) dead a millions-strong recall petition that was constitutionally protected. 2017 then proved everything beyond the state and its tamed society is now illegal. 2018 came with utter collapse, shortages, and famine, but did not challenge his mandate, and 2019 showed that the nation is truly irrelevant to Maduro's will to power.

From mid-spring to mid-summer 2017 Venezuela was engulfed in protests, which could more accurately be described as a revolution. For about one hundred days straight, tens (and sometimes hundreds) of thousands of citizens were on the streets demanding *political* change. In addition to better favors for its clients and shriller propaganda, the regime responded primarily with mass violence. Tanks and combat-geared secret police, along with armed thugs, the colectivos, blocked marches and fired live bullets. The surveillance and security machine is trained, supplied, advised, and commanded by Cuban colonists. Far more than one hundred people were confirmed killed in broad daylight on the wide Latin boulevards of the formerly beautiful, now decrepit metropolis of Caracas. It was chaotic: mass protests and brash violence. Hundreds were documented imprisoned over a year later. The *desaparecidos* are uncounted. The slaughter and the regime and its movement's unshakeable will[61] to ensure that Maduro remained in power eventually forced the protestors to stay home.

Aside from the philosophical and moral standpoint of human dignity, Maduro's rule has been a disaster for the basic survival in everyday life. In

---

[60] Langdon and Tismaneanu, *Putin's Totalitarian Democracy*, 165–77.
[61] Sibylla Brodzinsky and Ana Sofia Romero, "Chávez loyalists hold firm amid chaos in Venezuela: 'We are Doing Things Right,'" *The Guardian*, August 08, 2017, https://www.theguardian.com/world/2017/aug/08/venezuela-hugo-Chávez-ruben-avila-interview-political-chaos.

2016, 74% of Venezuelans lost more than 17 pounds.[62] The figures for 2017, 2018, and 2019 are unimaginable, as the economic collapse has become exponential. The country does not have enough food within its borders. Currency is worthless because of the massive artificiality of the official exchange rate, so the black-market is a daily necessity. Condoms are scarce and at one point cost $755 per pack.[63] The birth control pill is rare, too, so teenage pregnancy is soaring.[64] This is bad since there are no jobs or food. It is also bad because hospitals have almost no medicine. One typical hospital reported that in a single day, "by nightfall, four more newborns had died." The elderly and sick languish daily with no treatment. If they get a bed, they are lucky; no one gets medicine.[65] Only 5% of medicine stocks are available—that is, not for sale or affordable, but literally present anywhere within the country's borders at all. It is among the worst economic and social collapses short of total war in modern history.[66] Crime has soared, making Venezuela one of the most dangerous countries on earth; many people have been kidnapped for ransom. Meanwhile, there is no work because there is no electricity (consider the two-day workweek Maduro mandated). The totalitarian obligation to take everything from citizens has been achieved. Through 2018 and 2019 the humanitarian material crisis has continued and intensified, with more than five million refugees, at least, fleeing Venezuela. Meanwhile, regime violence increases and power remains unchallenged, while President Guaidó and the will of the people are blatantly ignored and violently overpowered.

Some of this reminds us of life in the Soviet Union in the 1980s, but the collapse under Gorbachev is not even close. Just as it is worth discussing the reality of life in Venezuela for moral reasons, because all should be outraged

---

[62] Loren Meléndez, "Encovi 2016: 74% de los venezolanos perdió más de 8 kilos de peso el año pasado," *Runrunes*, February 18, 2017, online edition, http://runrun.es/rr-es-plus/297797/encovi-2016-74-de-los-venezolanos-perdio-mas-de-8-kilos-de-peso-el-ano-pasado.html#.

[63] Rafael Romo, "$755 for a Box of Condoms? No Protection from Shortages in Venezuela," *CNN*, February 06, 2015, online edition, https://edition.cnn.com/2015/02/05/americas/venezuela-expensive-condoms-shortage/index.html.

[64] Katy Watson, "Venezuela Pill Shortage Triggers Rise in Teenage Pregnancies," *BBC*, January 10, 2018, online edition, http://www.bbc.com/news/world-latin-america-42620379.

[65] This report is from two years ago, which means it has only gotten unimaginably worse. Nicholas Casey, "Dying Infants and No Medicine: Inside Venezuela's Failing Hospitals," *New York Times*, May 15, 2016, online edition, https://www.nytimes.com/2016/05/16/world/americas/dying-infants-and-no-medicine-inside-venezuelas-failing-hospitals.html.

[66] Anatoly Kurmanaev, "Venezuela's Collapse Is the Worst Outside of War in Decades, Economists Say," *New York Times*, May 17, 2019, online edition, https://www.nytimes.com/2019/05/17/world/americas/venezuela-economy.html.

that this is happening to people, the intensity of the material misery of life in Maduro's totalitarianism illustrates the difference between the average communist and a Jacobin.

Jacobins

Few things are more outrageous to communists than anarchy,[67] yet a Jacobin reign is precisely chaos. This contradiction demonstrates how Jacobinism is a different form of communism. Unlike anarchism, Jacobinism's total disorganization is not on purpose—it is an unavoidable result of its unmatched extremism. The intensity of deprivation in Venezuela is stunning, and it is complemented by the savagery of unrestrained violence. In prison, there is no torture to obtain confessions as under Stalin, there is just sadism—torture with no objective.[68] Besides Maduro, only six modern ideological movements have been in a state of chaotic ruin which was *this deep* for *so long*—Robespierre, Leopold's colony in Congo, Lenin, Mao, Pol Pot, and Bashaar. The reason that Venezuela has reached an unprecedented level of earth-in-hell is that never before, besides those five, has a Jacobin regime held power.

Jacobinism is a particular version of communism. The difference is that, for Jacobins, their philosophy is more intensely pessimistic, and so their political program is more intentionally transformative, their actions more severely violent, the people's suffering more horrific. Scholars widely agree the Cultural Revolution is the most ideologically intense and savagely violent period of Mao's reign. This is because it was China's only Jacobin period, when mobs killed in the streets, rather than secret police in camps and prisons. That demonstrates the clearest difference: Communism is a state effort, but in Jacobinism the state is a mob.

To understand the difference that a more intense ideology can make, remember the fin-de-siècle bourgeoisie brutalized and slaughtered in Africa, but its children, the mob, exterminated Jews, Roma, and other social and cultural groups.[69] The intensity of their ideology is the difference between Jacobins and communists. In this regard, there are four specific distinctions.

---

[67] See George Orwell, *Homage to Catalonia* (Orlando: Harcourt, Inc., 1952), 150–79.

[68] Maru Morales, "Obligaron a comer pasta con excremento a procesados en justicia militar," *El País*, May 16, 2017, online edition, http://www.el-nacional.com/noticias/politica/obligaron-comer-pasta-con-excremento-procesados-justicia-militar_182436.

[69] See Hannah Arendt, *The Origins of Totalitarianism*, "Part Two: Imperialism" (Orlando: Harcourt, Brace & World, 1968).

The first is that communism's purpose is ending alienation and achieving freedom, while the Jacobins aim for happiness. To communists, material necessity in the age of industry has mutated man's harmony into mastership and slavery, leaving the masses exploited and alienated. Eliminating private property will end the reign of necessity, in whose place the kingdom of freedom can begin. The Jacobins, meanwhile, do not care about freedom. Happiness is a collective virtue that all worthy men must participate in. Property, economics, and exploitation are not on their minds. Unlike Marxists, they do not mourn a lost period of bliss between all men. Free pursuit of your potential is the Marxist concept of man in utopia, while the Jacobins only see utopia as everyone being militantly committed to the cultish idolization of virtue—essentially little more than simultaneous violence and celebration eternally. Marxists want men to realize themselves (it is an fundamentally misogynist philosophy); the Jacobins insist men follow the Committee's directive. At its base, it is a long-winded argument for conformity. For communists, roboticism is liberty. The communists' freedom has logical consistency at least, while the Jacobins' happiness is a single-minded focus on nothing. And they pursue it. Wipe out civilization, so that men (Jacobins are similarly patriarchal) live as units little different from plants in a forest—wholly perfect, individually inconsequential.

The second distinction is that Jacobins are more destructive, because they are frantic. Of course, communists are destructive and frantic too, but Jacobins are to communists like communists are to democrats. Jacobins' fanaticism and impulse is far more intense than other communists. In Jacobin eyes, the enemies of happiness are so powerful that victory is impossible. Not only defeat, but annihilation, is imminent. Communists are soldiers seeking to win the war and build their peace after, while Jacobins are suicide bombers, hopeless in their prospects and so even more fervent in the pursuit of their cause. For them every political and social moment is happening in the midst of a literal battle of guns, explosions, and death. The goal is not planning the long game to triumph, where macro-thinking introduces a touch of reason and calculation as with the communists, but to play the most micro-level role, to take down with you as many enemies as you can. Defeat is acknowledged, so immediate destruction is the only objective.

Rather than the working class, Jacobins serve the "General Will." Communists favor the proletariat as a class. But Jacobins hate everyone. No one is worthy of the universe; all must die. So, while communists fight for a group, and the members of that group are theoretically a bit safer than others, Jacobins intend to fight and destroy everyone. This has huge effects, it explains the different levels of violence, destruction, and chaos. Communists believe the proletariat is worthy of utopia; Jacobins are not convinced anyone is. Death is so much more public, random, brutal, and widespread under Jacobinism because no one has worth; total destruction is the right thing to do, and there should probably be no survivors. They are beyond pessimistic. No one can ever live up to virtue which the supernatural universe has called on man to fulfill. Disgusted with the world, they have realized that everyone deserves to die. Jacobins slaughter anyone and tolerate meltdown because everyone is an enemy of Happiness. No one is righteous. This is quite different from communism. The General Will, whatever version each Jacobin movement conceives of, is a supernatural being, what man (as they see humanity) ought to and has to be. For their god of morality the Jacobins purify civilization, with the smallest chance that maybe this will bring redemption for a very few. Urgency means incompetence: Jacobins lynch anyone in the streets rather than follow the basic totalitarian rule of killing in isolation. With contempt, they serve something higher than humanity.

Finally, Jacobins believe society has two classes: teachers and the rest. When nine-tenths of people are slaves, everyone will be happy. If the Jacobins' premises are accepted, their logical conclusions are correct: if there is a truth to human nature, that people will be happy when they are all equal in spirit and material, there must be instruction and command. A few people know what is right, the rest have to be taught. The education must be strict because the people are stupid and enemies feed them lies. Allowing people independence would be to deny them heaven, and that is cruel. For communists, a proletarian cannot sin because they are the only good cause in the world. But for the Jacobins, all people are sin, barley worthy of the truth. No one can be trusted except the divine Committee.

Venezuela is a slaughterhouse. For twenty years there has been no plurality, so no humanity, so no justice or equality. For four years there has been no food. Few in history have been in greater despair than a Venezuelan today. The country is in a one-way war, and the people are losing. The level and length of the catastrophe shocks those who do not realize the distinctiveness of the disciples of Robespierre. The world for any number of reasons fails to do anything meaningful.[70] The Venezuelans are trying everything. But *Presidente interino* Guaidó and the majority who support him are destined to be unable to defeat shameless power, as years of stunning defeat prove. Terror and barbarism will go on until a revolution liberates the people by conquering the regime. Civil society, an active public, equality, and human dignity must return to Venezuela immediately but likely will not. The paradox of Jacobinism is the imminent annihilation it fears and induces is highly durable. Jacobins do not surrender or moderate. They will go on until not even a trace of either they or their enemies exists anymore. Bashaar's fascist regime "hates its people," and this is what compelled it to carry out extermination.[71] The Jacobins' equivalent extremism leaves it almost indistinct from fascism like Hitler and Bashaar. After all, Carlos Fuentes saw Chávez as a "tropical Mussolini."[72] Similarly to the Syrian holocaust, Venezuela's Jacobins never stop conquering their own people. Ideological empires must devour communities. To stop the harrowing price paid in innocent suffering, when faced with Jacobinism the world's choice is to tolerate extermination or act with solidarity.

---

[70] It is a double standard, like always: North Atlantic leftists wouldn't tolerate this happening to them. But it's not. It's happening to someone else so they're fine with it. See Moisés Naím, "Lo que Sabe Zapatero," *El País*, February 24, 2018, online edition, https://elpais.com/elpais/2018/02/24/opinion/1519491858_220756.html?id_externo_rsoc=FB_CM.

[71] Yassin al-Haj Saleh, *The Impossible Revolution: Making Sense of the Syrian Tragedy*, trans. Ibtihal Mahmood (Chicago: Haymarket Books, 2017), 70–73.

[72] Anthony DePalma, "Carlos Fuentes, Mexican Man of Letters, Dies at 83," *New York Times*, online edition, May 15, 2012, https://www.nytimes.com/2012/05/16/books/carlos-fuentes-mexican-novelist-dies-at-83.html.

PART FOUR
Society and Culture

COMMUNIST RHETORIC AS OFFICIAL PRACTICES OF DISCOURSE

Making Epideictic Arguments on Authority and National Identity

Noemi Marin

In the hundred years of communist regimes of the world, can we talk about communist rhetoric as a pervasive genre of public discourse enforced by the Soviet-modeled regimes?

While this particular chapter argues the answer is affirmative, the rhetorical challenge lies in specifying which of the multiple persuasive characteristics engage with communist, authoritarian, and totalitarian discourse, in turn bringing in cultural caveats, multiplicity of histories, and, just as importantly, an immense gap of rhetorical studies on the matter.[1] Can we examine communist rhetoric without specifying what are the conditions for public discourse mandated by the each of the countries part of (S)tate communist rule?[2] What consequences can communist rhetoric bring into the public sphere of the countries where shared ideological, political and policy making structures impact inherently the discursive styles utilized by regime leaders to address people, to promise different political future while remembering national histories of the respective countries? An expected answer would be the inevitable post-communist, nationalist political claims and appeals that continue to rattle the public spheres in these regions. To what extent culturally specific rhetorical strategies used in public discourse

---

[1] Communist rhetoric of the last hundred years has been studied extensively through research pertinent to political science, history, anthropology, sociology, and literary studies. Ironically, such rhetorical discourse is to be almost missing within the body of rhetorical studies in the United States. In the last two decades, writing on Eastern European communist rhetoric has proved to be more of a niche-like research effort mainly due the lack of scholarly studies that treat communism as their scope.

[2] My approach to the term "(S)tate" does not focus on a specific country, rather I use "(S)tate" as an argumentative framework of authority imposed on its citizens by all communist regimes.

in separate communist countries mark dramatic differences in political governance? When we look back and assess a hundred years of authoritarian and centralized political regimes, can we find a common set of rhetorical practices and strategies shared by most communist countries?[3]

This study examines several normative qualities of communist rhetoric as official practices examining discursive strategies promoted by the communist/ socialist (S)tate to engage public discourse and persuade its polis, its peoples, and the world of its legitimacy of governance. In previous works I explored totalitarian rhetoric, using the example of the extreme rhetorical discourse in Romania in the last decades of the twentieth century. In this chapter,[4] I examine epideictic strategies and practices shared throughout the geopolitical space of communist public discourse for the last hundred years.[5] As mentioned, for the last decade I provided extensive analyses on Romanian public discourse and Ceaușescu's speeches from the last part of his dictatorship; on rhetorical space and the discourse of national identity;[6] on the year 1989 as a historical cluster of discourse in crisis in Eastern and Central Europe; as well as on totalitarian rhetoric and its distinct rhetorical style, to name a few subjects.

In my research, I argue that most communist rhetorical claims and appeals to persuade the polis function within the epideictic framework of praise and blame, without any intervention from deliberative and/or argumentative discursive paradigms. Looking at most persuasive practices

---

[3] I refer mainly to countries like the former Soviet Union, all the Eastern European block, China, North Korea, Cuba, and African states whose regimes are considered to feature communist ideology central to their state governance.

[4] In this chapter I examine strategies used in official communist rhetoric as *the* discursive practices of public oratory developed and employed by Communist Party leaders.

[5] Noemi Marin, "History Ante Portas!: Nicolae Ceausescu's Speech in Response to Timisoara Events and the Beginning of 1989 Romanian Revolution," *Advances in the History of Rhetoric* 11–12, no. 1 (2011): 237–61; Noemi Marin, "Ceaușescu's Rhetorical Legacy: Totalitarian Rhetoric and Its Impact on Communist Romania," in *Twenty Years After: Central and Eastern European Communist Regimes as a Shared Legacy,* ed. Vojtech Ripka (Prague: Institute for the Study of Totalitarian Regimes, 2010), 1–11; Noemi Marin, *After the Fall: Rhetoric in the Aftermath of Dissent in Post-communist Times* (New York: Peter Lang, 2007); Noemi Marin, "From Banned Rhetoric to Public Legitimacy: Religion and National Discourse in Post-Communist Romania," *Forum Artis Rhetoricae,* 1–2, no. 8–9 (2007): 30–48; Noemi Marin, "The Other Side(s) of History: The Return of Rhetoric," in *Advances in the History of Rhetoric,* ed. Robert N. Gaines (College Park, MD, Routledge, 2007), 209–27.

[6] To add one more, see Noemi Marin, "Totalitarian Rhetoric and Ceausescu's Loss of Words," in *The End and the Beginning: The Revolutions of 1989 and the Resurgence of History,* eds. Vladimir Tismaneanu and Bogdan C. Iacob (Budapest: Central Europe University Press, 2012), 441–65.

part of communist political discourse, I consider epideictic rhetoric as the rhetorical genus legitimized as the strategic operational framework for political discourse engaged to serve the communist (S)tate. I define epideictic communist rhetoric as the official public discourse in use under the conditions explained by Carl J. Friedrich and Zbiegniew Brzezinski in their work on *Totalitarian Dictatorship and Autocracy*, a disturbingly current book in our nowadays world.[7] Accordingly, looking at one hundred years of communist experiments, this chapter addresses how characteristics of epideictic rhetoric and the rhetorical notion of "audience" become operative frameworks perti-nent to most communist regimes.

Why epideictic rhetoric? Because it is the one and only political discourse of the Party

The mechanism of the totalitarian system works in such a way that everything converts into its opposite. Proclaimed freedom is slavery; independence comes to mean total dependence; equality means the inequality of Party class structures; the "classless society" becomes a feudal differentiation of classes and sub-classes. But the most amazing transformation is when honest people turn, unawares, into accomplices of totalitarian crimes through their industriousness, their discipline and loyalty when personalities convert into nameless creatures and into faceless specters. Language is one of the magic means of these metamorphoses.[8]

For over a century, epideictic rhetoric–with its praise and blame, its demon-strative and tributary functions proving who is honorable and who is shameful (to quote Aristotle)–allows communist political discourse to display endless demonstrative speeches and addresses delivered in similar style by

---

[7]   From the very first pages of the book, Friedrich and Brzezinski list the major 6 qualifiers that determine dictatorial states: "[i] an official ideology…; [ii] a single mass party led typically by one man…; [iii] a system of terroristic police control…; [iv] a technologically conditioned near-complete monopoly of control in the hands of the party… [v] a similarly technologically conditioned near-complete monopoly…of all means of effective armed control; and [vi] a central control and direction of the entire economy…." See Carol J. Friedrich and Zbiegniew Brzezinski, *Totalitarian Dictatorship and Autocracy* (New York: Frederick A. Praeger, 1965), 9–10.

[8]   Blaga Dimitrova, "Language and Politics in Bulgaria," in *Towards a New Community: Culture and Politics in Post-Totalitarian Europe*, eds. Peter J.S. Duncan and Martyn Rady (London: LTV Verlag, 1993), 138.

Party and political leaders throughout the world.[9] Why epideictic discourse? Because epideictic rhetoric allows communist parties and its leaders to shape narratives of national identity where History takes a turn to define (one way) the past, present, and/or future of the nation.[10] Praise and blame argumentative frameworks assist all political discourse, but set in the hundred years context of communist practices of political discourse, these ideological clusters of words, slogans and vocabularies capture the *(right)* mission to save communist nations, legitimize tireless tirades of villains and heroes that create an easy to identify, singular *(communist)* language of the Party line, the communist language appropriate for use in the public realm *(the only one)*.[11]

While deliberative rhetoric, according to the Aristotelian cannon, might overlap with epideictic rhetoric in principle, under communism, the Party leadership's discursive praxis leaves deliberative and/or forensic rhetoric inoperative throughout.[12] As such, political discursive praxis does not engage with any other public action, leaving outside of its Party's appeals any other argumentative and/or participatory engagement from and by the people. This is not to say that epideictic rhetoric does not use arguments. Aristotle would be the first to explain that rhetorical arguments are highly necessary for epideictic praise and blame when composing political speeches, as well as the need to engage reason and emotion to create public and political justification for agreement and/or disagreement.[13]

---

[9]   George Kennedy presents Aristotelian definition of "epideictic" rhetorical genre from Book 1.9 and continues by stating that "at many times in history, praise and blame has been the chief form of speech under autocratic government" (Kennedy, 88). See George Kennedy, *Classical Rhetoric and its Christian and Secular Tradition from Ancient to Modern Times* (Chapel Hill: University of North Carolina Press, 1999).

[10] When all arguments *of* and *from History* in communist rhetoric take on a singular meaning, utilized in singular form of appeal, I consider it is necessary to use capital letters (History, Past, Nation, etc.). Throughout the chapter I write History with a capital H, since for all studies on communist rhetoric, History stands for an enthymematic approach to national history, selected in Burkean terministic screens only from the national repository of political and public action accepted and acclaimed by communist apparatchiks in charge with propaganda and official public discourse. Kenneth Burke, *Language as Symbolic Action: Essays on Life, Literature and Method* (Berkeley: University of California Press, 1968).

[11] It is impossible to leave out the use of irony specific vocabulary clusters identifying the communist era and its political speech patterns and accepted words. An International Dictionary of Communist Discourse would be a most needed compendium for all researchers studying a century of communist experiments, as the ideological language set for political persuasion includes always enthymematic claims on communist victory.

[12] Kennedy, *Classical*, 88.

[13] See Aristotle, Cicero, and Quintilian in their respective rhetorical treatises teach epideictic rhetoric and its appeals and arguments to be used for praise and blame. Of note that these strategies of discourse remain current for over two thousand years of public and political discourse.

And yet, communist epideictic discourse suppresses (at all costs) civic participation in the classical rhetorical sense, political leaders asking audiences to accept only persuasive claims and arguments enlisted as tributary narratives of the "nation" in its Party-line stories of heroes and foes, to recognize and obey communist governance as the only legitimate safeguarding public action. In an earlier study, I highlighted that for communist discourse, designed to be everlasting and victorious, epideictic rhetoric functions as an umbrella genre intended to solidify and strengthen public and political arguments and appeals, never to be questioned (*by the public*), always accepted as declamatory actions of communist activism.[14]

Who would need (or why, for that matter) deliberative rhetoric and non-partisan public debate, when the Party can solve all the problems for all its citizens? In a one political party public sphere, where the opposition cannot speak out against communism either as ideology and/or praxis, the rhetoric of the Party and (S)tate become a non-disputable set of public address strategies mandated to engage in political praise of the ruling regime, introducing audiences to the victorious new communist language recognized by Orwell to be *newspeak*.[15]

Let's unfold how epideictic rhetoric works in communist discourse.[16] Praise and blame as rhetoric strategies represent the normative frames of public discourse accepted and enforced by communist practitioners. What such discourse comprises of is narratives of (*the*) national identity, narratives of the new (S)tate and political leadership, homages to heroes, and powerful accusations of treason against anyone who opposes such governance. *newspeak* takes over *oldspeak*: the heroic past (pre-bourgeoisie) is used to praise the "glorious" present that the Communist Party envisions as the standard of living for its countrymen. What such governing discourse brings with it is a singular, rigid vocabulary for political and/or civic engagement; a propagandistic apparatus that censors any difference from communist linguistic, political, and/or cultural narratives; legislated public and private discourse that sustains political views of the regime.

---

[14] Marin, "Totalitarian Discourse and Ceausescu's Loss," 454.

[15] George Orwell in *1984* utilizes the term *Newspeak* as the one changing the public usage of language under new ideological rules. *Oldspeak* is out, *Newspeak* is in. Re-reading the entire chapter, one cannot but notice that such directives appear to be taken *ad literam* by propaganda and communist writers of public discourse in all countries under such regimes. George Orwell, *1984* (New York: Signet Classics, 1961).

[16] I remind the reader that I refer mainly to official political discourse of all Communist Party leaders that comprise mainly of communist ideologically-supported practices of public address.

It is worth noting two important caveats when examining the epideictic rhetoric of communism: (a) the notion of "wooden language" as the official vocabulary created and accepted by communist parties with all its arsenal of rigid linguistic attributes; and (b) communist propaganda as the ongoing official context to promote communist ideology. Both have been prevalent in *all* communist regimes, reinforced and reenacted for the last hundred years with different national flare, with distinct nationalist narratives and linguistic practices, and have been analyzed extensively in historical and political studies internationally. However, while an intrinsic part of communist discursive practices, these caveats require extensive description, and therefore they remain outside of the scope of this analysis.[17]

Epideictic as Frameworks of and for History. Inherent to epideictic rhetoric as used in all communist regimes for over a hundred years is the recovery of history. *All* political discourse engages history. Yet, the praise and/or blame structures of public argument part of political discourse in the name of and in light of communist national history and national identity within the constitutive frameworks of freedom/dominance carry narrative legitimation by having been recited over and over by all Communist Party leaders in order to instill national pride in their people. Metanarratives of the national past as a communist version of the past become the public argument *ad continuum* on which mandatory patriotic formulas legitimize the mandate for carefully-crafted acceptance of communist history as the only strategic arguments that motivate, invoke and reenact national pride in the name of the collective, never leaving any (rhetorical) space or place for narratives of difference or critical perspectives.[18]

Looking at American public discourse, Celeste Condit includes epideictic rhetoric as part of democratic discourse as well, defining it as one of the rhetorical genres (including, not excluding deliberative genre), a genre that forms and supports a community for speaker and audience, certainly beneficial

---

[17] Here is what I stated on this topic in previous work: "While scholarly debates conceptualizing differences between total propaganda and totalitarian rhetoric can add theoretical relevance to the theme of this collection, the scope of the study primarily reveals the relationship between rhetoric and collective persuasion, which influences history and politics through one of the most powerful human means of symbolic action-language." Marin, "Totalitarian Discourse and Ceausescu's Loss," 451.

[18] I refer here mainly to delivery of communist rhetorical appeals to national history and national identity as repeated *ad continuum* by all political leaders in endless official speeches. Such practices continue to be in effect nowadays in Chinese and North Korean official speeches to domestic audiences.

in times of crisis. Distinct from Condit's democratic context for epideictic speeches, communist praxis moves epideictic public discourse beyond communal dimensions by agreement, leaving no room for political deliberation or public debate to achieve consensus.[19] In most contexts, communist rhetoric entails one party speeches and discursive practices that use aggressive verbiage, superlatives, and emphatic forms, stripping public language of any non-communist cultural and public memory for and of its audience.[20] Accordingly, the recovery of history as a national salvation narrative comes in the form of a fundamental communist redemption theme for the collective (aka 'the people') as a sole, eternal cultural narrative that explains, motivates, and supports the aspirations of the people.[21]

All political regimes construe legitimacy through the powerful ethos offered by historical arguments, or as part of classical rhetoric logos, arguments from History. However, in communism, this political and discursive strategic practice is mandated by a powerful corrective, namely that History (read "communist history") is appropriated correctly only by and within communist narratives of salvation.[22] Abolition or condemnation of the near past (read "bourgeois" or "capitalist") in exchange for the exaltation of a communist version of national History add praise and blame political address to emphasize glorious present. Along with the State communist mission to change the country, this epideictic praxis shared by all Communist Party leaders construes *the* one and only legitimate narrative of national identity, authorized in *newspeak*,[23] assigned for use by all people with no right to question, justify or remember any other national narrative.[24]

---

[19] Celeste Condit, "The Function of Epideictic: The Boston Massacre Orations as Exemplar," *Communication Quarterly*, no. 33 (1985): 284–98.

[20] One major effect of communist epideictic rhetoric is "wooden language," studied mainly by scholars in the fields of linguistics, political science, history, and sociology. Unfortunately, very few rhetoricians study communist "wooden language" nowadays. One recent collection on "wooden language" is by Ilie Rad, ed. *Limba de Lemn in Presa* (Bucharest: Tritonic, 2009).

[21] Vladimir Tismaneanu, *Fantasies of Salvation: Democracy, Nationalism, ad Myth in Post-Communist Europe* (Princeton: Princeton University Press, 2009).

[22] I am reiterating here that in communist practices, metanarratives from *History* (my emphasis) call for the "true" History of and for the people, whether by Lenin, Stalin, Mao, Ceaușescu, and nowadays quite effectively Putin. Vladimir Tismaneanu's books, *Fantasies of Salvation* and *Stalinism for All Seasons* capture best such epideictic uses of History with a capital H in communist times. See Vladimir Tismaneanu, *Stalinism for All Seasons: A Political History of Romanian Communism* (Berkeley: University of California Press, 2003).

[23] Orwell, *1984*, 62–80.

[24] It is important to remind the reader that the vocabulary of communism, while it differs in tone and intensity in some of the eras and regimes, rests almost inevitably unchanged in terms of major arguments of political legitimation.

Messianic promises of *nation anew* have been and continue to be utilized in current political discourse throughout the world. However, for communist discourse, such promises glorify the only kind of history for one (only) kind of Nation, praising only one substantive narrative formulated by the Party for common use, which blames all "otherness" and difference for interrupting or dis-ordering political and public action. When studying epideictic rhetoric in communist regimes, it is almost impossible to leave out notes on explicative vocabulary, on the emphasis on capital letters, and on emphatic and enthymematic clusters of communist arguments.

After all, appeals for "peace," "democracy," and "unity of the people" permeate all political discourse throughout time. And yet, there is an enthymematic use of these themes in political discourse that qualifies these rhetorical appeals to be legitimized as the only correct *communist* qualifiers for democracy, peace, and unity of the people, markers to be found in all public addresses in totalitarian and authoritarian regimes. Maybe this distinct use to reconstitute history through enthymematic arguments for peace, democracy, or political unity might offer scholars an opportunity to reexamine how such appeals and argumentative strategies function within two frameworks of political discourse: communist vs. democratic rhetoric. Take as an example Romanian public discourse under Nicolae Ceaușescu. In a previous paper I noted that,

> the emphatic usage of "praise and blame" style of political presentations
> dominates the Romanian leader's political speeches, culminating in 1989 in
> a re-vamped vocabulary of foes and heroes, and a new grammar of victory...
> 'New era,' 'new state' 'new socialist economy,' 'new multi-developed and
> multilateral new man.' 'new Romanian future,' and many more such words
> provide endless descriptions of one and only communist-style promised
> future as depicted in Ceaușescu's own grammar of victory.[25]

Timothy Snyder in his excellent recent book, *On Tyranny,* reminds us of Hannah Arendt's warning about totalitarianism in that it blurs public and private to unfree the citizens and make them obey unconditionally.[26] When looking at national identity appeals in communism, such demonstrative strategies call for highly selective (read "amnesic") appeals to history to

---

[25]   Marin, "Totalitarian Discourse and Ceausescu's Loss," 454.
[26]   Timothy Snyder, *On Tyranny: Twenty Lessons from the Twentieth Century* (New York: Tim Duggan Books, 2017), 89.

maintain the political seduction around the "mythicized past."[27] And what better way than by removing from history the private memories of people for the sake of the unending public glorification of national history, wiping away all "other" parts of history that do not cohere with the grandeur narrative of communist salvation? This is an epideictic argumentative strategy towards History that continues in current times to mesmerize new societies like Russia under Vladimir Putin's governance.[28]

Epideictic communist discourse leaves out all deliberative practices, offering in exchange tributary addresses promoting (*ad continuum*)[29] communist heroes (always portrayed as saviors of the nation), while vilifying imperialist and capitalist people and societies as motivational foes that legitimize communist action.[30] This simple (and somewhat simplistic) discursive strategy gains rhetorical force due to its continuous repetition of such public praise/blame narratives as well as by a strategic *reductio* of narratives to a singular, reinforced, repetitive, legislated story of the nation. As Friedrich and Brzezinski note, the communist language of the Party when defining the enemy of the people brings to the forefront epideictic blame in its most powerful and vindictive tones:

> To the totalitarian, this "rotting corpse"[31] of the *ancient regime* is still a mortal enemy from whom the people must be protected. It makes no difference whether the people desire such protection of not. The totalitarian is convinced either that the masses are with him, or that they ought to be. And in either case,

---

27 Snyder, *On Tyranny*, 123.

28 In most of Putin's presidential addresses, World War II is an argument from History, called the Great War, by now Russian, no longer Soviet victorious war against the West, another promise to reach salvation with a narrative of national grandeur. For an extensive analysis, see Noemi Marin and David Cratis Williams, "Presidential Arguments in Post-Soviet Russia: An Enthymematic Return to National Identity as Argumentation of Citizenry?" in *Seventh Conference of the International Society for the Study of Argumentation—Conference Proceedings*, eds. Frans H. van Eemeren, Bart Garssen, David Godden, and Gordon Mitchell (Amsterdam: Rozenberg/Sciential International Center for Scholarship in Argumentation Theory Press, 2012), 1181–94.

29 Along with *ad continuum*, one can read also ad nauseum since the leaders of communist appeals repeat for hours at length the same arguments in the same rhetorical formula intended to instill persuasive force and legitimacy for their official addresses.

30 I do not want to speak here about Marxism and its uses in communist history, it is too large of a topic for this study. It is however understood that such paradigm of epideictic praise is fundamentally based on Marxist-Leninist dogma.

31 Reference to Lenin's quote: "When the old society dies, the corpse of bourgeois society cannot be nailed down in a coffin and put in a grave. It decomposes in our midst, this corpse rots and contaminates us," quoted in Friedrich and Brzezinski, *Totalitarian Dictatorship and Autocracy*, 138.

they have to be defended from the enemy who makes every effort to impede the process of indoctrination—to teach people to perceive the totalitarian "truth"—and even to overthrow the totalitarian system. This struggle against the enemies is a constant (my emphasis) one, and as suggested in the preceding section, often grows in intensity as the totalitarian regimes become stabler and firmer. The regime can then afford greater violence (my emphasis), and initial patience and expedient give way to unbridled terror.[32]

The **reductio ad unum** (my own phrase)[33]as a rhetorical strategy in communist discourse functions as a cluster of political thematic appeals, namely that no individual other than Communist Party-elected officials can speak for the people, and therefore the centralized singular and undisputable argument from the position of authority can and should never be challenged. Thus ownership of all public and national narratives carries the unquestionable (mandated) singular use of "we" with no space or place for deliberation and democratic debate.[34]

When examining communist metanarratives as presented in the public realm by political leaders, I consider two rhetorical dimensions that add salience to the epideictic practices enforced by communist regimes. First, the notion offered by Richard Weaver in his analysis of ultimate terms as a tri-partite rhetorical cluster (god-devil-charismatic) of embedded appeals articulate distinctive expectations from the collective inherent to all political realms, introducing a powerful perspective on communist usage of political and official discourse of the nation.[35] Notably, Weaver's rhetorical treatise conceptualizes such terms within democratic frameworks of public and political discourse, examining United States cultural and political spheres respectively.

Exploring rhetors' discursive constructs that present worldviews applied specifically to US culture, Richard Weaver identifies a triad of ultimate terms

---

[32] Brzezinski, *Totalitarian Dictatorship and Autocracy*, 138–39.

[33] I coined this phrase "communist *reductio ad unum*" to refer specifically to this paradoxical use of pronouns, namely to speak in the name of "we, the (communist) people" as "one" and that "one voice" is a singular that cannot be broken by individual voices.

[34] As mentioned previously, the "we" that communist vocabulary defines is the "we as one" and "we as the only voice of the General Secretary/Leader," an important distinction that calls for more rhetorical and cultural studies both for communist past practices and for totalitarian and authoritarian practices in public and political discourse currently in the world. See Marin, *After the Fall*.

[35] Richard Weaver, *The Ethics of Rhetoric* (South Bend, IN: Henry Regnery, 1953).

(god-term, devil-term and charismatic) on which public discourse relies. The rhetorician calls them "ultimate terms" as these words/clusters of arguments are easily identifiable and carry weight in cultural, political, and public spheres of a society. They are pretty self-explanatory in their denomination and use: a god term is a term "about which all other expressions are ranked as subordinate... its force imparts to the others their lesser degree of force, and fixes the scale by which degrees of comparison are understood," while devil terms, the counterpart of god terms, are "terms of repulsion" that designate whatever is perceived as the enemy of greatest evil in a society.[36] Ironically, one of Weaver's examples of devil terms in his treatise is *communism*, as his work in the 1950s reflected on the political framework of American discourse of the time.[37] Adding one more layer of irony is that Weaver's ultimate terms for such rhetorical analysis brings religious flavor to the atheist discourse of communist appeals.

Translating how ultimate terms work within communist political discourse, such lenses prove useful to examine both *newspeak* as wooden language and propaganda, as well as ideological enthymemes, the *-isms of communism* (my term).[38] The *-isms of communism* are mainly presented in the public arena as god-terms, if we were to create a rhetorical list on which political arguments engage leaders and narratives within the framework of communist victory. Praising the communist victories (again, ad continuum) of Marx-*ism*, Social-*ism*, Lenin-*ism*, Bolshev-*ism*, Stalin-*ism*, Mao-*ism*, (the list goes on), the ideological *-isms* create ideological political appeals that require audiences to constantly understand their lives within a highly ideological framework. On the blame side of the communist epideictic, fewer yet eternally threatening villains acquire devil-terms: Imperial-*ism* and Capital-*ism* for certain. Zion-*ism*, Barbar-*ism* (and many others) are left as charismatic terms, pending particular rhetorical contexts, timing, leaders' political style, countries, and era of communist governance.[39] Gorbachev's

---

[36] Weaver, *The Ethics of Rhetoric*, 211–12.

[37] Notably that Weaver's "ultimate terms" mentioned are not slogans, rather operational clusters of argumentative content recognized by the respective political culture both by speakers and audience alike.

[38] A suggestion would be to utilize Richard Weaver's "ultimate terms" for an extensive analysis of wooden language, moving from the linguistic and political into the rhetorical examination of strategic discourse of communism.

[39] The use of *-isms* part of authoritarian and totalitarian paradigm is not singular to past communist societies. Nowadays, public discourse on authoritarian(ism) includes *Trump-ism and Putin-ism* as two additional charismatic (for now) terms in current public sphere.

own discourse introduced two ultimate terms, *"perestroika"* and *"glasnost,"* both charismatic terms that were not appropriated as god-terms or devil-terms, and the debate on their rhetorical value continues within post-commun-*ism* (a charismatic term itself!).[40]

The second rhetorical perspective useful when examining communist praise and blame discursive practices of over one hundred years is Michael Calvin McGee's view on the role of "ideographs" in political, cultural, and, I would add, national discourse.[41] Introducing McGee's work on the "ideograph," Jasinski writes that

> McGee uses the term in his seminal article "The 'Ideograph': A Link Between Rhetoric and Ideology" which appeared in the *Quarterly Journal of Speech* in 1980.[42] He begins his essay by defining the practice of ideology as practice of political language in specific contexts—actual discursive acts by individual speakers and writers. The question this raises is how does this practice of ideology create social control. McGee's answer to this is to say that "political language which manifests ideology seems characterized by slogans, a vocabulary of 'ideographs' easily mistaken for the technical terminology of political philosophy."[43]

McGee offers his definition of "ideograph" as "an ordinary-language term found in political discourse. It is a high order abstraction representing commitment to a particular but equivocal and ill-defined normative goal. An *ideograph* is not just any particular word or phrase used in political discourse but one of a *particular* subset of terms often invoked in political discourse, yet which has no clear, univocal definition. Despite this, in political speeches, ideographs are often invoked precisely to give the sense of a clearly understood and shared meaning. This potency makes them the primary tools for shaping public decisions. It is in this role as the vocabulary for public values and decision-making that they are linked to ideology."[44]

---

[40] One interesting implication of Weaver's "ultimate terms" under the *-isms* of communist appeals is in my view the legitimation of other *-isms*, long time covered over by such regimes, surfacing in the last decades, National-*ism*, for one, utilized almost constantly after 1989, throughout post-communist political discourse.

[41] Michael Calvin McGee, "The 'Ideograph': A Link between Rhetoric and Ideology," *Quarterly Journal of Speech* (1980): 1–16.

[42] *Quarterly Journal of Speech* (QJS) is the oldest and most important academic journal for rhetorical studies in the United States (www.natcom.org).

[43] James Jasinski, *Sourcebook on Rhetoric: Key Concepts in Contemporary Rhetorical Studies* (Thousand Oaks, CA: Sage Publications, 2001), 308–10.

[44] McGee, "The 'Ideograph,'" 3.

Like Weaver, McGee provides a rhetorical perspective on the basis of American political discourse, arguing that words like *<liberty,>* *<property,>* *<freedom of speech,>* *<religion>* and *<equality>* constitute rhetorical ideographs without a specific referent, rather than invoking an abstraction that carries different cultural and political meanings based on context. It is within this kind of politically accepted word, like <liberty>, that the very mutability of the term ensures its rhetorical power/force for the audience. Such a general term in a sense can be thus stretched, extended, inferred, and repeated over and over in political contexts in which the public contributes support and adherence. For McGee, an "ideograph" comprises of cultural and political values thought to be shared by the public as a community, and therefore, even when defined differently by different speakers, this rhetorical cluster term can provide a powerful persuasive strategy for any political speaker. In his study, McGee offers an interesting example of this phenomenon, using Richard Nixon's attempt to defend his decision not to turn over documents to Congress during the Watergate Scandal by invoking the ideograph of *<the principle of "confidentiality>* against *<the rule of law>*. While the two ideographs in current use might not be opposite to each other, in this case, the American President was trying to focus on <confidentiality> as inherent in the ideograph, and with that, to show that such emphasis does interfere with <the rule of law>. Since that time, I would say that all presidential campaigns, debates, and victorious speeches use ideographs to justify shared cultural and political values, proposing politically agreed upon claims and strategies for the participant audiences.

The main reason I consider McGee's concept of "ideograph" useful when applied to communist political discourse is its potential to explain how practices of public discourse under such regimes reinforce and legislate the official language in use. For communist discourse, the construction of public arguments under the ideograph of <the Nation>is a constantly reinforced strategy to restrict pluralism and curtail its legitimate usage to a single ideological perspective.[45]In other words, only communist leaders in their political addresses can claim <the Nation> as the correct ideograph as a signifier of legitimate communist claims for the benefit of the people.

---

[45] McGee uses *brackets* when examining rhetorical cluster words that he identifies as *ideographs*. I utilized here the chevron brackets as indicated by McGee for the benefit of readership, when referring to official political addresses. As an example, I refer to <the Nation> as one such ideograph utilized throughout all communist discourse. McGee, "The Ideograph," 1.

Rhetorically, such ideographs reveal political language at work, they use ideological commitments to reduce public argument to an ideologically acceptable strategy of patriotic praise to glorify communist practices. McGee warns that an "ideograph" should not merely be conceptualized from a legal, historical, or linguistic approach. Rather McGee's "ideograph" as a rhetorical cluster of cultural appeals demonstrates its discursive power in political arena, enabling us to see how claims and public arguments are construed and practiced by political speakers and perceived by their participatory audiences. The ideograph of <the Nation> in communist times gained force, a century of such discourse does not leave the public arena without traces. This might explain some of nationalistic ideographic arguments and their continuous rhetorical use in post-communism. For while the ideograph functions in all political discourse, the *communist* ideograph of <the Nation> is an essential rhetorical argument that remains throughout the century a political and cultural appeal to unity of communist goals, reused over and over. In post-communist times, interestingly, the same ideograph, with similar political and cultural connotations get to be included in the public sphere throughout social media, movies, plays, music, educational texts, and historical narratives (to name a few mediums). As such, <the Nation> remains a very active *ideograph* in the public spheres that legitimizes both communist and post-communist discursive practices.[46]

The rhetorical use of both Weaver's *ultimate terms* and McGee's *ideograph* in understanding official political discourse helps explain how reductionist practices enforced by Party leaders define the epideictic rhetoric of communism. By using the same words repeatedly and discursive patterns for public appeals, the same terminology and same praise-blame frameworks, ideographs and ultimate terms help identify the rhetorical strategies reinforced by communist parties to narrow public participation. Official communist

---

[46] A caveat about the distinction between an ideograph and a slogan is important to state. An ideograph is constituted from a cultural and political abstraction, invoking cultural values pertinent to society and ready to be retrieved within political, civic, and ethical discourse and within an ideological call for action First and foremost, a slogan is part of a specific discourse, whether commercial, political or cultural. A slogan can be more than one word or phrase, and it can serve certain specific rhetorical purposes, from a Ciceronian view, either to persuade or to entertain. A slogan carries an appeal of a limited value, on basis of *Kairos*, of a limited timing in its contextual use. All mentioned characteristics of a slogan can share some values with ideographs, but never for a long time. For a more extensive explanation of *Kairos*, see John Poulakos, "Toward A Sophistic Definition of Rhetoric," *Philosophy and Rhetoric*, no. 16 (1983): 35–48.

appeals and their restrictive and restricted (read "unviable") strategies for participation in the public sphere, represent nothing *but a reductionist rhetoric*. This is probably the most challenging discursive strategy for any democratic analyst of communist rhetoric to fully comprehend. The political and discursive praxis to use a redux epideictic rhetoric for public engagement, to mold everything into a tight repetitive and monotone set of appeals leaving no rhetorical space accessible to citizens impacts all communist regimes, carrying discursive, political, and cultural implications both in the construction of audience members as citizens as well as in the construction and reconstruction of national identity.

Citizen to comrade or comrade to citizen: Which way is home?

What the epideictic rhetoric of communism achieved is the transition from citizens in pre-communist times to comrade-citizens, a profound and *effective* rhetorical action. Scholars studying communist epideictic rhetoric need to carefully examine how arguments of allure, the promise of salvation, seduction, and mythicized pasts actually affect audiences in the name of the nation/the people/the (S)tate/the country/ and of course the Party.[47]

Who are "the people"?

Argumentum ad populum stands as *the* communist appeal that expects the people to enact discursive political narratives (read "myths"), while single Party leaders assume no change of ideas or political and public adherence can occur. In the communist leaders' speeches, such a collapse of the appeals to and expectations of the "people" call citizens to take on only the roles prescribed in the political discourse *ad literam*. In his seminal "The Power of the Powerless" Havel asks how do we actually talk about a rhetorical audience when it comes to participation in political discourse.[48] Hannah Arendt provides an answer, describing the appeal for mass action in totalitarian societies:

---

[47] This is a generalization, but the aim is to bring into the discussion the notion of *audience as citizens* and from this angle, one can discuss communist epideictic rhetoric as a global phenomenon, in my view.

[48] Vaclav Havel, "The Power of the Powerless," in *From Stalinism to Pluralism: A Documentary History of Eastern Europe Since 1945*, ed. Gail Stokes (New York: Oxford University Press, 1996), 168–74.

Totalitarianism begins in contempt for what you have. The second step is the notion: "Things must change—no matter how, anything is better than what we have." Totalitarian rulers organize this kind of mass sentiment, and by organizing it articulate it, and by articulating it make the people somehow love it. They were told before, thou shalt not kill; and they didn't kill. Now they are told, thou shalt kill; and although they think it's very difficult to kill, they do it because it's now part of the code of behavior. They learn whom to kill and how to kill and how to do it together. This is the much talked about Gleichschaltung—the coordination process. You are coordinated not with the powers that be, but with your neighbor—coordinated with the majority. But instead of communicating with the other you are now glued to him. And you feel of course marvelous. Totalitarianism appeals to the very dangerous emotional needs of people who live in complete isolation and in fear of one another.[49]

In communist contexts, the official strategies to collapse the appeals to the "people" and appeals to the "masses" and the "nation" order participants to live as an uniformly shaped audience for the benefit of a mythical reality promised by the Party leaders. McGee examines fascist rhetoric to observe how all political myths use "the People" to objectify the reality of the audience as a group appeal in discourse. However, rhetorically it becomes difficult to explain the use of similar rhetorical expectations when turning the "people" into "persons."[50]

So how does a "comrade" become a "citizen"? One way is to examine audience from two distinct rhetorical frameworks, one democratic and deliberative, the other an epideictic, reductionist, communist perspective. Konrád's well-known description of the "antipolitician" marks precisely this transition from communist masses into individuals whose relationship with political governance brings forth discursive participation and civic engagement. As Konrád puts it, when looking at how "the People as comrades" can become persons as "citizens:"

(An antipolitician) ...wants to keep the scope of government policy (especially that of its military apparatus) under the control of civil society.

49 Hannah Arendt, "Hannah Arendt: from An Interview," *New York Review of Books*, Oct. 26, 1978, http://www.nybooks.com/articles/1978/10/26/hannah-arendt-from-an-interview/.
50 Michael Calvin McGee, "In Search of 'the People': A Rhetorical Alternative," *Quarterly Journal of Speech*, no. 61 (1975): 235–49.

The antipolitician is not a representative of spiritual authority, but rather, its repository. The politicians and their intellectual employees pollute the intellectual environment in the hope that the population whom they target through the media will be unable to think in any terms other than the ones they present. Their product is the cheerleader, the political dupe; the good party member (of any party);... the young people who can always be brought out for parades; the technicians of oppression who willingly commit atrocities because, if they have orders from above to do it, it cannot be an atrocity. Their product is the stultification of the average person.[51]

Looking at communist discourse, I consider as stated in other works as well that the brutal manipulation of political language remains for the greater part of the twentieth century shared by most Eastern and Central European countries informed by the ideologically shared Soviet-style of public address. This uniformity of a Soviet-imposed proletarian language advocated by all former communist regimes represents one of the main rhetorical dimensions that define communist public sphere.[52] Under this ideological formula to address people living in communist regimes, "audience(s)" lose their participatory powers in the public sphere, becoming transformed into "masses" rather than "publics." Thus, communist discourse prevents participants from engaging in the public sphere with opinions or civic action.[53] While this might seem a simple political, cultural, and discursive action, rhetorically it cannot be achieved without powerful strategies of coercion[54] The impoverishment of public language where only one (Party-approved) official vocabulary is accepted and reinforced under military-style supervision remains the rhetorical driving force that move audiences from

---

[51] György Konrád, "Antipolitics," in *From Stalinism to Pluralism: A Documentary History of Eastern Europe Since 1945*, ed. Gail Stokes (New York: Oxford University Press, 1996), 168–74.

[52] Marin, "Totalitarian Rhetoric and Ceausescu's Loss," 448.

[53] Michael Warner, *Publics and Counter-Publics* (New York: Zone Books, 2005).

[54] Audiences of communist discourse are expected to live in (as) the collective, never in the "I" when it comes to responses and participation in public sphere. Here is an excerpt of the analysis of totalitarian discourse in 1989 Romania: "As (Romanian) audiences could not speak in any other than through unequivocal adherence to the totalitarian 'praise and blame' discourse, the first person singular pronoun 'I' is no longer part of the political language of the 1989 public sphere. Rather, rhetorical prowess is given to the over-imposed collective pronoun 'we' as the ONLY enthymematic collective, a unison proud that justifies and legitimates the oneness with and the oneness of the voice of the General Secretary of the Romanian Communist Party, Comrade Nicolae Ceaușescu, the only voice intended to be heard in the political arena of a country." Marin, "Totalitarian Rhetoric and Ceausescu's Loss," 457.

citizens into comrades.[55] When it comes to communist practices of official discourse for over one hundred years, it is difficult to ignore how persons/people/peoples become transformed from communist audiences into victims and people without any voice. However, this study remains focused on rhetorical strategies inherent to official communist discourse, beyond coercion and militarization as daily actions and practices, to engage instead with the communist participation of the people.

A salient dimension that qualifies epideictic communist discourse and the role of audiences as comrades/citizens is *rhetorical space.*[56] *Rhetorical space* provides a critical perspective for understanding discursive strategies of access and control in communist public sphere, especially when examining the role of the audience, and its expected obedience under the regime. As I have previously argued, in communist rhetoric such space "underlines all strategies moves of discourse to control access and censor language and information, to monitor private and public life."[57] Conceptualized as a discursive strategy of control legislating public sphere under communist regimes, the *rhetorical space* of totalitarian appeals occupies both physical and discursive locations for rhetorical action controlling the entire public sphere through the official enactment of political discourse.[58] Here is one more example of the concept of *rhetorical space* at work, which I have pointed to before:

> It is always a challenge to explain an aberration of discourse such as totalitarian rhetoric, in communist forms and otherwise. By 1989, Romanian rhetorical space takes on strategic life where communist vocabulary enters deeper and deeper into the fabric of public life, where rules for public speech policies codify and ratify only one legal way to speak, write, and think—in

---

[55] Citizens in democracies vs. citizens in communism call for a major distinction. Comrades carry the specific communist agenda and as importantly the communist code of behavior with it. Notably, nowadays citizens in some authoritarian regimes, and I think here of Russia as one, the appeal to citizens can easily be translated into comrades: the words have changed, the public expectations of the political regime might not.

[56] Noemi Marin, "Rhetorical Crossings of 1989: Communist Space, Arguments by Definition, and Discourse of National Identity Twenty-Five Years Later," in *Rhetorics of 1989: Rhetorical Archaeologies of Political Transitions,* eds. Cezar Ornatowski and Noemi Marin (New York: Routledge, 2015), 167–86. This collection is published online as research supplement, see *Advances in the History of Rhetoric,* no. 18/1 (2015) https://www.tandfonline.com/toc/uahr20/18/sup1.

[57] Marin, "Rhetorical Crossings," 171.

[58] Marin, "Rhetorical Crossings," 174.

accordance with the regime's codex for Romanians as communist citizens. Knowing how rhetorical space was strategically utilized throughout the regime as a tool for rhetorical and political control, one can understand why the Romanian dictator could not accept dissent, even if imminent throughout Central and Eastern European political arenas"[59]

When looking at the relationship between the concept of "audience" and "rhetorical space" in communist regimes one cannot but observe that such strategic interaction highlights whether authoritarian or totalitarian regimes allow audience participation in the political spheres of post-communism.[60]

The never-ending quest for the nation

Epideictic communist rhetoric, beyond ultimate terms, ideographs or official appeals to the masses in praise-blame discourse, reveals that the legitimation of public arguments for the "Nation" under such regimes remains in post-communist arenas the "unifying strategy when it comes to political argument and national discourse."[61] The mystifying allure of nationalism constitutes an epideictic unifying myth that has been a demonstrable consequence of communist practices of discourse.[62] Many instances of public discourse in former communist countries continues to exhibit themes that strongly resemble (communist) nationalistic discourse, allegiance to nationalist ideals, and more. A casual look at Putin's political appeals, whether on the memory of the Great War or the rehabilitation of Stalin, of Viktor Orbán's discourse in Hungary, or of the current Chinese Party leader's speeches find many nationalistic themes that reinforce (yet again) the legitimation of former communist political action.[63] One inevitable argument stemming from nationalist discourse is the legitimation of violence. In post-communist rhetorical practice, war and violence continue to be politically and persuasively

[59] Marin, "Rhetorical Crossings," 175.
[60] In this study, I want to emphasize that "Putin's current ruling as an authoritarian leader over a reconstructed Soviet-turned Russian public sphere raises the question of the function of postcommunist rhetorical space in all countries formerly behind the Iron Curtain." I consider this question relevant nowadays as well. Marin, "Rhetorical Crossings," 180
[61] Marin, "Rhetorical Crossings," 180.
[62] Marin, "Totalitarian Rhetoric and Ceausescu's Loss," 449.
[63] Vladimir Tismaneanu and Marius Stan presented an outstanding lecture on Putin and Orbán at Florida Atlantic University invited by the Peace Studies Program in January 2016, addressing specifically these themes prevalent both in Russia and Hungary today.

explained using epideictic appeals to justify the crimes and destruction of the opposition (whatever that may be). It is interesting to note that from the beginning of communism, over a century ago, until now, its justifications for violence have not changed either in force nor in content.

Rhetoricians, historians, political scientists, and all researchers interested in the discourse of freedom need to continually revisit communist epideictic rhetoric as new authoritarian regimes are starting to reenact such practices throughout parts of the worlds. What happened to millions of audience members who for over a century, generation by generation, have not been allowed or encouraged to walk the road back to citizenry, to take the democratic and deliberative action of stepping back into public and political discourse? Does almost thirty years of post-communism provide enough time for audiences to become publics, politically and culturally, or does nostalgia for the communist "nation" rule over such changes? What is the role of silence under communist rhetoric? And why do the vocabularies of communist discourse continue to mystify its citizens, with so many arguing for a re-legitimization and a return to a comrade-status of sorts? The rhetoric of communist public discourse carries epideictic, descriptive, repetitive, and reductionist practices in all its glory. And yet, nowadays, political leaders still utilize such rhetorical appeals and communist promises to impact people in many countries. Thus, a century of communist rhetoric continues to posit unanswered questions for scholars and citizens of the world alike.

SELECTIVE REPRESSION AND DEMOCRATIC OPPOSITION IN POST-TOTALITARIAN HUNGARY

András Bozóki

As part of the Soviet bloc, Hungary had a long-lasting communist regime from 1948 until 1989, where censorship and the limitation of the right to freedom of speech was a vital part of the system. On closer scrutiny however, the communist period cannot be regarded as uniform. 1948 to 1962 (with the exception of the short period leading up to the 1956 revolution) was by and large totalitarian, while the period from 1963 until the dissolution of the system in 1989 may be considered post-totalitarian. There were variations, though, within the post-totalitarian period in the practice of power. The regime was reform oriented between 1963 and 1971; anti-reform trends dominated between 1971 and 1978; and finally 1979 to 1990 was period of gradual disintegration that saw a struggle between reformers and hardliners (alongside the rise of dissidents),[1] ended by an upsurge of the reformers and the ultimate collapse of the system.

Political pluralism in the declining communist dictatorship grew out of cultural pluralism, which was easier to openly represent. The signs of pluralism appeared most of all in debates among intellectuals, and so it is practical for us to start our study with an analysis of the structure and different levels of the public sphere. In the first part of this chapter, I shall describe the principles behind the regulation of the press and media as reflected by party resolutions, then examine censorship of the 1980s through an empirical approach. Secondly, I will examine a crucial debate among dissidents about the future which occurred in a samizdat journal between 1982 and 1984. My aim here is to describe the nature of the post-totalitarian system from different angles: its institutional regulations, the informal operations of power, and dissident strategies of resistance.

---

[1] Ervin Csizmadia, *Diskurzus és diktatúra* [Discourse and dictatorship] (Budapest: Századvég, 2001).

Selective repression: Censorship in a post-totalitarian regime

How did censorship work in Hungary in the post-totalitarian period of communist rule? There was no Press Act on the statutes until 1986. After the communists came to power in 1948 censorship was primarily ensured by political and informal means. The 1949 Constitution formally declared the freedom of the press, and, at the same time, announced that the leading force in society was the communist party. Naturally, these two constitutional declarations were contradictory; it was the unlimited political power of the party, which held sway. There was no legislation on censorship because the system did not need it; legislation would have meant the blunt acknowledgement of the limited freedom of the press, and it was easier to exercise party control without such legal norms. The politicians operating within the system often stated that there was no censorship in Hungary, and they were somewhat taken aback in 1981 when the writer István Eörsi demanded the introduction of censorship at the congress of the Hungarian Writers' Union, arguing that the boundaries would then become obvious and writers would know within what limits they could write "freely."

Normative regulations

The expectations of those in power concerning the press came in the form of party resolutions. The basis for the Hungarian Socialist Worker's Party's (MSZMP) media policy was laid down by a 1958 resolution. According to this decision, which was never withdrawn by the leadership, the "task" of the media was to follow and popularize the policies of the Central Committee of the MSZMP. Thus, the press was a means of propaganda that presented party policy, and its duty was to influence and educate public opinion along the lines expected by the party. The "critical" activities of the press were only needed to attack the negative tendencies that hindered the realization of party policy.[2] It was mandatory for all working journalists to join the Association of Hungarian Journalists, which was under party control. Hence a journalist who was not a party member and did not conform to the expectations of the party-state, could be called to hold responsible either "professionally" or "ethically" through the Association. Only party members could become

---

[2]   Tamás Fricz, *Az MSZMP és a tömegkommunikáció* [The MSZMP and mass communication] (Budapest: TK, 1988), 9.

editors-in-chief or leading associates of the more prominent papers. The editors-in-chief were under the control of the party leadership until 1989.

According to the party resolution of 1958, "the press should be partisan, it should base itself without reservations on the dictatorship of the proletariat, and its stand-point should always be a class stance. Party control should be asserted in the entire press, because only in this way can the partisan stance of the press be safeguarded properly and the assertion of views alien to Marxism-Leninism avoided."[3] At the same time, the Central Committee of the communist party started a battle against "oppositionism, carping, outsiderness, political non-membership, unsubstantiated charges that lack corrective judgment, and the hunting of sensations and curiosities, which are still present at some places."[4]

Gradually, from the mid-1960s, milder wordings were added to these initially tough positions, stressing "ideological persuasion" as the main instrument of control.[5] The new strategy of János Kádár that "whoever is not against us is with us" was a significant improvement. The official ideology was represented by the leading articles, and the other pieces had to be loosely formed to them. By then the party itself was making a demand that "the entire quantity of information" be presented to the public, except for facts whose publication would be detrimental to national interest.[6] This was expressed even more strongly—the duty of providing information was not optional—in the 1986 Press Act, which was the only legislative act on the press in the Kádár-era. But since the criteria for national interest was not expressed in practice, each organ of the state had the authority to decide what information it wished to share with the public, and what it would classify. As such, the need for comprehensive information and the duty to supply it remained a dead letter.

The party resolution of 1975 is a good example of the spirit of the anti-reform campaign of the seventies. For the first time, in addition to the need

---

[3]   Zoltán Jakab, ed., *A tömegkommunikáció a Magyar Szocialista Munkáspárt határozataiban és dokumentumaiban* [Mass communication in the documents and declarations of the Hungarian Socialist Workers' Party] (Budapest: TK, 1987), 15.

[4]   Quoted by Rudolf Rajti, *A sértődékeny állam: a sajtóirányítás szociológiai vetülete, 1944–1973* [The resentful state: the sociological perspective of the control of the press, 1944–1973] (Budapest: ELTE, 1995), 18.

[5]   Jakab, *A tömegkommunikáció*, 40.

[6]   The publication of the weekly journal *Magyarország* and the newspaper *Magyar Hírlap* signaled the opening up in the 1960s.

to set positive objectives, it referred to the Party's ideological adversaries, even if they were not precisely defined: "We will strengthen the ideological struggle against bourgeois and petit bourgeois ideology and against the different unscientific world views and we take a resolute stand against the enemy ideas and the malpractices detrimental to socialist public thinking. For this purpose the radio, television and the press would also be put to their proper use."[7]

Practical limitations

Though it has never been written down, it was common knowledge among Hungarian journalists that they were not supposed to touch on certain taboo issues. These were: 1. Criticism on the Soviet Union; 2. Questioning Hungary's membership in the Soviet military system (the Warsaw Pact) and the stationing of Soviet forces in Hungary; 3. Criticism of the socialist economic and political system; and finally, 4. Any real assessment of the revolution of 1956. The suppression of the last was the genesis of Kádárism, which officially deemed 1956 a "counter-revolution."

In addition, some issues were temporarily taboo because of the political needs of the day. These covered a broad range of topics. For example in the late the 1970s, when the Communist Party demanded that the euphemism "a situation of multiple disadvantage" should be used instead of economic poverty of people but not out of any desire to be politically correct. Mention of the lack of political representation for Hungarian minorities living abroad was also taboo, because—according to the official stance—it would have endangered the good relationships with neighboring countries, which were also members of the same communist system. The political leadership loosened the rein on this question in the mid-1980s when they sensed the people's growing lack of confidence in them. This loosening happened mostly *ad hoc*, in an unpredictable way.

In the 1980s a dual objective was clear in the party control over the press, reflecting the struggle between hardliners and reformers within the party. Living standards were declining and the political leadership responded with economic liberalization. However, this liberalization simply made the regime's lack of legitimacy even more transparent. State socialism, it turned

---

[7]   Jakab, *A tömegkommunikáció*, 85.

out, was only acceptable to large segments of the population as long as it brought improvement in living conditions. This became evident in a backlash against the previously successful strategy of Kádár, which—lacking political legitimacy—tried to maintain social peace through "material compensation."[8] As regime's performance worsened, people turned further away from it.

Regular samizdat publications began to appear in Hungary from the end of 1981. These underground periodicals had a very limited circulation, but since they were featured on Radio Free Europe their uncensored articles reached broader and broader groups in the country. The political leadership was well aware that it could not afford to have a brutal showdown with the emerging opposition groups among the intelligentsia. Doing so would have put in jeopardy the possibility of drawing on the foreign credit necessary to keep up the level of consumer consumption (and social tranquility) and would have destroyed MSZMP's positive international image as a reformist, liberalizing dictatorship. Thus, the objective of the political leadership was to divide and marginalize the emerging opposition groups.

The reformers within the Party believed that the propaganda role of the press should be changed and its mediating function allowed to work in both directions. It was the hardliners who held that precisely because conditions were becoming more difficult and people more uncertain, direct control of the press needed to be maintained, as an important task of the press was to strengthen "confidence in socialism." At that time there was an open dispute within the party over how the press could meet its contradictory requirements: the objectives of the political leadership and the demands of public opinion. Party reformers and hardliners reacted differently to Gorbachev's *glasnost*: reformers demanded further liberalization, while hardliners wanted to limit the effect of Gorbachev's position to Soviet internal policy only, saying that *glasnost* was simply a delayed version of what had already been accomplished in Hungary in the 1960s.

As a result of these struggles, in the eighties Party lost control over the press, and the rise of ad hoc interferences often made conditions for the working press unpredictable. However, unpredictability made journalists more resourceful since any adjustment to a "central line" was made impossible. Opportunities for tactical journalism were greatly enhanced. All this

---

8   For details see Miklós Szabó, "A legitimáció történeti alakváltozásai" [The historical trans-
     formation of legitimacy], *Medvetánc* no. 1 (1988); Miklós Szabó, *Politikai kultúra Magyar-
     országon, 1896–1986* [Political culture in Hungary, 1896–1986] (Budapest: Medvetánc, 1989).

gave more room to maneuver for those working in the official press, thus the accelerating the pluralization of press.

In analyzing these conditions, which were often difficult to comprehend and which had become chaotic by the second half of the decade, one could differentiate between preliminary control and retrospective adjustment of the press.[9] Preliminary control was exercised through the Hungarian News Agency (MTI) screening news and information, which had a monopoly position in this regard. Consequently, the MTI's operation,[10] became totally intermingled with those of the political authorities. Screening the news was done by the MTI in cooperation with the agitprop department of the Party and under its guidance. The official news agency was particularly keen on only getting news about Warsaw Pact countries from news agencies in those countries themselves, and not from any Western source. The ironic consequence of this policy was that the public often learned about an event abroad from an announcement published as a disclaimer from a particular news agency. In many cases MTI did not even publish a disclaimer, choosing complete silence instead. Incidentally, the fact that the communist states would only incorporate each other's official news outlets caused serious problems. At the time of the Chernobyl nuclear catastrophe in April 1986, the information given out by the Soviets was simply not sufficient for the Hungarian public, and so they tried to get the information from other sources. In such cases MTI chose to publish false information with the objective of soothing people's worries, thus discrediting itself even more in the eyes of the public.

The agitprop department of the Central Committee of the Communist Party and the Information Bureau (a state organ) also institutionalized internal information. At regular meetings high-ranking functionaries provided information on the party and government's current positions. In addition, appeals were made to the press on whether it should or should not deal with certain topics; or if it was a question of more important domestic or foreign events, a press plan was put forward which spelled out precisely in what way certain papers should deal with certain events[11] Apparently there were no direct, formal prohibitions. These were expressed in practically each case

---

[9]   István Hegedűs, *Sajtó és irányítás* [Press and control] (Budapest: MTA, 1988). For the latest edition see István Hegedűs, "Sajtó és irányítás a Kádár-korszak végén" [Press and control at the end of the Kádár-regime], *Médiakutató*, no. 2 (2001): 45–60.

[10] Hegedűs, *Sajtó és irányítás*, 13.

[11] Hegedűs, *Sajtó és irányítás*, 16.

in the form of "requests" or "recommendations," which were nonetheless compulsory. The agitprop department held a meeting for editors at least once a month, and once a week for the editors of the national dailies (who were members of the Party anyhow). This was presided over by the secretary of the Central Committee in charge of the media.

However, it was the individual responsibility of the editors that proved to be the best means of censorship. The appointment or dismissal of editors was carried out at the highest level (Politburo), so editors depended on the elite of the *nomenklatura* for his very living. The editors of the party's national daily newspaper and its theoretical monthly journal were members of the Central Committee. There was a frequent cross-assignment between party headquarters and *Népszabadság*: not infrequently, its editor continued his career in the party headquarters and his place was taken by someone from another newspaper, but also from the party headquarters. However, the principle of individual responsibility of editors resulted in a slackening of censorship and more room for journalists to maneuver, causing some less politically exposed papers to grow. In editors of these papers were often closer to the journalists than to the bigwigs on party headquarters and thus performed their role as a censor to a lesser degree. It frequently happened that he or she was willing to take the blame at the party headquarters to defend the paper for articles considered more politically problematic.

The Party's cultural policy tolerated these anomalies until they acquired political undercurrents. One of the Party's main objectives in controlling the press was to hinder politically tendentious publications. For a decade the efforts of a group of populist writers to launch a journal of their own were frustrated (because they were deemed politically dangerous), yet the editors of practically all periodicals could be easily included in the camp of populist writers. It was easier for the individual responsibility of the editors to control those heterodox politics on their own. Some younger writers' request for a literary periodical aimed at their own generation was also turned down. Nevertheless, the same circle evolved spontaneously around the literary magazine *Mozgó Világ*, which the authorities attempted to break up by appointing a loyal, outside editor. The editorial staff, however, supported their former editor (who was also a party member), which led to the dismissal of the entire editorial staff, in one of the biggest press scandals of the 1980s.[12]

---

[12]   Cf. György Németh, *A Mozgó Világ története, 1971–1983* [The history of the *Mozgó Világ*, 1971–1983] (Budapest: Palatinus, 2002).

The system of control enforced self-censorship in addition to these tactics. No freedom of writing existed in the press as such until 1988. Yet a kind of latent pluralism was able to develop through readers' ability to read between the lines. In the 1980s, *Magyar Nemzet* was the favorite newspaper of the intelligentsia who were not members of the communist party. Of the weeklies it was the most reformist, though it still employed the neutral language of economic technocracy.

Selective repression and cultural policy

At the turn of the 1970s and '80s a new problem was posed to the authorities by the appearance of an underground opposition press (*samizdat*), which did not seek any license to publish, bypassing censorship altogether. In 1979 when independent political thinker István Bibó died, a group of dissidents published a collection of articles to which several eminent intellectuals contributed.[13] In a way of retrospective adjustment, party headquarters classified these contributors along a scale of political loyalty and opposition. Here again the objective was to hinder the development of an alternative camp. Consequently, certain contributors to the *Festschrift* did not suffer reprisal, primarily those whom party headquarters wanted to retain in the first, official public sphere. Others were summoned to party headquarters, where they were subjected to severe "discussions." A third group was allowed to retain their jobs but not to teach at university. There were some who were removed from their jobs and were unable to find state employment for years. Finally, there was a group who had no jobs to begin with, and who were subjected to official monitoring. The Party had their phones tapped and used other methods of intimidation, such as withdrawing their passports.[14]

Communist cultural politics was summarized by leading communist politician György Aczél as "Prohibit, Tolerate, Support."[15] The Party supported works by writers committed to socialism and by "progressive" fellow-travelers; tolerated ideologically neutral works or writings not sympathetic with the system but of marginal influence; and finally prohibited works classified

---

[13] The *Bibó Emlékkönyv*, a volume in honor to István Bibó, originally appeared in Budapest as a samizdat publication in 1979.

[14] For details see Ervin Csizmadia, *A magyar demokratikus ellenzék* [The Hungarian democratic opposition] (Budapest: T-Twins, 1995).

[15] Péter Agárdi, "Közelítések a Kádár-korszak művelődés-politikájának történetéhez" [The history of the cultural policy of the Kádár-regime], *Eszmélet*, no. 20 (1994): 129–65.

as "oppositional-hostile." The system was not rigid: for "good behavior" (making gestures of loyalty) a writer could move upwards in classification, and conversely for "bad behavior" one could move downwards. It happened that some authors were condemned to one year's "silence," while others were put on a list of prohibited works for a longer or shorter period of time.[16] In addition, those in charge of cultural policy made efforts to widen those fault lines (particularly populists vs. liberals), which had long existed within the Hungarian intelligentsia, with the view of dividing the opposition and semi-opposition groups.

The Kádár regime typically applied the tactics of selective repression against people in the grey zone (i. e. those who were not supported but officially not prohibited either) enforced social isolation against the anti-regime opposition. These tactics had been used relatively successfully for some years: those active in Hungarian democratic opposition did not increase in number and they were unable to communicate their message to the rest of society in the way that their Polish counterparts had succeeded in doing. Dissidents felt for years that they had been living in a hermetically isolated intellectual ghetto.[17] Nevertheless the circle of those who became not only consumers but producers of oppositional ideas gradually expanded, primarily in the rock-punk subculture and in literary groups forming within the younger generations. What typified them was irony, escapism, ideological value-neutrality, and a radical attitude. There was an author, Péter Esterházy, who incorporated the words "self-censorship" into his text, making it visible and, as such, ridiculous. When he reached a point in a sentence, which could be considered questionable, he put the word "self-censorship," and then continued the sentence.[18]

Since the dissidents appealed to human rights acknowledged by the Helsinki conference, pursued a strategy of self-limiting radicalism, and later became relatively well-known abroad because of Radio Free Europe, it became increasingly difficult for the political leadership to take stern measures against them. The names of the leading opposition figures were well publicized in the West as well, which provided them some protection.

---

[16] For details see Csizmadia, *A magyar demokratikus ellenzék.*

[17] Cf. János Kenedi, *A demokratikus ellenzék válsága* [The crisis of the democratic opposition] (Budapest: Samizdat, 1983).

[18] Cf. Péter Esterházy, *Kis magyar pornográfia* [Small Hungarian pornography] (Budapest: Magvető, 1984).

The control of the press in the 1980s can be described as selective repression compared to the earlier totalitarian period. For instance, policymakers consciously permitted certain periodicals to perform a safety-value function for the intelligentsia, and in this manner maintained a regulated flow of criticism. Thus, criticism in the official press was almost automatically treated as "constructive criticism," and what was not concluded in it was necessarily "destructive." In many instances, this form of censorship meant that the means and place of publishing a text was more important than the content itself.

In Hungary in the 1980s there was no formal censorship office working under a uniform pattern. The practice of censorship was through different, preliminary, and subsequent screening systems. There was always a chance of a "delicate" product to get through, but this could not be counted on in advance. The "soft" dictatorship of the late Kádár era had an indirect censorship, which was "velvet" in its operation.[19]

The system of selective repression can be best described as one of concentric circles, where political control was strictest in the circle closest to the center (that is the party leadership), and control gradually weakened moving outwards. However, what characterized the first part of the 1980s was the dualism of the legal (first) and the illegal (second) public sphere. Readership of the samizdat periodicals were growing in number, and the proportion of authors publishing in these papers under their real name and not a *nom de plume* also grew. The topics and the critical tone gradually influenced the press, making it increasingly critical. The grey zone, with its mediating role developed around the mid-eighties, had an important role in this, as the ideas expressed in the second sphere were brought to a broader public. Members of the opposition received invitations more frequently to address different university clubs and meetings organized by individuals acting without official sanction. At the same time, reformers were also becoming increasingly radical. Party reformers were speaking of the need for consent—this demand took on a critical edge in the party internal struggles. However, by that time it was evident that no consent could be imagined under the given circumstances and a general agreement with the hardliners of the party on transformation of the political system was simply not possible.[20]

[19]   Cf. Miklós Haraszti, *The Velvet Prison: Artists Under State Socialism* (New York: Basic Books, 1987).
[20]   Cf. Mihály Gálik, Gábor Halmai, Richárd Hirschler, and Guy Lázár, "Javaslat a nyilvánosság reformjára" [Recommendations on the reform of the public sphere], *Kritika*, no. 4 (1988): 53–59.

From 1988 onwards taboos, earlier regarded as untouchable, were challenged one after another. At first the need for Hungarian membership in the Comecon was questioned, then the need for reform increasingly shifted to a demand for a change of regime. In 1988, the Publicity Club was founded, which brought together journalists working in the official press who were critical of the regime. All the taboos were overturned by verbal challenges in 1989 and communist leaders had nothing left to say: the framework of discourse, which they were familiar with, had undergone radical change.[21]

Debating the future: The dissidents of the samizdat *Beszélő*

The basic experience of the generation growing up in the 1970s was the loss of perspective. Around 1980 national and international political events suddenly occurred and brought serious changes: the accumulation of unsolved social problems in domestic affairs; prices were radically raised for the first time in the Kádár era; the second oil crisis "crept in"; the Hungarian debt-crisis began; the Soviet Union invaded Afghanistan; several Western countries boycotted the Moscow Olympic Games; and Poland began its self-limiting revolution.[22] The internal situation of the country, created by the atmosphere of the new round of Cold War, became very sensitive.

In this altered situation, it was even more difficult for the communist politicians to rationalize their "right" to the power. They no longer said that state socialism would bring more freedom or greater equality than the capitalist democracies of the West. References to the "equitableness" of the system or to a "better future" disappeared from their arguments. Their picture of steady development had crashed. The raising of prices and low wages prevented communist politicians from referring to the cheapness of goods. While the communist leadership grew more open to communication by the eighties, it gradually ran out of arguments.

In order to keep up the "legitimacy" of the system the communist political leaders tried to make the past appear darker than it was, especially the

---

[21]   Cf. Iván Szelényi, *A posztkommunista átmenet társadalmi konfliktusai* [The social conflicts of post-communist transition] (Budapest: MTA PTI, 1992); András Bozóki, "Intellectuals and Democratization in Hungary," in *A New Europe? Social Change and Political Transformation,* eds. Chris Rootes and Howard Davis (London: UCL Press, 1994), 149–75.

[22]   Neil Ascherson, *The Polish August: The Self-Limiting Revolution* (New York: Penguin, 1981); Jadwiga Staniszkis, *Poland's Self-Limiting Revolution* (Princeton: Princeton University Press, 1984).

interwar Horthy-regime. They endeavored to point out that Hungary kept its solvency, and that the system of János Kádár was still more flexible, livable, and bearable than the communist systems of surrounding countries. They pointed out that the intelligentsia was less censored in Hungary and even able and competent elements could become members of the leadership. They endeavored to prove that besides the hardships, the management of the country was in good hands. Nobody spoke of the superiority of communist ideology anymore; they simply stated that they were able deal with the deepening crisis pragmatically and competently.

The Jaruzelski *coup d'état* on December 13, 1981 ended the Polish "self-limiting revolution," suppressed Solidarity, and declared a state of emergency. The pay-off happened according to the usual Eastern European scenario, except for the fact that Soviet troops did not invade the country. Central European intellectuals were shocked, seeing this as a severe defeat for attempts at democracy. Some were expecting an anti-reform, conservative turn and a new, long "ice age" of restoration of Stalinism.

The marginalized Hungarian radical thinkers and intellectuals who clustered around the samizdat journal *Beszélő* had to make a decision. They had to decide whether they wanted to stick to the habit of the cultural opposition, as had become normal between 1977 and 1981, or whether they should attempt to articulate their opinions through political means. A leading figure of the incipient opposition, philosopher János Kis, published an essay[23] in 1982 that resulted in a debate among the dissidents about the oppositional strategy and thus played a vital role in their decision of taking up the role of political opposition.

In this article,[24] Kis argued against those in the opposition with more pessimistic expectations. "I would like to convince my friends," he wrote, "that (...) whatever the fate of the oppositional groups will be, the status quo will not be consolidated." Kis supported this audacious statement by describing the declining economic situation of Central Europe, arguing that this was no temporary downturn. Polish Solidarity had broken the legitimacy of existing socialist systems for good. The word "reform" was again mentioned in Hungary but not as a part of a comprehensive social and economic change but as the only hope for political survival. The relative legitimacy of the regime became obsolete, because it was based only on material rationality.

---

[23] János Kis, "Gondolatok a közeljövőről" (Thoughts on the near future)," *Beszélő*, no. 3 (1982).
[24] Kis, "Gondolatok a közeljövőről."

And when one accepts the dimension of material rationality, one excludes the dogma of infallibility at the same time, inevitably leading to pluralism in the long run.[25]

The democratic attempt in Poland had not only supported anti-totalitarian principles— as its predecessors in 1956 and 1968 did—but also for economic guarantees of living. The working-class movement came up against the "the state of the proletariat." Based on this fact, Kis said, "the beginning of the eighties was not only the time of restoration and reaction in Eastern Europe, but also of the growing economic and political crisis." This crisis, according to him, would not spare the Soviet Union either:

> The Soviet leadership at present wants to do only one thing in Eastern Europe: to keep up the order by all means. Its successors will have to decide however, what they wish to do with the bankrupt heritage they get. Their decision will surely reflect the means by which they find a way out of the inner crisis and unstable position of the Soviet Union as a world power.[26]

Following the ideas of Polish dissident leader, Adam Michnik, the Hungarian dissidents put forward that both the revolution of 1956 and the top-down reform of the system in 1968 were not successful attempts because those aimed to change the state. However, radical reformism, or "new evolutionism," as Michnik called it, could be a fruitful strategy because it was oriented toward civil society. This strategy did not concentrate on the transformation of the regime but on the strengthening of social autonomies.[27] Interestingly, throughout the debate neither Kis nor the majority of the speakers mentioned the strategy of civil society explicitly, showing that the Hungarian opposition was not prepared to be effective outside its own circles yet. Human rights-oriented, legalist oppositional literature was considered the sign of its weakness by the party leadership. However, what Kis wanted to do was to put an end to this attitude and argue for the necessity of a new form of oppositional activity: "No matter if we have been doing it right or wrong: we cannot go on the same way."[28]

---

[25] Ambrus Oltványi, "A közel- és távolabbi jövőről, avagy a demokrácia kilátásai Magyarországon" [About the near and far future: chances for democracy in Hungary], *Beszélő*, nos. 5–6 (1982).

[26] Kis, "Gondolatok a közeljövőről."

[27] Adam Michnik, "A New Evolutionism," in *Letters from Prison and Other Essays* (Berkeley: University of California Press, 1987), 135–48.

[28] Kis, "Gondolatok a közeljövőről."

As Kis thought, the political initiative could only come from within the opposition circles, because this was the only group outside the "consensus" of the Kádár regime. But he added that this group could start on the road of political opposition only if it had an ideology. The suggested pillars of this ideology were human rights, liberal democracy, national independence, and some of the useful elements of the socialist tradition. Whereas his starting point for the ideological debate was not fully developed, it had already contained the components of a possible radical, left-liberal political worldview.

The debate started by this article lasted in *Beszélő* from May 1982 to February 1984. This debate gradually led to that circle around *Beszélő*'s new strategy in the second half of the 1980s.[29] This evolutionist strategy worked as a unique intellectual puzzle and from it the cornerstones of the political and ideological activities of the opposition took shape.

What they wanted

The contributors mostly agreed with Kis's opening proposal and the idea of consensus appealed to almost all the participants of the debate. As it appeared in the program of *Beszélő*,[30] dissidents wanted to create a new ground for future political consensus during crises and economic reform.

The dissidents were far from unified concerning their goals. Many of the contributors to the debate envisioned a generally leftist program. Someone talked about the socialization of the state,[31] another participant wanted an alternative socialism that was based on workers' democracy,[32] while philosopher G. M. Tamás claimed that "the ideology of the opposition should be anti-state and anti-authoritarian."[33]

Political theorist Pál Szalai was inclined to the idea of a multi-party system based on democratic socialism, in which the means of production were given to the workers collectives, where there was an agreement about the property relations, but where pluralism existed not only among the parties.

---

[29] Kis, "Gondolatok a közeljövőről."
[30] János Kis, "Hogyan keressünk kiutat a válságból?" [How to find a way out of the crisis?], *Beszélő*, nos. 5–6 (1982).
[31] András Lányi, "A magyar ellenzék programja" [The program of the Hungarian opposition], *Beszélő*, nos. 5–6 (1982).
[32] József Székely, "Reform és ellenzék" [Reform and the opposition], *Beszélő*, nos. 5–6 (1982).
[33] Gáspár Miklós Tamás, "Amiért mégis" [Against the odds], *Beszélő*, no. 8 (1983).

He seemed to admit the need for a market economy, but he also added that "the strengthening of it without worker's councils would be no more than the tug of war between the central bureaucracy and the company bureaucracy."[34] The sociologist Erzsébet Szalai wrote about the "social conditions of the liberal alternative," but by liberal alternative she meant "the possibility for multiple producing economic entities to live side by side," which would have happened parallel to the splitting of economic and political institutions.[35] She was convinced that a liberal alternative had to be completed alongside the realization of a democratic alternative. In such a system "the broadest layers of society—mostly large-scale industry workers—will or at least could establish their own institutions," by which she most probably meant worker's councils and trade unions. According to Szalai, "these means a guarantee that new— although historically well known—exploiting relationships could not emerge from the existence of all sorts of production relations."[36] Hence, to prevent the liberal alternative from leading to capitalism, the democratic representation of interests could have been guaranteed. In her article, democracy and capitalism were mutually exclusive, so the "liberal alternative" for her actually did not exceed the borders of the socialist paradigm.

Almost all the contributors referred to the national problem. The writer György Konrád named self-determination as a goal,[37] while sociologist Bálint Magyar emphasized the development of the *citoyen*.[38] Ambrus Oltványi, who had already stated in the title of his article that his aim was to speak about democracy, made one of the most up-to-the-point ommentaries.[39] Here, Oltványi proved to have outstanding foresight. He claimed that the probability of achieving democratic, pluralistic development should be expected in the short run. He considered the shape of a self-limiting market to be the key question, because for him a market economy was more easily imaginable without democracy than democracy without a market economy. With this, he presaged the next half decade of Hungarian political debate on this topic. Unlike many other contributors at that time, he did not believe in

---

[34] Pál Szalai, "Remény – remény nélkül" [Hope – without hope], *Beszélő*, no. 4 (1982).

[35] Erzsébet Szalai, "A liberális alternatíva társadalmi feltételeiről" [About the social criteria of the liberal alternative], *Beszélő*, no. 7 (1983).

[36] Szalai, "A liberális alternatíva társadalmi feltételeiről."

[37] György Konrád, "Adottságainkból kell kiindulni" [Our starting point should be our capability], *Beszélő* no. 8 (1983).

[38] Bálint Magyar, "Polgárokká válni" [To become citizens], *Beszélő*, no. 4 (1982).

[39] Oltványi, "A közel- és távolabbi jövőről."

democratic socialism, and he stated that socialism should be kept alive as a counter-tendency against the main tendency of capitalism, but it should not be realized. The opposition had learned the lesson of the economic reforms of 1968, and so never believed that reforms coming from above would be enough to reach their desired objective. When I describe the democratic opposition as radical reformers I do not refer mainly to the differences in their demands—even though those were notable compared to the vague ideas of the reformers within the system—but of the differences in their strategy. While the reformist communists of the age—who sat in different "reform committees" behind closed doors—spoke mostly to the men in power, the opposition tried to speak to the society as well.

Strategies for change

All but one person agreed the radical reformist strategy proposed by Kis. The journalist István Orosz stated "we need to step away from the margin and bear the consequences." He thought that there was no midway and so the opposition had to decide whether it wanted to pursue a popular front policy "with the reformer intelligentsia or with the working class."[40] In this dilemma, he clearly proposed a rather revolutionary strategy.

Many contributors drew a line between those standing inside and outside the Kádárist "consensus," emphasizing that the democratic opposition must avoid social isolation because it could lead to a political avant-gardism. According to István Eörsi, the problem with standing "inside" or "outside" the regime cannot be restricted to a moral question. The good strategy might be, he said, a rapprochement between the radical opposition and the reformists based on some kind of division of labor, and on the conscious changing of "insider" and "outsider" behavior.[41]

The philosopher Mihály Vajda was probably the most modest about the future role of the dissidents when he wrote: "The new democratic political community does not have to form the opposition itself but it should ensure, through critical publicity, that a real opposition is formed within the power elite."[42]

---

[40] István Orosz, "A Hivatal-védte ellenzékiség" [Opposition defended by bureaucracy], *Beszélő*, no. 4 (1982).

[41] István Eörsi, "Csto gyélaty?" [What to do?], *Beszélő*, no. 4 (1982).

[42] Mihály Vajda, "Ellenzék vagy kritikai nyilvánosság" [Opposition or critical public sphere], *Beszélő*, no. 8 (1983).

According to Pál Szalai, the opposition should not strategize along the lines of "inside" and "outside" but by content. He did not think it advisable to start cooperation with the leftist wing of MSZMP or the anti-liberal, middle-class heirs of noble nationalism. At the same time, "attention should be given to the democratic trends within MSZMP" and "to the revival within Hungarian Catholicism." Here, Pál Szalai elaborated on some topics that became important in the future: 1. the need of the opposition to have more than one ideology; 2. the anti-democratic traditions of the aristocratic middle class, and the dangers of cooperating with certain groups within these circles.[43] Who would have suspected that the organization of 'népi' (popular) writers called Hungarian Democratic Forum (MDF), after coming to power in 1990, would divide into two groups representing two tendencies. One group was the conservative Christian middle-class, and the other was the former gentry and some plebeians advocating for a right-wing radicalism.

Most of the contributors emphasized the need for cooperation with groups that were not part of the opposition, which should be done at a strategic level. But they emphasized different points. The moderate in this topic was Tamás Bauer who stated that the reform initiatives should come basically from the "good king, the party leadership, [and] the government," while the radical thinkers should act as a catalyst to "reveal and formulate the social needs and endeavors"[44]

Ambrus Oltványi stressed that the first and second public sphere should be more traversable, but legality should not be achieved by holding back or giving up on oppositional views but by acknowledging them. After all, the acceptance of political autonomy was just as alien to the nature of the Kádár-regime as the open tolerance of the opposition. Oltványi counted on the power and the opposition to "live permanently side-by-side," and he trusted that the autonomic powers of the society would be allowed to take part in creating the reforms from above.

Again prophetical, he called attention to the fact that once in world history: "although four decades after the dictatorship came into power, such a transition proved to be realizable in Spain after Franco."[45] To support his statement, Oltványi quoted Adam Michnik directly: "If I searched for a

---

[43] Szalai, "Remény – remény nélkül."
[44] Tamás Bauer, "Az optimista alternatíva körvonalai" [Outlines of an optimist alternative], *Beszélő*, nos. 5–6 (1982).
[45] Oltványi, "A közel- és távolabbi jövőről."

suitable example for the tasks ahead of us, I would mention Spain: behold a society, which—thanks to the more sensitive forces of the power and the opposition—found its way out of a shameful dictatorship to democracy."[46] However unbelievable it is, Michnik wrote these lines already in the mid-1970s. We might even say that the transition in Spain was something like the first evidence of the "self-freeing by self-delimiting" strategy Michnik described.

Oltványi also emphasized the importance of generational change, through which "possibly more and more of those will enter the apparatus who—unlike those members who dominate and can be there only because of counter-selection—will be able to stand their ground among the conditions of pluralism and competition with the help of their training and efficiency, and thus will not have to cling to the dictatorial means of power at any price."[47] These hypotheses were proved correct by the changes of 1989.

Most of those who contributed to the debate at that time found it important to maintain pluralism of ideas within the opposition, pointing out that those who want pluralism in the society cannot endeavor to suppress it within their own circles. They insisted on pluralism as a precondition of democracy and not just an outcome of it.

Looking back, one might tend to simplify things and treat the decade of the 1980s as the triumphal procession of the ideology of civil society. Yet, few people in opposition called for civil society. The task of civil society, such as it was, was to "free itself from the guardianship of the state."[48] "Civil society and political state are by nature struggling with each other," stated Vajda. For Konrád, "the organizational space of civil society was the world of informal relationships," which is characterized by autonomous speech, its primal bearer being the young intelligentsia.[49] Neither Vajda nor Konrád agreed that the dissidents should form a political opposition, because then it would have had to strive for power. According to the anti-political Konrád, the opposition "is democratic not if it is political but when it is a social opposition." Meanwhile, Vajda said that it is not a political opposition that needed to be established but a critical public sphere where the "social criticism of politics" could be exercised.[50]

---

46 Cf. Adam Michnik, "A New Evolutionism," in Adam Michnik, *Letters from Prison and Other Essays* (Berkeley: University of California Press, [1976] 1987), 135–148.

47 Oltványi, "A közel- és távolabbi jövőről."

48 Oltványi, "A közel- és távolabbi jövőről."

49 Konrád, "Adottságainkból."

50 Vajda, "Ellenzék."

One could argue from an anti-political approach that the dissidents were almost genetically anti-power, not only against the communist power but against power as such. But this was not true. A large part of the opposition was thinking not in terms of powerlessness, but in terms of balance in power, of a "new consensus" and a "social contract."

Konrád thought of striving for power as a heritage of communism and he rejected it on those grounds. For him, political opposition seemed inherently anti-democratic: "The *sine qua non* of democratic opposition is that it should be democratic, i.e. post-communist in its operation and its self-image, and thus it should deeply revise itself for the traces and habits of the communist opposition."[51] Vajda warned prophetically that the basis of the new democratic political community cannot be restricted to the dissidents, for it can easily happen that most of the members come from somewhere else.[52] Konrád said the following about the same phenomenon: "Our task is to help *others* to gain their freedom."[53]

Roads split at this point over the question of a political or non-political opposition. It is obviously not by accident that neither Vajda nor Konrád became professional politicians. Others, like Bálint Magyar, modified their views and pursued political careers in the 1990s. In the years following the 1990 elections, János Kis became the first president of SZDSZ, but soon he departed from party politics and returned to his academic profession.

A greater group of contributors agreed with the proposition of János Kis's article and thus hurried to openly create a political opposition. "We need to acknowledge that political goals can only be achieved by political means," wrote András Lányi.[54] Within the political opposition, many highlighted different aspects of the overall strategy. Some wanted confrontation, others social pressure, but G. M. Tamás, besides demanding political reforms, emphasized the need for an "ethical renewal."[55] Others believed that "even a historical compromise can come about between the government and the opposition on the common platform of advancement and national interest."[56]

---

[51] Konrád, "Adottságainkból."
[52] Vajda, "Ellenzék."
[53] Konrád, "Adottságainkból."
[54] András Lányi, "A magyar ellenzék programja" (The program of the Hungarian opposition), *Beszélő*, nos. 5–6 (1982).
[55] Gáspár Miklós Tamás, "Amiért mégis."
[56] Zoltán Krasznai, "Jelszavaink legyenek: haza és haladás" [Our slogans shall be: homeland and progress], *Beszélő*, no. 7 (1983).

After the debate ended, the option of forming a political opposition gained support, leading to a conference on the 1956 revolution in 1986, various lectures in the illegal "flying university" and other places on the forming of the *Social Contract* program in 1987,[57] and finally, the formation of the Network of Free Initiatives in 1988. Without this choice of opening up, and made to form a political opposition, the dissident intellectuals of the 1980's could have easily become insignificant in the period of transition.

Conclusions

From the viewpoint of history of ideas, the road of the Hungarian opposition led from Marxist philosopher György Lukács to liberal democratic political thinker István Bibó, that it to say from revisionism to radical reformism. Or, in other words, from the neo-Marxism of 1968 to the radical human rights activism of the Czech and the Polish opposition after 1977. It was a symbolic road from the Budapest School of philosophy to the "Gdańsk School" of social involvement. The *Beszélő* debate of 1982–84 did not bring along anything new from an ideological point of view, for the participants broke with the Marxism of György Lukács earlier, already in the 1970s.[58] But it was new in raising the question of strategy and ideology in speaking about it openly. There appeared a wide scale of conceptions, starting from democratic socialism to liberal democracy. As the effect of the debate, the group started to consider itself a political opposition instead of a marginalized subculture, and from this emerged new political programs.

The early 1980s was the Bibóist period of the democratic opposition—not only in that they tried to follow István Bibó's political legacy but also in that they accepted Bibó's concept of liberal socialism as a broad common basis. The contributors supported the development of the market economy, but they believed—without using the term "capitalism"—that its negative effects on society (i.e. the widening of social inequality) could be eliminated according to the Bibó theory. Yet the real importance of the debate in *Beszélő* lay not so much in ideological innovation but in their astute judgement of the situation, and in formed a political strategy and following it. The positive

---

[57] Miklós Haraszti, János Kis, Ferenc Kőszeg, and Ottília Solt, *Társadalmi Szerződés* [Social Contract], special issue, *Beszélő* (1987).

[58] Csizmadia, *A magyar demokratikus ellenzék*, 1995.

impact of István Bibó was not only in setting that goal but, more importantly, in how they reconciled "tactics with ethics."

The contributors could not foresee the fall of the communist system. But in carefully analyzing the Polish "self-limiting revolution" and the situation in Central Europe, it must have been clearer to them than to anyone else that the fall was bound to happen in the near future. Many even formulated its conditions. Pál Szalai was probably the most exact when he said that: "Democracy can break through in this region, 1) if democratic movements take action in several Eastern European countries at the same time, 2) if democratization makes progress within and outside of the communist party in parallel, 3) if the Soviet leadership is enlightened enough to admit that its only goal is to conserve a military zone of interest, while at the same time, it is willing to deal with the Eastern European movements at least enough to allow a limited democracy."[59]

How can we respond to this prediction with the hindsight of the past few decades? Szalai had a stupendously clear vision of the future. 1) Communist systems did fall like dominoes in Central and Eastern Europe. 2) The transition in most countries happened peacefully because the communist leadership was divided. 3) An enlightened communist leader, Gorbachev, appeared, who was willing to give up the "Brezhnev-doctrine" and let these countries go their own way. While Pál Szalai logically deduced the details of the change of regime, Zoltán Krasznai made an event more exact prophesy in 1983, writing: "If the equalization tendency resulting from economic recession proves to be permanent, then the crisis may hit many countries in Eastern Europe at the same time. This could take place in the second part of the 1980s."[60]

Though the crises of the Central and Eastern European countries did not come exactly at the same time and did not reach the same depth, the crisis of the Soviet Union provided an opportunity for change. The legacy of dissent helped out the process of democratization in the most difficult times of transformation.

Maybe they did not realize that the radical rightist, nationalist values of the pre-communist Hungary persistently stayed alive in the loam of Kádár's post-totalitarian dictatorship. Probably they had illusions about the

---

[59] Szalai, "Remény – remény nélkül."
[60] Krasznai, "Jelszavaink legyenek."

viability of the state-socialist economy. Certainly they paid less attention to the alliance with workers than their counterparts in Poland. Moreover their ideology was, in some ways vague. This is not so surprising since it was not primarily the positive values but the marginalized and isolated social position and the opposition to the power that bound them together. They had to approach people who were in a very different situation than them. Yet, those within the circles of the democratic opposition were able to develop the civil techniques by which they kept their integrity and also made it possible for others to use them when changes were coming.

LOST IN PROTOCHRONIA

Ideological Dada in Ceauşescu's Romania

Mircea Mihăieş

Two enormous scandals shook the intellectual circles of late Romania communism. Both were consequences of and chapters in a Ceauşescu's bizarre "cultural revolution" with Levantine-Asian nuances, started by the 1971 "July Theses." The dictator's ambition to gain total control over Romanian society was precipitated by a few years of more relaxed propaganda and the loosening of the Party's dogmatic reins (1964–1970). A state visit to China and Korea exposed the semi-illiterate leader to a version of dictatorship that resonated with his own ideal of Stalinism, one he could adapt to Romanian conditions. This ultimately was the national-communism that governed Romania between 1974 and 1989. In order to perpetuate his power, Ceauşescu had to change not only his position (being the party's general secretary no longer sufficed; he was preparing to become head of the state as well), but, if we may, his ontological status as well. He was no longer satisfied with the title "working-class hero" (as John Lennon would have put it), he rather aspired to super-manhood. To that particular end, it was necessary for him to strengthen the confines of the Party's monolithic thinking, to embolden the indisputable ideology of the leader, to further the repression of dissident voices and of initiatives that did not bear the "leading light's" seal of approval.

In 1977, when the party decided to do away with the five academic specializations in the socio-humanities (which included sociology and psychology) and to redistribute their students to strongly ideological departments (philosophy and history), the regime's intolerant attitude was evidently and brutally marked. The "Transcendental Meditation" Affair, when two hundred and fifty intellectuals were laid off, reached its climax in 1982, and proved that the communist regime did not tolerate any disobedience to its dogma. In the repressive apparatus's morbid imagination, those who participated in the Transcendental Meditation's meetings to learn relaxation techniques were part of a global conspiracy. To the Eastern despot, mental exercises equaled perverse, dangerous plans to overthrow the neo-Bolshevik order.

The state's gigantic propaganda machine, as well as other cultural and ideological publications servile to the cult of the leader and of national-communism, exhibited one of the strangest trends of the communist era, exalting the primordial nature of Romanian art and science as compared to all other countries, particularly capitalist ones. The premise was simple: Romania, a country everybody hated, whose values were ignored, despised, or appropriated by enemies from abroad, had long anticipated a host of universally notable creations. The campaign's emphasis lay less on *value* than on *primacy*. In the works and words of the zealots of national communism, Romania presented itself as the initiator, inventor, and, paradoxically, victim of a volcanic eruption of ideas, theories, and discoveries of planetary importance, which, incidentally, no one had ever heard of before. The term coined by Edgar Papu to designate this unprecedented plenitude aimed at illustriousness itself: *protochronism*, a forced contraction of the Greek terms *protos* and *chronos*, "that which has happened for the first time" (and, undoubtedly, in the first place as well).

The initiative demonstrated an inferiority complex that party officials were trying to turn into a superiority one. The "fortress under siege" mentality fought back at "historic misfortune" with a mixture of deviousness and affection that characterizes the complexed character, whose despair makes him bluff. This situation is more common than one would be inclined to believe. In his *Dacopathia*, Dan Alexe starts from an older version of the protochronist zaniness, whose pioneer is, presumably, Nicolae Densuşianu (1846–1911), a Romanian ethnologist and collector of folklore. A monk of Mount Athos, admirer of *Prehistoric Dacia*, Densuşianu's best-known work, stunned Alexe with the following reasoning: "As its own tradition tells us, Rome was founded by the Trojans. The Trojans were Thracians, thus a kind of Dacians. Therefore, the founders of Rome were nothing but a handful of Dacians, which had fled Troy with Eneas and taken their language along into the Italic exile so that, when Trajan returned to conquer Dacia, he and his mixed-blood Latins discovered that Dacians spoke the same language as themselves, only much more clearly. That is why the two peoples merged so easily: the languages they spoke were fairly similar. Consequently, it is not Romanian that comes from Latin but rather, reversely, it was the Dacians who taught Latin to Italic tribes."

Such grotesquely comical fables are often found in conversations between amateur "scholars." They become atrocious, however, when they leave the private sphere (such as Mount Athos, in Dan Alexe's narrative) and become the vulgate of a state or of high representatives in its administration. In the mid-'80s, one of the most brutal proponents of Romanian communism, Eugen Florescu, firmly stated: "It should be understood, once and for all: protochronism is neither the ideology of the *Luceafărul* magazine, not Edgar Papu's; it is an ideology created by Comrade Nicolae Ceaușescu."[1] These examples invoke the supreme authority: Emperor Trajan and the presidential scepter-bearer, Nicolae. Every ideology needs validation from an intangible mystique of power.

Drawing a resourceful comparison, Dan Alexe proves that "the malady of primacies" is not an exclusively Romanian ailment, nor is it necessarily tied to the existence of communist parties. The particularity rests in the fact that a respected intellectual, Edgar Papu, termed the phenomenon *protochronism*, and the propagandists wove around it flabbergasting tales of the greatness of the nation. Just as, according to psychologists and sociologists, identical situations create identical effects, inferiority complexes can become an easily recognizable symptom, regardless of their time and place of manifestation. Dan Alexe notes that "protochronism is a sticky disease of small and uncertain nations, wherein one or several groups of people of arguable culture and no training in history or linguistics ally to invent a past greatness of the nation of cosmic proportions."[2]

Romancing the past is one of the guaranteed success formulae in politics. All populations live in the mythology of a glorious beginning, mythical by the very belief that it *must* have existed, despite the obnubilation, the cecity, the despise of big, "imperialist" cultures in communist ideology. In some cases, centuries had to pass for the official ideology's fabricated myths of illuminati to be declared unequivocal truths via an archeology oozing "originality" itself. These "Imaginary primacies" have, nevertheless, not been probed either in Albania, Croatia, or in the former Soviet Bloc. Similarly, they could not be traced—as they are virtually irretrievable. In the case of daydreams by champions of the "glorious past" from countries with histories marked by humiliation and failure.

---

[1] Vladimir Tismăneanu and Mircea Mihăieş, *O tranziție mai lungă decât veacul. România după Ceaușescu* (Bucarest: Editura Curtea Veche, 2011), 45.

[2] Dan Alexe, *Dacopatia și alte rătăciri românești* (Bucarest: Editura Humanitas, 2015), 103.

Let us, however, clarify something. In the history of science and culture there have, indeed, been moments and circumstances of "primacy" that have remained unknown for objective reasons (such as, for example, the lack of a systematic history of science in the Far East). Where there is no clear framework for debate, a functional "marketplace of ideas," revelation, inspiration, original achievement, even "epiphanies" are all doomed to fail. Communism was an agoraphobic ideology, *par excellence*, one loath to the public confrontation of ideas. No topic, no idea was sanctioned before a prolonged analysis in the party's manipulation laboratories. Birth control methods functioned, metaphorically, in all fields: thought, art, creation. You did not procreate when you wished, but when the party decided that you should.

In a story by Borges, the Chinese emperor who had the famous Wall built made yet another decree: "that all books written before his reign be burnt."[3] The Asian autocrat had a clear purpose: the abolition of the past. He proclaimed himself the zero moment of history and of the world. What the protochronists fantasize about is no different. They descend into the past in order to annihilate all social, scientific, and artistic history and evolution, ignoring the fact that society has moved on without their precious contributions.

Thus, even without denying the existence of certain so-called "protochronic deeds," the idea of protochronism as means of *a posteriori* self-affirmation can only be perceived ironically, as grotesque. The promoters of protochronism are individuals who simply cannot accept the thought that existence is not an uninterrupted series of victories, that failure is just as important a part of the game. They promote a mechanistic vision of the universe, which solely envisages the teeth of an immense wheel of history, not the movement, rotation, and energy that propel the whole. In fact, it is a process, an incessant trade between old and new, discovery, and confirmation. Their slogan seems to be: "Not only am I the only one, I was also the first." The fact that protochronist theories go hand in hand with conspiracy theories only emphasizes the drift of certain organized human groups, in order to at times, impose dictatorial political and historical identities.

The present lines are not an *in nuce* history of Romanian protochronism. I am interested in one thing alone: to identify the means by which, under the

---

[3] Jorge-Luis Borges, *Eseuri*, trans. Irina Dogaru, Cristina Hăulică, Andrei Ionescu, and Tudora Şandru-Mehedinţi (Iaşi: Editura Polirom, 2006).

circumstances of the Romanian consolidation of Ceaușescu's neo-Stalinist power, organized groups of intellectuals and propagandists turned the crass falsification of historical data into a *modus operandi* that comprised the entire society. It was not an absolute novelty. Dan Alexe speaks of a true protochronist plague in the Balkan area and the Middle-East, i.e. in the countries where historical processes have always been highly fluid. Thus, the Albanian Mathieu Aref write a book, *Albanie, ou l'incroyable odyssée d'un people préhellénique*, which based on historical and linguistic speculation, designated the Albanians the forefathers of the entire Mediterranean Basin, up to the Caucasus. As in the case of the "Dacopaths," the "Pelasgians" are proclaimed the ancestors of the Etruscans, Thracians, and Trojans.

The Etruscans and Trojans are also disputed by an imaginative "scholar" from Estonia, Edgar Saks. To him, the Estonians are the forebears of the entirety Western and Eastern Europe. The title of his 1966 book is very clear: *Esto-Europa: A Treatise on the Finno-Ugric Primary Civilization in Europe*. Later, in 1981, he published yet another, equally "original" study: *The Estonian Vikings*.

I have selected only two examples from an archipelago of madness. Dan Alexe's book provides innumerable other cases of protochronist deviations, scattered across the globe, from Central Europe to the Far East. From this point of view, I was somewhat disappointed: I would have liked our "Dacopaths" to at least be the first, if not the most, irrational of the primacy-seekers! We have, however, been defeated here as well. The pseudo-scientist's imagination is infinite and ubiquitous. If there is something therein that impresses (and amuses), it is the aura of seriousness and solemnity, the severe, supreme competence that envelops each of these scholars of the void. They are perfectly logical within their own reference system, but completely oblivious to reason and historical evidence.

After the *pacification* years that followed the retreat of Soviet troops from Romania, the country adopted a policy of controlled reforms. Unlike Hungary, with its "Goulash Communism" that allowed liberties that Romanian, Bulgarian, and Albanian citizens did not dare dream of, and unlike Poland, where the principle of multi-partyism had been (even if demagogically) accepted, Romania remained all throughout a bastion of totalitarianism. The one and only party was not challenged in any way, and liberalization measures in one field (such as cultural policies that permitted Romanian translations of authors such as Solzhenitsyn—though not *The Gulag Archipelago*—and Franz Kafka, who was banned in Czechoslovakia) were immediately countered by inhumane measures in another, like the anti-abortion law or the one that forbid contacts with foreigners.

It was in this context that an article by Edgar Papu that at first went almost unnoticed in the most liberal journal of the time, *Secolul 20*, turned in only a few years into a missile with countless sections and warheads. There is no clear explanation as why such a respected intellectual metamorphosized into the ideologue of a doctrine that was, at best, ridiculous, and into a zealous promoter of the absurdities embraced by the communist party. Nothing—or almost nothing—in his biography anticipated his career as the flag-bearer of a retrograde cultural-ideological trend, and his complete subjection to the ultra-reactionary forces in Romanian culture. He had made his editorial debut in 1936 and accomplished some promising work as a historian of ideas and philosophy. He was arrested and incarcerated in 1961 for his presumed participation in an anti-state plot (in fact, sentenced for his deep religious beliefs). Although barred from higher education, he did manage to publish a series of volumes of history and literary theory starting in 1967. He wrote prefaces to important works in the humanities and he translated, alone or in collaboration, authors such as Epicurius, Lucretius, and García Lorca. He is the co-author of the first full Romanian version of Cervantes' masterpiece, *Don Quixote de la Mancha.*

Exiled among books, Edgar Papu cultivated a melancholic ahistoricism, seeking refuge in perfectly obsolete concepts like "beauty," "dream," "baroque," "lyrical forms," etc. What is intriguing is precisely why such a character, with a biography placed at the antipodes of the party activist profile, should have stood been central to one of the biggest ideological obsessions of Romanian communism. Yet, Edgar Papu was not as naïvely unaware of the role that had been attributed to him, as proved by the fact that in the fall of 1977 he became an open collaborator of the Foreign Affairs Ministry's propaganda apparatus, an annex of the Securitate (the secret police). The visit of a "comrade" from the institution overjoyed him. Without hesitation, he put together "a sort of essay" that illustrated "the idea of protochronism." What follows surpasses any expectation: "I read the draft to him and, after taking note of certain remarks he made, I was to write the definitive text as well." It was the most degrading type of collaborationism, showing that the scholar did not completely lack practical sense: "I also suggested something else, and he accepted: that some of us give lectures on this topic in big foreign cultural centers. He found the suggestion very judicious."[4] Patriotism, patriotism, but a little reward never hurts!

Romanian historiography has never lacked "primordialists" and "supremacists"—to use two current terms. From Nicolae Iorga (sometimes explicitly, most often implicitly) to Nicolae Densuşianu's *Prehistoric Dacia* (1913) and Vasile Pârvan's *Getica* (1926), a mixture of wishful thinking, literary talent, scientific competence, and grand imaginary projections built a royal lineage that connected nineteenth century historical studies to the challenges of aggressive modernity after World War I. The traces have endured, such that even nowadays people think that the historian's main duty is not to tell the truth but to devotedly serve "national ideals." Browsing through the list of members of the Romanian Academy's History and Archeology section, one will be surprised by the preponderance of "crooks of the nation," as poet Mihai Eminescu once called them.

An individual with Edgar Papu's biography and psychological profile paid natural attention to such lasting movements in the Romanian society. He had certainly developed a sort of grateful dependence on those who had helped him after he left jail, people with high positions and influence in the communist propaganda system. The delicacy, modesty, shyness, and disbelief that could be easily decoded in his behavior had made him easy prey to the experienced, cynical operators of the ideological sphere.

One particularly relevant feature of the system's perversity is worth mentioning. Ceauşescu skillfully predicted the effervescent atmosphere after political convicts were freed from prison in 1964. The departure of Soviet troops had already inflamed "national sentiment," and lying on the basis of a totalizing Romanian ethos had been the natural consequence of the expressed aversion towards the Soviet occupation. Suddenly, the small country at the crossroads of three great empires discovered, in a romantically exalted formula, its own "titanism." It had functioned impeccably in Eminescu's work; according to this elated logic, it could not malfunction at the level of contemporary society.

Starting from Matei Calinescu study, *The Titan and the Genius in Mihai Eminescu's Work* (1965), Edgar Papu coined a phrase—"the titanism of small countries"—to subtly attack the collectivism propagated by the party apparatus. The exegete thus meant to emphasize "the role of personality in

---

[4] Vlad-Ion Pappu, *Edgar Papu şi protocronismul în spaţiul revistei „Luceafărul"*, (Bucarest: Eikon, 2005), 39.

history (against the grain of the official doctrine, which exalted the role of the "masses") and illustrated privileged moments at which small states, destined to play a minor part, caused major mutations in "the big history."[5] Such a position would have placed the author of the erudite studies on baroque and classicism in direct opposition with the Romanian Communist Party dogmas. Which, obviously, did not happen. The scholar had simply detected a pleasant-sounding tune and repeated it without hesitation.

Edgar Papu's public gestures gained influence over the acivity of some of his fellow intellectuals, people whom he respected and who enjoyed steady positions in public life, unlike himself, who was marginal, persecuted, ignorant. A dispute between Ovidiu Papadima, reputed professor and researcher from Cluj, and the Cluj academic Liviu Rusu, gave him the opportunity to make his voice heard. Liviu Rusu had published a study, *Eminescu and Schopenhauer* (1966), which focused on the dichotomy of influence and originality in the work of a major author. The book was flooded with haphazard critical references, as well as by the thaw (in Ilya Ehrenburg words) that characterized the post-Stalinist era. Ovidiu Papadima's reply emphasized both the weakness of the Cluj literary historian's information, and the crudeness of his approach.

Edgar Papu's intervention represents one of the first documented instances in which the scholar tried to resolve the debate (he had the gift of "conciliation," Vlad-Ion Pappu informs us), proposing a solution that would end the quarrel between the two irreconcilable positions: protochronism would show when for the first time cultural value appeared in the world.[6] One can ponder forever to what degree a debate that seemed to be purely theoretical (in values, originality, objectivity, truth etc.) may have been guilty of having helped consolidate the tyrannical grip of a totalitarian regime. Unfortunately, Edgar Papu's radically ethnicist choices, his growingly visible attachment to the nationalist-communist group surrounding the *Luceafărul* and *Săptămâna* magazines, as to the scientist's position.

The big issue with protochronism, in its incipient stage, was that it contested the only truly admirable position in the entire Romanian twentieth century culture: that of Lovinescu's *synchronism*. For a country that, in just one decade, had faced three bloody dictatorships (Carol the Second's monarchy, Antonescu's fascist dictatorship, and the communist rule), synchronism was

---

5   Vlad-Ion Pappu, *Edgar Papu*, 18–19.
6   Vlad-Ion Pappu, *Edgar Papu*, 23.

its only opportunity to escape the totalitarian curse. One of the leaders of the synchronist group in the '60s-'70s, Nicolae Manolescu, far from being a "progressive" (as he was disdainfully labeled), acted as an inflexible supporter of European values. The reasoning was simple: in each of the country's experiences with totalitarianism, Romania had not endured catastrophe out of too much Europeanism, but rather out of excessive ethnocentrism, localism, and identitarianism.

No matter how many attenuating circumstances we might find in Edgar Papu's life, there is no denying that he was directly responsible for opening a true Pandora's box. Never and nowhere has the exaltation of tribal values resulted in general happiness, only in suffering, exclusion, and destruction. A theory that contributes to the strengthening of a despotic regime is to be blamed, no matter how "noble" its intentions. The numerous public debates in which Edgar Papu defended his position do not lend to the idea that he was a mad scientist. He knew very well both his allies and his enemies, and, against all evidence, he opted for retrograde forces, for the primitivism of the Securitate's assault troops in the *Luceafărul* and *Săptămâna* magazines.

In a desperate attempt to diminish his father's guilt, Vlad-Ion Pappu brings up Ion Constantinescu's book, *The Legacy of the Moderns*, which "invokes more Romanian priorities" than the ones that appear in the studies of the inventor of *protochronism* as a term.[7] The explanations are relevant: officials must have ignored Constantinescu because, on the one hand, he never attacked synchronism and, on the other, he did not "shake the hierarchies established in the fifties," i.e. the ones imposed by communist ideologues of Jewish origin. Yet, demonstrable reality shows that Edgar Papu's adversaries (mainly the critics around the *România literară* magazine and a few intellectuals from outside of Bucharest) were the champions of European values, in the Maiorescu-Lovinescu line, while his allies kept to the ethno-centrist, isolationist, xenophobic line of the interwar era. Edgar Papu's beliefs were, thus, in perfect accord with the new policy of ethnic closing and cleansing within the cultural zone created by Ceaușescu after 1971, as convincingly illustrated by Katherine Verdery[8] and amply exemplified by Alexandra Tomița (2007).[9]

---

[7] Vlad-Ion Pappu, *Edgar Papu*, 33.

[8] Katherine Verdery, *National Ideology under Socialism: Identity and Cultural Politics in Ceausescu's Romania* (Berkeley: University of California Press, 1991).

[9] Alexandra Tomița, *O istorie „glorioasă". Dosarul protocronismului românesc* (Bucarest: Editura Cartea Românească, 2007).

The conclusions are self-evident: Edgar Papu was chosen because he was an *anti-synchronist*, (i.e. *anti-European*), and, to the mind of upper party members, he bordered on antisemitism with his implicit cultural convictions. These two features were, in fact, the pillars of Ceaușescu's ideology after 1971. Looking back in 1985, Artur Silvestri saw protochronism as "the most notable critical idea in the Romania of the time," its essence being the creation of premises for the "de-Europeanization" of Romanian culture.[10] *De-Europeanization*: no more, no less! Edgar Papu was alive, but he did not bother to dismiss this preposterous claim.

Papu's *From our Classics*[11] is usually considered the Bible of Romanian protochronism. As we know, however, it is not his first contribution to the topic. Cobbling together studies revolving around the obsessive idea of the primacy of various Romanian creations over works from other meridians, the book can be also read in a psychoanalytical, if not psychiatric key. Under the guise of a coherent discourse, one finds cultural history musings (regarding Cantermir, Xenopol, Vasile Conta) and absurdities cited by authors who would certainly never have written them. For instance, while quoting Gelu Ionescu, the protochronist exegete finds superiority where the young critic saw, in a comparative manner, mere similarities: prestigious artistic works of Western literature today (such as the theme of the protagonist's tragic solitude) were generally comparable to the state of mind that generated Ion Vinea's poetry. Papu rushes to point out: Vinea's work had been written "about four decades before."[12] Nevertheless, in no way does Gelu Ionescu proclaim any superiority, but rather the possible ("partial," "broad") similarity! No causality, mere fate.

The aim of Papu's book is declared in the very first sentence: "My intention has been to reveal several illustrations of universal anticipation, which have occurred in Romanian literature throughout the centuries."[13] Highlighting the backwardness of literary studies as compared to scientific ones, the author begins to break the barriers that have kept hidden from humankind at large the works and ideas that first surfaced precisely in our part of the world. As in science, he notes "what a waste of ingeniousness and creativity

[10] Artur Silvestri, „Sinteza ideii de specific național," *Luceafărul*, no. 29 (1985): 4.
[11] Edgar Papu, *Din clasicii noștri. Contribuții la ideea unui protocronism românesc* (Bucarest: Editura Eminescu, 1977).
[12] Papu, *Din clasicii noștri*, 16.
[13] Papu, *Din clasicii noștri*, 5.

had marked our planet throughout the centuries, before others could reach the same conquests of the mind."[14]

The question that arises is how humankind has managed to survive "throughout the centuries" without feasting on the Romanians' "outstanding" capacity to invent scientific theories and create artistic beauty? The complicated history of the twentieth century has shown that what matters indeed is not *primacy*, but *value*. Every second, humankind produces extremely many things *for the first time*. Yet, they are acknowledged only if they prove their utility and expressive force. Otherwise, they remain mere oddities, bizarre fabrications of inflamed minds, to the benefit of some Guinness Book of World Records. Saddened, Papu regrets that he cannot employ in all analyzed cases the phrase borrowed from I. Constantinescu, "prophetic value," completely satisfactory to the tastes of the communist ideology of the moment. Protochronism is, to the author, "the simpler and, simultaneously, more comprehensive term" for the anti-synchronist assault encouraged by the party ideologues. Explicitly, Papu claims paternity of the "*Romanian protochronism* concept, meant to oppose the idea of *synchronism*, i.e. the aspiration behind a retarded consciousness."[15] To put it bluntly, whoever considered himself European was "retarded!"

For Papu, taking into account the values acknowledged by the European marketplace of ideas meant having a "peripheral identity." In solidarity with Dan Zamfirescu and Paul Anghel, he felt it was his duty to "transform it into a central, nodal one." Beyond the involuntary and suicidal humor of such endeavors, one can detect the inflexibility of totalitarian thinking. The way in which Edgar Papu summarizes, for instance, Paul Anghel's von Arghezi is itself an example of a schizoid protochronism, which exposes the low intellectual level and the despise for logic of the self-designated flag-bearers of Romanian "prophetism": "He is a great poet of matter... Arghezi has anchored himself in this theme of birth and degradation of matter... His vision is an immense gift that world poetry receives at a time when the great turmoil of the contemporary era makes Arghezi's lyrical gift salutary." Let us admit it: one needs a truly protochronist intelligence to understand the meaning of the "salutary gift," conveyed by Paul Anghel's unparalleled inebriation with words.

---

[14]   Papu, *Din clasicii noștri*, 6.
[15]   Papu, *Din clasicii noștri*, 9.

Beyond the mystical-ideological nature of protochronism, this aberration of the last 15 years of pure and unforgiving Ceauşescu ideology raise a few issues regarding the power relations between politics and culture within Romanian communism. Papu carefully emphasized the ultimate importance of the 1970–1974 period. The preface to *From our Classics* is as categorical as possible: 1970—"and everything after"—represented a new epoch in history. The book's chronology overlaps with the era inaugurated by the "July Theses" of 1971 and concluded with Nicolae Ceauşescu's "ascent to the throne" as the first president "of monarchic right" in the history of Romania. Protochronism was, therefore, conceived in the context of the rediscovery of absolute power, the distinctive trait of a new "golden era." Just as Ceauşescu embodied, almost divinely (as suggested by some works in the arts, literature, and cinema), the great leaders of world history, his *culture* descended into the past to demonstrate its prophetism and primacy.

Instead of being noisily embraced, protochronism should have indicated the painful absence of a marketplace of ideas from Romanian culture. Value cannot be imposed by administrative measures and dictatorial interjections, but by the incessant selection and comparison of works. In culture, the ones who are meant to last are the ones who build a marketplace of ideas. In an exceptional book on cultural ideology, *On Ideas and Blockages*, Horia-Roman Patapievici explains the endemic precariousness of art that refuses dialogue. The causes of the instability are not, however, related to the creation itself, but rather in the way in which the creation has always been treated by the authorities: "Romania is far from being a cultural desert. On the contrary, from the point of view of the values that spring from it, like all living cultures, it resembles a garden. Yet, it is a paradoxical garden, wherein the flowers which fully bloom are only the ones cultivated upon the guidance and care of others, outsiders, while all the flowers that were not lucky enough to attract the attention of gardeners from abroad remain tiny and inchoate. Romanian culture is a garden that lies shapeless in the hands of local gardeners and flourishes lushly in the hands of Western ones [...] The paradox of the Romanian cultural environment is that, although it produces values, it is incapable of ensuring their acknowledgement, brilliance, or universal recognition."[16]

This is why: the necessity of building a confirmation space, in accepting competition and information exchange. The marketplace of ideas is never

---

[16]   Horia-Roman Patapievici, *Despre idei & blocaje* (Bucarest: Editura Humanitas, 2007), 15.

just internal and it never sleeps. That is exactly why it excludes surprises. Everything that is valuable is already known, as the product of a geometrically variable reality, where excellence is negotiated every second and at every possible level. Protochronism invented the method of obscure, oblique, downward recognition, refusing direct confrontation. Thoughtlessness was codified, and discovery and knowledge were rejected. While feeling that they were rising to the Pantheon, the protochronists were ridiculously and degradingly falling, refusing to put cultural marketplaces in contact. They believed that if they forcefully plunged themselves into leading positions of the universal values platoon, their gesture would impress. It triggered condescending smiles at best. Instead of building a framework for validation and flexible and independent dialogue, the authorities turned to mercenaries, illuminati, and fanatics. Opaque to argument and logic, the communists chose the imposition by decree of everything that was "valuable," "original," and "representative." Although in positions of power, they consequently confessed their impotence, and Edgar Papu is one of the names of the powerless.

Particularly relevant—and insufficiently emphasized by the majority of those who have studied the topic—is the place where Papu's first articles were published: the *Secolul 20* journal. The publication apparently represented a bastion of anti-totalitarian thought, a "valve" that helped Romanian intellectuals breathe a different air from the party propaganda's fetid one. Slow to gestate (part of the seduction protocol that editor Dan Hăulică was not a stranger to), the journal appeared infrequently, like a colorful surprise against the dirty, grey backdrop of the times. Read from today's perspective, *Secolul 20* was, in fact, only one or two steps removed from the Romanian cultural communism's official publications. The journal largely followed the meanders of Ceaușescu's foreign affairs policy, oftentimes baroque and unpredictable. Browsing the table of contents indicates a certain preference for the leftism and "progressivism" of emerging cultures—particularly the South-American ones—but also an affinity for certain communist writers who had "trouble" in their own countries (not of course Milan Kundera or the Hungarian dissidents and only once Alexandr Solzhenitsyn, with an excerpt that hardly does justice to the greatness of this anti-Soviet writer).

The testimony of a former editor of the journal, an admirable intellectual and ex-political convict, Andrei Brezianu, shows that there was a clear coordination between *Secolul 20*'s topics and Romania's foreign policy. Ceaușescu's visits abroad were frequently prepared by the journal's special issues, which the editor-in-chief Dan Hăulică was in charge of distributing in culturally and politically strategic places. So, even a journal that seemed to evade the propaganda avalanche played a carefully thought out part in the Party propaganda. In fact, in the editorial board—which determined the journal's main publishing directions—one could find devotees to the communist cause, like Ion Hobana, Mihnea Gheorghiu, Vasile Nicolescu, Ion Brad, and Zoe Dumitrescu-Bușulenga.

Thus, there was, undoubtedly, premeditation, even if the practical forms in which it manifested itself are hard to demonstrate. It was, however, customary for Romanian communism to use its former ideological enemies as promotion agents for "mankind's golden dream." After the release of the political prisoners, the publication *Glasul patriei* (later *Tribuna Românie*) became, simultaneously, a weapon and at arget for political convicts freed in 1964. Irreconcilable enemies such as Nichifor Crainic, theoretician of the "ethnocratic state," and the legionaries Virgil Carianopol and Radu Gyr, sentenced to many years in prison, , under their own name or various pseudonyms wrote uplifting texts about the "new order" put in place by communists.

In this context, the publication of Papu's two articles, "Romanian Protochronism" (issue 5–6/1974) and "Protochronism and Synthesis" (issue 7–9/ 1976), in *Secolul 20*, could not have been accidental. The first article, at least, was commissioned by the editorial board. Both the journal and the author were, to the educated reader, highly reliable. It was far easier to make an aberration plausible if you formulated it in a respectable place, such as *Secolul 20*, than if it appeared in magazines whose Securitate-related communist fanaticism was well-known, such as *Luceafărul*, *Flacăra*, or *Săptămâna*. The fact that Dan Hăulică was a complicated character is demonstrated by an episode in the '80s: laid off under the almighty Elena Ceaușescu's order, he was given his job back in no time. The question that will never find the answer to is who was so influential, well into Ceaușescu's "reign," to undo the decision of "the people's most beloved daughter"?!

Even after 1990, Dan Hăulică has not excelled in supporting open society either. His name does not appear on any of the lists of reformist intellectuals of the 90s, although he was invited every time to join various activities directed against the neo-communist regime. Might that have had to do with the fact that his first important position, at less than thirty years old, was that of head of the arts department of the Communist Party's journal, *Scânteia*?

He was further promoted to head of a publication whose explicit role was to provide foreign countries with the image of a Romania that was open to dialogue, appreciated, and promoted values and liberties. It is not by sheer accident that, after 1990, both Papu and Hăulică received accolades from the *România Mare* magazine, the upgraded version of *Săptămâna*, the bastion of basic, aggressive nationalism and hateful chauvinism.

This is why articles that seemed merely obedient pieces, like others frequently published by the journal, like Papu's texts, had such an outrageous effect. Coincidentally or not, starting in 1977 (which was marked by two events of capital importance: the earthquake of March 4 and the uprising of the miners in the Jiu Valley, in August), the protochronist campaign took off strong. The disaster the earthquake produced tested the administration's ability to react under extremely dramatic circumstances, and the failure was evident. The miners' strike tested the regime's openness to dialogue, and the outcome was, once more, disastrous. To Vladimir Tismăneanu, proto-chronism represented the very "basis of Ceaușescu's nationalist tyranny."[17] In this context, the decision to strengthen the country's isolation process and to repress inconvenient opinions, which opposed the Great Leader's, became a priority.

Ethnocentrism, isolationism, xenophobia, the "fortress under siege" mentality, nationalism, and anti-Europeanism were commandments that gathered a quite diverse group of followers. It included nostalgia for the interwar Far Right (Ion Coja, Dan Zamfirescu), zealous executors of party orders (Ilie Bădescu, Paul Anghel, Pompiliu Marcea, Ilie Purcaru, M. Ungheanu, etc.), ruthless self-promoters like Corneliu Vadim Tudor, Eugen Barbu, and Adrian Păunescu, as well as a new generation of literary critics such as Artur Silvestri, Constantin Sorescu, Adrian Dinu Rachieru, and Dan Ciachir, eager to occupy dominant positions by ruthlessly attacking the Western-oriented trend in Romanian culture. It did also benefit from the discreet, yet massive, support of a journal like *Secolul 20*, which seemed rather devoted to Lovinescu's synchronism.

Protochronism proved to be an excellent vehicle for both the justice-seeking aspirations of an ignored culture and Nicolae Ceaușescu's personal delusions of grandeur. Starting in 1975–1976, *Secolul 20* took on the mission of publishing, almost every issue, articles and groups of texts with titles such

---

[17]   Vladimir Tismăneanu, *Stalinism for All Seasons* (Berkeley: University of California Press, 2003), 353.

as "The Revelation of Romanian Genius," "Romanian Humanist Traditions on European Roads," "The Getian Utopia," etc. The situation was strange. Paradoxically, the entire party apparatus wanted to simultaneously prove that Romanians were everyone's forebears while also severing all of the country's communication with the outside world. The desire expressed by one of the radical supporters of protochronism to promote "a new universal mission of the Romanian creative genius, to match the amplitude of contemporary history"[18] was totally ludicrous. Such texts, which appeared to address the outside world, in fact targeted the country itself. The population had to be proud of the prominent part it played in the world, despite the fact that not even leftist Western publications were permissible any longer.

The truly deplorable aspect of all of this is that Papu continued to fulfill the role he had been assigned even after Ceauşescu's disappearance. The fall was all the more shameful as the eulogies were no longer for classical writers and artists like Neagoe Basarab, Cantemir, Negruzzi, Creangă, Caragiale, and Brâncuşi, but for Ceauşescu's zealot, Corneliu Vadim Tudor.[19] The end of the story is filled with bitter irony. Eventually, Papu found himself deprived of his best known creation. Ceauşescu's claim to be the true author of the protochronist theory puts us in a perfectly Borges-like position. Romania is not only the native country of protochronism, but also that of protochronism before protochronism…

Beyond all that, the protochronist aberration should again cause alarm now, when nationalist discourses, resentful and frustrated, are gaining ground once more. Despite the warnings of Horia-Roman Patapievici and other intellectuals who have been accused of supporting dialogue, not even today, in 2018, in a democratic society, is a reasoned public debate much better off than forty years ago. Structurally, morphologically, and rhetorically, we still live in a closed society, dominated by the paranoid monologue of neo-communist ideology avatars, intensely, hysterically, and brutally supported by state institutions.

---

[18] George Arion, "Suntem printre cei care aşază pietrele de temelie," interview with Dan Zamfirescu, *Flacăra*, no. 15 (1977): 9.

[19] See *România Mare*, no. 23 (1990).

THE ROAD TO LIBERATION THEOLOGY

Experiments at the Intersection of Confessional and Secular Religion

Piotr H. Kosicki

Any study of communist experiments implies a certain engagement with the long-standing thesis that communism has historically, to varying degrees in different contexts, represented a "secular religion."[1] Understood as laboratories of political anthropology, communist ideologies, regimes, and systems have carried religious undertones even without crossing over into the transcendental, theistic realm. Rather, it is communism's secular promise of salvation—what theologians call a soteriology, or salvation doctrine—that led to its memorable encapsulation as "the god that failed."[2]

The goal of this chapter is to explore the non-secular variety of experimentation connected to communism in the twentieth century. I propose that, for a moment, we put aside the thesis of secular or political religion, returning instead to traditionally conceived confessional religion—and to the transcendental realm.

For scholars of the communist world, Roman Catholicism was long reducible to either a repressed "Church of silence" or a heroic "resistance Church." John Paul II, the pope (and, since 2014, officially a saint) from behind the Iron Curtain, became the embodiment of the latter narrative.[3] But the fact of the matter is that Roman Catholicism has historically shared far greater spaces of overlap and affinity with variously defined socialism,

---

[1] See Emilio Gentile and Robert Mallett, "The Sacralization of Politics: Definitions, Interpretations, and Reflections on the Question of Secular Religion and Totalitarianism," *Totalitarian Movements and Political Religions* 1, no. 1 (2000): 18–55; Vladimir Tismaneanu, *The Devil in History: Communism, Fascism, and Some Lessons of the Twentieth Century* (Berkeley: University of California Press, 2012).

[2] Richard H. Crossman, ed., *The God that Failed* (New York: Columbia University Press, 2001).

[3] For a critical account of these concepts, see for example Piotr H. Kosicki, "Introduction," in *Vatican II behind the Iron Curtain*, ed. Piotr H. Kosicki (Washington, DC: Catholic University of America Press, 2016), 1–26. On John Paul II, George Weigel, *Witness to Hope: The Biography of John Paul II* (New York: HarperCollins, 2005).

Marxism, and communism than immediately meets the eye. Conceived as intellectual and social projects, communism in particular shared with Catholicism, especially in the twentieth century, certain goals of building a just society on earth. The idea of social solidarity was common to both, though of course it manifested in different ways. Communists believed in solidarity internal to a given class (hence the dictatorship of the proletariat), which was to enable the ultimate pivot to universal freedom and a classless society. Meanwhile, Catholic social theorists advocated collective action across class lines: solidarity in secular affairs was to pave the way toward salvation in the afterlife.[4]

Without presuming to seek parallels between Catholic ideas of eternity and Marxist ideas of the leap to freedom, we can nonetheless recover a rich empirical story of Catholic experimentation with socialism, Marxism, and communism spanning the nineteenth and twentieth centuries. Some commentators have even argued, in reference to Pope Francis's various pronouncements, that this story has yet to reach its conclusion, even as we enter the third decade of the twenty-first century.[5]

This chapter is structured around three concepts, which offer at once an empirical and a heuristic account of Catholicism's significance for the history of communist experiments. This is but a small slice of a much richer account that can be given of the spaces of overlap and contestation between confessional and secular religion in the history of communism. The first concept is Catholic social teaching; the second, Catholic socialism; and the third, liberation theology.

Catholic social teaching emerged in the nineteenth century in direct opposition to the rise of revolutionary socialism—especially its Marxist variant. And yet Marx's brother-in-arms in the International Workingmen's Association, Ferdinand Lassalle, carried on a rich correspondence with mid-nineteenth-century Mainz bishop Wilhelm Emmanuel von Ketteler. Lassalle and Ketteler's exchanges do not, on their own, explain how the Catholic

---

[4] On Marxism and communism see for example Andrzej Walicki, *Marxism and the Leap to the Kingdom of Freedom: The Rise and Fall of the Communist Utopia* (Stanford, CA: Stanford University Press, 1995). On Catholicism see for example Paul Misner, *Social Catholicism in Europe: From the Onset of Industrialization to the First World War* (New York: Crossroad, 1991); Józef Tischner, *The Spirit of Solidarity*, trans. Marek B. Zaleski and Benjamin Fiore (San Francisco: Harper & Row, 1984).

[5] See for example Andrea Tornielli and Giacomo Galeazzi, *This Economy Kills: Pope Francis on Capitalism and Social Justice*, trans. Demetrio S. Yocum (Collegeville, MN: Liturgical Press, 2015).

Church began to compete with and contest the secular discursive space of "revolution." In 1891, however, Pope Leo XIII gave the Vatican's imprimatur to these conversations, reframing the competition for the souls of Europe's working classes in a way that made clear that socialism was Catholicism's antagonist.[6]

That said, by the time that Leo XIII handed down the famous encyclical *Rerum Novarum* (Of New Things), Catholic social teaching already existed as a long-standing, if diffuse, discursive tradition among Catholic social and political theorists. In fact, it was neither the International Workingmen's Association nor the Second International that first inspired Catholic engagement with socialism. Utopian socialists and Marxists alike sought to appropriate the legacies of the French Revolution and of the Peoples' Spring of 1848, and the Catholic Church—anathema as "revolution" was to its leadership—found throughout the nineteenth century that its theorists consistently prevented socialists from monopolizing the secular pursuit of a just society. Therein lie the origins of the second major concept under consideration in this chapter: Catholic socialism. This is a concept that I have explored at length in my 2018 book *Catholics on the Barricades*.[7]

But the story of Catholic socialism as I have previously reconstructed it for the mid-twentieth century has roots in the early-to-mid-nineteenth century. Already in the decades following the French Revolution, with Catholic political thought fracturing along a wide spectrum from the ultramontane monarchism of Joseph de Maistre to the radical utopianism of Henri de Saint-Simon, it was Saint-Simon who first experimented with the possibility of marrying Christian theology with a communitarian program for reorganizing secular society. His basic precept was that "men should treat one another as brothers; this principle carries within itself all that is divine

---

[6]   See Wilhelm Emmanuel von Ketteler, "The Working Class and Christianity" (1864), in *The Social Teachings of Wilhelm Emmanuel von Ketteler: Bishop of Mainz (1811–1867)*, trans. Rupert J. Ederer (Washington, DC: University Press of America, 1981). On Lassalle and Ketteler's mutual fascination and influence, see Franklin A. Walker, "Bishop Ketteler and Ferdinand Lassalle," *CCHA Study Sessions* 34 (1967): 47–56; Francesco Saverio Nitti, *Le Socialisme catholique* (Paris: Guillaumin, 1894), 370. On Leo XIII and *Rerum Novarum*, see for example George Weigel and Robert Royal, eds., *A Century of Catholic Social Thought: Essays on "Rerum Novarum" and Nine Other Key Documents* (Washington, DC: Ethics and Public Policy Center/University Press of America, 1991).

[7]   Piotr H. Kosicki, *Catholics on the Barricades: Poland, France, and "Revolution," 1891–1956* (New Haven, CT: Yale University Press, 2018).

within the Christian religion."[8] Saint-Simon's "New Christianity" never actually became the basis for any real secular political project, but his legacy permeated widely across modern European political and social thought.

In fact, throughout the successive revolutions that defined nineteenth-century France, the idea of marrying Christianity and socialism returned again and again. Well before his rise to national prominence in the context of the short-lived Second Republic launched in February 1848, Philippe Buchez, briefly president of the Constituent National Assembly, likewise proposed a "Christian socialism." Buchez's concept presupposed the utopian reorganization of human society around a classless vision of cooperative political economy—with a modicum of acceptance for republican government, predicated on state guarantees of basic social welfare.[9] While Saint-Simon's radicalism had led him to abandon religious orthodoxy, Buchez insisted on keeping Catholicism's doctrine of eternal salvation front and center in his vision for reorganizing secular society. In his words, "Many principles, including the most important that revolution has to offer, lose their meaning if they are not explained in reference to Christianity."[10] Buchez married a distinctly transcendental salvation doctrine to a communitarian vision of social ethics to be fulfilled in the secular realm.

What drove both Saint-Simon and Buchez was the experience of watching both France and Europe writ large industrialize at a breath-taking rate. Social and political unrest went hand in hand as old models of political economy fell away, rendered anachronistic by industrial capitalism. Both thinkers were responding to the Industrial Revolution, yet neither was able to rise above theories best suited to small-scale communal life—in effect, proposing escape routes from macro-level industrial society, rather than a means for living and dealing with its challenges on an ongoing basis. Perhaps this is because the Industrial Revolution was still a relatively new phenomenon in their day.

---

[8]   Quoted in Klauspeter Blaser, "Le christianisme social avant le socialisme chrétien," *Autres Temps* 61 (1999): 79–89, 79. On de Maistre's place in the history of ultramontanism, see Émile Perreau-Saussine, *Catholicism and Democracy: An Essay in the History of Political Thought*, trans. Richard Rex (Princeton, NJ: Princeton University Press, 2012), 13–36; on Saint-Simon, see Pierre Musso, "Religion and Political Economy in Saint-Simon," *European Journal of the History of Economic Thought* 24, no. 4 (2017): 809–27.

[9]   See especially Buchez, *Essai d'un traité complet de philosophie du point de vue du catholicisme et du progrès social* (Paris: E. Éveillard, 1838–1840), 3 vols.; Jean-Baptiste Duroselle, *Les débuts du catholicisme social en France (1820–1870)* (Paris: PUF, 1951).

[10] P.J.B. Buchez, *Traité de politique et de science sociale* (Paris: Amyot, 1866), II, 528.

Fundamentally, the promiscuous marriage of Catholicism and socialism was a product of the arrival of the second wave of the Industrial Revolution in Europe.[11] Like industrialization itself, the cross-pollination of confessional and secular faith was chronologically and geographically differential across the European continent. Seen teleologically from the standpoint of the twentieth century, in a world reckoning with the Bolshevik Revolution, the Red Army, and Joseph Stalin, Catholic socialism would become a matter of Catholics growing accustomed to following the lead of socialists. At their best, these twentieth-century radical Catholics would attempt to reformulate a socialist idiom in a way that would enable the Catholic Church to "catch up" to Europe's revolutionary vanguard.

Yet, in the late nineteenth century, the situation in fact looked completely different. If we forego all teleology, we see in fact that the origins of the hybrid grammar of Catholic socialism lay in certain projects of Catholics seeking, from a position of strength, to incorporate socialist gains into their own social and political theory. In other words, late-nineteenth-century Catholics believed themselves to be fundamentally in the right because of their salvation doctrine, and they sought to appropriate for themselves the best of what was working for the new radical experiments resulting from the Industrial Revolution—including revolutionary socialism, and specifically Marxism. The guiding premise was that "there was an identification between the progress of the [C]hurch and the welfare of the proletariat."[12]

Much ink has been spilled detailing the Austrian political movement known as Christian Socialism, whose leader Karl Lueger was perhaps one of *fin-de-siècle* Europe's best-known anti-Semites. Yet despite painting international socialism as the purview of a Jewish conspiracy fundamentally inimical to the Catholic Church, Lueger warmly embraced "municipal socialism," seeking to cater to the everyday material needs of Vienna's working classes just as the Catholic hierarchy attended to their spiritual needs.[13] The Austrian case of Catholicism's marriage with socialism was unique in the intensity of its predication on an exclusionary nationalism, but

---

[11] On cross-denominational projects of marrying Christianity and Socialism—which exploded in number in late-Victorian England, roughly contemporaneously with continental Catholic socialism—see Peter d'Alroy Jones, *The Christian Socialist Revival, 1877–1914: Religion, Class, and Social Conscience in Late-Victorian England* (Princeton, NJ: Princeton University Press, 1968).

[12] Walker, "Bishop Ketteler and Ferdinand Lassalle," 51.

[13] John Boyer, *Culture and Political Crisis in Vienna: Christian Socialism in Power, 1897–1918* (Chicago: University of Chicago Press, 1995), 6.

its success hints at a much larger, transnational conversation taking place outside German-language Europe—most notably, in the French and Italian languages.

For example, the Italian economist Francesco Saverio Nitti and the Dominican friar Antonin-Dalmace Sertillanges, writing in the 1890s and the early 1900s, laid the foundations of a transnational Catholic socialism. There was a profound tension to this program. On the one hand, *fin-de-siècle* Catholics were responding to Pope Leo XIII's formal 1891 call for a Catholic social teaching, granting that socialism was the Church's antagonist. And yet, at the same time, they intended to draw on the best of what socialism had to offer as they dealt with the exigencies of political economy in an industrializing world. Nitti explained, "the socialist ideal manifests certain essential affinities with the Christian ideal, if not in its entirety than at least to a substantial degree."[14]

Paradoxically, one of the results of *Rerum Novarum*'s declaration of war on socialism was a program that Nitti, Sertillanges, and others described as Catholic socialism. The word "Catholic" was the modifier here, not the subject, yet the assumption underlying Catholic socialism was that Catholics alone possessed the moral and spiritual authority to absorb secular lessons from social theory and political economy, without derailing the mission of the Church. The implication, then, was that socialism, too, had morality on its side (to a degree). As Nitti put it, "Whether or not socialist systems are false, contradictory, or utopian, the morality of socialism is very much superior to that of its adversaries."[15] This lesson proved extremely important also for Eastern Europe following the Bolshevik ascendancy.

We now move on to our third and final conceptual frame: liberation theology. It is crucial to note that, unlike Catholic social teaching or Catholic socialism, the noun "theology" implies a qualitatively new, radical break in Catholics' willingness to countenance the secular experiments of communism. "Theology," after all, does not describe everything that relates to religious thought.[16] Rather, theology is a set of conclusions derived from revealed truth. The very foundation of theology is that transcendental truth

[14] Nitti, *Socialisme catholique*, 24; Antonin-Dalmace Sertillanges, *Socialisme et christianisme* (Paris: V. Lecoffre, 1905).

[15] Nitti, *Socialisme catholique*, vi.

[16] For a contrasting view, see for example Gerd-Rainer Horn, *Western European Liberation Theology: The First Wave (1924–1959)* (Oxford: Oxford University Press, 2008).

has been revealed. And so, theology *cannot* be secular. Theology cannot be simply a matter of understanding concepts connected to God in a secular context. The vocabulary of "political theology" that we associate with Carl Schmitt has challenged, distorted, and marred this fundamental grammatical premise of theology as a discipline connected to revealed truth.[17]

The fact of the matter is that, once we move past "-isms" and instead start talking about theology, we have moved beyond politics. Therein lies the fundamental point of this chapter: by the mid-point of the twentieth century, experiments in the hybridization of Catholicism and Marxism that had begun a century earlier—in some sense, *avant la lettre*, even before Marx gained fame with *The Communist Manifesto* and his subsequent writings—had surpassed the secular realm and entered the realm of theology. After the Russian Revolutions of 1917, the long-standing secular project of Christian (Catholic) socialism became intertwined with a transcendental, confessional agenda.

This, in some sense, is the true paradox: that secular religion has never really broken free of the confessional. (*This* is the wisdom of Schmitt's political theology, not that theology carries lessons for politics or that politics becomes the foundation of theology.)[18] In other words, if one scratches deep enough beneath the surface in the study of secular religion—in this case, in the study of communism and its resultant political experiments—one finds also an actual pretense of non-secular, transcendental revealed truth. I am not speaking here about the cult of personality surrounding Joseph Stalin, Mao Zedong, or other communist national leaders. Rather, I am talking about the idea that the secular and the transcendental take on a unique value when fused together.

And so, the question returns—why liberation theology? Marx's basic assumption of the need for a leap to the kingdom of freedom, seen from the standpoint of Catholic theologians in the 1930s and 1940s, made sense.

---

[17] See for example the important interpretation offered by Hans Blumenberg, *The Legitimacy of the Modern Age*, trans. Robert M. Wallace (Cambridge, MA: MIT Press, 1985), 92–93. See also Matilda Arvidsson, "From Teleology to Eschatology: The *Katechon* and the Political Theology of the International Law of Belligerent Occupation," in *The Contemporary Relevance of Carl Schmitt: Law, Politics, Theology*, eds. Matilda Arvidsson, Leila Brännström, and Panu Minkkinen (London: Routledge, 2016), 223–36.

[18] The key point of reference is Schmitt's much-quoted line: "All significant concepts of the modern theory of the state are secularized theological concepts." Carl Schmitt, *Political Theology: Four Chapters on the Concept of Sovereignty*, trans. George Schwab (Cambridge, MA: MIT Press, 1985), 36.

Radical Dominican and Jesuit thinkers like Marie-Dominique Chenu, Yves Congar, or Henri de Lubac worried about the ongoing attrition of Catholic faithful who, simply put, believed that the Church was no longer capable of catering to their needs. In Congar's words, "As long as we talk about Marxism and Bolshevism in Latin, as I've seen it done in classes and at conferences of theologians, Lenin can sleep in peace in his Moscow mausoleum."[19] For Catholics, the alternative was to take Marx seriously, because the empirical reality of class struggle needed to be taken seriously.

Some of the most radical mid-century clergy simply read Marx and Lenin, while others went out and joined the ranks of the industrial proletariat—creating the so-called "worker-priest" experiment that became infamous in the 1930s and 1940s in France and Belgium. The Dominican priest (and dock-worker) Jacques Loew argued in the late 1940s that workers could hardly be expected to remain loyal to a Church that had abandoned them in their daily lives. And so, "This is our first task: we must come to the people not primarily as priests, not primarily as Christians, nor even as brothers and friends: our primary task is to live amongst them and win their acceptance as men."[20]

To recapitulate—a newly secular political ideology emerged in the late nineteenth century: one that was Catholic but drew on socialism in its various forms as well. Following the success of the Bolshevik Revolution and the spread of communist influence across the European continent, that ideology began to take on the sheen of theology, but without actually proposing transcendental truth. In other words, that theological sheen was predicated on the confusion of two separate ideas, representing two distinct domains of human society. One has to do with political economy; the other, with claims about the ability to save souls, in other words, a salvation doctrine.

For the Catholic Church, the underlying goal was evangelization, just as it always had been. What that meant in practice was seeking to go out and convert—to help others to see the light of Christ. The proper domain of evangelization was pastoral activity: the task of clergy and laity alike—of all believing Catholics—was to help others to find ways to believe. If we look at the worker-priests, if we look at the Dominican and Jesuit theologians reading Marx and Lenin in the 1930s, upon whom the Vatican began to frown

---

[19] Quoted in Jürgen Mettepenningen, *Nouvelle théologie—New Theology: Inheritor of Modernism, Precursor of Vatican II* (New York: T&T Clark, 2010), 44; see also Kosicki, *Catholics on the Barricades*, 193–94.

[20] M.R. (Jacques) Loew, *Mission to the Poorest*, trans. Pamela Carswell (New York: Sheed and Ward, 1950), 70; see also Kosicki, *Catholics on the Barricades*, 189.

severely—what all of these men were trying to do was to find new pastoral fodder for reconnecting in the secular realm with the working masses alienated from the direct experience of contact with the Catholic Church as an earthly institution. What this *did not* imply was the reformulation of Christianity in a Marxist idiom. What it *did* imply was the exploration of what had worked sociologically for Marxists, followed by the translation of those sociological lessons into a Catholic idiom—in other words, into a Catholic socialism.[21]

The danger lay in the belief that certain Catholic theologians reached in the 1940s and 1950s that, in fact, Marxism had a legitimate and essential contribution to make to Catholic theology. Two different paths opened up. The difference was determined first and foremost by the outcomes of World War II, specifically, by whether or not the Catholic thinkers in question found themselves living in territories occupied by the Red Army.

Behind the nascent Iron Curtain, a young generation of Catholic philosophers, journalists, and essayists had come of age during World War II and were trying to find their way through university and into professional life just as Eastern Europe was passing from the popular-front phase of fledgling communist regimes into full-blown Stalinism. Among others, the young Polish Catholic activists Janusz Zabłocki, Tadeusz Myślik, Wojciech Wieczorek, and—the best-known today from among this group, for his eventual turn to dissidence and his rise to the office of Poland's prime minister in 1989—Tadeusz Mazowiecki, argued that the young Karl Marx's 1850s writings about personhood held the key to making Catholicism relevant to the new social reality arising behind the Iron Curtain in the 1950s.[22] These young men did not go so far as to argue that Christ should be understood in a different light, but they did claim that Catholic evangelization should change, and that the Catholic vision of a just society should change, too. In 1950, the twenty-three-year-old Mazowiecki insisted that it was the task of reframing personhood—in Catholic theology, the key to understanding human beings as being made in God's Image—around "the content of socialist revolution that ought to endow Catholic thought with its proper form."[23] In other words,

---

[21] For another approach to mid-century Catholic socialisms—especially in the work of Austrian thinker Ernst Karl Winter—see James Chappel, *Catholic Modern: The Challenge of Totalitarianism and the Remaking of the Church* (Cambridge, MA: Harvard University Press, 2018), 123–32.

[22] For a fuller explanation, see Kosicki, *Catholics on the Barricades*, 249–56.

[23] Quoted in Kosicki, *Catholics on the Barricades*, 252. On Marx's understanding of personhood, see Warren Breckman, *Marx, the Young Hegelians, and the Origins of Radical Social Theory: Dethroning the Self* (New York: Cambridge University Press, 1999), 66–75.

in the secular realm, communist Poland's young Catholic socialists insisted that all Catholics should follow the lead of Marxists.

This was distinctly different from what Catholic radicals in Western Europe were proposing at mid-century. What the Dominican and Jesuit "new theologians," for example, were proposing was a pastoral, not a political project: the goal was—as it always had been—to save souls through the Catholic faith, not to "correct" Catholicism's errors with Marxism. The next generation of Western Europe-trained theologians, however—born, like Mazowiecki's Eastern Europe-educated generation of postwar Catholic socialists, in the 1920s and 1930s—broke dramatically with their elders. Especially for those trained by Western Europe's faculties of Catholic theology—in Fribourg, in Louvain, or in Munich—many of this generation crossed the line from Catholic socialism into liberation theology.

In mainstream scholarship, even among specialists on Catholic affairs, the phrase "liberation theology" is often synonymous with a particular Latin American school of thought.[24] Iconic is the Peruvian Dominican Gustavo Gutiérrez's 1973 pronouncement,

> In Latin America the world in which the Christian community must live and celebrate its eschatological hope is the world of social revolution; the Church's task must be defined in relation to this. Its fidelity to the Gospel leaves it no alternative: the Church must be the visible sign of the presence of the Lord within the aspiration for liberation and the struggle for a more human and just society.

Gutiérrez was hardly the only voice of liberation theology—which even Latin American bishops appeared to endorse in its fledgling stages—but his advocacy of social revolution like none other blended Western Europe's pastoral radicalism with the belief that Latin American social problems demanded a theological, rather than a purely social, solution. Unlike his icons Congar and Chenu, Gutiérrez dismissed the line between secular and confessional religion, insisting that "the Church must allow itself to be inhabited and evangelized by the world."[25]

---

[24] See for example Christian Smith, *The Emergence of Liberation Theology: Radical Religion and Social Movement Theory* (Chicago: University of Chicago Press, 1991).

[25] Gustavo Gutiérrez, *A Theology of Liberation: History, Politics, and Salvation*, trans. Caridad Inda and John Eagleson (Maryknoll, NY: Orbis Books, 1973), 262, 261.

Borrowing from Hegel, Marx, and twentieth-century Western Marxists like Louis Althusser, the Peruvian friar insisted that, in the face of post-colonial modernity, Christian love must embrace class struggle. In Gutiérrez's words, "love does not mean that the oppressors are no longer enemies, nor does it eliminate the radicalness of the combat against them." In the end, a theological recognition of class struggle was to enable the Catholic Church "to discover the path by which it can free itself from that which now prevents it from being a clear and true sign of brotherhood."[26] Gutiérrez's aim was nothing less than a "new understanding of the mission of the Church," predicated on the joining of Catholic salvation doctrine with a secular ideology of revolution: "the Church must cease considering itself as the exclusive place of salvation and orient itself towards a new and radical service of people." In this new reality, "owners of the goods of this world would no longer be the 'owners' of the Gospel."[27]

A decade after the publication of Gutiérrez's landmark *A Theology of Liberation* (1973), the Vatican of Pope John Paul II came down hard on the full range of Latin American liberation theology. Joseph Cardinal Ratzinger—the Polish pope's enforcer of theological orthodoxy, himself ultimately destined to be become Pope Benedict XVI—issued in 1984 an "Instruction on Certain Aspects of the Theology of Liberation." Published in Ratzinger's own name in his capacity as prefect of the Vatican's Congregation for the Doctrine of the Faith, the instruction nonetheless carried the personal approval of John Paul II, and it did not mince words about liberation theology: "This system is a perversion of the Christian message as God entrusted it to His church," insofar as it "subordinates theology to the class struggle."[28] Although some, like Brazilian theologian Leonardo Boff, left the priesthood in response to Ratzinger's criticism, the Vatican's challenge never rose to the level of anathema or excommunication. As late as 2015, Gutiérrez still demurred, "Was it a very critical conversation? Yes. But there was never a condemnation."[29]

---

[26] Gutiérrez, *A Theology of Liberation*, 276, 278.

[27] Gutiérrez, *A Theology of Liberation*, 255, 256, 271. On liberation theology's revisions to Catholic soteriology, see for example Daniel M. Bell, Jr., *Liberation Theology after the End of History: The Refusal to Cease Suffering* (London: Routledge, 2001), 51–65.

[28] Quoted in John L. Allen, Jr., *Pope Benedict XVI: A Biography of Joseph Ratzinger* (New York: Continuum, 2000), 157.

[29] "Vatican never condemned liberation theology, Gustavo Gutiérrez insists," *Catholic Culture. org*, May 12, 2015, https://www.catholicculture.org/news/headlines/index.cfm?storyid=24898. One of Boff's key writings to attract Roman ire is Leonardo Boff, *Jesus Christ Liberator: A Critical Christology for Our Time*, trans. Patrick Hughes (Maryknoll, NY: Orbis Books, 1978).

In effect, however, the Latin American experiments criticized in the early years of John Paul II's papacy were but one part of a global story of Catholicism's *theological* encounter with communism. The Latin American *avant-garde* movement of the 1960s, 1970s, and early 1980s would actually conclude that, in light of Marxism, Catholics had no choice but to reform theology. This was not the same as following the worker-priests or Western European new theologians in learning socialist lessons about how to reach the poor. Rather, liberation theology represented a shift in how Catholics should conceive of the poor's position in Christian salvation doctrine. Its exponents, in other words, called for a new ecclesiology—a new understanding of the dogmatic composition and constitution of the Church—rooted in the assumption that the secular poor were also transcendentally closest to God.

Seen from the standpoint of the Gospels, this might sound like nothing new. After all, Matthew 19:24 records Jesus' famous quip that "it is easier for a camel to go through the eye of a needle than for a rich person to enter the Kingdom of God!" In a 1905 essay, none other than the socialist revolutionary Rosa Luxemburg claimed that socialists were closer to Christ than the Catholic hierarchy because socialists actually treated the poor as the holiest social class. Meanwhile, in the early 1900s, the Catholic Church—busy advocating for cross-class solidarity in order to defuse revolutionary tensions—explained the line from Matthew as an ethical exhortation to charitable living, rather than a theological privileging of the poor over all others. This is why Francesco Saverio Nitti could write, "The Church itself has recently admitted that the ideal society imagined by socialists in many respects resembles the Kingdom of Heaven established by Jesus Christ."[30]

Liberation theology, especially its Latin American variants, ultimately faced criticism from the Holy See precisely because its exponents tended to assume that a new vision of political economy required a modification of salvation doctrine. From the standpoint of Rome, this move risked open heresy—and an attempt to reformulate Catholic theology in terms of Marxist political economy.

***

---

[30] Nitti, *Socialisme catholique*, 24–25. For Luxemburg's reflections on Matthew 19:24, see Rosa Luxemburg, "Socialism and the Churches" (1905), *Marxists.org*, https://www.marxists.org/archive/luxemburg/1905/misc/socialism-churches.htm.

The road traveled in this chapter has, in fact, been full of twists and turns. First of all, we saw that the role of Roman Catholicism in communist political experiments in fact considerably predates the very emergence of the vocabulary of communism. Even before Karl Marx's mid-nineteenth-century rise to fame, Henri de Saint-Simon and Philippe Buchez pursued utopian communitarianism in the name of "Christian socialism." The progress of industrialization in Europe over the course of the nineteenth century changed the conditions of possibility for the cross-fertilization of Catholicism and socialism, translating what began as a hybridization of utopian socialism with Catholic salvation doctrine into an actual vision for political economy in an industrialized world.

Then, following the success of the Bolshevik Revolution and the creation of the Soviet Union, the terms of the story changed dramatically. What had been a secular ideology espoused by some Catholics evolved slowly, step by step, into two separate projects. On the one hand, to the east of the Iron Curtain, the young Catholic revolutionaries of the Stalinist Soviet Bloc sought a justification for Catholicism conceived in Marxist terms; what they demanded was the revision of Catholic understandings of political economy and a just society. To the west of the Iron Curtain, meanwhile, liberation theology began to take off when lessons about not just a preferential option for the poor but in fact the greater holiness of the poor and an attendant need for revolution to achieve their salvation changed the terms of Roman Catholicism's confrontation with communism.

By the 1970s and 1980s, what had been mere experiments at marrying Catholicism and Marxism in the secular realm evolved into a theology that the Vatican felt the need to target—most notably, with Joseph Cardinal Ratzinger of the Congregation of the Doctrine of the Faith inveighing against Latin American theologians like the Brazilian Leonardo Boff and the Peruvian Gustavo Gutiérrez. As John Paul II's friend and confidant Maciej Zięba put it, "from the outset of his pontificate he clearly opposed a horizontal reading of the Scripture, a replacement of the Christ of the Gospels by Christ-with-a-Machine-Gun, Christ-the-Revolutionary, Christ-the-first-Socialist, and took a stand against the location of a Third or Fourth Rome in Havana or Moscow."[31] In the mind of John Paul II, liberation in Catholic theology stood

---

[31] Maciej Zięba, *The Surprising Pope: Understanding the Thought of John Paul II*, trans. Karolina Weening (Lanham, MD: Lexington Books, 2000), 17.

not for secular empowerment of the poor through violent revolution, but instead for liberation from "structures of sin."

This story points to several larger lessons:

- First, even in the study of secular religion, confessional religion also has an important role to play that must not be neglected;

- Second, Roman Catholicism has shared spaces of intellectual and political overlap with socialism in its various forms, and especially communism in its political experimentation, over the course of the nineteenth and twentieth centuries;

- Third, communist political experiments resulted in a degree of confusion within Catholic philosophy and, by the second half of the twentieth century, Catholic theology as well—namely, a confusion of political, fundamentally secular aims with their pastoral, fundamentally transcendental counterparts.

Ministering to humankind, enlarging the community of Catholic faithful in order to achieve humankind's salvation—that was the purpose of the Catholic Church, and the logical extension of Catholic salvation doctrine. The sociological reformulation of political economy worldwide following the twentieth-century ascendancy of communist regimes—whether in the Soviet Union, the People's Republic of China, or the Soviet Bloc—may have changed the way in which radical theologians like Gustavo Gutiérrez understood the social relevance of Catholic social teaching in Latin America, but from the standpoint of the Vatican, Gutiérrez and others crossed a line when they pivoted from a social message to a revisionist soteriology. For this reason, liberation theology—while a logical outgrowth of spaces of contestation and overlap between Catholicism and Marxism spanning the nineteenth and twentieth centuries—went a bridge too far in a world in which communist political experiments in Eastern Europe and elsewhere (China, Cuba, Vietnam) seemed to threaten the very existence and essence of the Church's mission in the world.

John Paul II, to bring our story to a close, represents perhaps the most fascinating case of Catholic experimentation with communism, and I have written about him at length in my book *Catholics on the Barricades*.[32] As a

---

[32] Kosicki, *Catholics on the Barricades*, 198–209, 309–314.

PhD student in the 1940s, he was fascinated by the worker-priest experiment. The then-Karol Wojtyła, future pontiff, sought every means he could to bring salvation to the masses, in order to convert Europe's industrial proletariat. But, for him, this task could never cross the line into revision of core theological precepts.

Between his graduate-student years in the 1940s and the first years of his pontificate in the 1970s and 1980s, when he condemned liberation theology, John Paul II understood two things as having happened. The first was that communist political experiments had threatened the integrity of the Catholic Church and its attendant vision of social justice and political economy in the world. The second was that he had come to distinguish between social theory and pastoral practice on the one hand and, on the other, theology understood as the exclusive domain of revealed truth. Social theory and theology, for John Paul II, needed to remain separate. By the time that Wojtyła became pope, he understood and articulated clearly—in words perhaps more familiar to us from Konrad Adenauer in the 1950s—"No experiments!"[33]

In the end, the brutal truth of Catholicism's place in the history of communist experiments is that, in the beginning as in the end of Catholic experiments with communism, Catholicism and communism shared fundamentally anti-liberal assumptions that never dissipated. And so it was that John Paul II, the pope renowned as a Cold Warrior who helped to bring down the Iron Curtain, already a full seven months *before* the dissolution of the Soviet Union turned his ire from communism to liberalism. For the centennial anniversary of Leo XIII's *Rerum Novarum*—in other words, one hundred years of Catholic social teaching, with its origins in opposition to revolutionary socialism—John Paul II proclaimed the free market and unchecked liberalism to be the greatest threats to humankind's salvation in Christ. In May 1991's *Centesimus Annus*, the Polish pope castigated capitalism, declaring,

> It seeks to defeat Marxism on the level of pure materialism by showing how a free-market society can achieve a greater satisfaction of material human needs than Communism, while equally excluding spiritual values. In reality, while on the one hand it is true that this social model shows the failure of Marxism to contribute to a humane and better society, on the other hand, insofar

---

[33] See for example Hans-Peter Schwarz, *Konrad Adenauer: German Politician and Statesman in a Period of War, Revolution, and Reconstruction*, vol. 2 *The Statesman, 1952–1967*, trans. Geoffrey Penny (Oxford: Berghahn Books, 1997), 275.

as it denies an autonomous existence and value to morality, law, culture and religion, it agrees with Marxism, in the sense that it totally reduces man to the sphere of economics and the satisfaction of material needs.[34]

And so, the coda to this chapter about Catholicism's role in the history of communist experiments is that, in the end, however implicated Catholicism indeed was in those experiments, the Church's leadership has persisted in targeting some of the very same antagonists that gave rise to communism in the first place. Scholars of Eastern Europe should recall that Vladimir Tismaneanu warned us already in the late 1990s that "anti-capitalist and anti-democratic sentiments, including paternalistic, corporatist, and populist nostalgias, could coalesce in new authoritarian experiments."[35] The twenty-first century has, unfortunately, already proven him right. Let us hope, then, that the Catholic Church, at least, can learn this lesson. Otherwise, even the anti-communist John Paul II will have left a dangerous legacy for future generations of Catholics: that, as long as Catholic salvation doctrine remains free of contamination by radical ideology, the Church's authorities can aspire to take the place of the authors of communist experiments.

---

[34] John Paul II, *Centesimus Annus* (May 1, 1991), Vatican.va, http://w2.vatican.va/content/john-paul-ii/en/encyclicals/documents/hf_jp-ii_enc_01051991_centesimus-annus.html.

[35] Vladimir Tismaneanu, *Fantasies of Salvation: Democracy, Nationalism, and Myth in Post-Communist Europe* (Princeton, NJ: Princeton University Press, 1998), 5.

PHILOSOPHICAL LESSONS FROM THE BOLSHEVIK EXPERIMENT

Marci Shore

Prologue

"It appears that certain periods of history quickly become, both for other societies and for those that follow them, the stuff of not especially edifying legend and the occasion for a good deal of hypocritical self-congratulations. If I may be permitted an editorial aside, allow me to say that in my opinion we must be cautious about passing moral judgment upon the Gileadeans. Surely we have learned by now that such judgments are of necessity culture-specific.... Our job is not to censure but to understand."[1]

So ends *The Handmaid's Tale*: no longer in totalitarian Gilead where the handmaid is a reproductive slave, but now two hundred years later at an International Historical Association Convention. It is perhaps not by chance that a new television series, based on Margaret Atwood's 1986 novel, premiered in 2017. One hundred years after the Bolshevik Revolution, we—not unlike the fictional historians of Gilead—are sitting in our conference room.

What have we understood?

"Karl Marx was a German philosopher."

This is the sentence with which Leszek Kołakowski begins *The Main Currents of Marxism*.[2] Kołakowski's statement is not trivial: Marx was a man of ideas, coming from a certain philosophical tradition. And the power of ideas should

---

[1] Margaret Atwood, *The Handmaid's Tale* (Boston: Houghton Mifflin Company, 1986), 302.

[2] Leszek Kołakowski, *Main Currents of Marxism: The Founders, the Golden Age, the Breakdown*, trans. P.S. Fall (New York: Norton, 2006), 5. Tony Judt writes of the epic-length *Main Currents of Marxism*, "It is quite impossible to convey in a short review the astonishing range of Kolakowski's history of Marxist doctrine. It will surely not be superseded: Who will ever again know—or care—enough to go back over this ground in such detail and with such analytical sophistication?" Tony Judt, "Goodbye to All That?" *New York Review of Books*, 21 September 2006.

not be taken lightly. "It was only toward the middle of the 20th century," the Polish poet Czesław Miłosz wrote, "that the inhabitants of many European countries came, in general unpleasantly, to the realization that their fate could be influenced directly by intricate and abstruse books of philosophy."[3]

Marx was not an aberrational lunatic. His ideas did not appear *ex nihilo*; they were—and are—beautifully explicable in the context of the history of European thought. When the philosophers of the Enlightenment relegated God to a minor role, they introduced, knowingly or not, the possibility that eventually God would disappear entirely. God had filled epistemological, ontological, and ethical roles. His disappearance left behind an enormous empty space. Neither the human cognition and reason proposed by Enlightenment thinkers, nor the human passion and will proposed by the Romantics, proved easily able to fill that space. God's marginalization-turned-death gave impetus to a search for a new transcendental signified; History, Human Reason, the Self being among the central contenders. The Enlightenment's shift from a predominantly cyclical to a predominantly linear temporality made possible the historicist chronotope. We were leaving the past behind, moving forward towards a future that opened new possibilities and lifted us upwards onto a higher plane.[4] In the context of these ideas, it was natural that visions of how the world ought to be would be dominated by the tension between the autonomy of human reason and the iron laws of History, between telos and subjectivity, between individual agency and historical determinism.

Liberalism is fragile

Miłosz defected from Stalinist Poland in 1951, and eventually made his home in California. He remained in the United States, even though it was difficult for him to take Americans seriously. They lacked the experiences that would instill a certain understanding: above all, that "[t]he habit of civilization is fragile."[5] Here Miłosz spoke from experience. As a student in the 1930s living between Hitler's Germany and Stalin's Soviet Union, he belonged to a group

---

[3]   Czesław Miłosz, *The Captive Mind*, trans. Jane Zielonko (New York: Vintage International, 1990), 3.

[4]   On the historicist chronotope—and its end, see Hans Ulrich Gumbrecht, *After 1945: Latency as the Origin of the Present* (Stanford: Stanford University Press, 2013).

[5]   Czesław Miłosz, *The Captive Mind*, trans. Jane Zielonko (New York: Vintage International, 1990), 122.

of young catastrophist poets attuned to an ever-darkening Zeitgeist. *"[C]louds white and silent,"* he wrote in 1935, *"I watch you at dawn with eyes full of tears and I know that in me there is haughtiness, lust and cruelty."*[6]

By the mid-1930s Polish democracy had become nationalist authoritarianism; at Polish universities Jewish students were relegated to ghetto benches. A few years later, Miłosz lived through a German invasion and a Soviet invasion of his country; he watched the Holocaust unfold before his eyes; he saw the Warsaw ghetto burn. And he listened as the melody of the carousel on his own "Aryan Side" of the ghetto wall drowned the sounds of bullets and cries of pain. Later he experienced the Warsaw Uprising, the remainder of the city going up in flames, and soon thereafter, the Stalinist takeover of postwar Poland. There was nothing irrational in his youthful foreboding of civilization's collapse.

"Civilization" was a neologism of the Enlightenment. All good things, Enlightenment thinkers believed, were harmonious: reason led to truth; truth led to virtue; virtue led to happiness. Conceived as the antithesis of barbarism, "civilization" suggested a society that had overcome the disorder and brutality of the state of nature. The center of civilization was naturally Paris, where in 1789 French revolutionaries stormed the Bastille and declared The Rights of Man and of the Citizen.

Classical liberalism, seemingly then triumphant, was the politically codified version of Enlightenment rationalism. Based on the consent of the governed, freedom of speech, popular sovereignty, and autonomous subjects possessing natural rights enshrined in a social contract, liberalism assumed a serendipitous harmony of virtue and self-interest.

The Romantics rebelled against the exaltation of reason. For Johann Wolfgang von Goethe, Enlightenment philosophers like Moses Mendelssohn treated beauty the way entomologists treated butterflies. Scientific analysis impoverished feeling. The Enlightenment had taken its concept of the human subject from René Descartes' *cogito ergo sum*: "I think, therefore I am." To the Romantics, the Cartesian *cogito* was a mind with no soul. They countered with *volo ergo sum*: "I desire, therefore I am." Fyodor Dostoevsky's Underground Man articulated the limitations of reason with merciless honesty: "Civilization merely develops man's capacity for a greater variety of sensations,

---

6   Czesław Miłosz, "Obłoki," *Trzy zimy* (Wilno: Związek Zawodowy Literackich Polskich, 1936); "i wiem, że we mnie pycha, pożądanie/i okrucieństwo..."

and ... absolutely nothing else. And, through the development of this capacity, man may yet come to find pleasure in the spilling of blood ... man is
sometimes extremely fond of suffering, to the point of passion, in fact."[7]

Just four years after the storming of the Bastille, the Declaration of the
Rights of Man gave way to the guillotine. The Revolution became the Jacobin
Terror. It was an early lesson in liberalism's fragility.

By the time of the Terror, the revolutionaries should have sensed that
democracy and liberalism were in fact not the same thing. In his Pulitzer
Prize-winning *Fin-de-siècle Vienna: Politics and Culture*, Carl Schorske
reminded us that in the Habsburg Empire, it was precisely as the franchise
expanded that the liberals lost power. Among the three portraits in Schorske's
text is that of Theodor Herzl, a Viennese journalist and a liberal—until 1894
when he was sent as a correspondent to cover the espionage trial of Captain
Alfred Dreyfus in Paris. Dreyfus, a wealthy French Jew and a military officer,
was falsely accused of treason. Modern Zionism was born of Herzl's watching
the mob on the streets in Paris—*Paris, the center of civilization*—shouting
"Death to the Jews!" For Herzl the Dreyfus trial revealed the failure not only
of Jewish emancipation, but also of Enlightenment liberalism.[8] For Hannah
Arendt, the Dreyfus trial revealed still more: the mob, now identified with
"the people," had come onto the historical stage. Arendt located the origins
of Nazism in the German bourgeoisie's secretly delighting in the mob's
irreverence. For the fun of having the curtain pulled on their own hypocrisy,
Arendt describes, the elite "did not at all object to paying a price, the
destruction of civilization."[9]

At the end of his life, the philosopher Edmund Husserl, repressed as a
Jew in Nazi Germany, despaired that Enlightenment rationalism had been
conceived too superficially: in understanding truth as mere scientific facts, in
failing to grapple with the subjectivity of the truth-seeker, we had lost a sense
of the meaning of human existence. Rationality had proven too existentially
thin. This superficial rationality had left us vulnerable to irrationality. And
irrationality had led us into barbarism.[10]

---

[7]   Fyodor Dostoevsky, *Notes from the Underground*, trans. Mirra Ginsburg (New York: Bantam
      Classic, 2005), 22, 34.
[8]   Carl E. Schorske, "Politics in a New Key: An Austrian Trio," *Fin-de-siècle Vienna: Politics and
      Culture* (New York: Vintage Books, 1981): 116–80.
[9]   Hannah Arendt, *The Origins of Totalitarianism* (San Diego: Harcourt Brace and Company,
      1973), 332.
[10] Edmund Husserl, *The Crisis of European Sciences and Transcendental Phenomenology* (Evanston:
      Northwestern University Press, 1970).

Like Enlightenment reason more generally, liberalism has often proven emotionally unfulfilling and inept at cultivating solidarity. It has failed to grasp the power of the instinctual realm, and has ignored a darker, more anguished side of human nature in favor of a stubborn insistence on rationality. Long after his youthful succumbing to fascism and later abandonment of Romania for Paris, the twentieth century Romanian philosopher E. M. Cioran asked, "And what, basically, is the West, what is the great French civilization, the idea of courtesy, other than a boundary that one accepts on account of reason?"[11]

The great problem of modernity is the problem of alienation

Marxism and Freudian psychoanalysis were both responses to the weaknesses of liberalism. Marx saw the causes of this in the fact that under the alleged freedom of capitalism, grotesque inequality, exploitation and alienation reigned. Freud countered that our irrational desires—sexual and aggressive—could be buried in our unconscious but never made to disappear from our deepest selves. These two men, who otherwise agreed on little, shared an understanding that the great problem of modernity was the problem of alienation. Man was unhappy in the modern world. He was unhappy by virtue of estrangement not only from that world, but also from himself.

This was arguably the starting point of modern philosophy: from Hegel, Marx and Freud to Kafka, Lukács, Heidegger, and Arendt: the great problem of European modernity was the problem of alienation. Arguably, the problem began with our inability to ever fully know the world, to ever reach epistemological certitude and truth. For Freud the problem went still deeper: not only could we never fully know the world, but moreover we could never fully know ourselves. The self would always remain hidden from the self; what was deepest and most essential was precisely what was inaccessible to consciousness. ("What have I in common with Jews? I have hardly anything in common with myself," Kafka wrote in January 1914.[12]) The unconscious was filled with what consciousness could not bear to see. This repression was the necessary precondition for civilization, and "every emotional affect, whatever its quality, is transformed by repression into morbid anxiety."[13]

---

[11] Michel Jacob, "Wakefulness and Obsession: An Interview with E.M. Cioran," *Salamagundi* 103 (Summer 1994): 122–45.

[12] Franz Kafka, *The Diaries of Franz Kafka 1914–1923*, ed. Max Brod (New York: Schocken Books, 1965), 11.

[13] Sigmund Freud, "The Uncanny," (1919) trans. Alik Strachey, MIT, http://web.mit.edu/allanmc/

Hannah Arendt blamed Immanuel Kant (whom she loved) for destroying the classical identity of thought and Being and in this way rendering us homeless—hence "the distinctive melancholy" of modern philosophy.[14] Kant left us with a gaping abyss between the *Ding-an-sich* and the world as it appeared to us: the *Ding-an-sich* would forever be beyond the reach of the "*Ich denke.*" And the "*Ich*" in Kant's "*Ich denke*" was existentially thin. "No truly living I can ever emerge from 'I think,'" explained Arendt, "but only an I that is a creation of thought."[15] Kant's epistemological modesty came with a certain fatalism. How could be we ever again be made to feel at one with the world?

Hegel answered this question: alienation had its origins in the sin of individualism. To fail to self-identify with History was to suffer from alienation. Antigone, the philosopher Jay Bernstein argued, played such an enormous role in *Phenomenology of Spirit* because she exemplified the one who did the impermissible: she asserted the individual against the universal and thereby alienated herself from the totality.[16] For Hegel, the ethical was the universal. To separate oneself as Antigone did was both unethical and self-alienating.

Hegel, while unsentimental, did not suffer from Kantian fatalism. On the contrary, he promised the resolution of *Entfremdung* in an ever-restless, edgy-but-dependably-forward-moving *Geist*. "*Das Wahre ist das Ganze,*" he asserted. Only from the perspective of wholeness could we arrive at truth. *Geist*, driven by dialectics onwards and upwards, would eventually bring us to the reconciliation of subject and object, to seamless wholeness. Arendt described *Phenomenology of Spirit* as the last great attempt to (re)unite thought and Being and thereby "reconstitute a world now shattered into pieces."[17]

Hegel satisfied the longing for wholeness, but his resolution lay largely in the realm of the metaphysical. Marx provided concrete illustrations of alienation—and a concrete path to overcoming it: capitalism resulted in a shift from use-value to exchange-value. Mechanization and the assembly line fragmented the process of production. "[T]his fragmention of the object of production necessarily entails the fragmentation of its subject," Georg Lukács

---

www/freud1.pdf, 12; Sigmund Freud, *Civilization and Its Discontents*, trans. James Strachey (New York: W. W. Norton and Company, 1989).

[14] Hannah Arendt, "What Is Existential Philosophy?" *Essays in Understanding 1930–1954*, ed. Jerome Kohn (New York: Schocken Books, 1994), 163–87, quotation 172.

[15] Arendt, "What Is Existential Philosophy?" 169.

[16] See Jay Bernstein's remarkable lecture course on *The Phenomenology of Spirit*, recorded by Todd Kesselman and Scott Shushan; notes by Lucas Ulrich, Sonia Ahsan and Devan Musser: http://www.bernsteintapes.com/hegellist.html

[17] Arendt, "What Is Existential Philosophy?" 164.

explained.[18] The worker was no longer connected to the product of his labor—nor was he any longer connected to his labor itself. "A man's own activity, his own labour," Lukács described, "becomes something objective and independent of him."[19] The person performing the labor sold himself by the hour: "Through the subordination of man to the machine the situation arises in which men are effaced by their labour," Marx explained, ". . .Time is everything, man is nothing; he is at the most the incarnation of time."[20] The worker had become a commodity, an object rather than a subject. His relations with others had been commodified as well, and so—Lukács explained—"a relation between people takes on the character of a thing."[21]

The bourgeoisie, not performing work but rather parasitically exploiting the labor of others, was also alienated from itself. The difference though, Marx explained, was that the bourgeoisie did not mind:

> The property-owning class and the class of the proletariat represent the same human self-alienation. But the former feels at home in this self-alienation and feels itself confirmed by it; it recognises alienation as its own instrument and in it it possesses the semblance of a human existence. The latter feels itself destroyed by this alienation and sees in it its own impotence and the reality of an inhuman existence.[22]

For Freud, too, alienation was universal. It could not be otherwise, for the necessary condition for civilization was the repression of our instincts. This was why civilization would always make us unhappy. Yet there was no other way. The alternative was barbarism. Psychoanalysis could cajole some of the dark contents of the unconscious into consciousness, and in this way alleviate some neurotic symptoms of repression. Success, though—Freud cautioned—could only ever be partial. In essence we were condemned never to fully understand ourselves. We were fated to unhappiness.

For Hegel, in contrast, we were always on the move towards eventual reconciliation. Marx made this much more explicit: eventually the proletariat would come to class consciousness; understand that no one problem could be

---

[18] Georg Lukács, *History and Class Consciousness*, trans. Rodney Livingstone (Cambridge: MIT Press, 2002), 89.

[19] Lukács, *History and Class Consciousness*, 87.

[20] Karl Marx, *The Poverty of Philosophy* (1847) quoted in Lukács, *History and Class Consciousness*, 89.

[21] Lukács, *History and Class Consciousness*, 83.

[22] Karl Marx and Friedrich Engels, *The Holy Family*, quoted in Lukács, *History and Class Consciousness*, 149.

solved without solving them all; unite, rise up and overthrow the bourgeoisie; abolish private property; and ultimately (following a necessarily violent dictatorship of the proletariat) institute a borderless, classless society in which everyone would work according to his ability and receive according to his need. Eventually everything would fall into place; alienation would be forever overcome; and we would live happily ever after.

Hence, the "Hegelian bite," as Miłosz called it.

The Czech philosopher Jan Patočka was just over forty when he watched Stalinism come to power in Czechoslovakia. There were purges and show trials, arrests, torture, executions. There was also tremendous genuine enthusiasm for the new regime. "And so it happened," Milan Kundera described, "that in February 1948 the Communists took power not in bloodshed and violence, but to the cheers of about half the population. And please note: the half that cheered was the more dynamic, the more intelligent, the better half."[23]

Kundera was among those who cheered. Patočka was not—nor was he among those who emigrated, nor was he among those who took great risks to resist. Instead he sat at home, reading philosophy, returning to Hegel and Marx, making notes in his journal. The "February Revolution," he concluded, was based on a misunderstanding: Marxists believed that they had found a solution to the problem of alienation. Yet in fact, Patočka noted in his diary, Marxism failed to solve the problem of alienation. This failure was due not to bad faith, but rather to a misunderstanding: "[Marxism] knows about human alienation, but it imagines this alienation as being of a similar kind and nature as an illness, something that can be cured by technical means. That a person can be without it. That alienation is an 'imperfection' in the sense of 'not-yet-perfectedness.'"[24] Patočka grasped the error: Marx had understood alienation to be a worldly, economic fact, contingent upon socio-economic conditions. He understood self-alienation as arising from the fact that man was *not whole*, as opposed to the fact that man was *not himself*. The true problem was not incompleteness but otherness, otherness to oneself.

---

[23] Milan Kundera, *The Book of Laughter and Forgetting*, trans. Michael Henry Heim (New York: Penguin Books), 8.

[24] Entry dated 12 May 1948. Patočka děník, Sešit VIII: 3.III.1948–10.VII.1948, Jan Patočka Archive, Center for Theoretical Studies, Prague. "Možná lépe vyjádřit: marxismus si zastírá otázku cele, ví o lidském odcizení, ale představuje si, že toto odcizení je podobného řádu a rázu jako nemoc, že leze je léčit technicky. Že člověk múze být bez něho. Že odcizení je 'nedokonalost', tj. nedokonanost."

"Self-alienation, the fact that man is not at home in the world, that hurt that Marx wants to heal," Patočka wrote in his diary that spring, "is incurable."[25]

Subjectivity contains its own dialectic

Could subjectivity ever then be consummated?

Stalinism was not only repressive but also productive of identity, the historian Jochen Hellbeck has argued:

> With its stress on subjective involvement in the revolutionary cause, the Bolshevik regime was pursuing a quintessentially modern agenda of *subjectivization*, of fostering conscious citizens who would become engaged in the program of building socialism of their own will. Soviet revolutionaries sought to remove all mediation between the individual citizen and the larger community, so that the consciousness of the individual and the revolutionary goals of the state would merge.[26]

The Bolshevik project very much allowed for, in fact demanded, the constitution of subjectivity—Hellbeck insists—we only need to understand that subjectivity is not necessarily *liberal subjectivity*, that "illiberal subjectivity" is just as real.

The perfect consummation of subjectivity has always been a hair's breadth away from its total negation. Both the Soviet project in particular and the phenomenon of revolution more universally are predicated upon the exploitation of the fragile border between the fulfillment of subjectivity and the effacing of subjectivity—or rather the *Aufhebung* of the individual subject into the collective. Communist "self-criticism" harkened back to Hegel's preoccupation with Antigone's self-alienating transgression: *samokrytyka* was the ritualistic act of purging the vestiges of the particular that were not identical with the universal. The infamous Marxist distinction between the subjective and the objective functioned dialectically: the fullest achievement of the subjective was its being brought into identity with the objective.

---

[25] Entry dated 23 May [1948]. Patočka děník, Sešit VIII: 3.III.1948–10.VII.1948, Jan Patočka Archive, Center for Theoretical Studies, Prague. "Sebeodcizení, fakt, že člověk není ve světě doma, tato rána, kterou chce Marx zacelit, je nezhojitelná."

[26] Jochen Hellbeck, "Working, Struggling, Becoming: Stalin-Era Autobiographical Texts," in *Language and Revolution: Making Modern Political Identities* ed. Igal Halfin (London and Portland: Frank Cass, 2002), 136.

Theodor Adorno and Max Horkheimer, upon learning of Auschwitz while in American emigration, probed this dialectic of subjectivity: "The strain of holding the I together adheres to the I in all stages; and the temptation to lose it has always been there with the blind determination to maintain it."[27] The drive towards both solidarity and transparency is the desire to overcome alienation, to consummate subjectivity through an act of identity with the totality. This desire belongs to the human condition; it will never entirely leave us.

Revolution discloses natality

Revolution is a *Grenzerfahrung*; it pushes us to places beyond what we have known. It is also a moment of what Viktor Shlovsky called *ostranenie*: the familiar becomes strange. Time itself takes on an unfamiliar form.

"It is important to realise," wrote Lenin in March 1917, shortly after Tsar Nicholas II's abdication, "that in revolutionary times the objective situation changes with the same swiftness and abruptness as the current of life in general."[28] "*Es schwindelt*," Lenin told Trotsky in 1917, making a circular motion.[29] *It makes one dizzy.* John Reed's *Ten Days That Shook the World* has lasted as a classic work perhaps above all for capturing this vertigo.[30] Time hurled forward. "And in the rain, the bitter chill," wrote Reed, "the great throbbing city under grey skies rushing faster and faster towards—what?" A person could fall asleep and awaken hours, or even just minutes, later to find that absolutely everything was now different. In Petrograd that October Reed encountered a Bolshevik leader who told him, "The game is on."[31] It was an existentialist moment of decision-making. From total chaos emerged mad certainty.

"In revolutionary times the limits of what is possible expand a thousand-fold," Lenin noted parenthetically in a March 1917 letter.[32]

---

[27] Theodor Adorno and Max Horkheimer, *Dialectic of Enlightenment*, trans. John Cumming (New York: Continuum, 1996), 33.

[28] V. I. Lenin, "Letters from Afar," *Revolution at the Gates*, ed. Slavoj Žižek (London: Verso, 2002), 15–55, quotation 46.

[29] Quoted. in Yuri Slezkine, *The House of Government: A Saga of the Russian Revolution* (Princeton: Princeton University Press, 2017), 181.

[30] On *Nacherleben*, see Wilhelm Dilthey, "The Rise of Hermeneutics," trans. Frederic Jameson, *The New Literary History* 3, no. 2 (Winter 1972): 229–44.

[31] John Reed, *Ten Days That Shook the World* (New York: Penguin Books, 1977), 62 ("in the rain..."), 77 ("the game is on").

[32] V. I. Lenin, "Letters from Afar," 40.

Jean-Paul Sartre began his philosophy of time by acknowledging the paradox of the instantaneous present: "everyone knows that this does not exist at all but is the limit of an infinite division, like a point without dimension."[33] For Sartre the present was less a point than a border, the border between the *en-soi* and the *pour-soi*. The limit of the determinate past was the border of the present, which was the moment of the beginning of the *pour-soi*. "In contrast to the Past which is in-itself, the Present is for-itself," he writes.[34] Revolution is the *obnazhenie* of this border between the *en-soi* and the *pour-soi*; it illuminates the moment when we pass from the realm of facticity into the realm of the possibility of the negation of facticity—that is, into the realm of transcendence. It is as if, to quote Blanche in *A Streetcar Named Desire*, "you suddenly turned a blinding light on something that had always been half in shadow."[35]

Hannah Arendt called this crossing of the border "natality," which is— she wrote—"the miracle that saves the world, the realm of human affairs, from its normal, 'natural' ruin."[36] Revolution is the revelation of natality, of this capacity to begin anew, that capacity most often forgotten in our every- day lives. The consequences of what we set in motion cannot be foreseen, for actions—as Hegel insists—not only occasionally but as a rule have con- sequences in excess of their intentions. This is so, Arendt writes, due to the "boundlessness of human interrrelatedness":[37] "the story that an act starts is composed of its consequent deeds and sufferings. These consequences are boundless...."[38]

Naked empiricism is existentially unbearable

In his epic *The House of Government: A Saga of the Bolshevik Revolution*, Yuri Slezkine situates Bolshevism in a very long history of millenarian sects. Yes, there were many precedents—Slezkine concludes—*but not on this scale*. No one had ever attempted a social engineering experiment of such vastness.[39]

---

[33]   Jean Paul Sartre, "Phenomenology of the Three Temporal Dimensions," *Being and Nothingness*, trans. Hazel E. Barnes (New York: Washing Square Press, 1956): 107–29, quotation 107.

[34]   Sartre, "Phenomenology of the Three Temporal Dimensions," *Being and Nothingness*, 120.

[35]   Tennessee Williams, *A Streetcar Named Desire* (New York: Signet, 1974), 95.

[36]   Hannah Arendt, *The Human Condition* (Chicago: University of Chicago Press, 1998), 247.

[37]   Arendt, *The Human Condition*, 190.

[38]   Arendt, *The Human Condition*, 190.

[39]   Yuri Slezkine, *The House of Government*.

It was a social engineering experiment that confirmed Tony Judt's observation that the more perfect the solution, the more monstrous the consequences. It revealed the extraordinary human capacity to normalize the abnormal. And it justified the poet Wisława Szymborska's insistence on modesty, for *"we know ourselves/[only] in so far as we have been tested."*[40]

The Bolshevik Revolution was also a lesson in radical contingency: had anything happened to that sealed train car, had Lenin not appeared in Petrograd in April 1917, there would quite likely have been no Bolshevik Revolution. And the entire twentieth century would have been a different one.

The Bolshevik experiment is, at the same time, a lesson in our inability to face that uncertainty. Kołakowski articulated this especially clearly: history itself, in its raw empirical existence, provides us with no meaning, and hence no solace. "It is necessary," Kołakowski writes, "to surpass history by an act of faith if one wants to accord it a meaning."[41] He wrote this sympathetically, aware that "this act of faith is certainly indispensable to man."[42] The radical contingency revealed by naked empiricism is existentially unbearable. For Kołakowski, the impulse to seek recourse in myth, in a transcendental key that would sweep life together as a whole and give it some sense, was deeply human. This choice is a Kierkegaardian Either/Or: either we impose this transcendental key—be it Divine Providence or History and its iron laws or something else—or we face with eyes wide open our empirical, contingent existence, the fact that we are *Sein-zum Tode*. Few of us, as Kołakowski knew, were heroic enough to choose the latter.

---

[40] The line is from Wisława Szymborska's poem "Minuta ciszy po Ludwice Wawrzyńskiej," published in *Wołanie do Yeti* (Cracow: Wydawnictwo Literackie, 1957).

[41] Leszek Kolakowski, "Historical Understanding and the Intelligibility of History," *A Leszek Kolakowski Reader*, ed. Charles Newman (Evanston: Northwestern University Press, 1971): 103–17, quotation 115.

[42] Kolakowski, "Historical Understanding and the Intelligibility of History," 116.

LIST OF CONTRIBUTORS

Leon Aron is Director of Russian Studies at the American Enterprise Institute. He has published several books and over 300 essays and articles. He is the author of a biography of Boris Yeltsin and of *Roads to the Temple*, which explores the collapse of the Soviet Union within the history-of-ideas tradition. He is completing a book about the ideals, beliefs, and political imperatives that inform Vladimir Putin's domestic and foreign policies.

Paul Dragos Aligica is a Senior Research Fellow at the F. A. Hayek Program for Advanced Study in Philosophy, Politics and Economics, Mercatus Center at George Mason University, and KPMG Professor of Governance at the University of Bucharest. Among his most recent publications are *Public Governance and the Classical Liberal Perspective. The Political Economy Foundations* (with P. Boettke and V. Tarko), Oxford University Press, 2019 and *Public Entrepreneurship, Citizenship, and Self-Governance*, Cambridge University Press, 2018.

András Bozóki is Professor of Political Science at the Central European University in Vienna. He was recurrent visiting professor at Columbia, and other universities. His research interest includes comparative politics, democratization, political ideas, and the role of the intellectuals. His books include *Intellectuals and Politics in Central Europe* (1999), *The Roundtable Talks of 1989* (2002), and *Rolling Regime Change* (in Hungarian, 2019). He received the 2009 István Bibó Prize of the Hungarian Political Science Association.

Michael S. Bernstam is Research Fellow at the Hoover Institution, Stanford University. His research focuses on the centrality of income redistribution in the taxonomy and evolution of economic systems, long-run economic growth, social revolutions, and stability of inter-communal societies. His books include *Below-Replacement Fertility in Industrial Societies* (with Kingsley Davis), *Resources, Environment, and Population* (with Kingsley Davis), *The Wealth of Nations and the Environment, Fixing Russia's Banks* (with Alvin Rabushka), and *From Predation to Prosperity* (with Alvin Rabushka).

Serguey Braguinsky was born in Moscow, USSR, and graduated from Moscow State University. His doctoral degree in economics is from Keio University in Japan. He coauthored with Grigory Yavlinsky the book *Incentives and Institutions: The Transition to a Market Economy in Russia* (Princeton University Press, 2000) and has published scholarly papers in *American Economic Review, Journal of Law and Economics, Journal of Economic History, Strategic Management Journal, Review of Economic Dynamics*, and other leading journals.

Venelin I. Ganev is Professor in Political Science and a faculty associate of the Havighurst Center for Russian and Post-Soviet Studies at Miami University of Ohio. His main fields of interest are postcommunist politics, democratization studies, constitutionalism, and modern social theory. He is the author of more than thirty peer-reviewed articles and chapters, and of the book *Preying on the State: The Transformation of Postcommunist Bulgaria*, published by Cornell University Press in 2007.

Jeffrey Herf is Distinguished University Professor in the Department of History at the University of Maryland, College Park. Specializing in twentieth century history of Germany, he teaches the intersection of ideas and politics in modern European history. His works includes *The Jewish Enemy: Nazi Propaganda During World War II and the Holocaust* (Harvard University Press, 2006), *Nazi Propaganda for the Arab World* (Yale University Press, 2009; pb. 2010), *Undeclared Wars with Israel: East Germany and the West German Far Left, 1967–1989* (Cambridge University Press, 2016), and *Reactionary Modernism: Technology, Culture and Politics in Weimar and the Third Reich* (Cambridge University Press, 1984).

Piotr H. Kosicki is Associate Professor of History at the University of Maryland. He is the author, among others, of *Catholics on the Barricades: Poland, France, and "Revolution," 1891-1956* (Yale University Press) and editor/co-editor, among others, of *Christian Democracy across the Iron Curtain* (Palgrave Macmillan), *Christian Democracy and the Fall of Communism* (Leuven University Press), *The Long 1989* (CEU Press), and *Vatican II behind the Iron Curtain* (Catholic University of America Press). Kosicki has published 20 refereed articles and book chapters, and he has also written for *Commonweal, The New Republic, The TLS,* and the *Washington Post.*

Mark Kramer is Director of Cold War Studies at Harvard University, Director of Harvard's Sakharov Seminars on Human Rights, and a Senior Fellow of Harvard's Davis Center for Russian and Eurasian Studies. In addition to publishing his own books and articles, he has long been editor of the *Journal of Cold War Studies*, a quarterly journal published by MIT Press, and of Harvard's Cold War Studies Book Series, published by Rowman & Littlefield.

Jordan Luber is a 2023 JD candidate at American University Washington College of Law, and a staff writer for the *Human Rights Brief*. He was the research assistant to Vladimir Tismaneanu while in undergrad at the University of Maryland, College Park. Jordan has interned for the State Department at the US Embassy in Kyiv, Ukraine, was an editorial intern for *New Eastern Europe* in Kraków, Poland, and received his MA from Charles University's Václav Havel Joint Master's Programme. Jordan's specialty is Latin American and European history and politics, with a focus on human rights, modernity, mass politics, and dictatorship.

Noemi Marin is Professor of Rhetorical Studies at Florida Atlantic University, author of *After the Fall: Rhetoric in the Aftermath of Dissent in Post-Communist Times* (2007), and co-editor of several edited volumes: *Rhetorics of 1989* (2015); *Collocutio, Advances in the History of Rhetoric* (2011, 2007). Dr. Marin's research focuses on communist and post-communist rhetoric, with over thirty-five book chapters and journal articles. Currently, she works on a new book project on totalitarian rhetoric.

Mircea Mihaies is emeritus professor of English and American literature at the University of the West in Timisoara, Romania, editor-in-chief of the cultural monthly *Orizont*, weekly columnist for the country's leading literary magazine *Romania Literara*, and author of numerous scholarly articles and books in Romanian including monographs on William Faulkner, James Joyce, and Leonard Cohen. In 2013, Lexington Books published his volume *The Metaphysics of Detective Marlowe*. Together with Vladimir Tismaneanu he co-authored several books about Romanian post-communism.

Margaret M. Pearson is Dr. Horace E. and Wilma V. Harrison Distinguished Professor of Government and Politics, University of Maryland, College Park. Her research focuses on China's political economy, bureaucratic and regulatory behavior, and Chinese foreign economic policy. She received her Ph.D. in Political Science from Yale University.

Mykola Riabchuk is a Senior Research Fellow in the Institute of Political and Nationalities' Studies at the Academy of Sciences of Ukraine and a lecturer at the University of Warsaw and Ukrainian Catholic University in Lviv. He penned a dozen books on postcommunist transformation, state-nation building, national identity and nationalism, including the last one, in English, *At the Fence of Metternich's Garden. Essays on Europe, Ukraine and Europeanization* (Stuttgart: ibidem Verlag, 2021).

Steven Rosefielde is Professor of Economics at the University of North Carolina, Chapel Hill. He received his Ph.D. in Economics from Harvard University, and is a member of the Russian Academy of Natural Sciences (RAEN). Most recently, he published *Kremlin Strikes Back: Russia and the West after Crimea's Annexation* (Cambridge University Press, 2017), *Putin's Russia: Economic, Political and Military Foundations* (World Scientific Publishers, 2020), *Progressive and Populists* (with Quinn Mills) (World Scientific Publishers, 2020).

Peter Rutland is a Professor of Government at Wesleyan University in Middletown, CT, where he has taught since 1989. Before that he taught at the University of Texas, Austin and London University. He has a BA from Oxford and a PhD from the University of York. He has been a Fulbright visiting professor at the European University of St. Petersburg and Sophia University, Tokyo, and a Leverhulme visiting professor at the University of Manchester.

Marci Shore is Associate Professor of History at Yale University. She is the translator of Michał Głowiński's *The Black Seasons* and the author of *Caviar and Ashes: A Warsaw Generation's Life and Death in Marxism, 1918–1968, The Taste of Ashes: The Afterlife of Totalitarianism in Eastern Europe,* and *The Ukrainian Night: An Intimate History of Revolution.* In 2018 she received a Guggenheim Fellowship for her current project titled "Phenomenological Encounters: Scenes from Central Europe."

Marius Stan is a Romanian political scientist and research director of the Hannah Arendt Center at the University of Bucharest. He holds a Ph.D.

in Political Science from the University of Bucharest and served as the editor of the journal *History of Communism in Europe*. He is the author of books published in several languages and of numerous articles in international scholarly journals. Together with Vladimir Tismaneanu, he co-authored *A Stalin Dossier: The Genialissimo Generalissimo* (Bucharest, Curtea Veche Publishing, 2014), *A Lenin Dossier: The Magic of Nihilism* (Bucharest, Curtea Veche Publishing, 2016), and *Romania Confronts its Communist Past: Democracy, Memory, and Moral Justice* (NY: Cambridge University Press, 2018). His research and teaching interests include twentieth-century European communism and fascism, revolutionary political ideologies and movements, transitional justice, and the main intellectual biographies and debates during the Cold War.

Vlad Tarko is Assistant Professor at University of Arizona in the Department of Political Economy and Moral Science. His work was published in *American Political Science Review, Governance, Comparative Economic Studies, Public Choice, Journal of Institutional Economics, Review of Austrian Economics*, and others. He is the author of *Elinor Ostrom: An Intellectual Biography* (Rowman & Littlefield International 2017), co-author with Paul Dragos Aligica of *Capitalist Alternatives* (Routledge 2015), and co-author with Paul Dragos Aligica and Peter Boettke of *Public Administration and the Classical Liberal Perspective* (Oxford 2019).

Vladimir Tismaneanu is Professor of Comparative Politics at the University of Maryland, College Park. His research focuses on communism, fascism, and twentieth century Central and Eastern European politics. In 2006 he chaired the Presidential Commission for the Analysis of the Communist Dictatorship in Romania. His works include *Putin's Totalitarian Democracy: Ideology, Myth, and Violence in the Twenty-First Century*, coauthored with Kate. C. Langdon (Palgrave Macmillan 2020), *Romania Confronts its Communist Past: Democracy, Memory, and Moral Justice*, coauthored with Marius Stan (Cambridge University Press, 2018), *The Devil in History: Communism, Fascism, and the Lessons of the 20th Century* (University of California Press, 2012), and *Fantasies of Salvation: Democracy, Nationalism and Myth in Post-Communist Europe* (Princeton University Press, 1998).

INDEX

Notes are indicated by note numbers after the letter "n"; tables are denoted by the letter "t" and figures are denoted by the letter "f" following their respective page numbers.